T0261430

This comprehensive summary of the history, rationale, current status, and future directions of the *Total Worker Health* initiative will be an excellent resource for researchers and practitioners who are looking for examples of successful, integrated interventions. And, as director of one of the first U.S. *Total Worker Health* certificate programs, I believe this book will be a valuable resource for our students.

—**Laura A. Linnan, ScD,** Director, Carolina Collaborative for Research on Work and Health, University of North Carolina Gillings School of Global Public Health

From the minds of leading experts flows this wellspring of knowledge that refreshes the evidence base and provides a landmark compendium on *Total Worker Health*. It is the definitive resource that will irrigate the growth of future innovative initiatives in worker safety, health, and well-being.

—**Ron Loeppke, MD, MPH, FACOEM, FACPM,** Vice Chairman, U.S. Preventive Medicine, Inc., Jacksonville, FL

Truly a landmark book in the emerging field of *Total Worker Health*. With contributions from a diverse and distinguished group of scholars, many of whom were directly responsible for the field's emergence, it provides a state-of-the-art examination of this important and comprehensive approach to occupational health and safety. Essential reading for both researchers and practitioners who seek to make work a safer and healthier endeavor.

—**Joseph J. Hurrell Jr., PhD,** past Editor, *Journal of Occupational Health Psychology*

Dealing with health and well-being in the context of work implies the challenge of focusing on specific issues while being aware of the overall situation and the broader context. This book demonstrates how to do the first without losing sight of the second.

—**Norbert Semmer, PhD,** Professor Emeritus for the Psychology of Work and Organizations, University of Bern, Bern, Switzerland

For anyone wanting to get up to speed on *Total Worker Health*, start with this book. It provides a fantastic launchpad for integrated intervention and implementation research around *Total Worker Health* efforts.

—**Kimberly Jinnett, PhD,** President, Center for Workforce Health and Performance, San Francisco, CA

Here's the book we've been waiting for! A broad sweep of 20 years of NIOSH-led innovation in the bold vision of *Total Worker Health*, documenting the evolution of the idea, providing rich examples of how the idea has flowered in workplace settings, and offering important thoughts about future directions. There is something for everyone.

—**Cameron Mustard, ScD,** President and Senior Scientist, Institute for Work & Health, Toronto, Canada

This comprehensive framework for employee health is timely and adaptive to the needs of occupational and environmental medicine professionals, employers, and research investigators. An essential and unique resource in occupational and environmental health.

—**Martín-J. Sepúlveda, MD, ScD,** IBM Fellow, FACOEM, FACP, FAAP; retired Vice President, IBM Corporation

It is refreshing to read a book that, just like the National Institute for Occupational Safety and Health's (NIOSH) 2016–2026 *Total Worker Health* Agenda itself, emphasizes the true drivers of workplace health and safety—drivers that require the coordination of many initiatives across many departments, with no easy fixes. The good news is that this volume presents a detailed road map to do exactly that. My uncle, former Acting NIOSH Director Dr. Michael Lane, would be very impressed.

—**Al Lewis, JD,** CEO, Quizzify; author of *Why Nobody Believes the Numbers: Distinguishing Fact From Fiction in Population Health Management*

Total Worker Health

Total Worker Health

EDITED BY

Heidi L. Hudson, Jeannie A. S. Nigam,
Steven L. Sauter, L. Casey Chosewood,
Anita L. Schill, and John Howard

AMERICAN PSYCHOLOGICAL ASSOCIATION
Washington, DC

Copyright © 2019 by the American Psychological Association. All rights reserved. Except as permitted under the United States Copyright Act of 1976, no part of this publication may be reproduced or distributed in any form or by any means, including, but not limited to, the process of scanning and digitization, or stored in a database or retrieval system, without the prior written permission of the publisher.

The Foreword, the Introduction, and Chapters 2, 3, 13, 14, and 17 were coauthored by employees of the United States government as part of official duty and are considered to be in the public domain.

TOTAL WORKER HEALTH® is a registered trademark of the US Department of Health and Human Services. Participation by other organizations named herein does not imply endorsement by HHS, the Centers for Disease Control and Prevention, or the National Institute for Occupational Safety and Health.

The opinions and statements published are the responsibility of the authors, and such opinions and statements do not necessarily represent the policies of the American Psychological Association.

Published by
American Psychological Association
750 First Street, NE
Washington, DC 20002
https://www.apa.org

Order Department
https://www.apa.org/pubs/books
order@apa.org

In the U.K., Europe, Africa, and the Middle East, copies may be ordered from Eurospan
https://www.eurospanbookstore.com/apa
info@eurospangroup.com

Typeset in Meridien and Ortodoxa by Circle Graphics, Inc., Reisterstown, MD

Printer: Sheridan Books, Chelsea, MI
Cover Designer: Beth Schlenoff Design, Bethesda, MD

Library of Congress Cataloging-in-Publication Data
Names: Hudson, Heidi, editor. | Nigam, Jeannie A. S., editor. |
  Sauter, Steven L., 1946- editor.
Title: Total worker health / edited by Heidi L. Hudson, Jeannie A. S. Nigam,
  Steven L. Sauter, L. Casey Chosewood, Anita L. Schill, and John Howard.
Description: Washington, DC : American Psychological Association, [2019] |
  Includes bibliographical references and index.
Identifiers: LCCN 2018061043 (print) | LCCN 2019017619 (ebook) |
  ISBN 9781433831164 (eBook) | ISBN 1433831163 (eBook) |
  ISBN 9781433830259 (hardcover) | ISBN 1433830256 (hardcover)
Subjects: LCSH: Industrial hygiene. | Industrial safety.
Classification: LCC HD7261 (ebook) | LCC HD7261 .I558 2019 (print) |
  DDC 658.3/82—dc23
LC record available at https://lccn.loc.gov/2018061043

http://dx.doi.org/10.1037/0000149-000

Printed in the United States of America

10 9 8 7 6 5 4 3 2 1

Dedicated to all people who work.

CONTENTS

CONTRIBUTORS

Amanda Allisey, PhD, Deakin University, Geelong, Victoria, Australia

W. Kent Anger, PhD, Oregon Health & Science University, Portland

Sherry Baron, MD, MPH, Queens College, City University of New York, Queens, NY

Jamie F. Becker, MS, LCSW-C, Laborers' Health and Safety Fund of North America, Washington, DC

Todd Bodner, PhD, Portland State University, Portland, OR

Shelly Campo, PhD, University of Iowa, Iowa City

Claire C. Caruso, PhD, RN, FAAN, National Institute for Occupational Safety and Health, Cincinnati, OII

Martin G. Cherniack, MD, MPH, University of Connecticut Health Center, Farmington

L. Casey Chosewood, MD, MPH, National Institute for Occupational Safety and Health, Atlanta, GA

Isabel Cuervo, PhD, Queens College, City University of New York, Queens, NY

David M. DeJoy, PhD, University of Georgia, Athens

Jack T. Dennerlein, PhD, Northeastern University, Boston, MA; Harvard T. H. Chan School of Public Health, Boston, MA

Ron Z. Goetzel, PhD, Johns Hopkins University, Bethesda, MD

James W. Grosch, PhD, MBA, National Institute for Occupational Safety and Health, Cincinnati, OH

Leslie B. Hammer, PhD, Oregon Health & Science University, Portland; Portland State University, Portland, OR

Steven Hecker, MSPH, University of Oregon, Eugene

John Howard, MD, MPH, JD, LLM, MBA, National Institute for
Occupational Safety and Health, Washington, DC

CDR Heidi L. Hudson, MPH, U.S. Public Health Service, National
Institute for Occupational Safety and Health, Cincinnati, OH

David A. Hurtado, ScD, Oregon Health & Science University, Portland

Nadia Islam, PhD, New York University School of Medicine, New York, NY

Tessa Keegel, PhD, MS, La Trobe University, Melbourne, Victoria,
Australia

Kevin M. Kelly, PhD, University of Iowa, Iowa City

Karen B. Kent, MPH, Johns Hopkins University, Baltimore, MD

Anthony D. LaMontagne, ScD, MA, MEd, Deakin University, Geelong,
Victoria, Australia

Angela Martin, PhD, University of Tasmania, Hobart, Tasmania, Australia

Katherine McCleary, MS, CHES, Johns Hopkins University, Baltimore, MD

Deborah L. McLellan, PhD, MHS, Harvard T. H. Chan School of Public
Health, Boston, MA; Dana-Farber Cancer Institute, Boston, MA

Robert K. McLellan, MD, MPH, FACOEM, FAAFP, The Dartmouth
Institute for Health Policy & Clinical Practice, Lebanon, NH

Allison J. Milner, PhD, MEpi, University of Melbourne, Melbourne,
Victoria, Australia

Eve M. Nagler, ScD, MPH, CHES, Harvard T. H. Chan School of Public
Health, Boston, MA; Dana-Farber Cancer Institute, Boston, MA

Lee S. Newman, MD, MA, Center for Health, Work, & Environment,
University of Colorado, Aurora

Jeannie A. S. Nigam, MS, PhDc, National Institute for Occupational
Safety and Health, Cincinnati, OH

Andrew J. Noblet, PhD, Deakin University, Geelong, Victoria, Australia

Ryan Olson, PhD, Oregon Health & Science University, Portland

Kathryn M. Page, PhD, Deakin University, Geelong, Victoria, Australia

Sudha P. Pandalai, MD, PhD, National Institute for Occupational Safety
and Health, Cincinnati, OH

Alicia Papas, DPsych, Deakin University, Geelong, Victoria, Australia

Kelsey Parker, PhD, Oregon Health & Science University, Portland

MacKenna L. Perry, PhD, Oregon Health & Science University, Portland

Nicolaas P. Pronk, PhD, FACSM, FAWHP, HealthPartners Institute,
Bloomington, MN; Harvard T. H. Chan School of Public Health,
Boston, MA

Laura Punnett, ScD, University of Massachusetts Lowell, Lowell

Anjali Rameshbabu, PhD, Oregon Health & Science University, Portland

Nicola J. Reavley, PhD, University of Melbourne, Melbourne, Victoria,
Australia

Enid Chung Roemer, PhD, Johns Hopkins University, Baltimore, MD

Diane S. Rohlman, PhD, University of Iowa, Iowa City

Erika L. Sabbath, ScD, Boston College, Boston, MA; Dana-Farber Cancer
Institute, Boston, MA

Steven L. Sauter, PhD, AECOM N&C Technical Services, LLC, Cincinnati, OH

Anita L. Schill, PhD, MPH, MA, National Institute for Occupational Safety and Health, Washington, DC

Scott P. Schneider, MS, CIH, Retired, Laborers' Health and Safety Fund of North America, Washington, DC

Juliann C. Scholl, PhD, MA, National Institute for Occupational Safety and Health, Cincinnati, OH

Paul A. Schulte, PhD, National Institute for Occupational Safety and Health, Cincinnati, OH

Kenneth Scott, PhD, MPH, Denver Public Health, Denver, CO

Peter M. Smith, PhD, MPH, University of Toronto, Toronto, Ontario, Canada

Glorian Sorensen, PhD, MPH, Harvard T. H. Chan School of Public Health, Boston, MA; Dana-Farber Cancer Institute, Boston, MA

Liliana Tenney, MPH, Center for Health, Work & Environment, University of Colorado, Aurora

Emma K. Tsui, PhD, MPH, City University of New York Graduate School of Public Health & Health Policy, Queens, NY

Gregory R. Wagner, MD, Harvard T. H. Chan School of Public Health, Boston, MA

Wylie Wan, PhD, Oregon Health & Science University, Portland

Mark G. Wilson, HSD, University of Georgia, Athens

Bradley Wipfli, PhD, Oregon Health & Science University, Portland; Portland State University, Portland, OR

Katrina Witt, DPhil, Monash University, Clayton, Victoria, Australia

FOREWORD

In the spring of 2011, leaders of the National Institute for Occupational Safety and Health (NIOSH) *Total Worker Health*® program, including all of the editors of this volume, set a goal to publish a book focused on this emerging area of interest by 2020. Such is the power of goal setting: The book is 1 year ahead of schedule! The volume you hold in your hands is the first of its kind—a book dedicated to the *Total Worker Health* (TWH) approach.

Even in the early days of the TWH program, NIOSH leaders realized it would be essential to collect the work of authors, nationally and internationally, into one volume in order to capture the TWH story in an authoritative publication accessible to a wide audience. It was the vision then, and remains the vision today, that this volume would share the work of thought leaders engaged in both TWH research and practice to disseminate the knowledge gained beyond peer-reviewed scientific journals. During the last 15 to 20 years, NIOSH has learned much about this paradigm-shifting approach to occupational safety and health—an approach that recognizes the wholeness of each worker, where what's work-related and non–work-related are integrated, not separated. Yet it is only through the adoption of this approach by practice communities dedicated to worker safety, health, and well-being that the ultimate goals of improving the physical spaces where work is done, improving the design and organization of work itself, protecting workers from safety and

This chapter was authored by an employee of the United States government as part of their official duty and is considered to be in the public domain. The findings and conclusions in this report are those of the author and do not necessarily represent the official position of the National Institute for Occupational Safety and Health, Centers for Disease Control and Prevention.

health hazards related to their work, and advancing worker well-being through work will be achieved.

The editors of this volume are current or former NIOSH scientists who have spent significant portions of their careers charting the new direction in occupational safety and health that has become the TWH approach to worker safety, health, and well-being. Together, the editors have worked to create new ways of addressing long-standing challenges in occupational safety and health. At the same time, NIOSH has considered shifts in the sociocultural environment; their impacts on work and workers; and how these shifts have created unmet needs that sometimes threaten worker safety, health, and well-being.

The editors believe that this book has something for everyone interested in the TWH concept. Readers who are very familiar with the TWH approach will find programmatic details, nuanced perspectives, and practical applications that will augment their understanding and contribute to their pursuit of the TWH discipline. Those who are new to the TWH approach will learn from authoritative sources what it is, and what it is not, including fundamental concepts, empirical research findings that provide rationale for the approach, and ideas for program implementation. All readers will gain insights that will assist with their efforts to protect worker safety and health and advance worker well-being in an integrated way.

The challenges facing the American workforce are greater than ever. The TWH approach provides a key strategy for support of a workforce that is prepared to respond to the constantly changing demands related to 21st-century work. A strong economy depends on a workforce that is innovative and resilient. At a minimum, these qualities are possible only when work is safe, is free from health hazards, and promotes worker well-being. Realizing the full potential of the workforce becomes more likely when work enhances individual well-being both on and off the job. The TWH approach can be used to benefit individual workers, employers, communities, and the national economy.

—John Howard, MD
Director, National Institute for Occupational Safety and Health

ACKNOWLEDGMENTS

The editors gratefully acknowledge members of the NIOSH Office for Total Worker Health who provided support in the development of the volume. Special thanks go to NIOSH and CDC staff, including Pauline Benjamin, Sarah Mitchell, Reid Richards, Romina Stormo, Alice Kelley, Paul Middendorf, Roger Rosa, and John Piacentino.

Total
Worker
Health

Introduction

Heidi L. Hudson, Jeannie A. S. Nigam, Steven L. Sauter,
L. Casey Chosewood, Anita L. Schill, and John Howard

Today's on-demand, increasingly competitive global economy is redefining what it means to be someone who works. Although some may find opportunities, these complex economic times have threatened and continue to threaten the employment and welfare of many workers, their families, and their communities. Long working hours, nonstandard work arrangements, and reporting to multiple employers while juggling the competing demands between work and life have become the norm for many in today's workforce. Either by choice or necessity, many of today's workers are working beyond the "traditional" retirement age and pursuing multiple careers throughout their lives. Beyond the potential, overt safety and health risks faced at the workplace, it has become increasingly clear that these conditions have the potential to also impact overall health and well-being outside of work—influencing, for example, individual health behaviors, caring for family members, relationships, and family nutrition—with consequent effects on the development of acute and chronic health conditions in workers and their families.

Employers in the 21st century are challenged by fierce, global economic pressures while managing their work environments and workforce. Employers are required to provide safe and healthful working conditions that protect workers from recognized workplace safety and health risks, such as traumatic

This chapter was authored by employees and contractors of the United States government as part of their official duty and is considered to be in the public domain. The findings and conclusions in this report are those of the author(s) and do not necessarily represent the official position of the National Institute for Occupational Safety and Health, Centers for Disease Control and Prevention.

http://dx.doi.org/10.1037/0000149-001
Total Worker Health, H. L. Hudson, J. A. S. Nigam, S. L. Sauter, L. C. Chosewood, A. L. Schill, and J. Howard (Editors)

injury and chemical exposures. At the same time, employers are confronted with complex, emerging workforce issues, such as the shift in employment relationships, recruitment and retainment of workers in highly competitive labor markets, an aging workforce, and the uncertainty of how best to manage a workforce with multiple chronic health conditions while containing ever-growing health-care costs. Successfully balancing these issues has implications for both the safety and health of workers and organizational sustainability.

Occupational safety and health (OSH) leaders and practitioners recognize that the safety, health, and well-being of workers are influenced by workplace risks (e.g., unsafe working conditions, hours of work, wages, workload and stress, lack of access to paid leave), by societal risks beyond the workplace (e.g., lack of access to health care, social and environmental exposures), and by individual factors (e.g., gender and genetic predispositions). Furthermore, a growing body of evidence points to the relationship between chronic health conditions afflicting society today (e.g., cardiovascular disease and obesity) and conditions in the workplace. In addition, there is growing concern over the health protection of workers due to the recent shifts in employment practices, such as the movement toward nonstandard work arrangements (Howard, 2017) and fissuring of the workplace (Weil, 2014). Such practices are intensifying the entanglement of personal and work-related exposures and risks because many of these jobs are performed outside traditional work settings.

When seen in aggregate, shifts in the demands of the changing economy, new work arrangements and employment practices, and longer and more diverse work for many all argue for a more comprehensive look at safety and health of workers. The traditional siloed, or reductionist, approach is likely to be inadequate to safeguard the safety, health, and well-being of workers. These complex realities are driving multiple efforts to broaden the approach to worker safety and health, thereby reducing the impact and cost of injuries and illness and providing a pathway to create work and work environments that are safe and health enhancing.

Leaders in OSH are calling for comprehensive and systems-level prevention strategies to better address risks to the safety, health, and well-being of workers and the success of organizations in today's global economy. In fact, in 2003, the National Institute for Occupational Safety and Health (NIOSH) started the *Steps to a Healthier US Workforce* initiative to explore the benefits of integrating the protection of workers from work-related safety and health hazards with efforts to promote health and prevent disease. In 2015, NIOSH trademarked the expression *Total Worker Health*® in reference to policies, programs, and practices that take into account the work environment—both physical and organizational—while addressing safety and health risks arising from beyond the workplace, as described by Schill, Chosewood, and Howard in Chapter 2, this volume. In 2010, the World Health Organization published *Healthy Workplaces: A Model for Action*, which applies a comprehensive approach to worker health. This international framework embraces a new way of thinking about worker health using a public health approach addressing work-related physical and psychosocial risks, promotion and support of healthy behaviors, and broader social and environmental determinants of health. The model also incorporates criteria for a continual improvement process to protect and promote the health, safety, and well-being of all workers and the sustainability of the workplace. The Deutsche Gesetzliche Unfallversicherung (DGUV), Germany's primary agency for social accident insurance institutions, recognized important trends in the future of work. In 2016, DGUV published a position paper that describes 21st-century changes to work and its impact on worker safety and health and discusses the consequences and potential solutions for employers. The paper serves as a framework to inspire broader and more comprehensive prevention research and practice for worker safety and health, and it provides recommendations to companies on issues related to "new forms of work" and new social and labor market policies.

This volume brings together state-of-the-art research and practice in comprehensive and integrated prevention strategies from the most accomplished scholars and practitioners in the field. Owing to the still emergent status of the *Total Worker Health* (TWH) field, a unified model or framework for the TWH approach does not yet exist. Thus, throughout the volume are varying descriptions of TWH concepts. The variation between the present authors in how they approach or portray integration is only natural and to be expected—not withstanding that all chapters in the volume clearly converge in the general understanding of TWH policies and integration as the blending of workplace safety and health programs, including health promotion. This perspective is preserved for the readers so they can fully appreciate the evolution and development of this field. As discussed in the opening two chapters, the integrated approach to safety and health is rapidly evolving and is being applied in science and practice at academic centers of excellence, in labor organizations, and in industry.

This book is designed for multiple professional audiences with interests in the safety, health, and well-being of workers. It aims to inform these professionals of integrative approaches to safety, health, and well-being to further prevent adverse worker health and safety outcomes from contemporary work and work environments. A primary audience includes professionals from the field of OSH (e.g., occupational medicine physicians, occupational health nurses, industrial hygienists) and those who share a common goal of identifying hazardous conditions, materials, and practices in the workplace and assisting employers and workers in eliminating or reducing the associated risks. Another audience includes professionals who self-identify as TWH practitioners and scientists. This speaks to those professionals who, soon after learning about the TWH concept, quickly realized the value of an integrated approach and began to adopt and promote the philosophy within their day-to-day responsibilities and business operations. An additional audience includes those who have responsibility for the overall of health of the workforce and public and comprises professionals in the fields of public health, health promotion, health education, risk management, human resource management, employee assistance, occupational health psychology, and organizational sciences. Although these professionals expand beyond the traditional OSH field, their perspective is critical for a broader application of policies, practices, and programs that can comprehensively address determinants that further protect worker health and well-being.

This book can serve as a handbook for practitioners in these fields, whether from management or labor, on state-of-the-art practices for interventions that integrate elements of OSH protection with organizational policies, programs, and practices to advance worker health and well-being. Researchers will be informed by the chapters in this volume that provide updates on the current scientific evidence base and the knowledge gaps pertaining to the design and effectiveness of integrated interventions. This volume can also serve as a textbook for newly developed professional training programs and coursework on integrated approaches to worker safety, health, and well-being that are being created in academic centers in the United States and abroad.

This book is organized into three parts and 17 chapters. Part I, Historical, Theoretical, and Empirical Foundation of *Total Worker Health*®, traces the historical developments for this emerging field and provides a comprehensive overview of the theoretical rationale and seminal research that supports the argument for integrative workplace prevention strategies. The historical movement of integrated programming in OSH is introduced by DeJoy and Wilson with a discussion on modern challenges and opportunities for advancing TWH research and practice. Within the opening chapter, the authors discuss broad considerations for adoption and implementation of the TWH approach in research and practice. In Chapter 2, Schill, Chosewood, and Howard introduce readers to a fundamental understanding of the TWH concept and proceed with an insider's view of the development and implementation of the NIOSH TWH program. They describe a national call for research, practice, policy, and capacity building and discuss the future vision for the field of TWH. In Chapter 3, Schulte and Pandalai lay the scientific groundwork for a TWH approach by describing evidence of the interaction of occupational risk factors with personal risk factors in the etiology of occupational illness and injury. They also briefly discuss ethical implications pertaining to interventions that arise from the interplay of personal and occupational risk factors. In Chapter 4, commenting on the empirical foundations for TWH, Anger and colleagues review studies on the effectiveness of TWH interventions and discuss the limitations of this research. They proceed with a dialogue of opportunities to further develop the science. Part I concludes with a description and application of two complementary theoretical frameworks for TWH research and application from two academic centers. Sorensen and colleagues present a conceptual model to inform the design, implementation, and evaluation of integrated approaches and review applications of this model. Within their discussion, they mention factors critical to successful implementation of policies, programs, and practices. In Chapter 6, Cherniack and Punnett provide a framework for participatory action research and practice as applied to a TWH approach. They share compelling preliminary findings from four case studies and discuss practical implications of implementing and evaluating integrated interventions within the high-risk work environments, such as health care and corrections.

Part II, Organizational Approaches to *Total Worker Health*® Interventions, comprises four empirical chapters that describe applications for integrated interventions and evidence of their effectiveness in different occupational contexts. This section includes models for large, medium, and small organizations; a labor management approach; and an integrated community–workplace intervention model. Opening the second part, Campo, Kelly, and Rohlman provide an overview of findings on the prevalence of OSH and well-being programs of varying complexity in the Midwest. Drawing from the health care sector, McLellan shares a detailed case description of how to create a sustainable TWH approach in a mature and large health-care organization with a culture that traditionally treated occupational health and safety and personal health as separate concerns. Chapter 8 also reflects on the various roles of a TWH practitioner in implementing an integrated safety, health, and well-being program, such as navigating internal politics and obstacles, building teams, and evaluating program effectiveness. In Chapter 9, Newman and Tenney summarize research on the application of integrated safety, health, and well-being interventions in small and medium-sized businesses and suggest a systematic approach to developing sustainable, scalable solutions in these organizations. The authors briefly describe a TWH practitioner's responsibilities and discuss obstacles and facilitators within the context of applying TWH interventions in small and medium-sized organizations. In the following chapter, Becker and Schneider provide a labor-management perspective and discuss challenges and opportunities for implementing a TWH approach in the multiemployer industry of construction. Concluding Part II, Baron, Tsui, Cuervo, and Islam discuss how recent changes in the workforce influence the need to expand the reach of TWH programs beyond the worksite and into the community. Then Baron and colleagues describe a framework that aims to bring together the fields of OSH and community health that supports a TWH approach.

In Part III, A Spectrum of *Total Worker Health*® Applications, six chapters describe integrated interventions that target specific health and safety risks of central concern in occupational and public health today—mental health, aging, fatigue and sleep, and work–life conflict. Commencing this part, LaMontagne and colleagues outline the evidence on workplace mental health interventions and propose a new comprehensive intervention approach to optimize both the prevention and management of mental health problems in the workplace. Within this chapter, the authors discuss initial results on the effectiveness of an integrated workplace mental health intervention as well as cautionary risks and challenges of such approach. In Chapter 13, Grosch, Hecker, Scott, and Scholl examine the changing age structure of the workforce and provide a new framework, called productive aging, for addressing occupational health and safety concerns in an aging workforce. Next, Caruso reviews the science linking both workplace exposures and risk factors beyond the workplace with sleep disorders and fatigue. She provides an overview of strategies for managers and workers to reduce risks from inadequate sleep and discusses various resources for organizations and workers to use to promote healthy sleep. In Chapter 15, Hammer and Perry share a comprehensive review of research and practice on interventions aimed at reducing stress arising from work and life demands, including successes and challenges of implementing work–life interventions. Then they discuss recommendations for interventions that apply TWH practices and strategies. Rounding off the section by drawing upon experiences across industry, Goetzel and colleagues explore the evolution from traditional workplace health promotion programs to broader culture-of-health models within organizations and emphasize the full value of interventions—moving beyond the limited focus on return on investment. Also described in Chapter 16 is how employers have begun to implement, measure, and evaluate the value on investment of culture of safety and health programs, and a business case is presented for expanding such programs into the community. In the concluding chapter of the volume, Hudson and Nigam highlight three cross-cutting themes that are driving a paradigm shift in the area of OSH. Then the authors discuss opportunities for the TWH approach to move the OSH field forward through investments in training, science, and practice, and they close by proposing a new direction for achieving well-being through work.

This collection of thoughtful chapters offers insights on how the science and practice of the TWH field is forming, as well as new directions for implementation, political and ethical considerations, and evaluation of impact. We hope this volume provides an important reference for improved practice, inspiration for discovery of new knowledge, and opportunities for collaboration among all those dedicated to protecting worker safety and health and advancing worker well-being.

REFERENCES

Deutsche Gesetzliche Unfallversicherung. (2016). *New forms of work new forms of prevention. Work 4.0: Opportunities and challenges.* Berlin, Germany: Author. Retrieved from http://publikationen.dguv.de/dguv/pdf/10002/dguv-nfda_en_accessible.pdf

Howard, J. (2017). Nonstandard work arrangements and worker health and safety. *American Journal of Industrial Medicine, 60,* 1–10. http://dx.doi.org/10.1002/ajim.22669

Weil, D. (2014). *A fissured workplace: Why work became so bad for so many and what can be done to improve it.* Cambridge, MA: Harvard University Press.

World Health Organization. (2010). *Healthy workplaces: A model for action. For employers, workers, policy-makers and practitioners.* Geneva, Switzerland: Author. Retrieved from http://www.who.int/occupational_health/publications/healthy_workplaces_model_action.pdf

HISTORICAL, THEORETICAL, AND EMPIRICAL FOUNDATIONS OF *TOTAL WORKER HEALTH*®

1

Total Worker Health®

Evolution of the Concept

David M. DeJoy and Mark G. Wilson

This chapter traces the development of the *Total Worker Health®* concept in workplace safety and health. Integrated programming is the core idea underlying the *Total Worker Health* (TWH) approach. In the most basic sense, integrated programming involves combining health protection and health promotion; the former is concerned primarily with providing safe and healthful working conditions and the latter with improving personal health behaviors and general health status. As the concept has evolved, integration has come to involve a continuum or spectrum of prevention and protection activities across a variety of domains. Inherent in the TWH approach is the idea that efforts to improve the overall health status of workers should not be distinct from efforts to provide safe and healthful working conditions. Although 2003 is often identified as the formal beginning point for the TWH program (Schill & Chosewood, 2013), the antecedents of the TWH concept can traced back to the 1980s and even earlier, depending on the conceptual boundaries subscribed. In 2003, the National Institute for Occupational Safety and Health (NIOSH) started the *Steps to a Healthier US Workforce* initiative to explore the potential of integrative programming. Three white papers were commissioned to array the research base and stimulate discussion among researchers and practitioners alike (NIOSH, 2012). "Steps" was transformed into the WorkLife Initiative shortly thereafter, and the label *Total Worker Health* was introduced by NIOSH in 2011 (Schill & Chosewood, 2013) and became a registered trademark in 2015 (NIOSH, 2016b). As this initiative has

http://dx.doi.org/10.1037/0000149-002
Total Worker Health, H. L. Hudson, J. A. S. Nigam, S. L. Sauter, L. C. Chosewood, A. L. Schill, and J. Howard (Editors)
Copyright © 2019 by the American Psychological Association. All rights reserved.

continued to mature, the parameters and boundaries of integration have become better defined, research priorities have emerged, and efforts have been undertaken to fully assess the value-added of integration. For a more complete description of the NIOSH TWH vision and program, see Chapter 2, this volume.

Taking a historical approach is important to fully understanding the opportunities and challenges of the TWH approach. We begin this journey with brief historical summaries of the occupational safety and health (OSH) and workplace health promotion (WHP) movements, primarily as they have unfolded in the United States. Bringing these two traditions together is, after all, the essence of integration and the foundational principle for the TWH program. We then explore the basic idea of integration, tracing the major antecedent trends and events that brought forth this way of thinking. We argue that integration makes logical sense on several levels, but like most innovations or new ideas, it owes its creation to a number of forces and events. We conclude with a brief discussion of the current status of the TWH approach and some of the challenges and opportunities ahead.

HEALTH PROTECTION

Health protection (OSH) has been relevant for as long as people have held employment, and even before, as people have always performed work of one type or another, whether for pay or not, whether voluntarily or involuntarily. But it was not until widespread industrialization and the creation of the factory system that any serious consideration was given to the need to protect workers from harm while at work. The creation of factories propelled urbanization and created a large working class. These workers were almost universally impoverished, and many were newcomers to America. For example, in 1880, 42% of those employed in manufacturing and extractive industries in the United States were recent immigrants (Fink, 1982). The growing carnage of industrial accidents gradually drew the attention of reformers, the public, and ultimately governments, first in Europe and later in the United States. Early industries exposed workers to new and often poorly understood hazards, and typical living conditions for workers were often as hazardous as their work environments. The profit motive was dominant, and workers were plentiful and eager for employment. Steam power and locomotives only added to the casualties. Almost from the very beginning, the primary means to reduce work-related injuries and illnesses has involved legislation and government-imposed regulations. With its early textile industry, Massachusetts created the first factory inspection program in this country in 1867 and then subsequently enacted the first job safety laws in the United States (Geiser & Rosenberg, 2006). Social activists and organized labor played important roles during this period, agitating for safety laws in a number of industries and in multiple states across the nation. But most of these early laws and regulations were not very effective or widely enforced, and new hazards continued to enter the workplace. Ironically, the 14th Amendment to the U.S. Constitution, focused on civil rights and ratified in the aftermath of the American Civil War, was used quite effectively during this early period to thwart the enactment of OSH legislation (Hammer & Price, 2001). State laws intended to protect workers from hazardous working conditions were often seen as unduly limiting the individual's protected right to purse any lawful livelihood or avocation of his or her own choosing.

In response to the growing toll of workplace injuries and fatalities, and the need to provide assistance to victims and their families, workers compensation laws began to be enacted in one state after another. By 1920 almost every state had some type of workers compensation legislation (Fishback & Kantor, 1998). Liability without fault is a key undergirding principle for all workers compensation laws, and means that, in almost all instances, the worker is entitled to financial compensation for a work-related injury or illness regardless of fault or contribution on his or her part. Employers gave up the common law defenses of assumption of risk, fellow servant rule, and contributory negligence— defenses that had long been used by employers to avoid liability for worker injuries. But workers compensation laws fundamentally involved compromise; for their essentially assured benefits, workers gave up almost all their rights to sue their employer for negligence or wrongdoing.

World War II had significant ramifications for worker safety and health. The war effort underscored the importance of a healthy and productive workforce, and workers were in limited supply due to the large number of men called to military service. But after the war, not much happened until the 1960s. Injury rates increased markedly in the 1960s, and in 1968 a major mine disaster killed 74 workers and galvanized public attention (Geiser & Rosenberg, 2006). The Federal Coal Mine Health and Safety Act was passed in 1969 (Public Law 91-173), and in 1970, the Occupational Safety and Health Act (Public Law 91-596) was passed. The Occupational Safety and Health Act was the first piece of comprehensive federal legislation to protect workers. This legislative action led to the creation of the Occupational Safety and Health Administration (OSHA) and NIOSH.

The Occupational Safety and Health Act set the lofty goal that no employee should experience material impairment of health or functional capacity from a lifetime of occupational exposure. Under the Occupational Safety and Health Act, workers are protected primarily through the promulgation and enforcement of workplace safety and health standards. Employers are responsible for complying with standards; maintaining records of employee injuries, illnesses, and deaths; and keeping records of employee exposures to toxic materials and harmful physical agents. They must keep employees apprised of health and safety matters and of accidents and alleged safety violations; they must also refrain from discriminating against employees who file complaints. Workplaces are subject to inspection, and employers are cited and fined for noncompliance with pertinent standards. Many of the original OSHA standards were based on existing voluntary or industry consensus standards. Over time the process of promulgating new standards, or improving old standards, has become difficult and time-consuming due to the involvement of many parties with different views and priorities at stake.

Hale and Hovden (1998) described the history of modern OSH in terms of three major periods or epochs: (a) the technology period, (b) the systems perspective, and (c) the culture period. In the technology epoch, primary attention was given to engineering controls and the well-known hierarchy of hazard controls, where preference is given to actions that eliminate hazards, followed by those that control or otherwise contain hazards. Lowest priority is assigned to actions that may be helpful but that do not directly remove or alter the hazard, such as warnings or personal protective equipment. By and large, the hierarchy of controls is how OSHA has approached worker protection through its standards and enforcement procedures.

The second epoch takes a more comprehensive view and looks at injuries and other losses as arising from causal factors that reside at multiple levels within complex sociotechnical systems. Human systems interaction is one version of this type of thinking (Booher, 2003). Human systems interaction focuses on the interaction of people, tasks, and equipment and technology operating within some broader environmental context. Work systems are basically open systems and subject to influence by both internal and external factors. This type of thinking brings different perspectives to the protection of workers. Many employers today take this more comprehensive approach to worker safety and health, and OSHA has moved in this same direction. In 1989, OSHA issued recommended guidelines for the effective management and protection of worker safety and health. According to these guidelines, an effective program includes the systematic identification, evaluation, and prevention or control of general workplace hazards, specific job hazards, and potential hazards that may arise from foreseeable conditions. The clear emphasis is on comprehensiveness and multilevel detection and analysis of potential safety and health problems.

The third epoch focused on organizational culture and was certainly prompted by a series of high-profile disasters such as the Chernobyl nuclear disaster (Pidgeon & O'Leary, 2000). Safety culture has been defined in different ways, but there is a general consensus that it involves an organization's shared values, assumptions, and beliefs specific to workplace safety (DeJoy, 2005; Wiegmann, Zhang, von Thaden, Sharma, & Gibbons, 2004). Simplifying this even more, safety culture is about the relative importance of safety within an organization. More recently, we have seen some attention given to the idea that organizations also have health cultures (Aldana et al., 2012). The creation of strong and positive safety or health cultures depends largely on the actions taken or not taken by management. These requisite actions most often involve the implementation of a comprehensive and systematic approach to managing workplace safety and health that assigns primary importance to worker protection. The third epoch essentially built upon the first and second and brings the organization and its leadership directly into the mix of analysis and action.

In summary, there are at least four takeaway points from this brief history. First, OSH has basically focused on avoiding or minimizing adverse effects—keeping workers from becoming injured or ill due to hazards in the workplace. By mandate, this is fundamentally an employer responsibility. Second, legal and regulatory actions have been the primary tools used to prevent or reduce worker injuries and illnesses. Third, for most of this history, emphasis has been on developing and enforcing specific standards that target specific hazards. This approach can sometimes engender a "compliance mentality" among employers whereby the primary goal becomes compliance rather than protection. Fourth, there have always been trade-offs between maximizing worker safety and health and other organizational priorities such as productivity or cost.

HEALTH PROMOTION

The WHP efforts are of much more recent origin. How recent depends to some extent on what counts as health promotion (O'Donnell & Ainsworth, 1984; Wilson, 1999). For example, certain businesses operated medical clinics that provided basic care in addition to treating work-related injuries or health problems. For decades, organizations have sponsored softball teams or bowling leagues largely intended to improve employee morale rather than employee fitness. Some early fitness facilities emerged in the 1950s and early 1960s, usually at a company's headquarters and primarily for executives as a "perk" and to hedge against losing a top executive to a heart attack.

The late 1970s up through the mid-1980s witnessed growing interest in conducting health promotion or wellness efforts at the workplace. Much of this acceleration was due to increased awareness of the huge burden of preventable, lifestyle-related disease, disability, and premature death (Hartunian, Smart, & Thompson, 1980; Luce & Schweitzer, 1978; McGinnis, 1980). Some have argued that this was also a period of deregulation and the questioning of health protection measures in the workplace (DeJoy & Southern, 1993; Walsh, Jennings, Mangione, & Merrigan, 1991). Some economists pinpoint the 1970s as the starting point of systemic economic restructuring and shifting employment patterns (Galbraith, 2000). Also, at about this same time, several rather high-visibility reports appeared, including Lalonde's (1974) report in Canada, *Healthy People* in the United States (U.S. Department of Health, Education, and Welfare, 1979), and the Ottawa Charter sponsored by the World Health Organization (WHO; 1986). In their own ways, each of these reports called for a departure from a sole focus on the medical or treatment model of health and increased emphasis on disease prevention and health promotion. The Ottawa Charter contained what is arguably the best-known definition of health promotion:

> Health promotion is the process of enabling people to increase control over, and to improve, their health. To reach a state of complete physical, mental and social well-being, an individual or group must be able to identify and to realize aspirations, to satisfy needs, and to change or cope with the environment. (WHO, 1986, p. 1)

This ambitious definition notwithstanding, most early health promotion programs were more disease prevention than health promotion (Breslow, 1999).

From a basic public health perspective, workplaces are good places to find large numbers of people for the purposes of educating them about health and for delivering basic health screenings and other preventive services. A large percentage of the adult population is employed and spends a significant portion of most days at work. Workplaces are also social systems, so it was thought that these social systems could be activated in support of health promotion goals. Employer cooperation was not envisioned as a major barrier, in that most employers would be supportive of having a healthier and more productive workforce. This was especially so in the United States, where employers often provide health insurance coverage for many or all of their employees. And for the most part, WHP was not envisioned as interfering with work performance or as requiring modifications to jobs or operational processes.

From the beginning, most WHP initiatives emphasized personal health behaviors and individual responsibility, with the primary goal of preventing or reducing adverse outcomes (Fielding & Piserchia, 1989). WHP in the United States has focused much more on physical than mental health, with mental health typically the purview of employee assistance programs or confined to stress and stress management programs and activities. In the late 1980s especially, we begin to see more programs targeting multiple risk factors and offering a variety of screening and educational programming. Rising health care costs and the desire of organizations to control or contain them were important drivers here. Indeed, in the mid- to late 1980s, health care costs in the United States were increasing by 17% to 19% annually (Mercer Human Resources Consulting, 2002). As these programs began to expand and mature, greater attention was given to more formalized behavior change initiatives in such areas as physical activity and nutrition and weight management (DeJoy, Dyal, Padilla, & Wilson, 2014). As WHP programs became more popular, there was a commensurate expansion of the related research literature. Research and evaluation findings influenced program development in at least three important ways. First, the increasing popularity of social-ecological or multilevel models led to interventions and programs that made greater use of environmental and policy initiatives to encourage and support positive health behavior change (McLeroy, Bibeau, Steckler, & Glanz, 1988; Stokols, 1992). Second, evidence was also accumulating suggesting the advantages of multicomponent or comprehensive programs (Heaney & Goetzel, 1997; Pelletier, 2005). Third, research studies were increasing the focus on financial outcomes, primarily on health care costs initially but rather quickly expanding to include presenteeism and productivity-related costs (Goetzel et al., 1998).

Much of the interest in financial outcomes has revolved around cost-effectiveness and return on investment, the main idea being that health promotion programming should save an organization at least as much as it costs (of course, we worry much less about financial returns when the topic is treatment rather than prevention). Up until quite recently, research on financial outcomes had shown generally positive returns for employer investments in WHP (e.g., Aldana, 2001; Baicker, Cutler, & Song, 2010; Pelletier, 2005, 2009). More recent analyses, however, have been less supportive (e.g., Cherniack, 2013; Mattke et al., 2013, 2014). It is clear, though, that healthy employees cost less than unhealthy employees and that total productivity-related costs far exceed health care costs for most organizations (Brady et al., 1997). Goetzel et al. (2012) examined 10 modifiable health risks (high blood pressure, excess weight, high blood glucose, etc.) and reported that these 10 factors accounted for more than 20% of health care expenditures for seven employers (> 90,000 employees). Other recent evidence suggests that specific program components such as disease management may be particularly important drivers of cost savings (Caloyeras, Liu, Exum, Broderick, & Mattke, 2014).

As we move closer to the present, comprehensive WHP programs still seem to be more the exception than the rule. This conclusion rests somewhat on how you define a comprehensive program. Healthy People 2010 (U.S. Department of Health and Human Services, 2010) identified five key elements of comprehensive WHP programs: health education, supportive environment, program integration, linkage to related programs, and screening. Healthy People 2010 also set a related objective—that 75% of all employers should offer such programs by 2010. But as of 2004, progress toward that objective was quite poor. According to a national survey conducted at that time, less than 7% of sampled worksites with 50 or more employees included all five elements in their WHP programs (Linnan et al., 2008). Even among the largest worksites (those with 750 or more employees), only 24% did so.

In summary, WHP, for the most part, has focused on avoiding or minimizing adverse health effects. The idea of optimizing multiple dimensions of health and well-being as featured in prominent definitions of health promotion and wellness has not been a primary focus of WHP to date. Second, WHP initiatives are almost completely voluntary on the part of both employers and employees, although there has been some recent controversy about required employee participation and the use of potentially punitive or discriminatory financial incentives in some WHP activities (Madison, 2016). Third, to a considerable degree, WHP programming has not involved substantial modifications to or disruption of jobs, work processes, or operations. This may change, however, in view of growing interest in topics such as worker well-being, work–family balance, and the idea of work as a social determinant of health. Fourth, cost containment and return on investment, along with productivity enhancement, have become important justifications for investments in WHP, in some respects outweighing other outcomes.

INTEGRATED PROGRAMMING

Integrated programming, like most innovations, is not really a singularly unique idea. In many respects, there has been movement in this general direction for some time. A few examples help illustrate this point. In 1974, Lalonde's report in Canada called attention to the complex interplay of environmental and behavioral risks in population health, including working conditions. As we saw in the brief histories of OSH and WHP, both of these domains have veered toward more ecological or systems views of causation and prevention, beginning sometime about 1980. In a program-planning document produced in 1984, NIOSH argued the merits of simultaneously addressing OSH and WHP to create a "synergy of prevention." Dalton and Harris (1991) called for a comprehensive approach to corporate health management in 1991, and DeJoy and Southern (1993) argued specifically for integration of OSH and WHP and presented a conceptual model and general strategy for implementation in 1993. Almost from the start, models of integrated programming have followed a general social ecological or systems perspective and called for the development of complementary behavioral–environmental interventions. Sorensen et al. (2002) were among the first to actually test such an intervention in the WellWorks trial. They examined whether the addition of OSH components would enhance the effectiveness of WHP with regard to smoking cessation in manufacturing settings where hazardous exposures were common. Although somewhat forgotten today, early discussions of integration had much to do with using this as a strategy to reach underserved and/or hard-to-reach groups of employees (DeJoy & Southern, 1993; Sorensen, Stoddard, Ockene, Hunt, & Youngstrom, 1996). The core idea is that it would likely be difficult to change the personal health behaviors of workers when these same workers are being exposed to hazardous and unhealthy working conditions on a daily basis. That some stakeholders might be resistant to combining OSH and WHP was also recognized relatively early (Walsh et al., 1991).

The general idea of integration has been evident in several related initiatives, including research on creating healthier work organizations (Danna & Griffin, 1999; DeJoy & Wilson, 2003; Sauter, Lim, & Murphy, 1996; Wilson, DeJoy, Vandenberg, Richardson, & McGrath, 2004); workplace health circles and other similar comprehensive programs, primarily in Europe (Aust & Ducki, 2004); psychologically healthy workplaces (Grawitch, Gottschalk, & Munz, 2006; Kelloway & Day, 2005); and well-being at work (Harter, Schmidt, & Keyes, 2003; Schulte & Vainio, 2010). According to the American Psychological Association, psychologically healthy workplaces share five key characteristics (Grawitch et al., 2006): employee involvement, employee health and safety, work–life balance, employee growth and development, and employee recognition. In 2005, the Institute of Medicine (2005) published a report that offered a framework for integrating employee health at the National Aeronautics and Space Administration. In 2010, the WHO published a Healthy Workplace model that features four interacting spheres: physical work environment, personal health resources, enterprise community involvement, and psychosocial work environment. Indeed, the European Network for Workplace Health Promotion (2007) has espoused an agenda that highlights topics such as work organization, the work environment, worker participation, and personal development going back to the Luxembourg Declaration in 1997.

In many respects, the occupational health psychology (OHP) movement itself has been both a contributor to, and a product of, integration. David Ferguson, an Australian occupational physician, is often credited with being one of the earliest advocates of OHP (Sauter & Hurrell, 2017). In the 1970s, Ferguson (1977) argued for a broad-based approach to occupational health that would be multidisciplinary in scope and draw upon the skills of clinical, social, occupational, organizational, and applied experimental psychologists. He essentially called for a multilevel, holistic approach to worker health, safety, and well-being and emphasized the need to address primary, secondary, and tertiary prevention as they apply to the total occupational context. Significant and ongoing changes to workforce demographics, labor market conditions, employment structures, information and other technologies, globalization, and the blurring of lines between work and nonwork have all fueled interest in OHP and actively expanded the approaches taken to improving worker health, safety, and well-being.

An essentially similar trend has been evident within occupational and environment medicine. Within this medical specialty, there have specific calls for breaking down the silos that have traditionally separated health protection, health promotion, employment benefits, and related areas in many organizations. In 2011, the American College of Occupational and Environmental Medicine issued a guidance statement calling for the integration of health protection and promotion (Hymel et al., 2011). The introduction to the article by Hymel and colleagues concludes with the following statement:

> Stated simply, workplace health protection and promotion is the strategic and systematic integration of distinct environmental, health, and safety policies and programs into a continuum of activities that enhances the overall health and well-being of the workforce and prevents work-related injuries and illnesses. (p. 695)

Probably the strongest argument for integration is that it simply makes sense from both the health and business perspectives. A wealth of biomedical evidence exists showing the interaction of occupational and personal risk factors in disease and injury (Hymel et al., 2011; Schulte, Pandalai, Wulsin, & Chun, 2012). This interaction is evident in etiology as well as prevention, treatment, and rehabilitation. Using obesity or excessive body weight as a case in point, obesity is a risk factor for Type 2 diabetes, heart disease, and cancer (Must et al., 1999); it is also associated with greater absenteeism and higher health care costs (Finkelstein, DiBonaventura, Burgess, & Hale, 2010). Obesity is also a risk factor for certain occupational musculoskeletal injuries and disorders (Wearing, Hennig, Byrne, Steele, & Hills, 2006). At the same time, we know that certain working conditions can contribute to weight gain, including sedentary work, shiftwork, long work hours, and certain job stressors (Schulte et al., 2007).

From the business perspective, integration should limit the redundancy of workplace health and safety programs and services. It also offers the potential for more comprehensive and strategic programming. Today, in many organizations, related functional areas such as occupational safety, employee assistance, health promotion, and human resources operate independently in distinct departments or silos, with little interaction and sometimes in direct competition for resources. Integration offers the potential for greater sharing of knowledge and information and for developing more comprehensive initiatives and making better decisions about program priorities and resources. All of these factors make good business sense. The move toward integration also seems appropriate when we take into consideration the changing compositions of our economy and workforce: less manufacturing and more service and knowledge-oriented jobs, an older and more diverse workforce, and a host of new work settings and employment relationships.

As thinking and research on integrated programming have expanded, three issues have garnered increased attention. The first of these issues concerns making the business case for integrated programs in terms of cost reduction and improved productivity. As with WHP, there is the assumption that the adoption of more elaborate and comprehensive programming should be accompanied by a rational business case that shows them to be good financial investments. Although evidence is accumulating, the business case for integration has not been convincingly demonstrated (Anger et al., 2015; Pronk, 2013). Two questions are pertinent here: Do integrated programs provide a good return on investment? Are they superior to more traditional, nonintegrated programs? The second issue focuses on the interrelatedness of work and nonwork factors in health and disease (Cherniack et al., 2011). Integrative initiatives have begun to focus more on the total life space of the person (i.e., work, home, and community) and not confined to the workplace and work time. The third issue concerns the importance of employee involvement in program development and execution. For example, good use has been made of participatory strategies from the field of ergonomics (Henning, Warren, Robertson, Faghri, & Cherniack, 2009). Such strategies fit well with making simultaneous changes to the work environment and to individual behavior. Participatory and action research strategies, as iterative processes, can also be useful for building employee capacity that will help with making and sustaining future changes. All of these early and more recent integrated program developments create a foundation for NIOSH activities to advance TWH as a new prevention strategy in OSH, as presented in Chapter 2, this volume.

THE TWH PROGRAM: STATUS AND FUTURE DIRECTIONS

The TWH program has been launched, it makes sense for both workers and employers, and concerted efforts have been made to build infrastructure to support and coordinate related research and practice. But much more needs to be done. At present, the evidence base for the TWH approach remains quite limited in terms of both worker and financial outcomes (Anger et al., 2015; Feltner et al., 2016). Obviously, a key task is to build a body of research sufficient for drawing firm conclusions, but additional questions exist specific to the burden of proof. Must integrated interventions and programs be both more effective and less costly than nonintegrated or traditional interventions and programs? Must the benefits be synergistic in magnitude—that integration has a multiplier effect? We also need to know about program transfer and sustainability. Can a stockpile of interventions and programs be accumulated that can be deployed across industries and occupations? Once implemented, will integrated programs be sustained and supported by employers and workers? Effectiveness, adoption, and sustainability are related. Effective programs are more likely to be adopted and to be continued. That we do not yet have answers to these questions should not be viewed as a fault. One central challenge to furthering the science of the TWH program is funding. Although NIOSH has made a significant financial commitment to the TWH approach, the creation of a definitive and generalizable body of field-based research is expensive and ultimately will require partnerships with other federal agencies and funding sources.

The future of the TWH program involves both the "what" and the "how." Concerning the what, for example, the definition of *Total Worker Health* has evolved during its short history. In the transition from the NIOSH Steps to WorkLife initiatives, the term *well-being* entered the definition (NIOSH, 2008). In large part, this change was a reflection of the growing international literature on well-being at work (Hassan et al., 2009; McLellan, 2017; Schulte & Vainio, 2010). This term is also consistent with established definitions of health (WHO, 1948) and health promotion (WHO, 1986), and the ideas that health and well-being are related but not the same and that both are multidimensional. The term *well-being* emphasizes the positive and not simply the avoidance of adverse effects. Growing interest in viewing work as a social determinant of health has also increased the salience of well-being. Well-being also brings economics and behavioral health into the mix, and the reality that work can be a positive influence on health and well-being. Well being might also qualify as a suitable replacement for the terms *wellness* and *health promotion*, which have generated concern among those suspicious of integrated programming. The current definition of *Total Worker Health* retains the term *well-being* and emphasizes NIOSH's core vision of safer, healthier workers (NIOSH, 2016b). As currently defined, the TWH program involves the "policies, programs, and practices that integrate protection from work-related safety and health hazards with promotion of injury and illness–prevention efforts to advance worker well-being" (NIOSH, 2016a, p. 2).

Switching to the how, two broad considerations require attention going forward. The first consideration involves the how of designing and conducting research in support of the TWH concept. A number of authors have addressed this issue, and this topic has been prominent on the agendas of a number of TWH meetings and workshops. Sorensen et al. (2016; see also Chapter 5, this volume) proposed a conceptual model for integrated programming that draws upon a variety of theoretical perspectives. This model provides a framework for both research and intervention. In this model, the conditions of work (physical environment, work organization, etc.) are centrally positioned and important determinants of health and safety outcomes. Conditions of work also serve to mediate effects on health behaviors. Conditions of work are influenced by enterprise and workforce characteristics, which also can affect the implementation of various policies and programs.

The other consideration involves promoting and facilitating the adoption and successful implementation of integrated programs by business and industry. As we saw earlier in this chapter, the traditions and approaches of health protection and health promotion are quite different. They also have something important in common: aiding the worker. The general topic of adoption was addressed recently at a summit sponsored by the American College of Occupational and Environmental Medicine and Underwriters Laboratory in 2014. The guidance report produced by this summit (Loeppke et al., 2015) concluded that the uptake of integration in the workplace remains quite limited. The report identifies a number of areas in which improvement is needed, including a clearer demonstration of the value proposition of integration, a set of metrics for measuring effectiveness, and practical guidelines for implementing integrated programs applicable to a wide variety of employers. This report also featured recommendations focusing on the need to create incentives to motivate employers, the importance of partnerships and readily available technical assistance, and the maintenance of confidentiality and trust in handling the health-related data of employees. So, basically the challenge here is not to simply offer an implementation model but to create interest, motivation, and capacity among employers. NIOSH is aware of and working on these issues as evidenced in recent publications (NIOSH, 2016a, 2016b).

Adoption and implementation of the TWH program invariably calls forth the topic of organizational culture, or perhaps more specifically, organizational health culture. Interest in the concept of health culture is growing, but progress lags well behind that of safety culture (Aldana et al., 2012). As Loeppke and colleagues (2015) argued, the uptake of integration in an organization depends to a considerable extent on how well the health culture is developed. These same authors went on to argue that integration may itself be a key ingredient of a supportive health culture, but this becomes somewhat of a circular argument. Organizations wishing to change their health cultures face the challenges of creating readiness and building capacity. Doing so, of course, depends on leadership initiative, and both the actions and words of leadership matter (DeJoy & Della, 2014). Although the recent TWH research agenda makes little direct mention of culture or culture change, the expressed goals for all four of the priority areas (i.e., research, practice, policy, and capacity building) speak to the importance of culture.

In closing, the TWH program is a new way of thinking about the work–health relationship, a new paradigm. It offers a comprehensive and unified method for identifying safety and health needs and priorities. It opens up new options for intervention and for allocating resources across functional areas. It makes sense for today's workplaces and workforce. It offers more creative possibilities for making workplaces safer and healthier and for maximizing worker well-being. At this juncture, we have established priorities for future research and created infrastructure that makes the needed research possible. Increased attention is also being given to achieving the stakeholder input and buy-in that are crucial to adoption and sustainability. The stage is pretty well set to advance the TWH agenda.

REFERENCES

Aldana, S. G. (2001). Financial impact of health promotion programs: A comprehensive review of the literature. *American Journal of Health Promotion, 15*, 296–320. http://dx.doi.org/10.4278/0890-1171-15.5.296

Aldana, S. G., Anderson, D. R., Adams, T. B., Whitmer, R. W., Merrill, R. M., George, V., & Noyce, J. (2012). A review of the knowledge base on healthy worksite culture. *Journal of Occupational and Environmental Medicine, 54*, 414–419. http://dx.doi.org/10.1097/JOM.0b013c31824be25f

Anger, W. K., Elliot, D. L., Bodner, T., Olson, R., Rohlman, D. S., Truxillo, D. M., . . . Montgomery, D. (2015). Effectiveness of total worker health interventions. *Journal of Occupational Health Psychology, 20*, 226–247. http://dx.doi.org/10.1037/a0038340

Aust, B., & Ducki, A. (2004). Comprehensive health promotion interventions at the workplace: Experiences with health circles in Germany. *Journal of Occupational Health Psychology, 9*, 258–270. http://dx.doi.org/10.1037/1076-8998.9.3.258

Baicker, K., Cutler, D., & Song, Z. (2010). Workplace wellness programs can generate savings. *Health Affairs, 29*, 304–311. http://dx.doi.org/10.1377/hlthaff.2009.0626

Booher, H. R. (Ed.). (2003). *Handbook of human systems integration*. Hoboken, NJ: Wiley & Sons. http://dx.doi.org/10.1002/0471721174

Brady, W., Bass, J., Moser, R., Jr., Anstadt, G. W., Loeppke, R. R., & Leopold, R. (1997). Defining total corporate health and safety costs significance and impact: Review and recommendations. *Journal of Occupational and Environmental Medicine, 39*, 224–231. http://dx.doi.org/10.1097/00043764-199703000-00012

Breslow, L. (1999). From disease prevention to health promotion. *Journal of the American Medical Association, 281*, 1030–1033. http://dx.doi.org/10.1001/jama.281.11.1030

Caloyeras, J. P., Liu, H., Exum, E., Broderick, M., & Mattke, S. (2014). Managing manifest diseases, but not health risks, saved PepsiCo money over seven years. *Health Affairs, 33*, 124–131. http://dx.doi.org/10.1377/hlthaff.2013.0625

Cherniack, M. (2013). Integrated health programs, health outcomes, and return on investment: Measuring workplace health promotion and integrated program effectiveness. *Journal of Occupational and Environmental Medicine, 55*(Suppl.), S38–S45. http://dx.doi.org/10.1097/JOM.0000000000000044

Cherniack, M., Henning, R., Merchant, J. A., Punnett, L., Sorensen, G. R., & Wagner, G. (2011). Statement on national worklife priorities. *American Journal of Industrial Medicine, 54*, 10–20. http://dx.doi.org/10.1002/ajim.20900

Dalton, B. A., & Harris, J. S. (1991). A comprehensive approach to corporate health management. *Journal of Occupational Medicine, 33*, 338–347.

Danna, K., & Griffin, R. W. (1999). Health and well-being in the workplace: A review and synthesis of the literature. *Journal of Management, 25*, 357–384. http://dx.doi.org/10.1177/014920639902500305

DeJoy, D. M. (2005). Behavior change versus culture change: Divergent approaches to managing workplace safety. *Safety Science, 43*, 105–129. http://dx.doi.org/10.1016/j.ssci.2005.02.001

DeJoy, D. M., & Della, L. J. (2014). Culture, communication, and making workplaces healthier. In A. Day, E. K. Kelloway, & J. J. Hurrell (Eds.), *Workplace well-being: How to build psychologically healthy workplaces* (pp. 175–201). Chichester, England: Wiley Blackwell.

DeJoy, D. M., Dyal, M. A., Padilla, H. M., & Wilson, M. G. (2014). National workplace health promotion surveys: The Affordable Care Act and future surveys. *American Journal of Health Promotion, 28*, 142–145. http://dx.doi.org/10.4278/ajhp.121212-CIT-602

DeJoy, D. M., & Southern, D. J. (1993). An integrative perspective on work-site health promotion. *Journal of Occupational Medicine, 35*, 1221–1230.

DeJoy, D. M., & Wilson, M. G. (2003). Organizational health promotion: Broadening the horizon of workplace health promotion. *American Journal of Health Promotion, 17*, 337–341. http://dx.doi.org/10.4278/0890-1171-17.5.337

European Network for Workplace Health Promotion. (2007, January). *Luxembourg Declaration on workplace health promotion in the European Union.* Amersfoort, the Netherlands: Author.

Federal Coal Mine Health and Safety Act of 1969, Pub. L. No. 91-173, 83 Stat. 742 (1969).

Feltner, C., Peterson, K., Palmieri Weber, R., Cluff, L., Coker-Schwimmer, E., Viswanathan, M., & Lohr, K. N. (2016). The effectiveness of Total Worker Health interventions: A systematic review for a National Institutes of Health Pathways to Prevention Workshop. *Annals of Internal Medicine, 165*, 262–269.

Ferguson, D. (1977). The psychologist and occupational health. In J. Brebner (Eds.), *Proceedings of the Annual Conference, Ergonomics Society of Australia and New Zealand* (pp. 41–50). Adelaide, Australia: Department of Psychology, University of Adelaide.

Fielding, J. E., & Piserchia, P. V. (1989). Frequency of worksite health promotion activities. *American Journal of Public Health, 79*, 16–20. http://dx.doi.org/10.2105/AJPH.79.1.16

Fink, L. (1982). *Workingmen's democracy: The Knights of Labor and American politics.* Urbana: University of Illinois Press.

Finkelstein, E. A., DiBonaventura, M., Burgess, S. M., & Hale, B. C. (2010). The costs of obesity in the workplace. *Journal of Occupational and Environmental Medicine, 52*, 971–976. http://dx.doi.org/10.1097/JOM.0b013e3181f274d2

Fishback, P. V., & Kantor, S. E. (1998). The adoption of workers' compensation in the United States, 1990–1930. *The Journal of Law & Economics, 41*, 305–342. http://dx.doi.org/10.1086/467392

Galbraith, J. K. (2000). *Created unequal.* Chicago, IL: University of Chicago Press.

Geiser, K., & Rosenberg, B. J. (2006). The social context of occupational and environmental health. In B. S. Levy, D. H. Wegman, S. L. Baron, & R. K. Sokas (Eds.), *Occupational and environmental health: Recognizing and preventing disease and injury* (5th ed., pp. 21–38). Philadelphia, PA: Lippincott Williams & Wilkins.

Goetzel, R. Z., Anderson, D. R., Whitmer, R. W., Ozminkowski, R. J., Dunn, R. L., Wasserman, J., & the Health Enhancement Research Organization (HERO) Research Committee. (1998). The relationship between modifiable health risks and health care expenditures. An analysis of the multi-employer HERO health risk and cost database. *Journal of Occupational and Environmental Medicine, 40*, 843–854. http://dx.doi.org/10.1097/00043764-199810000-00003

Goetzel, R. Z., Pei, X., Tabrizi, M. J., Henke, R. M., Kowlessar, N., Nelson, C. F., & Metz, R. D. (2012). Ten modifiable health risk factors are linked to more than one-fifth of employer-employee health care spending. *Health Affairs, 31*, 2474–2484. http://dx.doi.org/10.1377/hlthaff.2011.0819

Grawitch, M. J., Gottschalk, M., & Munz, D. C. (2006). The path to a healthy workplace: A Critical review linking healthy workplace practices, employee well-being, and organizational improvements. *Consulting Psychology Journal: Practice and Research, 58*, 129–147. http://dx.doi.org/10.1037/1065-9293.58.3.129

Hale, A. R., & Hovden, J. (1998). Management and culture: The third age of safety. A review of approaches to organizational aspects of safety, health, and environment. In A. M. Feyer & A. Williamson (Eds.), *Occupational injury: Risk, prevention, and intervention* (pp. 129–166). London, England: Taylor & Francis. Retrieved from https://www.taylorfrancis.com/books/e/9780203212493/chapters/10.1201%2F9780203212493-18

Hammer, W., & Price, D. (2001). *Occupational safety and health management and engineering* (5th ed.). Upper Saddle River, NJ: Prentice-Hall.

Harter, J. K., Schmidt, F. L., & Keyes, C. L. M. (2003). Well-being in the workplace and its relationship to business outcomes: A review of the Gallup Studies. In C. L. M. Keyes & L. Haidt (Eds.), *Flourishing: Positive psychology and the life well-lived* (pp. 205–224). Washington, DC: American Psychological Association. http://dx.doi.org/10.1037/10594-009

Hartunian, N. S., Smart, C. N., & Thompson, M. S. (1980). The incidence and economic costs of cancer, motor vehicle injuries, coronary heart disease, and stroke: A comparative analysis. *American Journal of Public Health, 70,* 1249–1260. http://dx.doi.org/10.2105/AJPH.70.12.1249

Hassan, E., Austin, C., Celia, C., Disley, E., Hunt, P., Marjanovic, S., . . . van Stolk, C. (2009). *Health and well-being at work in the United Kingdom.* Cambridge, England: RAND Corporation.

Heaney, C. A., & Goetzel, R. Z. (1997). A review of health-related outcomes of multicomponent worksite health promotion programs. *American Journal of Health Promotion, 11,* 290–307. http://dx.doi.org/10.4278/0890-1171-11.4.290

Henning, R., Warren, N., Robertson, M., Faghri, P., & Cherniack, M. (2009). Workplace health protection and promotion through participatory ergonomics: An integrated approach. *Public Health Reports, 124*(Suppl. 1), 26–35. http://dx.doi.org/10.1177/00333549091244S104

Hymel, P. A., Loeppke, R. R., Baase, C. M., Burton, W. N., Hartenbaum, N. P., Hudson, T. W., . . . Larson, P. W. (2011). Workplace health protection and promotion: A new pathway for a healthier—and safer—workforce. *Journal of Occupational and Environmental Medicine, 53,* 695–702. http://dx.doi.org/10.1097/JOM.0b013e31822005d0

Institute of Medicine. (2005). *Integrating employee health: A model program for NASA.* Washington, DC: National Academies Press.

Institute of Medicine. (2014). *Promising and best practices in Total Worker Health: Workshop summary.* Washington, DC: National Academies Press.

Kelloway, E. K., & Day, A. L. (2005). Building healthy workplaces: What we know so far. *Canadian Journal of Behavioural Science/Revue canadienne des sciences du comportement, 37,* 223–235. http://dx.doi.org/10.1037/h0087259

Lalonde, M. (1974). *A new perspective on the health of Canadians.* Ottawa, Ontario, Canada: Government of Canada.

Linnan, L., Bowling, M., Childress, J., Lindsay, G., Blakey, C., Pronk, S., . . . Royall, P. (2008). Results of the 2004 National Worksite Health Promotion Survey. *American Journal of Public Health, 98,* 1503–1509. http://dx.doi.org/10.2105/AJPH.2006.100313

Loeppke, R. R., Hohn, T., Baase, C., Bunn, W. B., Burton, W. N., Eisenberg, B. S., . . . Siuba, J. (2015). Integrating health and safety in the workplace: How closely aligning health and safety strategies can yield measurable benefits. *Journal of Occupational and Environmental Medicine, 57,* 585–597. http://dx.doi.org/10.1097/JOM.0000000000000467

Luce, B. R., & Schweitzer, S. O. (1978). Smoking and alcohol abuse: A comparison of their economic consequences. *The New England Journal of Medicine, 298,* 569–571. http://dx.doi.org/10.1056/NEJM197803092981012

Madison, K. M. (2016). The risk of using workplace wellness programs to foster a culture of health. *Health Affairs, 35,* 2068–2074. http://dx.doi.org/10.1377/hlthaff.2016.0729

Mattke, S., Liu, H. H., Caloyeras, J. P., Huang, C. Y., Van Busum, K. R., Khodyakov, D., . . . Broderick, M. (2014). *Do workplace wellness programs save employers money?* Santa Monica, CA: RAND Corporation.

Mattke, S., Liu, H. H., Caloyeras, J. P., Huang, C. Y., Van Busum, K. R., Khodyakov, D., & Shier, V. (2013). Workplace wellness programs study: Final report. *RAND Health Quarterly, 3*(2), 7.

McGinnis, J. M. (1980). Trends in disease prevention: Assessing the benefits of prevention. *Bulletin of the New York Academy of Medicine, 56*, 38–44.

McLellan, R. K. (2017). Work, health, and worker well-being: Roles and opportunities for employers. *Health Affairs, 36*, 206–213. http://dx.doi.org/10.1377/hlthaff.2016.1150

McLeroy, K. R., Bibeau, D., Steckler, A., & Glanz, K. (1988). An ecological perspective on health promotion programs. *Health Education Quarterly, 15*, 351–377. http://dx.doi.org/10.1177/109019818801500401

Mercer Human Resources Consulting. (2002). *Rate hikes pushed employers to drop health plans and benefits in 2002, but average cost still rose. 2002 Mercer Health Care Survey Results.* New York, NY: Author.

Must, A., Spadano, J., Coakley, E. H., Field, A. E., Colditz, G., & Dietz, W. H. (1999). The disease burden associated with overweight and obesity. *JAMA, 282*, 1523–1529. http://dx.doi.org/10.1001/jama.282.16.1523

National Institute for Occupational Safety and Health. (1984). *Program of the National Institute for Occupational Safety and Health: Program plan by program area for FY 1984–1989* (NIOSH Publication No. 84-107). Washington, DC: U.S. Department of Health and Human Services.

National Institute for Occupational Safety and Health. (2008). *Essential elements of effective workplace programs and policies for improving worker health and well-being* (NIOSH Publication No. 2010-140). Washington, DC: U.S. Department of Health and Human Services.

National Institute for Occupational Safety and Health. (2012). *Research compendium: The NIOSH Total Worker Health Program: Seminal research papers* (NIOSH Publication No. 2012-146). Washington, DC: U.S. Department of Health and Human Services.

National Institute for Occupational Safety and Health. (2016a). *Fundamentals of Total Worker Health® approaches: Essential elements for advancing worker safety, health, and well-being* (NIOSH Publication No. 2017-112). Washington, DC: U.S. Department of Health and Human Services.

National Institute for Occupational Safety and Health. (2016b). *National occupational research agenda (NORA)/national Total Worker Health® agenda (2016–2026): A national agenda to advance Total Worker Health® research, practice, policy, and capacity* (NIOSH Publication No. 2016-114). Washington, DC: U.S. Department of Health and Human Services.

Occupational Safety and Health Act of 1970, Pub. L. No. 91-596, 84 Stat. 1590 (1970).

Occupational Safety and Health Administration. (1989). Safety and health program management guidelines: Issuance of voluntary guidelines. *Federal Register, 54*, 3904–3916.

O'Donnell, M. P., & Ainsworth, T. (Eds.). (1984). *Health promotion in the workplace.* New York, NY: Wiley Medical.

Pelletier, K. R. (2005). A review and analysis of the clinical and cost-effectiveness studies of comprehensive health promotion and disease management programs at the worksite: Update VI 2000–2004. *Journal of Occupational and Environmental Medicine, 47*, 1051–1058. http://dx.doi.org/10.1097/01.jom.0000174303.85442.bf

Pelletier, K. R. (2009). A review and analysis of the clinical and cost-effectiveness studies of comprehensive health promotion and disease management programs at the worksite: Update VII 2004–2008. *Journal of Occupational and Environmental Medicine, 51*, 822–837. http://dx.doi.org/10.1097/JOM.0b013e3181a7de5a

Pidgeon, N., & O'Leary, M. (2000). Man-made disasters: Why technology and organizations (sometimes) fail. *Safety Science, 34*, 15–30. http://dx.doi.org/10.1016/S0925-7535(00)00004-7

Pronk, N. P. (2013). Integrated worker health protection and promotion programs: Overview and perspectives on health and economic outcomes. *Journal of Occupational and Environmental Medicine, 55*(Suppl.), S30–S37. http://dx.doi.org/10.1097/JOM.0000000000000031

Sauter, S. L., & Hurrell, J. J. (2017). Occupational health contributions to the development and promise of occupational health psychology. *Journal of Occupational Health Psychology, 22*, 251–258. http://dx.doi.org/10.1037/ocp0000088

Sauter, S. L., Lim, S., & Murphy, L. R. (1996). Organizational health: A new paradigm for occupational stress research at NIOSH. *Japanese Journal of Occupational Mental Health, 4*, 248–254.

Schill, A. L., & Chosewood, L. C. (2013). The NIOSH Total Worker Health™ program: An overview. *Journal of Occupational and Environmental Medicine, 55*(Suppl.), S8–S11. http://dx.doi.org/10.1097/JOM.0000000000000037

Schulte, P. A., Pandalai, S., Wulsin, V., & Chun, H. (2012). Interaction of occupational and personal risk factors in workforce health and safety. *American Journal of Public Health, 102*, 434–448. http://dx.doi.org/10.2105/AJPH.2011.300249

Schulte, P. A., & Vainio, H. (2010). Well-being at work—Overview and perspective. *Scandinavian Journal of Work, Environment & Health, 36*, 422–429. http://dx.doi.org/10.5271/sjweh.3076

Schulte, P. A., Wagner, G. R., Ostry, A., Blanciforti, L. A., Cutlip, R. G., Krajnak, K. M., . . . Miller, D. B. (2007). Work, obesity, and occupational safety and health. *American Journal of Public Health, 97*, 428–436. http://dx.doi.org/10.2105/AJPH.2006.086900

Sorensen, G., McLellan, D. L., Sabbath, E. L., Dennerlein, J. T., Nagler, E. M., Hurtado, D. A., . . . Wagner, G. R. (2016). Integrating worksite health protection and health promotion: A conceptual model for intervention and research. *Preventive Medicine, 91,* 188–196. http://dx.doi.org/10.1016/j.ypmed.2016.08.005

Sorensen, G., Stoddard, A., LaMontagne, A., Emmons, K., Hunt, M., Youngstrom, R., . . . Christiani, D. (2002). A comprehensive worksite cancer prevention intervention: Behavior change results from a randomized controlled trial (United States). *Cancer Causes & Control, 13*, 493–502. http://dx.doi.org/10.1023/A:1016385001695

Sorensen, G., Stoddard, A., Ockene, J. K., Hunt, M. K., & Youngstrom, R. (1996). Worker participation in an integrated health promotion/health protection program: Results from the WellWorks project. *Health Education Quarterly, 23*, 191–203. http://dx.doi.org/10.1177/109019819602300205

Stokols, D. (1992). Establishing and maintaining healthy environments. Toward a social ecology of health promotion. *American Psychologist, 47*, 6–22. http://dx.doi.org/10.1037/0003-066X.47.1.6

U.S. Department of Health, Education, and Welfare. (1979). *Healthy people: The Surgeon General's report on health promotion and disease prevention* (DHEW [PHS] Publication No. 79-55071). Washington, DC: U.S. Government Printing Office.

U.S. Department of Health and Human Services. (2010). *Healthy people 2010: Understanding and improving health* (2nd ed.). Washington, DC: U.S. Government Printing Office, 2000.

Walsh, D. C., Jennings, S. E., Mangione, T., & Merrigan, D. M. (1991). Health promotion versus health protection? Employees' perceptions and concerns. *Journal of Public Health Policy, 12*, 148–164. http://dx.doi.org/10.2307/3342500

Wearing, S. C., Hennig, E. M., Byrne, N. M., Steele, J. R., & Hills, A. P. (2006). Musculoskeletal disorders associated with obesity: A biomechanical perspective. *Obesity Reviews, 7*, 239–250. http://dx.doi.org/10.1111/j.1467-789X.2006.00251.x

Wiegmann, D. A., Zhang, H., von Thaden, T. L., Sharma, G., & Gibbons, A. M. (2004). Safety culture: An integrative review. *The International Journal of Aviation Psychology, 14*, 117–134. http://dx.doi.org/10.1207/s15327108ijap1402_1

Wilson, M. G. (1999). Health promotion in the workplace. In J. Rippe (Ed.), *Lifestyle medicine* (pp. 901–911). Cambridge, England: Blackwell Science.

Wilson, M. G., DeJoy, D. M., Vandenberg, R. J., Richardson, H., & McGrath, A. L. (2004). Work characteristics and employee health and well-being: Test of a model of healthy work organization. *Journal of Occupational and Organizational Psychology, 77,* 565–588. http://dx.doi.org/10.1348/0963179042596522

World Health Organization. (1948). *World Health organization constitution.* Geneva, Switzerland: Author.

World Health Organization. (1986). *Ottawa Charter for Health Promotion* (WHO/HPR/HEP/95.1). Geneva, Switzerland: Author.

World Health Organization. (2010). *Healthy workplaces: A model for action for employers, workers, policy-makers, and practitioners.* Geneva, Switzerland: Author.

2

The NIOSH *Total Worker Health®* Vision

Anita L. Schill, L. Casey Chosewood, and John Howard

You never change things by fighting the existing reality. To change something, build a new model that makes the existing model obsolete.

—RICHARD BUCKMINSTER FULLER

The *Total Worker Health®* approach to safety, health, and well-being has attracted wide interest over the past 15 years. Not only is it intuitively appealing to a large portion of the National Institute for Occupational Safety and Health (NIOSH) stakeholder community, it has drawn stakeholders new to NIOSH, introducing them to extensive occupational safety and health (OSH) resources. The *Total Worker Health* (TWH) program has funded novel research and outreach efforts, forged dozens of new partnerships. and changed the focus of many workplace health programs in the private and public sectors. Yet, at times, the concept is applied in ways that are inconsistent with the NIOSH vision of the TWH program, creating uncertainty for some about what the TWH approach is and what it is not. This chapter presents an insiders' perspective on the TWH concept, including the formation of the original vision, the evolution and expansion of the vision, and the future vision. It provides information needed for a fundamental understanding of the TWH concept.

This chapter was authored by employees of the United States government as part of their official duty and is considered to be in the public domain. The findings and conclusions in this report are those of the authors and do not necessarily represent the official position of the National Institute for Occupational Safety and Health, Centers for Disease Control and Prevention.

http://dx.doi.org/10.1037/0000149-003
Total Worker Health, H. L. Hudson, J. A. S. Nigam, S. L. Sauter, L. C. Chosewood, A. L. Schill, and J. Howard (Editors)

FORMATION OF THE VISION

The NIOSH experience of well-meaning efforts to improve the health of the U.S. adult population is that little, if any, attention is paid to the fact that working people spend the greater part of their waking hours during each 24-hour cycle at work and a large part of most days each week at work. Over the years, NIOSH has also observed an overall lack of appreciation of the evidence that work can adversely affect a worker's general health. Such was the design of *Steps to a HealthierUS* (*Steps*), an initiative created by former U.S. Department of Health and Human Services (DHHS) secretary Tommy G. Thompson in 2003 to improve the health of the U.S. population (U.S. DHHS, 2004). Work as a contributor to people's health was forgotten largely because population health experts often lack the knowledge and skills to (a) recognize how working conditions contribute to creating a health hazard and (b) develop mitigation and prevention strategies to address those hazards. In addition, there has been a shortage of surveillance and research linking working conditions to population health outcomes, especially chronic disease outcomes.

Because OSH, including mandates by the Occupational Safety and Health Act of 1970, is such a niche area of public health, it is not surprising that efforts to promote population health often fail to recognize work as a contributor to general health outcomes. The Steps initiative provided a stimulus and an opportunity for NIOSH to contribute to its success by launching a complementary spin-off, *Steps to a HealthierUS Workforce* (NIOSH, 2004). The NIOSH initiative augmented the DHHS Steps initiative by adding specialized content about the ways that working conditions can adversely affect general health outcomes and ways to mitigate these effects. The goal of *Steps to a HealthierUS Workforce* was "to protect, support, and enhance the health of workers through comprehensive programs for safe and healthy work, integrated with health-supportive environments and access to adequate health care" (NIOSH, 2015d, para. 1).

Simultaneously, these developments provided an opportunity for reflection on why the OSH community was commonly forgotten in large population-based initiatives such as Steps. Perhaps the "fault" rested with the OSH community because its practitioners held an implicit understanding about the existence of a sharp division between what happened at work (occupational) and what workers experience outside the workplace (nonoccupational). This belief may have been grounded in experience with the state and federal workers' compensation laws that necessitate the evaluation of injury and illness as either "work related" or "not work related." This bright-line division does not allow for the integration of personal choices, lifestyle, after-work activities, or other individual factors, with working conditions to produce an integrated approach to worker health. Driven by workers' compensation laws, the administrative division between occupational and nonoccupational injury and illness tended to permeate all safety and health approaches to worker safety and health. This bifurcated approach became an obstacle to a population health approach to worker safety and health. NIOSH recognized this and sought to expand the world of "work-related" injury and illness to the broader world of "worker" injury and illness. Moreover, NIOSH observed that the strong and constant emphasis on the technical aspects of industrial hygiene and safety engineering ceded the field of worker health to health promotionists, who primarily used the worksite as a platform to promote individual behavior change, even if conditions at the worksite were unsafe and unhealthy. Even when the work environment was considered, the focus tended to be on amenities like fitness facilities, cafeterias, and vending machines, and not on working conditions.

The NIOSH *Steps to a HealthierUS Workforce* initiative provided a framework to enlarge the scope of practice for OSH practitioners. It was anticipated that this enlargement would (a) expand the scope of practice for the OSH profession, (b) better serve the worker and the employer, and (c) reveal the shortcomings of efforts that focused solely on worksite wellness and health promotion. The latter has often been an incomplete strategy that ignores the interaction of workers with the work environment and uses workers as a captive audience for health appraisals and disease management efforts by employers often guided by their interest in lowering skyrocketing employer-sponsored health care costs.

In 2005, the DHHS *Steps* initiative faded and the name of the NIOSH initiative was changed to the *WorkLife Initiative*. Focusing the program in this way acknowledged the intersection of work and life outside of work as a growing concern of workers and was responsive to stakeholder calls for NIOSH to continue its leadership in promoting research, policy, and practice in the areas of science, economics, and coordination of health protection and health promotion to improve the health of workers (NIOSH, 2015d). During these early years, the WorkLife Initiative continued efforts to address worker safety, health, and well-being in a more comprehensive way by considering both the work environment and general health-related decisions and behaviors of workers. In addition to supporting research, adoption of health-enhancing policies and practices, and transdisciplinary collaboration, the WorkLife Initiative endeavored to bridge the long-standing separation and, often, competition between the OSH and health promotion professional communities. From 2005 to 2010, funding for this NIOSH programmatic area was primarily extramural through NIOSH Centers of Excellence for *Total Worker Health*® (Centers; see Figure 2.1). In 2008, representatives of these Centers began to develop a long-range strategy for advancing the WorkLife Initiative. Their research, policy, and practice recommendations were released in 2011 (Cherniack et al., 2011).

By 2011, the vision to integrate health protection and health promotion to advance worker well-being and find common ground with the worksite health promotion community began to crystallize. To reflect the progression of programmatic development, NIOSH renamed its efforts the TWH program to emphasize a more holistic view of the health of workers. This name resonated more clearly with the stakeholder community. At this juncture, NIOSH broadened its commitment by developing an intramural research program and increasing efforts focused on research translation, communication, and partnership building. A time line of key events in the history of the TWH program is shown in Figure 2.1. To enable this expanded activity, a small team of dedicated staff was assigned responsibility for a rejuvenated NIOSH program to integrate

FIGURE 2.1. Key Events in the History of the NIOSH *Total Worker Health®* Program

TOTAL WORKER HEALTH®
ADVANCING WORKER SAFETY, HEALTH, AND WELL-BEING

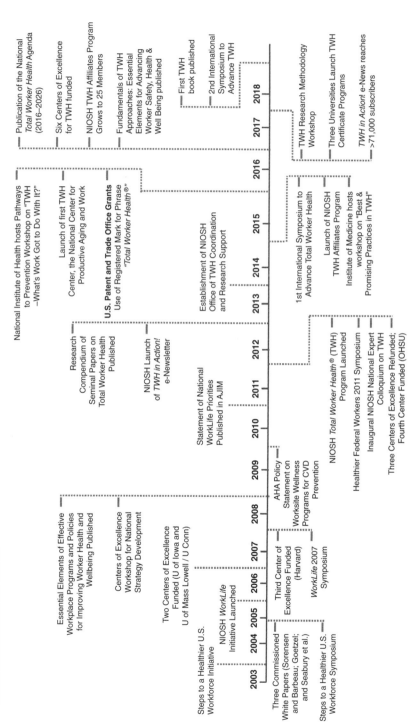

traditional safety and health protection with general health principles, policies, and practices.

Over the ensuing years, as the TWH program gained increasing traction with both intramural and extramural efforts, NIOSH was advised by key stakeholders that the foundational concept of safety and health protection for workers was sometimes diminished in favor of focusing on individual worker behavior change. Concerned by this misinterpretation and misapplication of the TWH approach to worker safety, health, and well-being, NIOSH made concrete programmatic changes with the goal of clearly articulating the vision that worker well-being can be advanced only when working conditions are safe and healthful. Through this approach, opportunities were created to expand knowledge about worker safety and health and enlarge the contribution that NIOSH can make to fulfill the mandate of the OSH Act "to assure so far as possible every man and woman in the Nation safe and healthful working conditions and to preserve our human resources . . . by developing innovative methods, techniques, and approaches for dealing with occupational safety and health problems" (Occupational Safety and Health Act, 2016, § 2(b)(5)).

EVOLUTION OF THE VISION

The purpose of the TWH predecessor program, the WorkLife Initiative, was "to better understand and promote the kinds of work environments, programs, and policies that result in healthier, more productive workers with reduced disease and injury and lower health care needs and costs" (NIOSH, 2009, p. 1). It was based on the idea that

> comprehensive practices and policies that take into account the work environment—both physical and organizational—while also addressing the personal health risks of individuals, are more effective in preventing disease and promoting health and safety than each approach taken separately. (NIOSH, 2010, p. 1)

It recognized that the worksite provides the unique opportunity to "implement programs and policies to prevent both work-related risks and chronic illnesses and injuries that are linked to behavior-related choices" (NIOSH, 2009, p. 2). Based on both early research findings (Sorensen et al., 1995; Sorensen, Stoddard, Ockene, Hunt, & Youngstrom, 1996) and field experience, *WorkLife* forged the path for a more comprehensive consideration of the safety, health, and well-being of workers.

As *WorkLife* transitioned to the TWH program (Figure 2.1), TWH was defined as "a strategy integrating occupational safety and health protection with health promotion to prevent worker injury and illness and to advance health and well-being" (Weisfeld & Lustig, 2014, p. 2). The addition of "well-being" to the TWH definition arose from emerging research in the previous 20 years that health was necessary, but not sufficient, for maximum positive functioning in life and that well-being is a more complete characterization of the ultimate goal. Well-being is a concept akin to "flourishing." Flourishing in life is based on three aspects of mental well-being—emotional well-being, psychological well-being, and social well-being (Keyes, 2002). What makes life positive is work that contributes to the overall well-being of the individual worker. Positive psychology has greatly increased the emphasis on happiness and well-being—positive emotions, engagement in life and work, meaning and accomplishment (Seligman, 2011).

This original TWH definition was intended to clearly convey the need to break down traditional organizational silos of OSH protection and health promotion to maximize worker well-being. With OSH protection efforts focused on reducing hazards and exposure through organizational change in the workplace, and traditional health promotion activities aimed at reducing lifestyle risk factors by promoting healthy behaviors through individual change, organizational resources tend to be inefficiently invested. Early research was supportive of integrated efforts being more effective than this "silo approach" (NIOSH, 2012).

As thinking about the TWH approach continued to evolve in response to NIOSH stakeholder input and the developing scientific evidence base, it became clear that the first TWH definition did not adequately convey the complexities of the concept. In 2015, the definition of TWH was revised to "policies, programs, and practices that integrate protection from work-related safety and health hazards with promotion of injury and illness prevention efforts to advance worker well-being" (NIOSH, 2015e, para. 1). Although the ultimate outcome of interest remains worker well-being, the revised definition better reflects the comprehensive approach, through policies, programs, and practices to addressing protection and illness and injury prevention in the workplace. Of note, the expression "promotion of injury and illness prevention efforts" was deliberately chosen instead of the term *health promotion* in order to clearly differentiate organizational approaches over individual behavior change. Integration, which means the connection of all relevant activities within the workplace, remains central to the approach. Integration itself can be thought of as an intermediate outcome of the TWH process. Without integration, the pathway to advancing worker well-being is hampered.

From a TWH perspective, worker well-being, the primary health outcome of interest, has been specifically defined as

> an integrative concept that characterizes quality of life with respect to an individual's health and work-related environmental, organizational, and psychosocial factors. It is the experience of positive perceptions and the presence of constructive conditions at work and beyond that enables workers to thrive and achieve their full potential. (Chari et al., 2018, p. 590)

The TWH worker well-being model has five domains: (a) physical environment and safety climate; (b) organizational policies and culture; (c) individual health status; (d) work evaluation and experience; and (e) home, community, and society (Chari et al., 2018).

The worker well-being definition and model are intended to accent the distinction between the TWH approach and more limited scope of worksite wellness programs. Unlike the typical worksite wellness program, the primary principle of TWH implementation is a fundamental focus on recognizing and addressing hazardous conditions of work and assuring provision of safe and healthful working conditions. The TWH approach is not a collection of health promotion efforts in a workplace that ignores the way work is organized and structured. The TWH approach is not consistent with workplace policies that discriminate against or penalize workers for their individual health conditions or create disincentives for improving health (NIOSH, 2015b). The TWH approach requires a strong commitment to better working conditions; a comprehensive approach to program development for worker safety, health, and well-being; the connection of all relevant parts of the organization; and a willingness to view the path to improved worker well-being as a continuum of progress from the simplest to the more sophisticated accomplishments.

Along with the revised TWH definition, in 2015 a completely revamped version of the list of issues relevant to TWH was released. Instead of the issues being grouped by workplace, workers, and employment, the issues were organized into nine topic areas (NIOSH, 2015b). The issue topics of concern to the TWH concept include (a) control of hazards and exposures, (b) organization of work, (c) built environment supports, (d) leadership, (e) compensation and benefits, (f) community supports, (g) changing workforce demographics, (h) policy issues, and (i) new employment patterns. These topics reflect the increasing breadth of issues related to 21st-century work that impact worker safety, health, and well-being. The list also places greater emphasis on the broad macroeconomic changes occurring in employment and in employment arrangements, as well as the emerging evidence of the societal and worker health effects of these changes (Howard, 2017).

Furthermore, the issues listed in the graphic make it clear that the TWH perspective does not emphasize individual behavior change. The public health community has long known that expectations of behavior change in the face of daily obstacles are an unreasonable expectation (Smedley & Syme, 2000). In fact, the OSH community has a long history of not relying on individual behavior change to assure worker safety and health, and this has been operationalized in the hierarchy of controls (NIOSH, 2015c). This traditional OSH strategy relies on hazard elimination as the most effective control and recognizes that controls that depend on human behavior, such as administrative controls or use of personal protective equipment, are the least effective means of protection. To strengthen the link between traditional OSH approaches and the TWH approach, NIOSH developed the hierarchy of controls applied to the TWH program (see Figure 2.2) to help organizations prioritize their efforts to advance worker safety, health, and well-being.

As in the traditional hierarchy, the controls and strategies are presented in descending order of anticipated effectiveness and protectiveness, as suggested by the cascading arrows. Application of this model begins with elimination of workplace conditions that cause or contribute to worker illness or injury or otherwise negatively impact worker well-being. The next level of the model focuses on replacement of unsafe, unhealthy working conditions or practices with safer, health-enhancing policies, programs, and management practices that

FIGURE 2.2. The Hierarchy of Controls Applied to NIOSH
Total Worker Health®, 2016

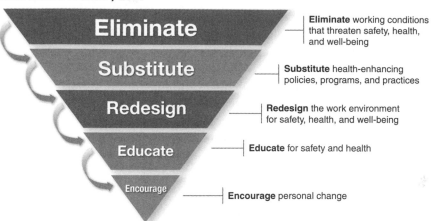

improve the culture of safety and health in the workplace. Redesign of the work environment, where needed, for safety, health, and well-being is the third level of control. The least effective approaches to the TWH concept rely solely on safety and health education for workers and personal behavior changes for improvements to safety, health, and well-being. When these less effective controls are used, education should be provided to enhance individual knowledge for all workers and support should be provided for healthier choice-making.

The scientific evidence to support the TWH approach to worker safety, health, and well-being is growing, but there is much work to be done to inform the development of evidence-based policies, programs, and practices. Through investments in research and the transfer of this research into practice, NIOSH's long-term vision of the TWH program to protect the safety and health of workers and to advance their well-being by creating safer and healthier work environments will move closer to reality. It is anticipated that this vision will be fulfilled through knowledge generation, translation of that knowledge into practice, development of policy guidance, and building workforce capacity. To make progress toward these goals, NIOSH led efforts in 2016 to create a TWH national agenda for the next decade (2016–2026), which culminated in the publication of *A National Agenda to Advance Total Worker Health® Research, Practice, Policy, and Capacity* (NIOSH, 2016c).

EXPANSION OF THE VISION

The 2016–2026 TWH agenda, the first by a NIOSH cross-sector program within the framework of the National Occupational Research Agenda, is designed to expand the scientific evidence base for the TWH vision; to stimulate and more finely focus research in this emerging area; and to broaden and engage the base of stakeholders who will, ultimately, move the TWH effort from research to practice.

Development of the agenda relied heavily on input from a broad, diverse group of academicians and researchers, worker representatives, private sector partners, and other stakeholders. The 2016–2026 TWH agenda calls for progress on four strategic goals for the nation to comprehensively advance the safety, health and well-being of workers: research, practice, policy, and capacity building.

Research

The 2016–2026 TWH agenda's *research* goal seeks to advance and conduct etiologic, surveillance, and intervention research that builds the evidence base for effectively integrating protection from work-related safety and health hazards with promotion of injury and illness prevention efforts to advance worker well-being. Funding NIOSH Centers to conduct TWH-related research was an early programmatic strategy to focus research efforts on building the evidence base for this approach. There are currently six Centers, each with an active research portfolio reflective of the selective issues of interest to the TWH agenda (see Table 2.1).

The six Centers accomplish work across 13 academic institutions in the United States. Their regional presence and expertise play an important role in conducting novel research on the important connections between work, safety, and health. Each Center collaborates with regional employers, labor partners, and stakeholders to conduct research, design interventions, evaluate intervention effectiveness, and translate findings for workers and employers. They provide start-up grants to spur innovation and intervention among local employers. Some Centers have extensive outreach programs that provide tool kits, web-based training, continuing education courses, online video series, and actionable guidance documents.

The Centers design and conduct research that strategically focuses on occupations or industries of high or emerging risk, including workers in hospital, home health, and nursing home settings; construction; corrections; and manufacturing. Populations targeted for study include high-risk workers, such as younger and older workers, low-wage workers, contingent and part-time workers, and workers employed in small businesses. Critical areas of research focus include workplace stress, obesity, productive aging, work organization, shift work, fatigue, chronic disease, and sleep with an emphasis on how these conditions influence workplace injury, illness, productivity, and health care costs.

Despite the active research portfolios of these Centers, the evidence base supporting the TWH approach is still evolving, and knowledge gaps remain as evidenced in review of the literature by Anger et al. (2015) and Feltner et al. (2016). These reviews contribute to understanding the state of the scientific evidence for the TWH approach, as well as gaps in understanding and research needs. The review by Anger et al. sought to identify, evaluate, and critique the

TABLE 2.1. National Institute for Occupational Safety and Health Centers of Excellence for Total Worker Health®

Center name	First year funded	University affiliation(s)	Examples of research, outreach, and areas of focus
Center for Health, Work & Environment	2016	Colorado School of Public Health, University of Colorado Anschutz Medical Campus http://www.ucdenver.edu/academics/colleges/PublicHealth/research/centers/CHWE/Pages/TheCenter.aspx#	Advances worker health, safety, and well-being by educating future leaders, conducting research, and designing practical solutions for small- and medium-sized businesses and high-risk industries.
Center for the Promotion of Health in the New England Workplace	2006	University of Connecticut, University of Massachusetts–Lowell http://www.uml.edu/Research/CPH-NEW/About/default.aspx	Improves worker health through participatory processes and models involving frontline employees and top-down organizational support; current projects with health care workers, low-wage workers, and public safety/correctional officers.
Harvard T.H. Chan School of Public Health, Center for Work, Health and Well-being	2007	Harvard University, Northeastern University http://www.centerforworkhealth.sph.harvard.edu	Optimizes worker safety/health and employer outcomes by improving conditions of work; expands evidence on integrated approaches through etiologic and intervention effectiveness research, translating, and disseminating best practices and policies.
Healthier Workforce Center of the Midwest	2006	University of Iowa, Washington University (St. Louis) http://www.HWCMW.org	Generates/disseminates evidence-based TWH practices; focuses on small enterprises, the regional economy; partnerships between Iowa, Missouri, Nebraska, and Kansas tackle regional challenges.
Oregon Healthy Workforce Center	2011	Oregon Health and Science University, Portland State University, University of Washington, Johns Hopkins University, University of Oregon http://www.ohsu.edu/xd/research/centers-institutes/oregon-institute-occupational-health-sciences/oregon-healthy-workforce-center/	Focuses on integration to improve the health, safety, and well-being of workers through effectiveness research, collaboration, dissemination of evidence; research centers on truck drivers, young workers, and call center, health care, and construction workers.
University of Illinois–Chicago Center for Healthy Work	2016	University of Illinois at Chicago http://www.publichealth.uic.edu/healthywork	Focuses on health of workers in precarious jobs and hardship neighborhoods, using participatory and community-based approaches; projects use systems analysis/action learning to identify strategies for change.

Note. TWH = *Total Worker Health.*

empirical intervention studies in the scientific literature that combined or integrated OSH interventions with prevention-related activities in the workplace, consistent with the NIOSH definition of TWH. Seventeen studies met the criteria for inclusion. Although their review drew from a limited evidence base, it concluded that TWH interventions addressing both work-related injury risks and chronic diseases can improve workforce health effectively and more rapidly than the alternative of separately employing more narrowly focused programs to change the same outcomes in a fragmented fashion.

The 2016 systematic review by Feltner et al. was commissioned by the National Institutes of Health (NIH) to establish a baseline of evidence of the effectiveness of TWH research and to evaluate the potential benefits and harms of such interventions. It served as the foundation for a much more comprehensive project funded through the NIH's Pathways to Prevention Program. Feltner et al. (2016) concluded that, although research in this field was early and sparse, findings related to the utility of integrated TWH interventions, such as those that target OSH along with diet and nutrition and sedentary lifestyles, are encouraging.

The NIH Pathways to Prevention Program is designed to assist new fields of study with public health relevance to establish a trajectory that will successfully impact population health. The TWH approach was fortunate to be selected for study by this program. As a Pathways to Prevention Program study, an impartial, independent panel of experts was convened to identify research gaps and future research priorities for TWH. The panel conducted their work in a workshop that was organized around TWH-related evidence presented by invited experts. The full workshop report, including eight recommendations, was published in a peer-reviewed medical journal (Bradley, Grossman, Hubbard, Ortega, & Curry, 2016). In the same journal issue, NIOSH published a response to the panel's report that details planned actions to accomplish major activities based upon these recommendations (Howard, Chang, Schill, & Chosewood, 2016).

The most pertinent panel recommendations related to expanding the TWH evidence base addressed development of a core set of measures and outcomes in TWH-related research. This recommendation inspired the University of Iowa to host a TWH Research Methodology Workshop in early 2017. This workshop reviewed current methodological approaches and shortcomings and identified the most promising methods and standards for this emerging field of research, including development of a core set of measures and outcomes that could be incorporated into future TWH-related studies. Proceedings from this workshop (Healthier Workforce Center of the Midwest, n.d.) provide researchers with critical tools to conduct inquiries and interventions in a more systematic, standardized fashion while still encouraging innovation and exploration in individual research studies (Tamers et al., 2018).

Practice

Advancing TWH *practice* is the focus of the TWH agenda's second goal, which aims to increase implementation of evidence-based programs and practices that are consistent with the TWH approach. To impact worker safety, health, and well-being, research knowledge must move into practice. The practice goal highlights the need to increase the implementation of evidence-based programs and practices that assess and improve the conditions workers face on the job while broadly working to prevent injuries and illnesses among workers, whether or not they are directly related to work.

A practice-oriented document published by NIOSH in 2016, *Fundamentals of Total Worker Health® Approaches: Essential Elements for Advancing Worker Safety, Health, and Well-being* (*Fundamentals*; NIOSH, 2016a), furthers the goal of increasing the uptake and implementation of TWH practices. The *Fundamentals* document focuses on five defining elements of TWH: demonstrating leadership commitment to worker safety and health at all levels of the organization, designing work to eliminate or reduce safety and health hazards and promote worker well-being, promoting and supporting worker engagement throughout program development, ensuring the confidentiality and privacy of workers during program design and implementation, and integrating relevant systems to advance worker well-being. The intention of the *Fundamentals* document is to accelerate the uptake and use of TWH concepts in day-to-day practice within organizations through practical self-assessment tools and the development of actionable steps for implementing changes.

The practice goal was written to inspire the development of novel interventions, within the research portfolios of NIOSH, the NIOSH Centers, and among a growing network of TWH Affiliates. Established by NIOSH in 2014, the NIOSH TWH Affiliates Program (NIOSH, 2017) is an unfunded volunteer collective of academic, government (state and federal), labor, industry, and nonprofit organizations with a mission of fostering an integrated approach to protecting and promoting worker well-being through active collaboration. TWH Affiliates work with NIOSH and with other affiliates to increase the visibility, uptake, and impact of TWH interventions. Their joint, complementary efforts greatly expand the limited reach of NIOSH intramural- and extramural-funded activities. Members of the TWH Affiliate network may assist NIOSH by conducting joint research or providing populations for intervention studies; by developing program materials, trainings, and other work products; collaborating on seminars, meetings, trainings, and educational events; and by cross-promoting and disseminating publications and other communication products. Many of the TWH Affiliates, both academic and nonacademic, serve as test beds for the development of promising practices, actively share learnings from pilot projects, and assist with dissemination of TWH research to their own regional or national networks.

Policy

Policy change often represents later, lagging evidence of programmatic or scientific influence from research, albeit an enduring influence. The TWH agenda's policy goal aims to promote adoption of policies that simultaneously protect workers and improve their health and well-being by focusing on policy development at the local, organizational, regional, and national levels. Although much work remains to be done, early efforts are underway in this area.

Comprehensive "tobacco free" workplace policies are a classic example of an organizational-level policy. When developed as a policy with integrated interventions that address both the workplace and individual workers, such policies serve to protect all workers from secondhand exposure to tobacco smoke and assist individuals with cessation efforts. Taking a TWH perspective, NIOSH developed a comprehensive *Current Intelligence Bulletin* to provide an authoritative source for workplace tobacco policies (NIOSH, 2015a).

Designing paid leave policies and other health-related benefits from a health-enhancing perspective is increasingly a focus at both the state and national level. NIOSH research on paid sick leave is helping to inform these decisions. For example, Asfaw, Pana-Cryan, and Rosa (2012) found that a reduced incidence of acute injury was seen among companies offering paid sick leave compared to companies not providing this benefit. With all other variables held constant, workers with access to paid sick leave were 28% less likely than workers without access to paid sick leave to be injured. The association between the availability of paid sick leave and the incidence of occupational injuries varied across occupations but was greatest in high-risk occupations. The authors concluded that, similar to other investments in worker safety and health, introducing or expanding paid sick leave programs might help businesses reduce the incidence of nonfatal occupational injuries, particularly in high-risk sectors and occupations.

Capacity Building

The final goal of the agenda encourages building capacity to strengthen the TWH workforce and TWH field to support the development, growth, and maintenance of policies, programs, and practices that advance worker well-being. Capacity building helps NIOSH and others engaged in advancing TWH concepts ensure that a sustainable professional community will emerge to support and implement efforts for organizations over the long term. Important work with a number of high-visibility partners is moving this effort forward, and a number of activities to build capacity have been already initiated. For example, continuing education credits for physicians, nurses, industrial hygienists, safety professionals, health promotion professionals, and human resources professionals and others are available through the TWH webinar series and other NIOSH offerings. Several universities, some of which are TWH Affiliates, offer accredited, graduate-level certificate programs for students and early and mid-career OSH professionals looking to sharpen or retool their skill in this subject area. Many of the Centers also work to build capacity by offering recurring, continuing education courses and training modules, both live and on-demand, with some offering lengthier summer institutes in specialty areas related to the TWH program. Others offer weeklong, multidisciplinary executive training programs for business leaders and OSH professionals to help bridge historic divides among disciplines, leverage expertise, and support integrated efforts.

NIOSH also engages with academic partners, specialty societies, labor partners, and private-sector employers to better define the needs of professionals in fields related to and overlapping with TWH approaches. This work will help identify key competencies for professionals who deliver integrated safety and health interventions. These collaborations will inform the future development of a core curriculum for full undergraduate- and graduate-level degrees for TWH professionals. Collaborations with private industry representatives and other stakeholders throughout the curriculum development process will keep the focus on the needs of potential future employers of these academically prepared professionals. Long-term plans for the development of a professional society representing specialists and professionals within the TWH field are also under consideration.

FUTURE VISION FOR THE TWH PROGRAM

As the nature of work changes, and with it the demands placed on workers, the TWH concept must evolve to meet the needs of workers facing new challenges. The interdependence of economies; the pace of commerce; the drive for greater productivity; and rapid, just-in-time market cycles all lead to unprecedented demands upon workers that are increasingly complex. Traditional hazards encountered by workers stubbornly remain in many industries and occupations. Although legacy exposures persist, new ones appear with every technological advancement. In addition, the way in which work is accomplished; how work is organized and scheduled; how we interact around the globe; and, even more basically, how workers are employed are rapidly shifting. This complex, ever-changing environment demands approaches and strategies that comprehensively safeguard and promote the health of workers.

In alignment with this need, NIOSH's TWH program will continue to champion a broad, holistic approach to assessing and addressing the needs of workers facing this new world of work. The TWH focus will remain on the nature of the work itself, maintaining a steadfast commitment to advancing improvement of working conditions and using input from and participation of workers who are most affected by the work. Policy, program, and practice interventions will require customization by taking into account the specific safety and health challenges facing workers on and off the job. Any solutions that are one-size-fits-all; that do not account for workers' needs, preferences, wages, cultures, and personal challenges; or that do not account for the tremendous variability of risks among organizations of different sizes, geographies, industries, and occupations, will become increasingly inadequate.

The NIOSH TWH program will continue to advance the evidence base for interventions that address worker and organizational needs on a comprehensive and holistic basis. This direction will include focusing research on the impact of the dramatic shifts being seen in employment, work arrangements, work schedules, job design, and work organization. It will necessitate investments in surveillance systems (or augmentation of existing ones) to better track the connections between working conditions, occupation, industry and chronic diseases, like cancer, heart disease, diabetes, obesity, and depression.

Research investments must be used to inform our understanding of etiologies and antidotes for the epidemic of work-related stress, which is largely due to unhealthful working conditions, poorly organized work, and excessive physical and psychological demands on workers. Additional research is needed on the challenges faced by working families, exploring the links between societal roles and employment, characterizing and better understanding conflicts between work and family demands, and crafting new solutions. Critical new insights are needed into serving the health and safety needs of an increasingly diverse workforce and the myriad of safety and health issues that are impacted by cultural differences, disparities, and inequalities. Last, NIOSH and its partners will be challenged to better define, measure, and track individual, organizational, and national well-being in the context of work and employment.

CONCLUSION

The long-term vision of the TWH program is to protect the safety and health of workers and to advance their well-being by creating safer and healthier work and work environments. This paradigm-shifting approach to OSH holds promise for thinking about existing problems in new ways, expanding the bounds of knowledge in new directions, and implementing solutions that match the changing world of work. This is a vision beyond what NIOSH can accomplish alone. It requires commitment from researchers, academics, practitioners, employers, workers, labor representatives, policymakers, and all those who share the vision that it is possible to design jobs that protect safety, enhance health and create work in which every worker has the opportunity to thrive.

REFERENCES

Anger, W. K., Elliot, D. L., Bodner, T., Olson, R., Rohlman, D. S., Truxillo, D. M., . . . Montgomery, D. (2015). Effectiveness of total worker health interventions. *Journal of Occupational Health Psychology, 20*, 226–247. http://dx.doi.org/10.1037/a0038340

Asfaw, A., Pana-Cryan, R., & Rosa, R. (2012). Paid sick leave and nonfatal occupational injuries. *American Journal of Public Health, 102*(9), e59–e64. http://dx.doi.org/10.2105/AJPH.2011.300482

Bradley, C. J., Grossman, D. C., Hubbard, R. A., Ortega, A. N., & Curry, S. J. (2016). Integrated interventions for improving Total Worker Health: A panel report from the National Institutes of Health Pathways to Prevention Workshop: Total Worker Health—What's work got to do with it? *Annals of Internal Medicine, 165*, 279–283. http://dx.doi.org/10.7326/M16-0740

Chari, R., Chang, C. C., Sauter, S. L., Petrun Sayers, E. L., Cerully, J. L., Schulte, P., . . . Uscher-Pines, L. (2018). Expanding the paradigm of occupational safety and health: A new framework for worker well-being. *Journal of Occupational and Environmental Medicine, 60*, 589–593. http://dx.doi.org/10.1097/JOM.0000000000001330

Cherniack, M., Henning, R., Merchant, J. A., Punnett, L., Sorensen, G. R., & Wagner, G. (2011). Statement on national worklife priorities. *American Journal of Industrial Medicine, 54,* 10–20. http://dx.doi.org/10.1002/ajim.20900

Feltner, C., Peterson, K., Palmieri Weber, R., Cluff, L., Coker-Schwimmer, E., Viswanathan, M., & Lohr, K. N. (2016). The effectiveness of Total Worker Health interventions: A systematic review for a National Institutes of Health Pathways to Prevention Workshop. *Annals of Internal Medicine, 165,* 262–269. http://dx.doi.org/10.7326/M16-0626

Healthier Workforce Center of the Midwest. (n.d.). TWH Workshop: Workshop resources. Retrieved from http://twhworkshop.com/resources/

Howard, J. (2017). Nonstandard work arrangements and worker health and safety. *American Journal of Industrial Medicine, 60,* 1–10. http://dx.doi.org/10.1002/ajim.22669

Howard, J., Chang, C. C., Schill, A. L., & Chosewood, L. C. (2016). NIOSH response to the NIH Pathways to Prevention Workshop recommendations. *Annals of Internal Medicine, 165,* 296–297. http://dx.doi.org/10.7326/M16-0904

Keyes, C. L. M. (2002). The mental health continuum: From languishing to flourishing in life. *Journal of Health and Social Behavior, 43,* 207–222. http://dx.doi.org/10.2307/3090197

National Institute for Occupational Safety and Health. (2004). *STEPS for workplace health, productivity are focus of October NIOSH symposium.* Retrieved from https://www.cdc.gov/niosh/updates/upd-09-16-04.html

National Institute for Occupational Safety and Health. (2009). *The WorkLife Initiative: Protecting and promoting worker health and well-being* (DHHS [NIOSH] Publication No. 2009-146). Washington, DC: U.S. Department of Health and Human Services.

National Institute for Occupational Safety and Health. (2010). *Essential elements of effective workplace program and policies for improving worker health and wellbeing* (DHHS [NIOSH] Publication No. 2010-140, pp. 1–4). Washington, DC: U.S. Department of Health and Human Services.

National Institute for Occupational Safety and Health. (2012). *Research compendium: The NIOSH Total Worker Health® program: Seminal research papers 2012* (DHHS [NIOSH] Publication No. 2012-146). Washington, DC: U.S. Department of Health and Human Services.

National Institute for Occupational Safety and Health. (2015a). *Current intelligence bulletin 67: Promoting health and preventing disease and injury through workplace tobacco policies, April 2015* (DHHS [NIOSH] Publication No. 2015-113). Washington, DC: U.S. Department of Health and Human Services.

National Institute for Occupational Safety and Health. (2015b). *Frequently asked questions: What is NOT Total Worker Health?* Retrieved from https://www.cdc.gov/niosh/twh/faq.html

National Institute for Occupational Safety and Health. (2015c). *Hierarchy of controls.* Retrieved from https://www.cdc.gov/niosh/topics/hierarchy/default.html

National Institute for Occupational Safety and Health. (2015d). *History.* Retrieved from https://www.cdc.gov/niosh/twh/history.html

National Institute for Occupational Safety and Health. (2015e). What is *Total Worker Health?* Retrieved from https://www.cdc.gov/niosh/twh/totalhealth.html

National Institute for Occupational Safety and Health. (2016a). *Fundamentals of Total Worker Health approaches: Essential elements for advancing worker safety, health, and well-being, December 2016* (DHHS [NIOSH] Publication No. 2017-112). Washington, DC: U.S. Department of Health and Human Services.

National Institute for Occupational Safety and Health. (2016b). Hierarchy of controls applied to *Total Worker Health.* Retrieved from https://www.cdc.gov/niosh/twh/letsgetstarted.html

National Institute for Occupational Safety and Health. (2016c). *National Occupational Research Agenda (NORA)/National Total Worker Health® Agenda (2016–2026): A national agenda to advance Total Worker Health® research, practice, policy, and capacity, April 2016* (DHHS [NIOSH] Publication No. 2016-114). Washington, DC: U.S. Department of Health and Human Services.

National Institute for Occupational Safety and Health. (2017). NIOSH *Total Worker Health* Affiliates. Retrieved from https://www.cdc.gov/niosh/twh/affiliate.html

Occupational Safety and Health Act of 1970, 29 U.S.C. § 651 et seq. (2016).

Seligman, M. E. P. (2011). *Flourish: A visionary new understanding of happiness and well-being.* New York, NY: Free Press.

Smedley, B. D., & Syme, S. L. (Eds.). (2000). *Promoting health: Intervention strategies from social and behavioral research.* Washington, DC: National Academies Press.

Sorensen, G., Himmelstein, J. S., Hunt, M. K., Youngstrom, R., Hebert, J. R., Hammond, S. K., . . . Ockene, J. K. (1995). A model for worksite cancer prevention: Integration of health protection and health promotion in the WellWorks Project. *American Journal of Health Promotion, 10,* 55–62. http://dx.doi.org/10.4278/0890-1171-10.1.55

Sorensen, G., Stoddard, A., Ockene, J. K., Hunt, M. K., & Youngstrom, R. (1996). Worker participation in an integrated health promotion/health protection program: Results from the WellWorks project. *Health Education Quarterly, 23,* 191–203. http://dx.doi.org/10.1177/109019819602300205

Tamers, S. L., Goetzel, R., Kelly, K. M., Luckhaupt, S., Nigam, J., Pronk, N. P., . . . Sorensen, G. (2018). Research methodologies for *Total Worker Health®*: Proceedings from a workshop. *Journal of Occupational and Environmental Medicine, 60,* 968–978. http://dx.doi.org/10.1097/JOM.0000000000001404

U.S. Department of Health and Human Services. (2004). *Diabetes: A national plan for action. Appendix A: Steps to a HealthierUS.* Retrieved from https://aspe.hhs.gov/report/diabetes-national-plan-action/appendix-steps-healthierus

Weisfeld, V., & Lustig, T. A. (2014). *Promising and best practices in Total Worker Health™: Workshop summary.* Washington, DC: National Academies Press. http://dx.doi.org/10.17226/18947

3

Interrelationships of Occupational and Personal Risk Factors in the Etiology of Disease and Injury

Paul A. Schulte and Sudha P. Pandalai

Work and workplace hazards are known to affect health and safety, and in turn, occupational safety and health (OSH) problems are associated with a large national burden (Loeppke, 2008). OSH can be affected by a large array of personal risk factors (PRFs), such as genetics, age, gender, obesity, smoking, alcohol use, and use of prescription drugs, to name a few (Loeppke, 2008; Schulte et al., 2017). Despite the awareness of all these various work and nonwork hazards, there has not been a strong emphasis in the OSH field on taking a holistic view of the health of working people. In fact, there are various barriers between work and nonwork factors. Historically, work has been viewed separately from other human activities. As mentioned in Chapter 2, this volume, this view is in part due to the contract nature of work and the practices of compensating injured or sick workers and determining the cause (Ringen & Smith, 1983). Although some work-related conditions are de facto triggers for compensation in various jurisdictions, and historical practice was to take the workers "as is," there are some compensation and tort system requirements to "apportion" the cause of an injury or illness among various work-related and nonwork factors and to compensate only the work-related causes (Poulter, 2001; Richter, 1997). However, the ability to

This chapter was authored by employees of the United States government as part of their official duty and is considered to be in the public domain. The findings and conclusions in this report are those of the author(s) and do not necessarily represent the official position of the National Institute for Occupational Safety and Health, Centers for Disease Control and Prevention.

http://dx.doi.org/10.1037/0000149-004
Total Worker Health, H. L. Hudson, J. A. S. Nigam, S. L. Sauter, L. C. Chosewood, A. L. Schill, and J. Howard (Editors)

accurately determine the extent to which a worker's illness or disability pertains to his or her work or nonwork factors is not a precise science.

Most of the diseases, injuries, and health conditions of working people are multifactorial in nature. The underlying evidence for the role of various risk factors in the overall health of working people is frequently underutilized in developing interventions. For the most part, the research focuses on one discipline or topic. An investigator interested in smoking, for example, when assessing smoking–disease relationships, treats all other factors as confounders or effect modifiers. Thus, smoking is the primary interest, and the total impact on the person's health—of all the risk factors that a person experiences—is not considered or studied. Similarly, in assessing workplace risk factors, PRFs (nonoccupational) are treated as confounders or sources of bias, and the totality of the work risk factors and PRFs that affect the health of working people is not comprehensively studied. This is partly because governments and other organizations/institutions that focus on health issues appropriate resources to address certain specific problems such as smoking, drinking, and occupational disease in a fragmented way. Societal programs rarely focus on research and intervention for the composite effect of those risk factors.

Understanding the interaction of various risk factors may help in targeting and determining the effectiveness of interventions. Specific problem-driven research focuses on what is colloquially referred to as a "main effect," which is technically a *marginal effect* that is averaged over the other risk factors in a given context. Such specific problem-driven research has also led to the lack of comprehensive research on the combined role of PRFs and occupational risk factors (ORFs) in work-related illness and injury. Not only are work risk factors and PRFs potential confounders or effect modifiers of associations of each with disease, but such factors may be directly related to each other. For example, shift work may lead to obesity or smoking, or use of prescription drugs may be interactive with workplace chemical exposures in affecting various organ systems.

Part of the practice of epidemiology and other disciplines is that factors are studied one at a time to isolate their effect while holding other factors constant or assuring that they are part of a uniformly distributed background, and hence disregarded in terms of interfering with the assessment of the "main effect." The challenge in epidemiologic research, however, is to identify major modifying factors when they are not uniformly distributed (Schoenbach & Rosamund, 2000). Determination of effect modification requires analysis by inclusion of interaction terms in statistical models or stratification based on the candidate variables. Identifying effect modification is important because failure to do so can lead to serious errors in interpreting exposure–disease relationships under study and to inefficiencies in developing interventions (Kleinbaum, Kupper, & Morgenstern, 1982; Vineis & Kriebel, 2006).

The overarching rationale for considering the interaction of ORFs and PRFs is that the health of the contemporary workforce in Western and other developed countries is critical to the well-being of the nation (Davis, Collins, Doty, Ho, & Holmgren, 2005; Schulte & Vainio, 2010; Tompa, 2002). The growing burden of illness and health risk and the subsequent increased use of health care services are driving up health care costs (Special Committee on Health, Productivity, and Disability Management, 2009). Ultimately, the impact of labor shortages and health-care costs on productivity and profitability can affect business and national economic health (Loeppke, 2008). Many developed nations with an aging population face the challenge of a need to increase work participation, especially at older ages (van den Berg, Elders, de Zwart, & Burdorf, 2009). To meet the challenge, governmental policies are being implemented to increase the age of full retirement to balance the ratio of dependent to employed persons, known as the dependency ratio (Holzmann, 2004).

In this chapter, we address various ways that ORFs and PRFs can inter-act. We reviewed the published scientific literature and developed a heuristic approach to describing the interaction of ORFs and PRFs among workers. The goal of this investigation is to begin to develop a theoretical framework for considering the health of working people in a comprehensive manner.

APPROACH TO DEVELOPING THEORETICAL MODELS OF OCCUPATIONAL AND PERSONAL RISK FACTORS

Evidence from epidemiological studies in the scientific literature was found to support the development of four conceptual models of the interrelationships between PRFs and ORFs (see Figure 3.1). Evidence to support these conceptual models was the result of structured searches of the published literature (Schulte, Pandalai, Wulsin, & Chun, 2012). We examined eight PRFs—genetics, age, gender, chronic disease, obesity, smoking, alcohol use, and prescription drug use—resulting in 32 examples (Schulte et al., 2012). The models presented here are not meant to delineate specific molecular/cellular/organ-level etiologic steps, epidemiological mechanisms, or statistical relationships with respect to the diseases discussed. Rather, these theorized models were developed to describe theoretical evidence-based frameworks by which PRFs and ORFs impact health outcomes.

Inclusion criteria guided the selection of literature underlying the examples chosen to illustrate each type of model for each PRF examined. These criteria

FIGURE 3.1. Models for the Effects of Occupational Risk Factors (ORFs) and Personal Risk Factors (PRFs)

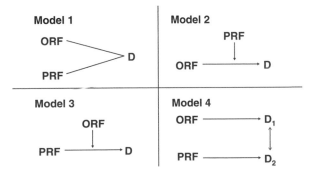

D = disease.

required that the studies included were peer-reviewed, original research papers; meta-analyses; or systematic reviews of epidemiological studies that used hypothesis testing and had calculated measures of effect such as relative risks, odds ratios, standardized mortality ratios, or other values.

In Model 1 (see Figure 3.1), a PRF and an ORF could both cause the same disease with possible simple independent effects. We define independent effects to mean that a given level of effect is seen if there is no relationship between the two sets of factors that cause a particular outcome (Weinberg, 2009). Examples of ways that Model 1 could transition into other model categories as evidence for possible relationships between ORFs and PRFs are potentially found through further research.

Models 2 and 3 conceptualize ORFs and PRFs, alternately, as variables that affect a risk factor–disease association. Thus, a PRF could affect an ORF–disease association. Conversely, an ORF could affect a PRF–disease association. Model 4 illustrates the situation in which ORFs and PRFs impact different diseases or disease stages with subsequent interrelationships between multiple diseases/disease stages.

Models 2, 3, and 4 can all have interrelationships among the risk factors presented in the illustrative examples. Inclusion of such interactions allows more accurate characterization and description of disease mechanisms. To illustrate the approach, a subset of each of these models is presented for specific PRFs with significant known impact on health outcomes (see Figures 3.2 and 3.3).

MODELS DEPICTING ORF–PRF INTERRELATIONSHIPS

Figure 3.2 shows selected examples of models depicting ORF–PRF interrelationships for a range of risk factors (Schulte et al., 2012). Model A1 indicates that hypertension (PRF) and occupational dioxin exposure (ORF) are independently associated with ischemic heart disease. Another example focuses on the risk factor of work-related fatigue, combined with the use of prescription sedatives, to affect risk of injury. Models B1 through C2 present examples in which one of the factors may affect an association of the other factor with a health or safety outcome. In Examples B1 and B2, a PRF, such as possessing a gene that is responsible for metabolizing chemicals used to make textile dyes NAT2 acetyltransferase, or alcohol use, can affect the ORF–adverse health outcome association of occupational aromatic amine exposure and bladder cancer, or job strain and hypertension, respectively. Alternatively, an ORF can affect a PRF–adverse health outcome association, as illustrated by exposure to organic solvents or have the ORF of employment grade (categorized as administrative, professional and executive, clerical, and "other" grades, e.g., messengers and other unskilled manual workers) affecting the association of age and hearing loss, or smoking and lung cancer, respectively.

In Examples D1 and D2, each factor leads to a separate outcome, with the outcomes possibly affecting each other. In Example D1, occupational solvent exposure can affect liver disease status and age can affect lipid disorder status,

FIGURE 3.2. Selected Conceptual Models Illustrating ORF/PRF/Outcome Associations

Description of model type	Illustration of model example	Specific example description
A: A PRF and an ORF independently affect an adverse health outcome		
A1. A chronic disease and an ORF are independent risks for an adverse health outcome	Occupational exposure to dioxin ↘ Ischemic heart disease ↗ Hypertension	Dioxin may be a risk for ischemic heart disease. Hypertension is risk for ischemia. Combined impact may be significant for the development of disease.
A2. Prescription drugs and an ORF are independent risks for an adverse health outcome	Occupational fatigue ↘ Injury ↗ Prescription sedatives	Both sedating medications and workplace factors, such as fatigue, can independently lead to occupational injuries.
B: A PRF affects an ORF-adverse health outcome association		
B1. Genetics affects an ORF-adverse health outcome	*NAT2* gene ↓ Aromatic amines → Occupational bladder exposure to cancer	Workers with certain *NAT2* genes, exposed to aryl amines, have an increased risk of bladder cancer.
B2. Alcohol modifies an ORF-adverse health outcome association	Alcohol ↓ Job strain → Hypertension	Job strain increases the risk of hypertension. Alcohol interacts with occupational risk factors in high strain but not low strain jobs.
C: An ORF affects a PRF-adverse health outcome association		
C1. An ORF modifies an age-adverse health outcome	Occupational exposure to organic solvents ↓ Age → Hearing loss	Hearing acuity decreases with age. Organic solvents impact age-related hearing loss.
C2. An ORF modifies a smoking-adverse health outcome association	Employment grade ↓ Smoking → Lung cancer	Smoking is associated with lung cancer. Employment grade may affect this association.

(figure continues)

FIGURE 3.2. (continued)

Description of model type	Illustration of model example	Specific example description
D: An ORF affects one adverse health outcome, a PRF affects another adverse health outcome, and the two outcomes have some association		
D1. Age is a risk for one disease/disease state, an ORF is a risk for another and the two diseases/disease states are associated	Occupational exposure to solvents → Liver disease ↑ Age → Lipid disorders	Dyslipidemias increase with age. Solvent exposure is linked to liver disease. Lipid disorders may account for 5% to 30% of U.S. "cryptogenic" hepatocellular carcinoma. Of relevance are the effects of lipid disorders and solvent exposure on workers' livers.
D2. Gender is a risk for one disease/disease state, an ORF is a risk for another and the two diseases/disease states are associated	Occupational stress → WMSDs ↕ Female → Depression	Psychosocial stress is associated with musculoskeletal disorders. Depression may impact the development of chronic musculoskeletal disease. Women have greater risk of depression. The interaction of depression and work-related musculoskeletal disorders (WMSDs) may vary by gender.

Note. These models were supported by literature searches based on keywords pertaining to the model components. Published literature from the PubMed database was searched, and publications of epidemiological studies that supported one of the four categories of models (A to D) with odds ratios, relative risks, attributable risks, standardized mortality ratios, or other measures of effect were selected. References for specific models can be found in Schulte et al. (2012), in which selected models are found and from which this figure was created. ORF = occupational risk factor; PRF = personal risk factor; CA = cancer; HTN = hypertension; WMSDs = work-related musculoskeletal disorders.

and the latter disease state can affect the former. In Example D2, stress can affect work-related musculoskeletal disorder, gender can affect depression status, and these two health effect outcomes can affect each other.

More in-depth assessment of risk factors, such as obesity, have been explored (Pandalai, Schulte, & Miller, 2013). Examination of obesity as a PRF, following the initial work by Schulte and colleagues (2012), was also notable for several reasons. First, as depicted in Figure 3.3, this work allowed the illustration that a PRF—in this case, obesity—could also be an outcome in certain occupational contexts, including exposures to both chemical and nonchemical hazards, or in association with other PRFs.

Figure 3.3 uses the same model structure shown in Figure 3.2 but examines a PRF, obesity, as an outcome. For example, evidence in the published literature supports an association between occupational activity/sitting/sedentary work

FIGURE 3.3. Conceptual Models of Where a PRF Can Also Be an Outcome: The Example of Obesity

Description of model type	Illustration of model type	Specific example description
A. An ORF and a PRF independently impact obesity	Occupational activity/sitting/sedentary work → Obesity; Age → Obesity	Occupational activity/sitting/sedentary work is a risk for obesity. Independently, obesity can increase with age.
B. A PRF impacts an ORF–obesity association	Gender; Endocrine-disrupting or lipid-metabolism altering xenobiotics (e.g., dioxins, phthalates) → Obesity	Exposure to endocrine-disrupting or lipid-metabolism-altering xenobiotic agents is a risk for obesity. Gender may affect this association.
C. An ORF impacts a PRF–obesity association	Job stress; Exercise activity/behavior → Obesity	Exercise activity/behavior affects obesity. Job stress may affect this association. Job stress may also affect exercise activity/behavior and obesity, independently.
D. An ORF impacts obesity; a PRF impacts another outcome; obesity and that health outcome can be associated	Shift work → Obesity; Diet and metabolism → Cardiovascular disease	Shift work has been associated with obesity. The association of diet/metabolism and obesity with cardiovascular disease is known. Shiftwork may also affect diet and metabolism.
E. A PRF impacts obesity; an ORF impacts another outcome; obesity and that health outcome can be associated	Noise → Cardiovascular disease; HTN; Diet and metabolism → Obesity	Noise is associated with cardiovascular disease and hypertension. The association of diet/metabolism and obesity with cardiovascular disease is known.

Note. These models were supported by literature searches based on keywords pertaining to the model components. Published literature in the PubMed database was searched, and publications of epidemiological studies that supported one of the five categories of models (A through E) with odds ratios, relative risks, attributable risks, standardized mortality ratios, or other measures of effect were selected. References for specific models can be found in Pandalai et al. (2013), in which selected models are found and from which this figure was created. PRF = personal risk factor; ORF = occupational risk factor; HTN = hypertension.

and obesity as an outcome (Model A). Other evidence suggests that job stress can affect exercise activity/behavior, known to be associated with obesity, which suggests a model involving these factors for further examination (Model C). Further additional evidence suggests that shift work can increase the risk for obesity (Model D). These examples suggest that behaviors, whether a personal, nonwork type of activity or work behaviors that may be due to specifics of occupational demands, can have health effects such as obesity. These examples also illustrate that behaviors can be PRFs, such as exercise activity, or ORFs, such as sitting as part of the occupational setting. Further, these examples along with all of those presented in Figure 3.3 reinforce the concept that a construct examined, sometimes predominantly, as a PRF (e.g., obesity) can also be an outcome due to ORFs. Similarly, other factors with a behavioral component that could also be outcomes in the occupational setting, such as smoking, alcohol use, or other factors, require evaluation for a role similar to that found for obesity in our work thus far (Hammer & Sauter, 2013).

IMPLICATIONS OF THE THEORETICAL MODELS

The idea that we should examine the interrelationship of ORFs and PRFs underpins a comprehensive view of workforce health. One example of such a view is the *Total Worker Health*® concept developed by the National Institute for Occupational Safety and Health (Schill & Chosewood, 2013). Changes in the nature of work, the workforce, and the workplace require a more comprehensive analysis than has been traditionally conducted because exposure, hazards, risks, and health and safety outcomes often cross over traditional boundaries of the workplace fence or shop floor (Hymel et al., 2011). Alternatively, even when they do not, the variability in worker exposure and response can be influenced significantly by nonwork factors (Neumann & Kimmel, 1998; Schulte et al., 2012). With theoretical models to aid us in identifying and categorizing these relationships, we can describe occupational interrelationships with specific risk factors, evaluate whether health protection or health promotion should be the main focus of interventions, design research that supports multivariable perspectives, and document the impact of work on personal health behaviors.

Using the interrelationships of ORFs and PRFs to guide development of interventions may have some ethical issues. These include blaming workers for unsafe work conditions because of inherent traits, failing to hold employers responsible for providing a safe and healthy workplace, and not keeping information about PRFs private and confidential (Schulte et al., 2007).

Describing Occupational Interrelationships With Specific Personal Risk Factors

Interventions to address workforce health need to account for a wide range of factors. To better enable practitioners, researchers, and decision makers to understand the range of ORF–PRF interactions, we are developing a web-based compendium of in-depth analyses of specific PRFs and their occupational inter-actions. The compendium will aid (a) hypothesis generation and research design, (b) the understanding and application of multiple factors in clinical activities, and (c) the integration of such factors into OSH prevention and inter-vention strategies.

Keeping Occupational Health and Safety Protection as the Dominant Focus

In considering models that include PRFs, it is critical that occupational health protection remain the dominant focus of workplace safety and health efforts (Howard, Chosewood, & Hudson, 2016; Lax, 2016). Great care must be taken to avoid the focus on PRFs at the expense of appropriate and necessary OSH efforts (Howard et al., 2016; Lax, 2016). This caution is because there are limited societal resources dedicated to investigating occupational hazards and there have been concerns (Lax, 2016) that these resources will be diluted if focus also includes PRFs. Nonetheless, although health protection is the pri-mary goal, increasingly that goal can be better achieved by also focusing on addressing PRFs (Sorensen, McLellan, et al., 2016; Sorensen, Nagler, et al., 2016). In this case, it is essential that appropriate OSH intervention and pre-vention strategies mitigate the occupational exposure to improve health.

Designing Research With Hypothesis-Generating Versus Causative Models

Assessing both the occupational and the nonoccupational published literature to hypothesize ORF/PRF/outcome associations can identify important PRFs that affect illness and injury outcomes, which may be important in working populations, and can identify workplace exposures that can affect outcomes not traditionally thought to be important occupational health effects. One lim-itation of this approach is that summary measures of effect are not calculated for any of the interrelationships suggested in the models developed. A more rigorous analytical approach to evaluate risk variables as confounders, media-tors, moderators, or independent causal factors is one avenue for future work (Howards, Schisterman, Poole, Kaufman, & Weinberg, 2012).

Evaluating the association of multiple risk factors and illness/injury states presents myriad challenges for understanding the level and quality of scientific support, determining the magnitude of such associations, and incorporating this information into clinical practice and developing prevention and interven-tion recommendations. The approach outlined here could help to organize and address challenging complex associations inherent, for example, in problems such as aggregate exposures and cumulative risk (Lentz et al., 2015) and meth-ods for cumulative risk assessment (Gallagher et al., 2015). Cumulative risk assessment is the analysis, characterization, and possible quantification of the combined risks to human health or the environment from multiple agents or stressors (U.S. Environmental Protection Agency, 2003). The continuation of the current approach is warranted, with need to expand the list of PRFs to major ones not yet addressed in depth, for example, age, alcohol consumption, and chronic diseases (in general and specifically) for each of these the occupational contexts.

Considering the interrelationships of ORFs and PRFs raises many issues, such as a need to contemplate multifactorial causative associations, blurring classic boundaries of the OSH field, implications for research funding, and workers compensation (Schulte et al., 2012). Causation may be the most fundamental and raises several questions. One question is whether causation can or should be apportioned or is a blended result (Schulte et al., 2012). Another is the need to extend concepts such as work-related and work-exacerbated to include risk factors previously not thought to be associated with occupational illness and injury, and common health effects previously not designated as being associated with occupational exposures. A new appreciation is needed that health effects not previously thought to be relevant to OSH may be affected by workplace factors, in the absence of nonwork risk factors, or in a combined effect with nonoccupational variables.

The approach in this chapter is an attempt to make explicit nonwork factors (PRFs) that may affect outcomes that are also affected by occupational exposures. In understanding these variables, one can help protect workers' health by comprehending if workplace exposures exacerbate PRF–outcome associations or if common health effects can also be the result of occupational hazards. In these cases, more attention to workplace variables can help address health issues in workers.

Supporting Multivariable and Multilevel Perspectives

A healthy workplace can be defined in terms of the hazards present in the workplace and characteristics that workers bring to it, which might include, for example, the underlying health status of workers. As seen in the models developed for obesity as an outcome, however, common health conditions may also result from workplace exposures, an important consideration for adequate and appropriate health protection in the occupational setting (Lax, 2016). For situations in which occupational hazards are associated with common conditions, even more aggressive mitigation of such hazards may be important, as attempts to treat such conditions may be ineffective without properly addressing workplace factors that contribute to the adverse health effect.

Examinations of ORF/PRF/outcome models highlight the need to fund and conduct research that addresses the multiplicity of factors related to work and workers (Sorensen, McLellan, et al., 2016). These include variables at multiple levels such as worker, enterprise, and population. Methods such as multilevel analysis are potentially important in this regard (Martin, Karanika-Murray, Biron, & Sanderson, 2016). For example, workforce health, which is affected by ORFs and PRFs, is also affected by and affects population well-being. Focusing on a single ORF–PRF interrelationship is only one part of the causal web.

In the modern workplace, work organization factors and overarching issues such as multiple job changes; underemployment; and contingent, precarious, and nonstandard employment arrangements may be work-related risk factors of importance (Schulte et al., 2017). These factors may have interrelationships with PRFs, overt workplace hazards, classic occupational health effects, and/or disease or injury outcomes not traditionally viewed as work related (Schulte et al., 2017).

Another systemic issue that may arise when considering the interrelationship of ORFs and PRFs relates to workers' compensation and personal health insurance. Workers' compensation systems are not comprehensive, and the personal health insurance system has covered many health problems with an occupational etiology (O'Leary, Boden, Seabury, Ozonoff, & Scherer, 2012; Spieler & Wagner, 2014). In some cases these adverse effects should have been addressed by the workers' compensation system (Spieler & Burton, 2012; Spieler & Wagner, 2014). There are many types of workers' compensation systems, generally with the goal of covering work-related health problems in exchange for no further redress by workers. Some systems apportion causality to distinguish work-related from non-work-related effects, but these systems may have challenges in the contemporary work context (Spieler & Wagner, 2014). For example, further research on ORF/PRF/outcome associations, using methods such as those discussed here, may produce additional support for the association of common medical problems with occupational exposures, as suggested by the work on obesity discussed earlier. In these situations, coverage of such conditions by workers' compensation systems becomes an important consideration.

In addressing the interrelationships of ORFs and PRFs, there is a need to be aware that these risk factors may be of different origins, responsibilities, and legalities. Interventions to address them may have to consider these differences.

Documenting the Impact of Work on Health Behaviors

Health behaviors (e.g., smoking, drinking) compose one category of PRFs. They may also be outcomes. One example described in this chapter involved obesity as an outcome of ORF and PRF exposure (Pandalai et al., 2013). More specifically, this raises the issue of behaviors that result from exposure to workplace hazards, which may lead to obesity. In the case of obesity as an outcome in the occupational setting, some hazards, such as exposure to endocrine-disrupting chemicals or engagement in shiftwork, can potentially lead to obesity due to direct effects on biochemistry or circadian rhythm processes. Shiftwork, however, can also be a risk factor for obesity by affecting lifestyle behaviors related to diet, for example, changes in the timing of meals due to work shifts. Other workplace exposures, such as job stress, may affect obesity via behavioral pathways such as engagement in exercise activity. In these cases, obesity is not a PRF but an outcome that would merit intervention based on physiologic and behavioral changes due to exposure to chemical or nonchemical ORFs.

CONCLUSION

Disease and injury in the workplace can be the result of the interaction of a variety of ORFs and PRFs. Historically, there was only a work-related focus regarding causes and interventions. This sufficed when workers tended to be exposed to large amounts or uncontrolled types of workplace hazards. However, although many of the historic risks of the workplace were increasingly being controlled, the workforce was also changing such that, at lower exposures, the variability of effects is potentially affected by PRFs as well. Consequently, there is a need for a holistic approach to address adverse workforce health and safety outcomes.

The approach suggested in this chapter begins a process of developing an evidence base for reliable determinations of the interaction of occupational and PRFs. This approach develops a hypothesized linkage between risk factors and outcomes substantiated by limited but significant scientific evidence from epidemiological studies. More empirical confirmation of these linkages is generally required. The *Total Worker Health* program reflects the understanding of the need for a holistic approach to workforce safety and health and systematically is moving forward in that regard with a program of etiologic, intervention, and translation research. The models described in this chapter may be seen as guideposts for future research. Taken as a whole, they point the way to addressing the health and safety needs of the current and future workforce.

REFERENCES

Davis, K., Collins, S. R., Doty, M. M., Ho, A., & Holmgren, A. (2005). Health and productivity among U.S. workers. *Issue Brief (Commonwealth Fund)*, *856*, 1–10.

Gallagher, S. S., Rice, G. E., Scarano, L. J., Teuschler, L. K., Bollweg, G., & Martin, L. (2015). Cumulative risk assessment lessons learned: A review of case studies and issue papers. *Chemosphere*, *120*, 697–705. http://dx.doi.org/10.1016/j.chemosphere.2014.10.030

Hammer, L. B., & Sauter, S. (2013). Total worker health and work-life stress. *Journal of Occupational and Environmental Medicine*, *55*(12, Suppl.), S25–S29. http://dx.doi.org/10.1097/JOM.0000000000000043

Holzmann, R. (2004). *Toward a reformed and coordinated pension system in Europe: Rationale and potential structure*. Washington, DC: World Bank.

Howard, J., Chosewood, L. C., & Hudson, H. L. (2016). The perils of integrating wellness and safety and health and the possibility of a worker-oriented alternative. *New Solutions*, *26*, 345–348. http://dx.doi.org/10.1177/1048291116656631

Howards, P. P., Schisterman, E. F., Poole, C., Kaufman, J. S., & Weinberg, C. R. (2012). "Toward a clearer definition of confounding" revisited with directed acyclic graphs. *American Journal of Epidemiology*, *176*, 506–511. http://dx.doi.org/10.1093/aje/kws127

Hymel, P. A., Loeppke, R. R., Baase, C. M., Burton, W. N., Hartenbaum, N. P., Hudson, T. W., . . . Larson, P. W. (2011). Workplace health protection and promotion: A new pathway for a healthier—and safer—workforce. *Journal of Occupational and Environmental Medicine*, *53*, 695–702. http://dx.doi.org/10.1097/JOM.0b013e31822005d0

Kleinbaum, D. G., Kupper, L. L., & Morgenstern, H. (1982). *Epidemiologic research: Principles and quantitative methods*. New York, NY: Wiley & Sons.

Lax, M. B. (2016). The perils of integrating wellness and safety and health and the possibility of a worker-oriented alternative. *New Solutions*, *26*, 11–39. http://dx.doi.org/10.1177/1048291116629489

Lentz, T. J., Dotson, G. S., Williams, P. R., Maier, A., Gadagbui, B., Pandalai, S. P., . . . Mumtaz, M. (2015). Aggregate exposure and cumulative risk assessment—Integrating occupational and non-occupational risk factors. *Journal of Occupational and Environmental Hygiene, 12*(Suppl. 1), S112–S126. http://dx.doi.org/10.1080/15459624.2015.1060326

Loeppke, R. (2008). The value of health and the power of prevention. *International Journal of Workplace Health Management, 1,* 95–108. http://dx.doi.org/10.1108/17538350810893892

Martin, A., Karanika-Murray, M., Biron, C., & Sanderson, K. (2016). The psychosocial work environment, employee mental health and organization interventions: Improving research and practice by taking a multilevel approach. *Stress and Health, 32,* 201–215. http://dx.doi.org/10.1002/smi.2593

Neumann, D. A., & Kimmel, C. A. (1998). *Human variability in response to chemical exposures, measures, modeling, and risk assessment.* Boca Raton, FL: CRC Press.

O'Leary, P., Boden, L. I., Seabury, S. A., Ozonoff, A., & Scherer, E. (2012). Workplace injuries and the take-up of Social Security disability benefits. *Social Security Bulletin, 72*(3), 1–17.

Pandalai, S. P., Schulte, P. A., & Miller, D. B. (2013). Conceptual heuristic models of the interrelationships between obesity and the occupational environment. *Scandinavian Journal of Work, Environment & Health, 39,* 221–232. http://dx.doi.org/10.5271/sjweh.3363

Poulter, S. R. (2001). Genetic testing in toxic injury litigation: The path to scientific certainty or blind alleys. *Jurimetrics, 41,* 211–239.

Richter, J. (1997). Taking the worker as you find him. *Maryland Journal of Contemporary Legal Issues, 8,* 189–236.

Ringen, K., & Smith, W. J. (1983). Occupational diseases and equity issues. *Virginia Journal of Natural Resources Law, 2,* 213–231.

Schill, A. L., & Chosewood, L. C. (2013). The NIOSH Total Worker Health™ program: An overview. *Journal of Occupational and Environmental Medicine, 55*(Suppl.), S8–S11. http://dx.doi.org/10.1097/JOM.0000000000000037

Schoenbach, V. J., & Rosamund, W. D. (2000). *Understanding the fundamentals of epidemiology: An evolving text.* Chapel Hill: University of North Carolina.

Schulte, P. A., Pana-Cryan, R., Schnorr, T., Schill, A. L., Guerin, R., Felknor, S., & Wagner, G. R. (2017). An approach to assess the burden of work-related injury, disease, and distress. *American Journal of Public Health, 107,* 1051–1057. http://dx.doi.org/10.2105/AJPH.2017.303765

Schulte, P. A., Pandalai, S., Wulsin, V., & Chun, H. (2012). Interaction of occupational and personal risk factors in workforce health and safety. *American Journal of Public Health, 102,* 434–448. http://dx.doi.org/10.2105/AJPH.2011.300249

Schulte, P., & Vainio, H. (2010). Well-being at work—Overview and perspective. *Scandinavian Journal of Work, Environment & Health, 36,* 422–429. http://dx.doi.org/10.5271/sjweh.3076

Schulte, P. A., Wagner, G. R., Ostry, A., Blanciforti, L. A., Cutlip, R. G., Krajnak, K. M., . . . Miller, D. B. (2007). Work, obesity, and occupational safety and health. *American Journal of Public Health, 97,* 428–436. http://dx.doi.org/10.2105/AJPH.2006.086900

Sorensen, G., McLellan, D. L., Sabbath, E. L., Dennerlein, J. T., Nagler, E. M., Hurtado, D. A., . . . Wagner, G. R. (2016). Integrating worksite health protection and health promotion: A conceptual model for intervention and research. *Preventive Medicine, 91,* 188–196. http://dx.doi.org/10.1016/j.ypmed.2016.08.005

Sorensen, G., Nagler, E. M., Hashimoto, D., Dennerlein, J. T., Theron, J. V., Stoddard, A. M., . . . Wagner, G. (2016). Implementing an integrated health protection/health promotion intervention in the hospital setting: Lessons learned from the Be Well, Work Well Study. *Journal of Occupational and Environmental Medicine, 58,* 185–194. http://dx.doi.org/10.1097/JOM.0000000000000592

Special Committee on Health, Productivity, and Disability Management, American College of Occupational and Environmental Medicine. (2009). Healthy workforce/ healthy economy: the role of health, productivity, and disability management in addressing the nation's health care crisis: why an emphasis on the health of the workforce is vital to the health of the economy. *Journal of Occupational and Environmental Medicine, 51,* 114–119. http://dx.doi.org/10.1097/JOM.0b013e318195dad2

Spieler, E. A., & Burton, J. F., Jr. (2012). The lack of correspondence between work-related disability and receipt of workers' compensation benefits. *American Journal of Industrial Medicine, 55,* 487–505. http://dx.doi.org/10.1002/ajim.21034

Spieler, E. A., & Wagner, G. R. (2014). Counting matters: Implications of undercounting in the BLS survey of occupational injuries and illnesses. *American Journal of Industrial Medicine, 57,* 1077–1084. http://dx.doi.org/10.1002/ajim.22382

Tompa, E. (2002). The impact of health on productivity: Macro and microeconomic evidence and policy implications. In A. Sharpe & K. Banting (Eds.), *The review of economic performance and social progress 2002: Towards a social understanding of productivity* (Vol. 2, pp. 181–202). Montreal, Quebec, Canada: Institute for Research on Public Policy.

U.S. Environmental Protection Agency. (2003). *Framework for cumulative risk assessment* (PA/630/P-02/001A). Washington, DC: Author.

van den Berg, T. I., Elders, L. A., de Zwart, B. C., & Burdorf, A. (2009). The effects of work-related and individual factors on the Work Ability Index: A systematic review. *Occupational and Environmental Medicine, 66,* 211–220. http://dx.doi.org/10.1136/oem.2008.039883

Vineis, P., & Kriebel, D. (2006). Causal models in epidemiology: Past inheritance and genetic future. *Environmental Health, 5,* 21. http://dx.doi.org/10.1186/1476-069X-5-21

Weinberg, C. R. (2009). Less is more, except when less is less: Studying joint effects. *Genomics, 93,* 10–12.

4

Effectiveness of *Total Worker Health*® Interventions

W. Kent Anger, Anjali Rameshbabu, Ryan Olson,
Todd Bodner, David A. Hurtado, Kelsey Parker,
Wylie Wan, Bradley Wipfli, and Diane S. Rohlman

Total Worker Health® is an integrated approach to safety, health, and well-being introduced by the National Institute for Occupational Safety and Health (NIOSH) in 2011 and refined in 2016. *Total Worker Health* (TWH) is defined as "policies, programs, and practices that integrate protection from work-related safety and health hazards with promotion of injury and illness prevention efforts to advance worker well-being" (NIOSH, n.d., para. 1). At its core, the TWH program aims to enhance worker well-being by informing the design of work and employment conditions in a way that will not only prioritize safety but also optimize physical and psychological outcomes. Although there are interventions focusing on occupational safety and health *and* well-being, the empirical evidence of such programs in the literature remains sparse (Anger et al., 2015; Feltner et al., 2016). The purposes of this chapter are to provide a systematic review of occupational safety, health, and well-being intervention research through April 2017 and to examine the effectiveness of those interventions.

Conflict of interest: Oregon Health & Science University (OHSU) and Drs. Anger and Rohlman have a significant financial interest in Northwest Education Training and Assessment (NwETA), a company that may have a commercial interest in the results of this research and technology. This potential individual and institutional conflict of interest has been reviewed and managed by OHSU. This chapter was funded by the National Institute for Occupational Safety and Health (NIOSH U19 OH010154). The chapter is solely the responsibility of the authors and does not represent the official views of NIOSH.

http://dx.doi.org/10.1037/0000149-005
Total Worker Health, H. L. Hudson, J. A. S. Nigam, S. L. Sauter, L. C. Chosewood, A. L. Schill, and J. Howard (Editors)
Copyright © 2019 by the American Psychological Association. All rights reserved.

SELECTION OF STUDIES FOR ANALYSIS

An initial search for publications focused on self-identified TWH interventions or "integrated occupational safety and health *plus* well-being interventions" linked to the NIOSH list of issues relevant to the TWH program (Chapter 2, this volume; NIOSH, 2015a). Entering these phrases independently or in combination into PubMed, Scopus, and PsycINFO produced 51,227 citations. Given that the emergent literature pool was impractical to tackle, the search strategy was modified to focus specifically on the phrase "total worker health," which would provide directly relevant results; a search for "total worker health" resulted in 30 hits via PubMed, 451 in Google Scholar, and 22 in Scopus. PsycINFO provided surprisingly few, mostly overlapping hits. The six NIOSH-funded TWH Centers of Excellence were contacted to identify published and in press articles on intervention results. Other sources included the NIOSHTIC-2 database (NIOSH, 2015b) and the systematic reviews of the TWH program (Anger et al., 2015; Feltner et al., 2016).

Each of the titles, abstracts, or full articles was examined to identify studies that met four inclusion criteria. First, the intervention addressed (attempted to change) both traditional safety and health *and* well-being issues; although there would appear to be a clear distinction between safety and wellness or well-being targets, crosscutting targets (viz., stress, sleep, sitting) were judged to simultaneously address both. Second, there was a degree of integration between safety and health *and* well-being in the intervention program. Third, the research was conducted as a designed study, employing quasi-experimental or randomized designs. Fourth, publications were in English. Thirty-eight studies met the inclusion criteria. Seven studies identified *"Total Worker Health"* in the publication, six of which have been published by authors in TWH Centers of Excellence.

KEY FEATURES OF THE INTERVENTIONS REVIEWED

Key features were extracted from each article (Table 4.1): (a) industry sector based on the Standard Industrial Classifications (Occupational Safety and Health Administration, n.d.); (b) country where the intervention was conducted; (c) goal of the intervention; (d) intervention dose based on the time schedule and length, and delivery mode—live or in-person presentations, online or computer presentation, paper-based information, and introduction of equipment/environment; (e) intervention target—employee, supervisor, and manager; (f) degree of integration (see next)—high, medium, and low; (g) sample size (at baseline); and (h) study design.

Because integration between the *occupational safety and health* and *well-being* components within an intervention is a salient feature of the TWH program, the degree of integration was assessed in each study. Although there is no established definition of "integration," the Indicators of Integration (Sorensen et al., 2013; Williams et al., 2015) and NIOSH's Fundamentals of Total Worker Health Approaches (NIOSH, 2016a) provided guiding frameworks.

TABLE 4.1. Key Features of the TWH Interventions

Author (year); *Name of intervention (if so identified)*	Intervention goal	Industry / Country	Dose	Mode	Integration target	Integration rating	n	Research design
Adeleke, Healy, Smith, Goode, & Clark (2017)	Reduce sitting	Public administration / Australia	12.9 w	E	E S M	M	137	Quasi—no C
Alkhajah et al. (2012)	Reduce sitting	Services / Australia	1 w, 3 m	E L P E	E	M	32	Quasi—w/ C & Pretests
Bertera (1990)	Improve lifestyle	Manufacturing / U.S.	2 y	L P E	E	H	43,888	Quasi—w/ C & Pretests
Bøggild & Jeppesen (2001)	Enhance shift scheduling	Services / Denmark	6 m	L P E	E S	H	101	Quasi—w/ C & Pretests
Carr et al. (2016)[a]	Increase physical activity	Unspecified ("Company") / U.S.	16 w	L O E	E	L	54	RCT comparing 2 treatment groups, no C (w/ Pretest)
Caspi et al. (2013); *Be Well, Work Well*	Encourage safe patient handling, fitness, improve ergonomics	Services / U.S.	3 m	L E	E S M	H	374	Quasi—pre–post, no C
Cherniack et al. (2016); *HITEC 2*[a]	Improve safety and well-being using participatory approach	Public administration / U.S.	5 y	L P	E S M	H	326	Quasi—2 conditions; pre–post; no C

(table continues)

TABLE 4.1. (continued)

Author (year); *Name of intervention (if so identified)*	Intervention goal	Industry / Country	Dose / Mode	Integration target	Integration rating	n	Research design
Coffeng, Boot, et al. (2014); Coffeng, Hendriksen, et al. (2014); *Be Active & Relax: Vitality in Practice*	Reduce need for recovery, stress; increase physical activity	Finance / Netherlands	? / L O P E	E S	M	412	RCT—Factorial Design
Dalton & Harris (1991)	Integrate company-wide safety, industrial hygiene, primary care, health promotion	Other ("Telecommunications") / U.S.	1,460–1,825 d / L P	E S M	H	6,600	Quasi—Interrupted Time Series
Danquah, Kloster, Holtermann, Aadahl, Bauman, et al. (2017); *Take a Stand!*	Reduce sitting	Unspecified ("Offices") / Denmark	? / L O E	E	H	313	RCT—Pre–post test w/ C
Dennerlein et al. (2017)[a]	Increase safe patient handling equipment use	Services / U.S.	7 m / L E	E S M	H	1,832	Quasi—Pretests w/ C
Eriksen et al. (2002)	Manage stress, improve lifestyle	Public administration / Norway	120 h / L	E	L	860	RCT—Multiple treatments & C w/ pretest
Glass et al. (2016); *IPV and the Workplace*	Prevent IPV via supportive work environment	Public administration / U.S.	1 session / O	S	L	941	RCT—Pre–post test w/ C
Hammer et al. (2016); *Work, Family, and Health Study*	Improve work-life balance	Services / U.S.	9 h + / L O	E S M	M	1,524	RCT + Pre–post test w/ C

Study	Goal	Industry / Country	Duration	Outcome	Rating	N	Design
Hammer et al. (2015); *SHIP*[a]	Increase effective supervision, team effectiveness	Construction / U.S.	5.83 h / L O E	E S	H	264	RCT—pre-post test w/ C
Konradt, Schmook, Wilm, & Hertel, (2000); *Health Circles*	Increase stress and coping	Multiple industries / Germany	15 h / L	E	L	17	Quasi—pre-post test
Kurowski, Gore, Roberts, Richardson Kincaid, & Punnett (2017)	Increase safe patient handling equipment use	Services / U.S.	2 y / L E	E	H	several centers	Quasi—no C
Lin, Lin, Chen, & Lee (2017); *Sit Less, Walk More*	Increase physical activity, reduce sitting	Other ("Aerospace industry") / Taiwan	12 w / L P E	E	M	99	Quasi—Pretests w/ C
Maes, Verhoeven, Kittel, & Scholten, (1998); *Brabantia Project*	Participatory management-employee work improvement	Manufacturing / Netherlands	3 y / L P E	E S	H	264	Quasi—Pretests w/ C
Okechukwu, Krieger, Sorensen, Li, & Barbeau (2009); *Mass Built*	Reduce smoking	Construction / U.S.	4 m / L P E	E	M	1,213	RCT + Pre-post test w/ C
Olson et al. (2009); *SHIFT* pilot	Encourage weight loss; improve safety	Transportation / U.S.	~ 8 h / L O P	E	L	29	Quasi—Pre-post, no C
Olson, Thompson, et al. (2016); *COMPASS*[a]	Create peer support groups; improve safety, lifestyle	Services / U.S.	30 h / L P	E	H	149	RCT + Pre-post test w/ C

(table continues)

TABLE 4.1. (continued)

Author (year); *Name of intervention (if so identified)*	Intervention goal	Industry —— Country	Dose —— Mode	Integration target	Integration rating	n	Research design
Olson, Wipfli, et al. (2016) *SHIFT*	Encourage weight loss; improve safety	Transportation —— U.S.	3.75 h + —— L O P	E	L	452	RCT—Pre-post test w/ C
Olson et al. (2015); *COMPASS pilot*[a]	Create peer support groups; improve safety, lifestyle	Services —— U.S.	6 m —— L P	E	H	16	Quasi—Pre-post, no C
Peters & Carlson (1999)	Manage stress; improve lifestyle	Services —— U.S.	7 h —— L E	E	L	50	RCT + Pre-post test w/ C
Pronk, Katz, Lowry, & Payfer (2012)[a]; *Take-a-Stand Project*	Reduce sitting	Public administration —— U.S.	4 w —— E	E	M	34	Quasi—Interrupted Time Series
Ramey et al. (2016)	Manage stress; increase resiliency	Public administration —— U.S.	2 sessions + 3 m —— L O E	E	M	38	RCT—Pre-post test w/ C
Rohlman et al. (2016)[a]; *PUSH*	Educate on worker rights, communication, lifestyle	Public administration —— U.S.	1 h —— O	E	L	255	RCT—Pre-post test w/ C
Snetselaar et al. (2016); *Be Hipp*	Manage stress; improve lifestyle, ergonomics	Multiple industries —— U.S.	3 y —— L	E S M	L	280	RCT—Pre-post test w/ C
Sorensen et al. (2007)[a]; *Tools for Health*	Reduce smoking; increase fruit/ vegetable intake	Construction —— U.S.	3 m (?) —— L P	E	L	582	RCT—Pre-post test w/ C

Study; Intervention	Goal	Industry / Country	Dose	Integration Target	Integration Rating	N	Research Design
Sorensen et al. (2005)[a]; *Healthy Directions-Small Business*	Reduce smoking, hazardous exposure; improve lifestyle	Manufacturing / U.S.	18 sessions / L O	E S M	H	974	RCT—Pre-post test w/ C
Sorensen et al. (2016)[a]; *Be Well, Work Well*	Improve ergonomics, lifestyle	Services / U.S.	? / L O P E	E S	H	452	RCT—Pre-post test w/ C
Sorensen et al. (1998)[a]; *WellWorks Study*	Reduce smoking, hazardous exposure	Manufacturing / U.S.	? / L P	E	H	2,386	RCT—Pre-post test w/ C
Sorensen et al. (2003)[a]; *WellWorks2*	Reduce smoking, hazardous exposure	Manufacturing / U.S.	? / L E	E S M	H	9,019	RCT—Alternative-treatments design w/ Pretest; no C
Sorensen et al. (2010)[a]; *Gear Up for Health Study*	Reduce smoking; encourage weight loss	Transportation / U.S.	5 sessions / L	E	L	215	Quasi—no C
Tsutsumi et al. (2009)	Improve workplace via participatory intervention	Manufacturing / Japan	48 w / L	E S M	H	97	RCT—Pre-post test w/ C
Tveito & Eriksen (2009); *Integrated Health Programme*	Manage stress	Services / Norway	123 h / L	E	M	40	RCT—Pre-post test w/ C
von Thiele Schwarz et al. (2015)	Integrate health protection and health promotion with continuous improvement	Services / Sweden	1.5 y / L	E S M	H	202	RCT—Pre-post test w/ C

Note. Intervention names are provided where applicable. Dose (+ = added components, ? = time not specified; h = hours, d = days, w = weeks, m = months, y = years); Mode (L = live, O = online/computer, P = paper, E = equipment/environment), Integration Target (E = employees, S = supervisor, M = managers); Integration Rating (H = high, M = medium, L = low); Research Design (RCT = randomized controlled trial; Quasi = quasi.-experimental; w/ = with; C = control); IPV = intimate partner violence.
[a]Interventions from National Institute for Occupational Safety and Health–funded TWH Centers.

We examined whether each intervention reflected three key factors: it addressed occupational safety and health *plus* well-being at the organizational level (e.g., included workplace policy change) and at the individual level (e.g., included lifestyle programs, safety trainings) and had leadership engagement (i.e., senior leaders were involved in the development and/or implementation of the intervention). An intervention was rated *high* if all factors were present and low if only one of the three factors was present. In most cases, the extent of integration was not made explicit in the publication, leaving us to infer from the description of the methods.

Intervention Goal

The intervention goals were diverse. Reducing sitting/increasing activity at work and stress management were the goals of four interventions, and the introduction of participatory interventions that involved both management and labor representatives was also a goal of four others.

Location and Industries

Most of the interventions occurred in the United States (26). The largest number of interventions were implemented in the area of services ($n = 12$), followed by public administration ($n = 7$), manufacturing ($n = 6$), construction ($n = 3$), transportation ($n = 3$), and finance ($n = 1$). Other studies fell into the "other" category ($n = 2$), two studies employed multiple industries, and another two studies did not specify a type of industry.

Intervention Dose and Mode of Delivery

The intervention dose—the specific duration or number of sessions—was difficult to extract from many of the publications as noted by a question mark in the body of Table 4.1. Of those identified, the range was from 1 hour (Rohlman, Parish, Elliot, Hanson, & Perrin, 2016) to (periodic activities over) 5 years (Cherniack et al., 2016). Examples of shorter intervention duration were 1 hour (Rohlman et al., 2016), 2.5 hours (Caspi et al., 2013), 4 to 8 hours (Olson, Anger, Elliot, Wipfli, & Gray, 2009; Olson, Wipfli, et al., 2016), or 12 hours (Snetselaar et al., 2016). Longer duration interventions included those of Sorensen et al. (2005) with a dose of 18 sessions and Olson, Thompson, et al. (2016) with a dose of 30 hours. Tveito and Eriksen (2009) included aerobic exercise and training for 123 hours over 9.03 months, and the Eriksen et al. (2002) intervention provided a dose of 120 hours over 12 weeks (Table 4.1).

The majority of studies ($n = 31$) delivered the intervention live (in person). Interventions delivered via online platforms, paper, and/or the work environment were often used in conjunction with in-person contact.

Intervention Target

One intervention targeted supervisors exclusively (Glass, Hanson, Laharnar, Anger, & Perrin, 2016). The other 37 were aimed at employees combined with managers and supervisors.

Degree of Integration

Contrary to many traditional wellness and safety efforts where the burden of responsibility lies on the individual employee, the TWH program emphasizes high integration between occupational safety and health *and* the well-being components of an intervention. Many of the studies in our review ($n = 19$) were judged as having a high degree of integration. That is, they included an organization-level focus and individual-level change and they engaged leadership. Eight studies were rated as having medium integration, and 11 studies were rated as having a low degree of integration. Only two of the studies compared an integrated TWH program to either a safety-only (Carr et al., 2016) or a health-promotion-only (Sorensen et al., 2003) program, and none compared an integrated program to safety-only *and* well-being-only programs. Studies measured the level of integration between health protection and health promotion (von Thiele Schwarz, Augustsson, Hasson, & Stenfors-Hayes, 2015) and measured employee understanding of the link between work and health (Coffeng, Boot, et al., 2014). Overall, although there are many types of employment structures (consider home care workers who work alone in a person's apartment or home), our assessment of integration was tailored to organizations with traditional hierarchical and policy structures.

Research Design and Sample Size

The designs of the majority of the included studies were conducted as randomized trials ($n = 21$); the others employed quasi-experimental designs. The intervention sample size ranged from 16 to 43,888; the mean sample size was 2,014, and the median was 264 participants.

INTERVENTION EFFECTS

The outcomes of studies designed as randomized trials ($n = 21$) are listed in Table 4.2. Both statistically significant and nonsignificant effects are listed to identify outcomes not changed by the interventions as well as those that were changed. Where available, secondary outcomes are identified, and when the distinction was not explicit in the publication, all outcomes are categorized as primary. In three studies, proximal outcomes were identified. Intervention effect sizes are included if listed in the article or if sufficient data were provided for a calculation. Six articles included measures of effect size.

TABLE 4.2. Significant and Nonsignificant Intervention Effects

Study	Significant effects	Nonsignificant effects
Carr et al. (2016)	Primary outcomes: % work time in light intensity physical activity	Primary outcomes: total occupational physical activity, % work time sedentary, % work time in moderate intensity physical activity, % work time in vigorous intensity physical activity
Coffeng, Boot, et al. (2014); Coffeng, Hendriksen, et al. (2014); *Be Active & Relax: Vitality in Practice*	Primary outcomes: Significant Ix effects for some Ix conditions on task performance, contextual performance, and work engagement (absorption and dedication) at some follow-up assessment wave (6 m or 12 m)	Primary outcomes: Need for recovery (6 m and 12 m follow-ups), nonsignificant Ix effects for some Ix conditions on presenteeism (absolute, relative and absenteeism), work performance (task performance, contextual performance, and counterproductive work behavior), work engagement (absorption and dedication) at some follow-up assessment wave (6 m or 12 m)
	Secondary outcomes: Significant Ix effects for some Ix conditions on work-related stress exhaustion, small breaks at work, physical activity stair climbing at work, sedentary behavior at work at some follow-up assessment wave (6 m or 12 m)	Secondary outcomes: Nonsignificant Ix effects for some Ix conditions on work-related stress exhaustion, detachment at work, detachment after work, relaxation at work, relaxation after work, small breaks at work, physical activity stair climbing at work, active commuting, leisure activities, sport activities, light physical activity, moderate physical activity, vigorous physical activity, sedentary behavior at work at some follow-up assessment wave (6 m or 12 m)
Danquah, Kloster, Holtermann, Aadahl, Bauman, et al. (2017); Danquah, Kloster, Holtermann, Aadahl, & Tolstrup (2017); *Take a Stand!*	Primary outcomes: Neck/shoulder pain (3 m follow-up)	Primary outcomes: Neck/shoulder pain (1 m follow-up), back pain (1 m and 3 m follow-ups), extremity pain (1 m and 3 m follow-ups), total pain score (1 m and 3 m follow-ups)

Study		
Eriksen et al. (2002)	Primary outcomes: Various subjective effects that depended on the particular intervention condition on health, work environment, physical fitness, work situation, muscle pain, stress, health maintenance	Primary outcomes: Subjective health complaints of musculoskeletal, pseudoneurological, gastrointestinal, allergy, and flu, job stress (domains of communication, leadership, relocation, workload, sick leave)
Glass et al. (2016); *IPV and the Workplace*	Primary outcomes: Workplace climate toward domestic violence Proximal outcomes: Intimate partner violence training knowledge	Primary outcomes: Providing incentives did not significantly moderate the Ix effect on workplace climate toward domestic violence
Hammer et al. (2016); *Work, Family, & Health Study*	Primary outcomes: Safety compliance (6 m follow-up, $d = 0.12$), organizational citizenship behaviors (12 m follow-up, $d = 0.16$), some significant moderated Ix effects were obtained for at least one follow-up period for the primary outcomes as a function of baseline Family Supportive Supervisor Behavior, perceived work–family climate, and control over work time values. Proximal outcomes: Control over work time (6 m follow-up, $d = -0.16$ [unexpected direction])	Primary outcomes: Safety compliance (12 m follow-up, $d = 0.08$), Organizational Citizenship Behaviors (6 m follow-up, $d = 0.09$), some non-significant moderated Ix effects were obtained for at least one follow-up period for the primary outcomes as a function of baseline Family Supportive Supervisor Behavior, perceived work–family climate, and control over work time values. Proximal outcomes: Family Supportive Supervisor Behaviors (6 m follow-up, $d = 0.08$, 12 m follow-up, $d = 0.10$), control over work time (12 m follow-up, $d = -0.11$), work-to-family conflict (6 m follow-up, $d = 0.03$, 12 m follow-up, $d = 0.06$), family-to-work conflict (6 m follow-up, $d = -0.04$, 12 m follow-up, $d = -0.02$)
Hammer et al. (2015); *SHIP*	Primary outcomes: Blood pressure ($\Delta R^2 = .015$)	Primary outcomes: Physical health ($\Delta R^2 < .001$), safety compliance ($\Delta R^2 = .001$), safety participation ($\Delta R^2 = .014$)
Okechukwu et al. (2009); *Mass Built*	Primary Outcome: Quit rates among smokers (30 days postintervention) Secondary Outcomes: Decrease in daily cigarette smoking of at least half a pack (6 m postintervention)	Primary Outcome: Quit rates among smokers (6 m postintervention) Secondary Outcomes: Smoking cessation attempts lasting more than 1 day, decisional balance that supports smoking cessation, number of days smoking

(table continues)

TABLE 4.2. (continued)

Study	Significant effects	Nonsignificant effects
Olson, Thompson, et al. (2016); *COMPASS*	Primary outcomes: Experienced community of practice (6 m follow-up, $d = 0.36$, 12 m follow-up, $d = 0.37$); talked about improving unsafe conditions (12 m follow-up, $d = 0.84$); corrected slip, trip, or fall hazards (12 m follow-up, $d = 0.45$); used new tool or techniques for moving objects (6 m follow-up, $d = 0.65$); used new tool or techniques for housecleaning (6 m follow-up, $d = 0.51$, 12 m follow-up, $d = 0.64$); fruit and vegetable intake (12 m follow-up, $d = 0.31$); meals brought from home (12 m follow-up, $d = <$minus>0.46 [unexpected direction]) Secondary outcomes: Client corrected slip, trip, or fall hazards (12 m follow-up, $d = 0.51$); client corrected other hazards (6 m follow-up, $d = .82$, 12 m follow-up, $d = 1.01$); client noted using new tool or technique for housecleaning (6 m follow-up, $d = 0.69$)	Primary outcomes: Talked about improving unsafe conditions (6 m follow-up, $d = 0.34$); corrected slip, trip, or fall hazards (6 m follow-up, $d = 0.13$); corrected other hazards (6 m follow-up, $d = -0.05$, 12 m follow-up, $d = 0.16$); used new tool or techniques for moving objects (12 m follow-up, $d = 0.17$); fruit and vegetable intake (6 m follow-up, $d = 0.12$); sugary snack intake (6 m follow-up, $d = -0.28$, 12 m follow-up, $d = -0.03$); sugary drink intake (6 m follow-up, $d = 0.00$, 12 m follow-up, $d = 0.05$); fast-food intake (6 m follow-up, $d = 0.00$, 12 m follow-up, $d = 0.06$); meals brought from home (6 m follow-up, $d = -0.13$); health physical activity (6 m follow-up, $d = 0.09$, 12 m follow-up, $d = 0.18$); SF-12 physical health composite (6 m follow-up, $d = -0.06$, 12 m follow-up, $d = -0.18$); SF-12 mental health composite (6 m follow-up, $d = -0.03$, 12 m follow-up, $d = 0.03$) Secondary outcomes: Sleep quality; perceived stress; musculoskeletal pain and discomfort; functional impairment with activities of daily living; work-related injuries and lost work time attributable to illness or injury; blood pressure; blood cholesterol; triglycerides; glucose; body mass index; hand strength; hamstring flexibility; walk test; client interpersonal conflict with home care worker (6 m follow-up, $d = -0.13$, 12 m follow-up, $d = -0.18$); client satisfaction with home care worker (6 m follow-up, $d = 0.08$, 12 m follow-up, $d = 0.06$); client talked about improving unsafe conditions (6 m follow-up, $d = -0.06$, 12 m follow-up, $d = 0.34$); client corrected slip, trip, or fall hazards (6 m follow-up, $d = 0.23$); client noted using new tool or technique for moving objects or self (6 m follow-up, $d = 0.39$, 12 m follow-up, $d = 0.44$); client noted using new tool or technique for housecleaning (12 m follow-up, $d = 0.33$)

Study		
Olson, Wipfli, et al. (2016); *SHIFT*	Primary outcomes: Body weight ($d = -0.13$), body mass index ($d = -0.14$), daily fruit/vegetable intake ($d = 0.33$), physical activity ($d = 0.34$) Secondary outcomes: Waist circumference ($d = -0.11$), % body fat ($d = -0.23$)	Primary outcomes: Energy usage from fat, sugary snack intake, sugary drink intake, fast food intake Secondary outcomes: Sleep quality, sleep duration, waist-to-hip ratio, systolic BP, diastolic BP, total cholesterol (plus HDL and LDL), triglycerides, blood glucose, driving safety incidents, days missed for illness or injury
Peters & Carlson (1999)	Primary Outcomes (at 3 m posttreatment): % overweight, exercise amount, health behavior changes, HSE general, HSE for exercise, HSE for stress management, curiosity, social support for health, positive environment for health	Primary Outcomes (at 3 m posttreatment): Systolic blood pressure, diastolic blood pressure, cholesterol, risk age, cigarettes smoked, HSE for nutrition, HSE for responsible practices, anxiety, anger, depression, intention to change for health, access to health care satisfaction, job satisfaction, health locus of control, injuries and absenteeism
Rohlman et al. (2016); *PUSH*	Primary outcomes: Safety behaviors ($d = -0.36$), health attitudes ($d = -0.37$), Safety attitudes ($d = -0.37$) Proximal outcomes: Safety and health training knowledge ($d = 0.40$)	Primary outcomes: Health behaviors ($d = -0.15$) Proximal outcomes: Nonsafety and health training knowledge ($d = -0.21$)
Snetselaar et al. (2016); *Be Hipp*	Primary outcomes: None	Primary outcomes: Absenteeism
Sorensen et al. (2007); *Tools for Health*	Primary outcomes: Smoking cessation (7 days or more), any tobacco use cessation, quit attempts, daily fruit and vegetable consumption	Primary outcomes: None reported
Sorensen et al. (2005); *Healthy Directions*	Primary outcomes: Multivitamin use, some significant moderated Ix effects obtained for the primary outcomes as a function of gender, race/ethnicity, occupational class, and education subgroup	Primary outcomes: Fruit and vegetable consumption, red meat consumption, physical activity, some nonsignificant moderated Ix effects were obtained for the primary outcomes as a function of gender, race/ethnicity, occupational class, and education subgroup

(table continues)

TABLE 4.2. (continued)

Study	Significant effects	Nonsignificant effects
Sorensen et al. (2016); *Be Well, Work Well*	Primary outcomes: None Proximal outcomes: Safety practices (unexpected direction)	Primary outcomes: Pain severity, any pain, work interference, fruit/vegetable intake, sugary snacks intake, sugary drinks intake, fast food intake, physical activity, minutes walking weekly, daily minutes sitting, sleep deficiency Proximal outcomes: Ergonomic practices, supervisor support, coworker support, meal break frequency
Sorensen et al. (1998); *WellWorks*	Primary outcomes: % calories consumed as fat, fruit and vegetable intake, moderated Ix effect on fiber consumption as a function of job category	Primary outcomes: Smoking cessation, fiber consumption
Sorensen et al. (2003); *WellWorks2*	Primary outcomes: None	Primary outcomes: Smoking prevalence, fruit and vegetable intake
Tsutsumi et al. (2009)	Primary outcomes: Health and work performance	Primary outcomes: General health
Tveito & Eriksen (2009); *Integrated Health Programme*	Primary outcomes: Neck pain Secondary outcomes: Subjective improvements in health, work environment, physical fitness, work situation, muscle pain, stress management, health maintenance	Primary outcomes: Sick leave; subjective health complaints in allergy, flu, musculoskeletal, pseudoneurology, and gastrointestinal domains Secondary outcomes: Coping, job stress, effort reward imbalance, demands, control, physical functioning, role physical, general health, bodily pain, vitality, social functioning, role emotional, mental health
von Thiele Schwarz et al. (2015)	Primary outcomes: None Proximal outcomes: Health promotion ($\eta^2 = .06$), integration ($\eta^2 = .09$) and Kaizen ($\eta^2 = .04$)	Primary outcomes: Workability ($\eta^2 = .03$), self-rated health ($\eta^2 < .01$), productivity ($\eta^2 = .03$), sickness absence duration, sickness absence frequency

Note. d, ΔR^2, and η^2 are effect size indicators. Ix = intervention effects; m = months; SF-12 = 12-Item Short Form Health Survey; BP = blood pressure; HDL = high-density lipoprotein; LDL = low-density lipoprotein; HSE = health self-efficacy.

Most studies do not report effect size, a significant gap in reporting. The attempt to distinguish occupational safety/health from well-being outcomes was limited given the lack of consistency in reporting. We recommend reporting standardized effect size as a practical indicator of the magnitude of intervention impact. Alternatively, researchers could develop "minimal clinically important differences" for unstandardized effects and discuss whether the intervention effects exceed these differences.

HIERARCHY OF CONTROLS APPLIED TO THE TWH PROGRAM

The intervention methods in the 38 studies can be described in relation to the Hierarchy of Controls as applied to the TWH approach (NIOSH, 2016b) in Table 4.3. NIOSH recommends that efforts to advance occupational safety and health *plus* well-being employ the five levels of the hierarchy in order of priority, with *eliminate* being the highest priority and *encourage* being the lowest:

- *Eliminate* negative working conditions and barriers to safety, health, and well-being.
- *Substitute* safer and healthier workplace policies, work processes, and practices.
- *Redesign* the work environment to enhance working conditions and improve safety, health, and well-being.
- *Educate* all employees and provide resources for improved knowledge.
- *Encourage* or reinforce adoption of safe and healthy practices.

The majority of studies in this review employed the *educate* approach to implement TWH, followed by *encourage* ($n = 30$), *redesign* ($n = 20$), and *substitute* ($n = 8$); only four interventions employed the strategy to *eliminate* a problem, the highest priority method of control. Three studies employed all five levels of control, and three others employed only one; most studies used two ($n = 17$) or three ($n = 13$) levels of control.

CONCLUSION

We find that there has been an increase in efforts to tackle health and safety outcomes within the workplace since earlier reviews (Anger et al., 2015; Feltner et al., 2016), although the inclusion criteria varied in these reviews. As of 2013, 17 TWH interventions were identified by Anger et al. (2015), whose inclusion criteria closely resembled those used here. Our review found that number to be 38 as of April 2017. Interventions most often were implemented in the healthcare industry; they ranged in duration from 1 hour (Rohlman et al., 2016) to periodically over 5 years (Cherniack et al., 2016), and most were delivered in person, targeted employees and supervisors, and were successful in addressing a wide range of occupational safety and health *and* well-being outcomes.

TABLE 4.3. Hierarchy of Controls Applied to the TWH Program

Study	Eliminate	Substitute	Redesign	Educate	Encourage
Adeleke et al. (2017)			Added sit–stand workstations		
Alkhajah et al. (2012)			Added sit–stand workstations	Oral instruction in work-station use: written ergonomic instructions on sitting, standing posture	
Bertera (1990)		Heart healthy options replaced cafeteria, vending machine options		Health Risk Appraisal with interpretation by medical personnel. Training for program coordination, implementation. Individual training in stress management, dental health, weight control, fitness, healthy back, blood pressure, nutrition, smoking cessation. Blood pressure and scales made available. Safety meetings.	Challenges and incentive programs to stimulate fitness, weight control, smoking cessation; individual counseling; program implementation committee
Bøggild & Jeppesen (2001)			Incorporated principles of shift scheduling and allowed workers to select beneficial shift schedules	Education on shift schedules, shift work problems, options for changing schedules	
Carr et al. (2016)			Added seated elliptical machine with daily pedaling tracker and feedback	Consultation on optimizing workstation ergonomics	E-mail prompts for rest breaks, posture variation, physical activity, work environment changes, reducing work stress

Study					
Caspi et al. (2013); *Be Well, Work Well Pilot*	Posters to encourage physical fitness	One-on-one safe patient handling training	Safety audits led to improved ergonomics		
Cherniack et al. (2016)	Participatory process designed to engage people across the organization and encourage change. Program viewed as a success if it progresses on a reliable schedule; implementation not required.	Participatory problem solving to improve fitness for duty; posters and educational materials on healthy eating	Developed plans to place noise-damping panels, replace headphones. New cleaning schedules; reduced temperature variability.	Added healthy vending choices	
Coffeng, Boot, et al. (2014); Coffeng, Hendriksen, et al. (2014) *Be Active & Relax: Vitality in Practice*	Group motivational interviewing to promote recovery; supported by social media platform	Motivational interviews provided education	"Vitality in Practice" zones for relaxation, background noise reduction, standing desks and meetings, recreation		
Dalton & Harris (1991)	Divisional competition to improve in safety; incentives to join HMO; on-site primary care: screening, chronic disease monitoring, counseling	Communications of programs, successes through newspaper, newsletters, videos, media; presentations to management on organizational stress management techniques	Organizational surveys, participant-directed task realignment, job redesign, safety, quality improvements. Medically related disability managed.	Targets for accident frequency. Self-funded insurance. Healthy foods in cafeteria, vending machines.	Cigarette vending machines removed; smoking prohibited in company buildings and vehicles

(table continues)

TABLE 4.3. (continued)

Study	Eliminate	Substitute	Redesign	Educate	Encourage
Danquah, Kloster, Holtermann, Aadahl, Bauman, et al. (2017); Danquah, Kloster, Holtermann, Aadahl, & Tolstrup (2017); *Take a Stand!*			Added standing tables for meetings; structured walking meetings; walking routes	Lecture on sedentary behavior and health	Health ambassadors for social support; manager commitment to act as role models; individual goal setting; e-mails and texts
Dennerlein et al. (2017)			Added safe patient equipment, building infrastructure. Process for maintaining equipment. Scheduled training for staff attendance. Began patient mobility needs assessment and care plan.	Instructions at bedside and on portable equipment; training on safe patient handling; new employees trained by champions (given added training, mentoring); patient education materials communicated program goals, benefits	Internal marketing campaign on safe patient handling
Eriksen et al. (2002)		New work practices on lifting, static work, repetitive motions		Integrated health program on nutrition, exercise pain, stress and coping; stress management	Aerobic dancing, physical exercise program for muscle strength, flexibility, relaxation and pain reduction

Study				
Glass et al. (2016); *IPV and the Workplace*			Supervisor training on Intimate Partner Violence, Family and Medical Leave Act	
Hammer et al. (2016); *Work, Family, & Health Study*		Teams developed plans to improve team workflow and processes	Supervisor training on how to support employees' personal and family lives. Behavior tracking of family-supportive supervisor behaviors.	30-, 60-, and 90-day check-ins where supervisors assessed progress with team effectiveness.
Hammer et al. (2015); *SHIP*			Supervisor training and behavior tracking on supportive supervisory behaviors; schedule flexibility to reduce work–life stress and prioritize safety; team effectiveness education in groups	
Konradt et al. (2000); *Health Circles*			5-hour group Health Circle sessions with a facilitator: information on stress coping strategies, and selection of strategies	Health Circle sessions: held informal and facilitated discussions to enhance motivation
Kurowski et al. (2017)	Follow-up meetings about use of resident transfer equipment	Added mechanical lifts, lifting protocols	Training, demonstrations of use and maintenance of transfer equipment; competency tests	
Lin et al. (2017); *Sit Less, Walk More*			Monthly newsletter providing health education	Self-monitoring, goal setting; pedometer challenge; prompts to increase activity, reduce sitting, walk route use; encouraged walk breaks

(table continues)

TABLE 4.3. (continued)

Study	Eliminate	Substitute	Redesign	Educate	Encourage
Maes et al. (1998); *Brabantia Project*	No-smoking policy in cafeteria		Reorganization of production by enhancing decision latitude, job autonomy, task rotation. Trained leaders, employees on ergonomics. Created on-site exercise facility.	Health & safety education; trained management in social skills, leadership	Partly paid exercise and health education time; health fair; health exhibition; advertising of program (posters, video); incentives to participate in health initiatives
Okechukwu et al. (2009); *Mass Built*				Two 1-hour classes on effects of tobacco, toxic exposures at work that synergized with tobacco smoke	Posters, written materials supporting tobacco cessation; tobacco counseling, nicotine replacement kit; quit-kit
Olson et al. (2009); *SHIFT Pilot*				Computer-based training and website with tailored information (sleep, body weight, occupational safety) and knowledge tests. Assessment to set weight loss goals. Motivational interviews provided education.	Weight loss and safety driving competition; behavioral self-monitoring; social interaction encouraged within teams; company communication prompts; biweekly individual and social comparison feedback; "certification" for meeting completion goals; cash incentives; motivational interviewing

Olson, Thompson, et al. (2016); *COMPASS*; Olson et al. (2015); *Pilot*	Scripted, peer-led meetings on occupational safety, health, well-being, communication	Individual and team goal-setting, behavioral self-monitoring emphasizing structured social support
Olson, Wipfli, et al. (2016); *SHIFT*	Computer-based training and website with tailored information (sleep, weight, occupational safety); knowledge tests. Interviews provided education. Assessment to set weight loss goals.	Weight loss competition with behavioral self-monitoring; motivational interviewing; "certification" for meeting completion goals; and cash incentives
Peters & Carlson (1999)	Professional Health Risk Assessment. Education on stress, stress management, exercise, sleep, smoking, health behaviors, lifestyle.	Behavioral self-contracting, goal setting, self-monitoring with results viewed in ongoing small group meetings
Pronk et al. (2012); *Take-a-Stand*	Added sit–stand devices on desks	3/day random text messages to ask if participants were sitting, standing, or walking
Ramey et al. (2016)	Educational class and "telementoring" on stress management, resiliency, physiological impact	In-field practice of learned skills with biofeedback
Rohlman et al. (2016); *PUSH*	Web-based training on workplace safety, health promotion, communication	

(table continues)

TABLE 4.3. (continued)

Study	Eliminate	Substitute	Redesign	Educate	Encourage
Snetselaar et al. (2016); *Be Hipp*				Monthly education sessions on nutrition, physical activity, stress management, and ergonomics	Used self-determination principles, group processes to motivate healthy lifestyle choices; modeled healthy food choices
Sorensen et al. (2007); *Tools for Health*				12–15 tip sheets on tobacco, nutrition, nature of laborers' work. Interviews provided education.	One-on-one motivational interviews (4) to encourage change
Sorensen et al. (2005); *Healthy Directions*	Created smoke-free workplace policies	Provided healthy food options at company meetings	Industrial hygiene consult led to systems-oriented approaches to occupational health	Tabletop displays and demonstrations	Smoking cessation program; signs to help workers meet physical activity guidelines. Health fairs.
Sorensen et al. (2016); *Be Well, Work Well*			Ergonomic walkthrough and work organization assessment with feedback to nurse managers; followed by up to 4 consultations with nurse managers on action plans	Kickoff health event; safe patient handling training. Healthy eating session (Eat Well). Presentation and conversation with sleep expert; ergonomic talks and individual assistance on safe patient handling, equipment and workstation setup; slip, trip, fall prevention; outside work activities. 10-week hospital nutrition and fitness program.	Pedometer challenge, competition among units to be physically active. Goal setting, health coaching (Plan Well). Mutual support of health and safety goals (Together We Are Well). Access to fitness center/personal training/nutritionist; telephone health coaching sessions on diet, physical activity, sleep hygiene, ergonomics. Social media page.

Sorensen et al. (1998); *WellWorks*	Engineering controls (e.g., ventilation systems) to reduce hazardous exposures. Protective equipment.	Tobacco control policies. Job redesign, rotations, administrative changes to minimize exposures. Industrial hygiene walk-through assessment and recommendations.	Nutritionist provided new recipes, suggested healthier foods; training program for food service manager, staff; opportunities to meet with nutritionist. Large- and small-group discussions to practice reviewing Material Safety Data Sheets, food labels. Activities for workers at all stages of readiness for change.	Workers involved in program planning and implementation. Management actions to communicate employer commitment to employee health. Promotions (e.g., posters, health fairs, brochures, self-assessments with feedback); quit-smoking contests.
Sorensen et al. (2003); LaMontagne et al. (2004); *WellWorks 2*	Safer chemicals replaced potential carcinogens. Include/substitute health food options in cafeteria, vending machines.	Industrial hygiene walk-through assessments with recommendations for reducing exposures	Self-assessment with feedback. Self-help activities, demonstrations.	Encouraged management to change policies, contests, practices, procedures on industrial hygiene, health promotion, occupational hazards. Behavior change tactics targeted smoking, fruits and vegetables (set goals, group discussions).
Sorensen et al. (2010); *Gear Up For Health*			Telephone counseling sessions with individualized feedback. Educational materials.	Individual counseling on work environment factors; nicotine replacement therapy, social context of work. Weekly meetings encouraged access to health counselors.

(table continues)

TABLE 4.3. (continued)

Study	Eliminate	Substitute	Redesign	Educate	Encourage
Tsutsumi et al. (2009)			Work station redesign, material storage, handling, clean up; use of appropriate tools, regular machine maintenance	Trained facilitators; supervisor education on positive mental health, improving work environment. Work-shops. Improvements checklist.	Workers involved in redesign plans; researchers encouraged workers to sustain autonomous activities for workplace improvement
Tveito & Eriksen (2009); *Integrated Health Programme*			Practical examination of workplace: members contributed experiences on organization and job coping. Physical exercise.	Health information; stress management training	
von Thiele Schwarz et al. (2015)			(Kaizen) Practices to integrate health promotion and protection with production, quality	Train-the-trainer to facilitate program. Coaching would have provided education.	Coaching

Note. HMO = health maintenance organization.

Important to note, 21 of the 38 studies identified here were randomized trials (59%), the strongest research design. By contrast, the earlier review by Anger et al. reported that nine of the 17 TWH interventions (53%) were randomized controlled trials. Thus, strong designs continue to be employed in this emerging field of study.

The highest priority method for implementing the TWH program in industry is to eliminate barriers or negative working conditions, but this approach was used in only four of the 38 interventions. Rather, education and encouraging change are the most popular approaches. Perhaps a combination of controls is preferable; providing TWH education and encouraging its use is certainly valuable once an organization has eliminated the barriers and negative conditions. The majority of studies in this review employed *education* ($n = 34$) when implementing TWH, many paired with *encouragement* strategies ($n = 30$). In many cases, *redesign* ($n = 20$) and *substitution* ($n = 7$) were selected as strategies. Three studies employed all five levels of control.

Although there are strengths in the emerging TWH intervention literature, the gaps are significant. As noted earlier, there is a lack of effect sizes reported in the TWH literature. In their systematic reviews of the TWH literature, both Anger et al. (2015) and Feltner et al. (2016) urged researchers to use randomized controlled designs and report intervention effect sizes, which would facilitate meta-analysis studies of the TWH research. Another gap is that integration, a defining concept of the TWH approach, is rarely addressed in published studies. Integration of safety and health, and well-being, must be further developed as a construct, drawing clear operational definitions and indicators to guide future intervention efforts and to provide a basis for evaluating this basic TWH concept. Similarly, no study has individually examined the components of the TWH approach while testing their integration against a control condition. Thus, the basic principles underlying the TWH approach have not yet been examined with studies designed to evaluate the effectiveness of integrated safety, health, and well-being interventions. Nonetheless, this chapter provides a summary of the growing evidence base to support the effectiveness of TWH interventions, be they integrated or not, for improving safety, health, and well-being. The greatest gap in the TWH literature is the lack of factorial research studies testing the effectiveness of integrated versus independent applications of safety, health, and well-being intervention components.

Overall, despite the caveats just noted, our review identified 21 randomized trials showing positive outcomes, suggesting that TWH interventions can be effective in improving workplace outcomes in safety, health, and well-being. Future intervention research can be expected to offer broad-based and meaningful TWH solutions for improving worker safety, health, and well-being.

REFERENCES

Adeleke, S. O., Healy, G. N., Smith, C., Goode, A. D., & Clark, B. K. (2017). Effect of a workplace-driven sit–stand initiative on sitting time and work outcomes. *Translational Journal of the ACSM, 2*(3), 20–26.

Alkhajah, T. A., Reeves, M. M., Eakin, E. G., Winkler, E. A., Owen, N., & Healy, G. N. (2012). Sit–stand workstations: A pilot intervention to reduce office sitting time. *American Journal of Preventive Medicine, 43*, 298–303. http://dx.doi.org/10.1016/j.amepre.2012.05.027

Anger, W. K., Elliot, D. L., Bodner, T., Olson, R., Rohlman, D. S., Truxillo, D. M., . . . Montgomery, D. (2015). Effectiveness of total worker health interventions. *Journal of Occupational Health Psychology, 20*, 226–247. http://dx.doi.org/10.1037/a0038340

Bertera, R. L. (1990). The effects of workplace health promotion on absenteeism and employment costs in a large industrial population. *American Journal of Public Health, 80*, 1101–1105. http://dx.doi.org/10.2105/AJPH.80.9.1101

Bøggild, H., & Jeppesen, H. J. (2001). Intervention in shift scheduling and changes in biomarkers of heart disease in hospital wards. *Scandinavian Journal of Work, Environment & Health, 27*, 87–96. http://dx.doi.org/10.5271/sjweh.594

Carr, L. J., Leonhard, C., Tucker, S., Fethke, N., Benzo, R., & Gerr, F. (2016). Total Worker Health intervention increases activity of sedentary workers. *American Journal of Preventive Medicine, 50*, 9–17. http://dx.doi.org/10.1016/j.amepre.2015.06.022

Caspi, C. E., Dennerlein, J. T., Kenwood, C., Stoddard, A. M., Hopcia, K., Hashimoto, D., & Sorensen, G. (2013). Results of a pilot intervention to improve health and safety for health care workers. *Journal of Occupational and Environmental Medicine, 55*, 1449–1455. http://dx.doi.org/10.1097/JOM.0b013e3182a7e65a

Cherniack, M., Dussetschleger, J., Dugan, A., Farr, D., Namazi, S., El Ghaziri, M., & Henning, R. (2016). Participatory action research in corrections: The HITEC 2 program. *Applied Ergonomics, 53 Pt A*, 169–180. http://dx.doi.org/10.1016/j.apergo.2015.09.011

Coffeng, J. K., Boot, C. R., Duijts, S. F., Twisk, J. W., van Mechelen, W., & Hendriksen, I. J. (2014). Effectiveness of a worksite social & physical environment intervention on need for recovery, physical activity and relaxation; results of a randomized controlled trial. *PLoS One, 9*(12), e114860. http://dx.doi.org/10.1371/journal.pone.0114860

Coffeng, J. K., Hendriksen, I. J., Duijts, S. F., Twisk, J. W., van Mechelen, W., & Boot, C. R. (2014). Effectiveness of a combined social and physical environmental intervention on presenteeism, absenteeism, work performance, and work engagement in office employees. *Journal of Occupational and Environmental Medicine, 56*, 258–265. http://dx.doi.org/10.1097/JOM.0000000000000116

Dalton, B. A., & Harris, J. S. (1991). A comprehensive approach to corporate health management. *Journal of Occupational Medicine, 33*, 338–347.

Danquah, I. H., Kloster, S., Holtermann, A., Aadahl, M., Bauman, A., Ersbøll, A. K., & Tolstrup, J. S. (2017). Take a Stand!—A multi-component intervention aimed at reducing sitting time among office workers—A cluster randomized trial. *International Journal of Epidemiology, 46*, 128–140.

Danquah, I. H., Kloster, S., Holtermann, A., Aadahl, M., & Tolstrup, J. S. (2017). Effects on musculoskeletal pain from "Take a Stand!"—A cluster-randomized controlled trial reducing sitting time among office workers. *Scandinavian Journal of Work, Environment & Health, 43*, 350–357. http://dx.doi.org/10.5271/sjweh.3639

Dennerlein, J. T., O'Day, E. T., Mulloy, D. F., Somerville, J., Stoddard, A. M., Kenwood, C., . . . Hashimoto, D. (2017). Lifting and exertion injuries decrease after implementation of an integrated hospital-wide safe patient handling and mobilisation programme. *Occupational and Environmental Medicine, 74*, 336–343. http://dx.doi.org/10.1136/oemed-2015-103507

Eriksen, H. R., Ihlebaek, C., Mikkelsen, A., Grønningsaeter, H., Sandal, G. M., & Ursin, H. (2002). Improving subjective health at the worksite: A randomized controlled trial of stress management training, physical exercise and an integrated health programme. *Occupational Medicine, 52*, 383–391. http://dx.doi.org/10.1093/occmed/52.7.383

Feltner, C., Peterson, K., Palmieri Weber, R., Cluff, L., Coker-Schwimmer, E., Viswanathan, M., & Lohr, K. N. (2016). The effectiveness of Total Worker Health interventions: A systematic review for a National Institutes of Health Pathways to Prevention workshop. *Annals of Internal Medicine, 165,* 262–269.

Glass, N., Hanson, G. C., Laharnar, N., Anger, W. K., & Perrin, N. (2016). Interactive training improves workplace climate, knowledge, and support towards domestic violence. *American Journal of Industrial Medicine, 59,* 538–548. http://dx.doi.org/10.1002/ajim.22601

Hammer, L. B., Johnson, R. C., Crain, T. L., Bodner, T., Kossek, E. E., Davis, K. D., . . . Berkman, L. (2016). Intervention effects on safety compliance and citizenship behaviors: Evidence from the Work, Family, and Health Study. *Journal of Applied Psychology, 101,* 190–208. http://dx.doi.org/10.1037/apl0000047

Hammer, L. B., Truxillo, D. M., Bodner, T., Rineer, J., Pytlovany, A. C., & Richman, A. (2015). Effects of a workplace intervention targeting psychosocial risk factors on safety and health outcomes. *BioMed Research International, 2015,* 836967. http://dx.doi.org/10.1155/2015/836967

Konradt, U., Schmook, R., Wilm, A., & Hertel, G. (2000). Health circles for teleworkers: Selective results on stress, strain and coping styles. *Health Education Research, 15,* 327–338. http://dx.doi.org/10.1093/her/15.3.327

Kurowski, A., Gore, R., Roberts, Y., Richardson Kincaid, K., & Punnett, L. (2017). Injury rates before and after the implementation of a safe resident handling program in the long-term care sector. *Safety Science, 92,* 217–224. http://dx.doi.org/10.1016/j.ssci.2016.10.012

LaMontagne, A. D., Barbeau, E., Youngstrom, R. A., Lewiton, M., Stoddard, A. M., McLellan, D., . . . Sorensen, G. (2004). Assessing and intervening on OSH programmes: Effectiveness evaluation of the Wellworks-2 intervention in 15 manufacturing worksites. *Occupational and Environmental Medicine, 61,* 651–660. http://dx.doi.org/10.1136/oem.2003.011718

Lin, Y. P., Lin, C. C., Chen, M. M., & Lee, K. C. (2017). Short-term efficacy of a "sit less, walk more" workplace intervention on improving cardiometabolic health and work productivity in office workers. *Journal of Occupational and Environmental Medicine, 59,* 327–334. http://dx.doi.org/10.1097/JOM.0000000000000955

Maes, S., Verhoeven, C., Kittel, F., & Scholten, H. (1998). Effects of a Dutch work-site wellness-health program: The Brabantia Project. *American Journal of Public Health, 88,* 1037–1041. http://dx.doi.org/10.2105/AJPH.88.7.1037

National Institute for Occupational Safety and Health. (n.d.). *Total Worker Health.* Retrieved from https://www.cdc.gov/niosh/twh/totalhealth.html

National Institute for Occupational Safety and Health. (2015a). *Issues relevant to advancing worker well-being through Total Worker Health.* Washington, DC: Author.

National Institute for Occupational Safety and Health. (2015b). NIOSHTIC-2 publications search. Retrieved from https://www2a.cdc.gov/nioshtic-2/default.asp

National Institute for Occupational Safety and Health. (2016a). *Fundamentals of total worker health approaches: Essential elements for advancing worker safety, health, and well-being.* Washington, DC: U.S. Department of Health and Human Services.

National Institute for Occupational Safety and Health. (2016b). Hierarchy of controls applied to *Total Worker Health.* Retrieved from https://www.cdc.gov/niosh/twh/letsgetstarted.html

Occupational Safety and Health Administration. (n.d.). SIC division structure. Retrieved from https://www.osha.gov/pls/imis/sic_manual.html

Okechukwu, C. A., Krieger, N., Sorensen, G., Li, Y., & Barbeau, E. M. (2009). MassBuilt: Effectiveness of an apprenticeship site-based smoking cessation intervention for unionized building trades workers. *Cancer Causes & Control, 20,* 887–894. http://dx.doi.org/10.1007/s10552-009-9324-0

Olson, R., Anger, W. K., Elliot, D. L., Wipfli, B., & Gray, M. (2009). A new health promotion model for lone workers: Results of the Safety & Health Involvement for Truckers

(SHIFT) pilot study. *Journal of Occupational and Environmental Medicine, 51,* 1233–1246. http://dx.doi.org/10.1097/JOM.0b013e3181c1dc7a

Olson, R., Thompson, S. V., Elliot, D. L., Hess, J. A., Rhoten, K. L., Parker, K. N., . . . Marino, M. (2016). Safety and health support for home care workers: The COMPASS randomized controlled trial. *American Journal of Public Health, 106,* 1823–1832. http://dx.doi.org/10.2105/AJPH.2016.303327

Olson, R., Wipfli, B., Thompson, S. V., Elliot, D. L., Anger, W. K., Bodner, T., . . . Perrin, N. A. (2016). Weight control intervention for truck drivers: The SHIFT randomized controlled trial, United States. *American Journal of Public Health, 106,* 1698–1706. http://dx.doi.org/10.2105/AJPH.2016.303262

Olson, R., Wright, R. R., Elliot, D. L., Hess, J. A., Thompson, S., Buckmaster, A., . . . Wipfli, B. (2015). The COMPASS pilot study: A Total Worker Health™ intervention for home care workers. *Journal of Occupational and Environmental Medicine, 57,* 406–416. http://dx.doi.org/10.1097/JOM.0000000000000374

Peters, K. K., & Carlson, J. G. (1999). Worksite stress management with high-risk maintenance workers: A controlled study. *International Journal of Stress Management, 6,* 21–44. http://dx.doi.org/10.1023/A:1021958219737

Pronk, N. P., Katz, A. S., Lowry, M., & Payfer, J. R. (2012). Reducing occupational sitting time and improving worker health: The Take-a-Stand Project, 2011. *Preventing Chronic Disease, 9,* E154. http://dx.doi.org/10.5888/pcd9.110323

Ramey, S. L., Perkhounkova, Y., Hein, M., Chung, S., Franke, W. D., & Anderson, A. A. (2016). Building resilience in an urban police department. *Journal of Occupational and Environmental Medicine, 58,* 796–804. http://dx.doi.org/10.1097/JOM.0000000000000791

Rohlman, D. S., Parish, M., Elliot, D. L., Hanson, G., & Perrin, N. (2016). Addressing younger workers' needs: The Promoting U through Safety and Health (PUSH) trial outcomes. *Healthcare, 4*(3), E55. http://dx.doi.org/10.3390/healthcare4030055

Snetselaar, A., Ahrens, L., Johnston, K., Smith, K., Hollinger, D., & Hockenberry, J. (2016). A participatory integrated health promotion and protection worksite intervention: A cluster randomized controlled trial. *Topics in Clinical Nutrition, 31,* 36–46. http://dx.doi.org/10.1097/TIN.0000000000000056

Sorensen, G., Barbeau, E. M., Stoddard, A. M., Hunt, M. K., Goldman, R., Smith, A., . . . Wallace, L. (2007). Tools for health: The efficacy of a tailored intervention targeted for construction laborers. *Cancer Causes & Control, 18,* 51–59. http://dx.doi.org/10.1007/s10552-006-0076-9

Sorensen, G., Barbeau, E., Stoddard, A. M., Hunt, M. K., Kaphingst, K., & Wallace, L. (2005). Promoting behavior change among working-class, multiethnic workers: Results of the healthy directions–small business study. *American Journal of Public Health, 95,* 1389–1395. http://dx.doi.org/10.2105/AJPH.2004.038745

Sorensen, G., McLellan, D., Dennerlein, J. T., Pronk, N. P., Allen, J. D., Boden, L. I., . . . Wagner, G. R. (2013). Integration of health protection and health promotion: Rationale, indicators, and metrics. *Journal of Occupational and Environmental Medicine, 55*(12, Suppl.), S12–S18. http://dx.doi.org/10.1097/JOM.0000000000000032

Sorensen, G., Nagler, E. M., Hashimoto, D., Dennerlein, J. T., Theron, J. V., Stoddard, A. M., . . . Wagner, G. (2016). Implementing an integrated health protection/health promotion intervention in the hospital setting: Lessons learned from the Be Well, Work Well Study. *Journal of Occupational and Environmental Medicine, 58,* 185–194. http://dx.doi.org/10.1097/JOM.0000000000000592

Sorensen, G., Stoddard, A., Hunt, M. K., Hebert, J. R., Ockene, J. K., Avrunin, J. S., . . . Hammond, S. K. (1998). The effects of a health promotion-health protection intervention on behavior change: The WellWorks Study. *American Journal of Public Health, 88,* 1685–1690. http://dx.doi.org/10.2105/AJPH.88.11.1685

Sorensen, G., Stoddard, A. M., LaMontagne, A. D., Emmons, K., Hunt, M. K., Youngstrom, R., . . . Christiani, D. C. (2003). A comprehensive worksite cancer prevention intervention: Behavior change results from a randomized controlled trial (United States). *Journal of Public Health Policy, 24*(1), 5–25. http://dx.doi.org/10.2307/3343174

Sorensen, G., Stoddard, A., Quintiliani, L., Ebbeling, C., Nagler, E., Yang, M., . . . Wallace, L. (2010). Tobacco use cessation and weight management among motor freight workers: Results of the gear up for health study. *Cancer Causes & Control, 21,* 2113–2122. http://dx.doi.org/10.1007/s10552-010-9630-6

Tsutsumi, A., Nagami, M., Yoshikawa, T., Kogi, K., & Kawakami, N. (2009). Participatory intervention for workplace improvements on mental health and job performance among blue-collar workers: A cluster randomized controlled trial. *Journal of Occupational and Environmental Medicine, 51,* 554–563. http://dx.doi.org/10.1097/JOM.0b013e3181a24d28

Tveito, T. H., & Eriksen, H. R. (2009). Integrated health programme: A workplace randomized controlled trial. *Journal of Advanced Nursing, 65,* 110–119. http://dx.doi.org/10.1111/j.1365-2648.2008.04846.x

von Thiele Schwarz, U., Augustsson, H., Hasson, H., & Stenfors-Hayes, T. (2015). Promoting employee health by integrating health protection, health promotion, and continuous improvement: A longitudinal quasi-experimental intervention study. *Journal of Occupational and Environmental Medicine, 57,* 217–225. http://dx.doi.org/10.1097/JOM.0000000000000344

Williams, J. A., Nelson, C. C., Cabán-Martinez, A. J., Katz, J. N., Wagner, G. R., Pronk, N. P., . . . McLellan, D. L. (2015). Validation of a new metric for assessing the integration of health protection and health promotion in a sample of small- and medium-sized employer groups. *Journal of Occupational and Environmental Medicine, 57,* 1017–1021. http://dx.doi.org/10.1097/JOM.0000000000000521

5

A Conceptual Model for Guiding Integrated Interventions and Research

Pathways Through the Conditions of Work

Glorian Sorensen, Deborah L. McLellan,
Jack T. Dennerlein, Eve M. Nagler, Erika L. Sabbath,
Nicolaas P. Pronk, and Gregory R. Wagner

There is a paradigm shift underway in protection and promotion of worker safety and health, as is evident in this volume. The National Institute for Occupational Safety and Health (NIOSH; n.d.) has led this shift through its *Total Worker Health®* program, which defines an integrated approach to worker safety and health as "policies, programs, and practices that integrate protection from work-related safety and health hazards with promotion of injury and illness prevention efforts to advance worker well-being" (para. 1). This approach builds on NIOSH's long-standing efforts to ensure that workers are

This research was funded by the National Institute for Occupational Safety and Health, Grant U19 OH008861 for the Harvard T. H. Chan School of Public Health Center for Work, Health and Well-being. This chapter is solely the responsibility of the authors and does not represent the official views of the National Institute for Occupational Safety and Health. We thank Linnea Benson-Whelan for her contributions to the production of this manuscript, including formatting of references. The work described here represents the efforts of multiple investigators, including Les Boden, Dean Hashimoto, Karen Hopcia, Jeffrey Katz, Maria Lopez Gomez, Justin Manjourides, Cassandra Okechukwu, Susan Peters, Emily Sparer, Anne Stoddard, Lorraine Wallace, and Jessica Williams. Many staff and students at the provided excellent assistance in data collection, coding, management, and analysis. Finally, we express our deep respect for the workers who participated in these projects.

http://dx.doi.org/10.1037/0000149-006
Total Worker Health, H. L. Hudson, J. A. S. Nigam, S. L. Sauter, L. C. Chosewood, A. L. Schill, and J. Howard (Editors)
Copyright © 2019 by the American Psychological Association. All rights reserved.

protected from harm at work by acknowledging the broad impact that working conditions have on worker health and well-being. For example, wages, work hours, workload, relationships with coworkers and supervisors, and stress levels at work may contribute not only to health, safety, and well-being but also to health behaviors that increase or decrease risk of chronic diseases (LaMontagne et al., 2014; Montano, Hoven, & Siegrist, 2014).

The recent trend toward adoption of this approach underscores the need for defining best practices and processes to ensure optimal results (Hammer & Sauter, 2013; Sorensen, Landsbergis, et al., 2011). This trend builds on growing evidence about the potential benefits of integrated approaches for improvements in health behaviors (Okechukwu, Krieger, Sorensen, Li, & Barbeau, 2009; Olson, Anger, Elliot, Wipfli, & Gray, 2009; Sorensen et al., 2002, 2005); enhanced rates of employee participation in programs (Hunt et al., 2005); potential reductions in pain, occupational injury, and disability rates (Pronk, Katz, Lowry, & Payfer, 2012; Shaw, Robertson, McLellan, Verma, & Pransky, 2006); strengthened health and safety programs (LaMontagne et al., 2004); potentially reduced costs (Goetzel, Guindon, Turshen, & Ozminkowski, 2001); and support for market performance of companies (Fabius et al., 2016). These findings are supported by multiple reviews of integrated interventions (Anger et al., 2015; Cherniack, 2013; Cooklin, Joss, Husser, & Oldenburg, 2017; Institute of Medicine [IOM], 2005; NIOSH, 2012; Pronk, 2013; Sorensen, Landsbergis, et al., 2011), although a recent systematic review concluded that although integrated interventions may improve health behaviors, there remains a need for further evidence on their impact on injuries and overall quality of life (Feltner et al., 2016).

Despite growing evidence, this field of inquiry is still in its infancy, needing further evaluation of the effectiveness of this approach. A common conceptual model can structure intervention research to elucidate the pathways through which occupational factors influence safety and chronic disease risk. Thus, a conceptual model is useful in making explicit the underlying assumptions of integrated interventions. The purpose of this chapter is to present a conceptual model that will guide research on determinants of worker safety and health and inform the design, implementation, and evaluation of integrated approaches to protecting and promoting worker safety and health. This model embeds worker health within the work environment, placing a focus on the conditions of work. The chapter also illustrates the application of this model to both social epidemiological and intervention research.

DEVELOPMENT OF THE CONCEPTUAL MODEL

This conceptual model was developed by the Center for Work, Health and Well-being at the Harvard T. H. Chan School of Public Health, a Center for Excellence within NIOSH's *Total Worker Health* (TWH) program. Based on the Center's previous research and to guide future research, investigators developed, used, and updated this conceptual model to specify the causal pathways through which integrated policies, programs, and practices are expected to influence worker safety and health outcomes (see Figure 5.1).

This conceptual model is based on the premise that addressing multiple pathways in an integrated manner with a focus on the conditions of work will contribute to greater improvements in worker health and enterprise outcomes than addressing each pathway separately. Critical to the model are workplace policies, programs, and practices that may concurrently operate through multiple pathways, including the physical work environment and the organization of work. These conditions of work, centrally located in the model as determinants of worker safety, health, and well-being outcomes, also mediate the effects of enterprise characteristics, workplace policies, programs and practices, and worker/workforce characteristics on worker proximal outcomes (e.g., health and safety behaviors). Integrated policies, programs, and practices may also contribute to improvements in enterprise outcomes such as turnover and health-care costs. At the same time, enterprise and worker outcomes may influence workplace policies, programs, and practices, creating a loop of integrated influence within the organization. It is important to recognize, in addition, that these relationships occur within the context of labor market and economic trends; legal and political forces; and social mores, norms, and influences.

This conceptual model represents diverse theoretical perspectives, including the social ecological model (Stokols, 1996), social contextual model of health behavior change (Sorensen et al., 2003), hierarchy of controls (Levy, Wegman, Baron, & Sokas, 2006), organizational ergonomics (Hendrick & Kleiner, 2002), participatory frameworks (Rivilis et al., 2008), job strain (Karasek & Theorell, 1990), and sociotechnical systems theory (Cooper & Foster, 1971). These theoretical foundations underscore the complex interplay of factors involving

FIGURE 5.1. Conceptual Model for Integrated Approaches to Worker Safety and Health

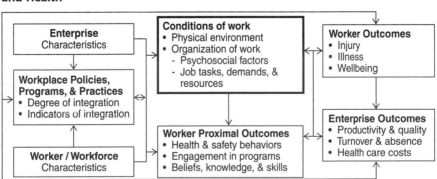

From "Integrating Worksite Health Protection and Health Promotion: A Conceptual Model for Intervention and Research," by G. Sorensen, D. L. McLellan, E. L. Sabbath, J. T. Dennerlein, E. M. Nagler, D. A. Hurtado, N. P. Pronk, and G. R. Wagner, 2016, *Preventive Medicine, 91*, p. 189. Copyright 2016 by Elsevier. Adapted with permission.

individual workers and the immediate work environment, characteristics of the larger contexts in which both the worker and the worksite are embedded, and proximal outcomes, such as individual health and safety behaviors and related factors of self-efficacy and risk perceptions that support improvements in these behaviors. Examples of feedback pathways are included in Figure 5.1, which underscore the complexity of the system and interrelationships across multiple dimensions. Each of the model's components is presented following discussion of indicators of integrated workplace policies, programs, and practices.

Indicators of Integrated Workplace Policies, Programs, and Practices

Implementation of integrated approaches operates on a continuum rather than as an all-or-none adoption of this approach. Organizations may implement change in varying sequences and may respond differently by industry sector, size of workplace, and extent of leadership and labor engagement (D. L. McLellan, Cabán-Martinez, et al., 2015). We have defined a set of indicators of integrated policies, programs, and practices that may directly or indirectly affect the conditions of work (see Table 5.1). First, leadership commitment, a necessary foundation for an integrated approach, reflects the key roles that senior leadership and middle management play in articulating the vision for worker and worksite health and ensuring availability of resources (i.e., human, financial, physical; IOM, 2005). Second, further reflecting the centrality of the conditions of work within this model, the indicators include policies, programs, and practices that foster working conditions that contribute to worker health, safety, and well-being, including the physical work environment and the

TABLE 5.1. Indicators of Integrated Policies, Programs, and Practices

Indicator domain	Definition
Leadership commitment	Leadership makes worker safety, health, and well-being a clear priority for the entire organization. They drive accountability and provide the necessary resources and environment to create positive working conditions.
Participation	Stakeholders at every level of an organization, including organized labor, help plan and carry out efforts to protect and promote worker safety and health.
Policies, programs, and practices focused on positive working conditions.	The organization enhances worker safety, health, and well-being with policies and practices that improve working conditions.
Comprehensive and collaborative strategies	Employees from across the organization work together to develop comprehensive health and safety initiatives.
Adherence	The organization adheres to federal and state regulations, as well as ethical norms, that advance worker safety, health, and well-being.
Data-driven change	Regular evaluation guides an organization's priority setting; decision making; and continuous improvement of worker safety, health, and well-being initiatives.

organization of work. These conditions of work are further described next. Fourth, integrated strategies are both comprehensive and collaborative. Rather than functioning independently, coordination and collaboration among occupational safety and health, worksite health promotion, employee benefits, and other workplace functions is needed to optimize benefits for worker safety and health (IOM, 2005). Fifth, integrated approaches ensure that organizations adhere to federal and state regulations and ethical norms that contribute to protecting and promoting safety, health, and well-being at worksites and for employees (Occupational Safety and Health Administration, 2008). Finally, workplace programs, policies, and practices are monitored and evaluated for both occupational health exposures and health-related behaviors and the relationships of exposures and behaviors to health outcomes, and these data are used in setting priorities for improvement (IOM, 2005).

Conditions of Work

This model illustrates the potential impact that these integrated policies, programs, and practices may have on worker safety and health outcomes through several pathways based primarily within the conditions of work. First, integrated policies and practices have a direct impact on the *physical work environment*, including on potential exposures on the job. For example, policies may impact physical demands related to biomechanical sources of strain, or may include purchasing policies that influence selection of safer versus more hazardous chemicals or equipment used in some work processes. The work environment may also support healthy behaviors among workers, for example, through worksite tobacco control policies or availability of healthy foods in cafeterias and vending machines. Second, the *organization of work* has been consistently shown to influence worker health and safety outcomes (Lipscomb, Trinkoff, Brady, & Geiger-Brown, 2004; Tullar et al., 2010) as well as health behaviors (Albertsen, Borg, & Oldenburg, 2006; Choi et al., 2010). *Psychosocial factors*, part of the organization of work, broadly include job strain, psychological demands and control (Karasek & Theorell, 1990), rewards (Siegrist, 1996), social support, harassment, and discrimination (NIOSH, 2008). For example, supervisor and coworker support and social norms that support health and safety behaviors are associated with improved health behaviors, such as physical activity and sleep quality (Choi et al., 2010; Nishitani & Sakakibara, 2010) and reduced risk of musculoskeletal disorders (Macfarlane et al., 2009). *Job tasks, demand,* and *resources*, including the extent to which high physical exertion is a requirement of the job, work hours and shift, and the pace of work, have been shown consistently to influence a range of safety and health outcomes (Lipscomb, Trinkoff, Geiger-Brown, & Brady, 2002). Changes in the conditions of work may ultimately contribute to transformational change in the organization toward a culture of worker safety, health, and well-being (Sorensen et al., 2013), by which we mean one that anticipates and mitigates potential workplace health risks; encourages worker identification and reporting of health and safety concerns without fear of reprisal; and provides health supportive programs, policies, and practices.

Enterprise Characteristics

Enterprise characteristics, such as industry sector and size, influence the conditions of work and the types of exposures that workers face and are likely to play significant roles in the uptake of integrated approaches (Harris, Hannon, Beresford, Linnan, & McLellan, 2014; Krieger, 2010). Employers also set pay scales and work hours, further shaping the resources and health outcomes that workers experience (Baron et al., 2014; Krieger et al., 2008).

Workforce–Worker Characteristics

It is also important to understand, for example, the changing needs of an aging workforce, the potentially differing work–family intersections for men compared to women workers, and potential vulnerabilities of immigrant workers compared to U.S.-born workers. Similarly, for example, young workers are twice as likely as older workers to be injured on the job (Estes, Jackson, Castillo, & Centers for Disease Control and Prevention, 2010) and often lack sufficient training in workplace safety practices and legal rights on the job (Rohlman, Parish, Elliot, Montgomery, & Hanson, 2013).

Outcomes (Including Worker Proximal Outcomes, Worker Outcomes, and Enterprise Outcomes)

Both individual- and organization-level outcomes are included in the model. The conditions of work contribute directly to risk of injury and illness as well as well-being. In addition, the conditions of work contribute to quality of life and health- and safety-related behaviors (e.g., job stress is associated with increased tobacco and alcohol use; Hammer & Sauter, 2013), as well as other proximal outcomes such as participation in safety or smoking cessation programs. At the organizational level, enterprise outcomes can include financial and economic outcomes, such as absenteeism, turnover, employer expenditures on health care, and intervention return on investment. Given that worksite interventions require employer support and commitment of resources, consideration of enterprise outcomes can help make the business case for integrated interventions.

APPLICATION OF THE CONCEPTUAL MODEL IN RESEARCH AND INTERVENTION DESIGN

We used this model to guide social epidemiological research in a study of hospital patient care workers in the Be Well, Work Well Study, conducted by the Center for Work, Health and Well-being. Findings from this research illustrate the roles of the conditions of work as critical pathways shaping worker health and safety outcomes (see Figure 5.2; Caspi et al., 2013; Sorensen et al., 2013;

FIGURE 5.2. Application of the Conceptual Model in the Be Well, Work Well Study

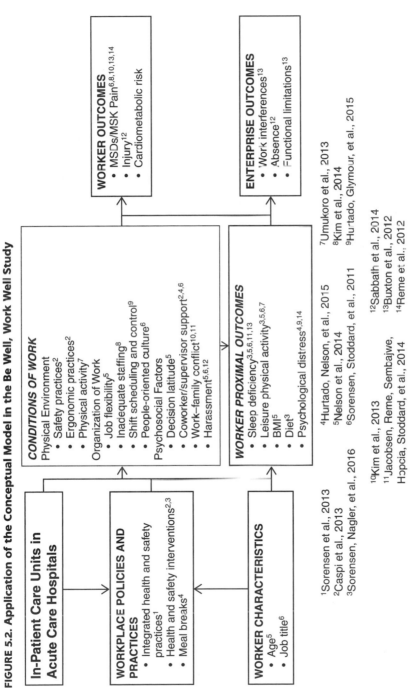

In-Patient Care Units in Acute Care Hospitals

WORKPLACE POLICIES AND PRACTICES
- Integrated health and safety practices[1]
- Health and safety interventions[2,3]
- Meal breaks[4]

WORKER CHARACTERISTICS
- Age[5]
- Job title[6]

CONDITIONS OF WORK

Physical Environment
- Safety practices[2]
- Ergonomic practices[2]
- Physical activity[7]

Organization of Work
- Job flexibility[5]
- Inadequate staffing[8]
- Shift scheduling and control[9]
- People-oriented culture[6]

Psychosocial Factors
- Decision latitude[5]
- Coworker/supervisor support[2,4,6]
- Work–family conflict[10,11]
- Harassment[5,6,12]

WORKER PROXIMAL OUTCOMES
- Sleep deficiency[3,5,6,11,13]
- Leisure physical activity[3,5,6,7]
- BMI[5]
- Diet[3]
- Psychological distress[4,9,14]

WORKER OUTCOMES
- MSDs/MSK Pain[6,8,10,13,14]
- Injury[12]
- Cardiometabolic risk

ENTERPRISE OUTCOMES
- Work interferences[13]
- Absence[12]
- Functional limitations[13]

[1]Sorensen et al., 2013
[2]Caspi et al., 2013
[3]Sorensen, Nagler, et al., 2016

[4]Hurtado, Nelson, et al., 2015
[5]Nelson et al, 2014
[6]Sorensen, Stoddard, et al., 2011

[7]Umukoro et al., 2013
[8]Kim et al., 2014
[9]Hurtado, Glymour, et al., 2015

[10]Kim et al, 2013
[11]Jacobsen, Reme, Sembajwe, Hopcia, Stoddard, et al., 2014

[12]Sabbath et al., 2014
[13]Buxton et al., 2012
[14]Reme et al., 2012

MSDs = musculoskeletal disorders; MSK = musculoskeletal; BMI = body mass index. From "Integrating Worksite Health Protection and Health Promotion: A Conceptual Model for Intervention and Research," by G. Sorensen, D. L. McLellan, E. L. Sabbath, J. T. Dennerlein, E. M. Nagler, D. A. Hurtado, N. P. Pronk, and G. R. Wagner, 2016, *Preventive Medicine, 91,* p. 191. Copyright 2016 by Elsevier. Adapted with permission.

Sorensen, McLellan, et al., 2016; Sorensen, Nagler, et al., 2016). We found that injury, musculoskeletal pain, and health behaviors share diverse determinants within the work environment and vary by the socioeconomic status of workers (Jacobsen, Reme, Sembajwe, Hopcia, Stoddard, et al., 2014; Kim et al., 2013). For example, several dimensions of the organization of work and the psychosocial work environment were associated with injury risk, including staffing adequacy (Kim et al., 2014), schedule control (Hurtado, Glymour, et al., 2015), supervisor support, and related organizational policies and practices (Hurtado, Nelson, Hashimoto, & Sorensen, 2015; Tveito et al., 2014). Similarly, we found that workplace culture reflected in policies and practices, such as effective ergonomic and other safety practices, jointly predicted lower back pain; improved sleep; and, to a lesser extent, physical activity (Buxton et al., 2012; Reme, Dennerlein, Hashimoto, & Sorensen, 2012; Sorensen, Stoddard, et al., 2011). In addition, these findings document the role of work organization and the psychosocial work environment in shaping safety and health behaviors and health outcomes (Nelson et al., 2014; Sorensen, Stoddard, et al., 2011; Umukoro et al., 2013). For example, nurses working on units with more shift flexibility had relatively less depression and anxiety (Hurtado, Glymour, et al., 2015). Higher levels of work–family conflict were also significantly associated with sleep deficiency in the short term and nearly two years later (Jacobsen, Reme, Sembajwe, Hopcia, Stiles, et al., 2014), and with multiple types of musculoskeletal pain (Kim et al., 2013). Also, harassment at work was associated with increased risk of chronic injury (Sabbath et al., 2014), obesity, and low levels of physical activity (Sorensen, Stoddard, et al., 2011). Collectively, these findings underscore the need for a comprehensive approach to safety and health interventions, consistent with our integrated model.

We also used the conceptual model to design an integrated intervention in response to specific settings and conditions of work, based on a systematic assessment, including input from employees (Pronk et al., 2016). We tested the feasibility of the intervention in three small- and medium-sized manufacturing businesses in Minnesota. As part of planning, we used the conceptual model to guide assessment of employee health indicators and the physical and organizational environment, and we provided feedback on the assessments to the sites. This intervention focused particularly on changes in working conditions, such as environmental supports for ergonomic and health promotion practices. For example, participating sites used technology to address ergonomic and physical hazards related to back pain, including improved lifting or moving devices on factory floors and sit-to-stand devices in some office spaces. Consultation and training with midlevel and upper management, including committees comprising those responsible for protecting and promoting worker health and safety, provided a further means of influencing working conditions. In addition, telephone health coaching and web-based resources that included integrated messages on back pain and safe movement were available for employees as part of this comprehensive integrated program. We identified factors critical to successful implementation of policies, programs, and practices, including multilevel management support and articulation of that support throughout the worksite; allocation of dedicated staff, budgets, and committees; collaborative organizational cultures that prioritized employee health and safety; engaging existing organizational processes, such as continual improvement, that could be leveraged for new approaches; and realistic implementation time lines to account for organizational changes (D. McLellan, Pronk, & Pember, 2015; Pronk et al., 2016). When these factors were not in place, implementation efforts lagged.

DISCUSSION

This model responds to the ongoing dialogue on the importance of a conceptual framework to guide research and intervention design related to worker health (Bradley, Grossman, Hubbard, Ortega, & Curry, 2016; Punnett, Cherniack, Henning, Morse, & Faghri, 2009; Schulte, Pandalai, Wulsin, & Chun, 2012). It provides a framework for research and interventions by specifying how the conditions of work can shape worker safety and health. The model serves as an evidence-based guide for prioritizing research questions, framing a standard approach to interventions, and steering practical applications toward effective processes to protect and improve worker health. Specifying the pathways through which the intervention is intended to affect worker safety and health can clarify the priorities for both the intervention and evaluation. A conceptual model can also guide mediation analyses for testing specific pathways (Anger et al., 2015).

This model highlights priorities for ongoing research that explores, for example, the extent to which integrated workplace policies, programs, and practices determine safety and health outcomes; the ways in which these policies, programs, and practices may shape physical and psychosocial work exposures; and the roles that worker and enterprise factors play in influencing these pathways. Research presented by others further illustrates the applicability of this model. For example, Schulte et al. (2012) emphasized how shared pathways focusing on conditions of work could impact enterprise and worker outcomes such as occupational hazards and obesity. Although prior research has examined ways in which the conditions of work influence chronic disease and its behavioral antecedents and risks associated with hazards on the job, as described earlier, additional research is needed to examine the synergies and interactions in these relationships, as well as their associations with improved enterprise outcomes. Responding to recommendations from a recent workshop with NIOSH and the National Institutes of Health (Bradley et al., 2016), this model can also guide further development of measures to assess the effects of an integrated approach, inform the design and testing of future integrated approaches to worker health, and offer a framework for increased attention to organizational change, central to the TWH approach yet underrepresented within research findings reported to date (Lax, 2016; R. K. McLellan, 2016). Use of a common conceptual model offers a platform for bridging these diverse perspectives and suggests shared vocabularies for understanding the influences on worker health (Sorensen et al., 2003).

In this model, improvements in the conditions of work—in the physical and psychosocial work environment, as well as the work organization—provide the foundation for protecting and promoting worker safety, health, and well-being. This focus builds on the hierarchy of controls approach, which the TWH program has employed to underscore the importance of elimination or control of workplace hazards, including the physical work environment and the organization of work (NIOSH, 2016). Interventions targeting changes in the conditions of work have been hypothesized to produce more sustainable benefits for worker health than those focusing solely on individual factors (Montano et al., 2014).

This model also informs translation from research to practice by outlining key components of effective implementation of TWH approaches. Although a growing array of guidelines and tools are available to support adoption of TWH approaches (Burton, 2010; Center for the Promotion of Health in the New England Workplace, 2013; D. McLellan, Moore, Nagler, & Sorensen, 2017; Velazquez, Baker, Dewey, Andrews, & Stock, 2010), implementation of these integrated policies, programs, and practices remains concentrated primarily among a select group of vanguard employers (Loeppke et al., 2015). There is urgent need for effective dissemination of evidence-based best practices and resources to build capacity in worksites across size and sector to improve the conditions of work and transform the work organization, thus improving worker health. Our work has shown, however, that employers often turn first to providing programs for individual workers rather than tackling system-level policies and practices, a tendency we have labeled "regression to the individual" (Sorensen, McLellan, et al., 2016). Effective implementation of TWH interventions requires that employers have the capacity to recognize and modify features of the work organization that are a risk to worker health (Mellor & Webster, 2013). This conceptual model provides a framework for employers to identify, develop, and implement interventions and strategies that will enable system-level changes in the conditions of work.

CONCLUSION

Traditionally, a focus on the conditions of work has been the domain of occupational safety and health; here, we aim to underscore the central role of the conditions of work, not only for classic occupational safety and health outcomes but also for chronic disease risk. An increasing number of workplaces are adopting integrated approaches to worker health that should be carefully evaluated. This chapter proposes a conceptual model to guide this inquiry and to frame the focus on the conditions of work as central to building a culture of safety, health, and well-being. This model further illustrates the potential for synergy in integrated approaches to worker health, offering opportunities for improvements in the conditions of work as well as for multiple worker health outcomes. Thus, this conceptual model may provide a valuable tool for future research aimed at testing the effectiveness of integrated approaches to worker safety, health, and well-being, as well as a framework for translating research to practice.

REFERENCES

Albertsen, K., Borg, V., & Oldenburg, B. (2006). A systematic review of the impact of work environment on smoking cessation, relapse and amount smoked. *Preventive Medicine, 43,* 291–305. http://dx.doi.org/10.1016/j.ypmed.2006.05.001

Anger, W. K., Elliot, D. L., Bodner, T., Olson, R., Rohlman, D. S., Truxillo, D. M., . . . Montgomery, D. (2015). Effectiveness of total worker health interventions. *Journal of Occupational Health Psychology, 20,* 226–247. http://dx.doi.org/10.1037/a0038340

Baron, S. L., Beard, S., Davis, L. K., Delp, L., Forst, L., Kidd-Taylor, A., . . . Welch, L. S. (2014). Promoting integrated approaches to reducing health inequities among low-income workers: Applying a social ecological framework. *American Journal of Industrial Medicine, 57,* 539–556. http://dx.doi.org/10.1002/ajim.22174

Bradley, C. J., Grossman, D. C., Hubbard, R. A., Ortega, A. N., & Curry, S. J. (2016). Integrated interventions for improving Total Worker Health: A panel report from the National Institutes of Health Pathways to Prevention Workshop: Total Worker Health—What's work got to do with it? *Annals of Internal Medicine, 165,* 279–283. http://dx.doi.org/10.7326/M16-0740

Burton, J. (2010). *WHO Healthy Workplace framework and model: Background and supporting literature and practices.* Retrieved from http://apps.who.int/iris/bitstream/10665/113144/1/9789241500241_eng.pdf?ua=1

Buxton, O. M., Hopcia, K., Sembajwe, G., Porter, J. H., Dennerlein, J. T., Kenwood, C., . . . Sorensen, G. (2012). Relationship of sleep deficiency to perceived pain and functional limitations in hospital patient care workers. *Journal of Occupational and Environmental Medicine, 54,* 851–858. http://dx.doi.org/10.1097/JOM.0b013e31824e6913

Caspi, C. E., Dennerlein, J. T., Kenwood, C., Stoddard, A. M., Hopcia, K., Hashimoto, D., & Sorensen, G. (2013). Results of a pilot intervention to improve health and safety for health care workers. *Journal of Occupational and Environmental Medicine, 55,* 1449–1455. http://dx.doi.org/10.1097/JOM.0b013e3182a7e65a

Center for the Promotion of Health in the New England Workplace. (2013, March). *Intervention Design and Analysis Scorecard (IDEAS) CPH-NEW intervention planning tool: Facilitator's guide.* Lowell, MA: Author. Retrieved from http://www.uml.edu/docs/FGuide_Mar3_Website_tcm18-102071.pdf

Cherniack, M. (2013). Integrated health programs, health outcomes, and return on investment: Measuring workplace health promotion and integrated program effectiveness. *Journal of Occupational and Environmental Medicine, 55*(12, Suppl.), S38–S45. http://dx.doi.org/10.1097/JOM.0000000000000044

Choi, B., Schnall, P. L., Yang, H., Dobson, M., Landsbergis, P., Israel, L., . . . Baker, D. (2010). Psychosocial working conditions and active leisure-time physical activity in middle-aged us workers. *International Journal of Occupational Medicine and Environmental Health, 23,* 239–253. http://dx.doi.org/10.2478/v10001-010-0029-0

Cooklin, A., Joss, N., Husser, E., & Oldenburg, B. (2017). Integrated approaches to occupational health and safety and health promotion: A systematic review. *American Journal of Health Promotion, 31,* 401–412. http://dx.doi.org/10.4278/ajhp.141027-LIT-542

Cooper, R., & Foster, M. (1971). Sociotechnical systems. *American Psychologist, 26,* 467–474. http://dx.doi.org/10.1037/h0031539

Estes, C. R., Jackson, L. L., Castillo, D. N., & Centers for Disease Control and Prevention. (2010). Occupational injuries and deaths among younger workers—United States,

1998–2007. *MMWR. Morbidity and Mortality Weekly Report, 59,* 449–455. Retrieved from http://www.cdc.gov/mmwr/preview/mmwrhtml/mm5915a2.htm

Fabius, R., Loeppke, R. R., Hohn, T., Fabius, D., Eisenberg, B., Konicki, D. L., & Larson, P. (2016). Tracking the market performance of companies that integrate a culture of health and safety: An assessment of corporate health achievement award applicants. *Journal of Occupational and Environmental Medicine, 58,* 3–8. http://dx.doi.org/10.1097/JOM.0000000000000638

Feltner, C., Peterson, K., Weber, R. P., Cluff, L., Coker-Schwimmer, E., Viswanathan, M., & Lohr, K. N. (2016). The effectiveness of Total Worker Health interventions: A systematic review for a National Institutes of Health Pathways to Prevention workshop. *Annals of Internal Medicine, 165,* 262–269. http://dx.doi.org/10.7326/M16-0626

Goetzel, R. Z., Guindon, A. M., Turshen, I. J., & Ozminkowski, R. J. (2001). Health and productivity management: Establishing key performance measures, benchmarks, and best practices. *Journal of Occupational and Environmental Medicine, 43,* 10–17. http://dx.doi.org/10.1097/00043764-200101000-00003

Hammer, L. B., & Sauter, S. (2013). Total worker health and work–life stress. *Journal of Occupational and Environmental Medicine, 55*(12, Suppl.), S25–S29. http://dx.doi.org/10.1097/JOM.0000000000000043

Harris, J. R., Hannon, P. A., Beresford, S. A., Linnan, L. A., & McLellan, D. L. (2014). Health promotion in smaller workplaces in the United States. *Annual Review of Public Health, 35,* 327–342. http://dx.doi.org/10.1146/annurev-publhealth-032013-182416

Hendrick, H. W., & Kleiner, B. M. (Eds.). (2002). *Macroergonomics: Theory, methods, and applications.* Mahwah, NJ: Erlbaum. http://dx.doi.org/10.1201/b12477

Hunt, M. K., Lederman, R., Stoddard, A. M., LaMontagne, A. D., McLellan, D., Combe, C., . . . Sorensen, G. (2005). Process evaluation of an integrated health promotion/occupational health model in WellWorks–2. *Health Education & Behavior, 32,* 10–26. http://dx.doi.org/10.1177/1090198104264216

Hurtado, D. A., Glymour, M. M., Berkman, L. F., Hashimoto, D., Reme, S. E., & Sorensen, G. (2015). Schedule control and mental health: The relevance of coworkers' reports. *Community, Work & Family, 18,* 416–434. http://dx.doi.org/10.1080/13668803.2015.1080663

Hurtado, D. A., Nelson, C. C., Hashimoto, D., & Sorensen, G. (2015). Supervisors' support for nurses' meal breaks and mental health. *Workplace Health & Safety, 63,* 107–115. http://dx.doi.org/10.1177/2165079915571354

Institute of Medicine. (2005). *Integrating employee health: A model program for NASA.* Washington, DC: National Academies Press.

Jacobsen, H. B., Reme, S. E., Sembajwe, G., Hopcia, K., Stiles, T. C., Sorensen, G., . . . Buxton, O. M. (2014). Work stress, sleep deficiency, and predicted 10-year cardiometabolic risk in a female patient care worker population. *American Journal of Industrial Medicine, 57,* 940–949. http://dx.doi.org/10.1002/ajim.22340

Jacobsen, H. B., Reme, S. E., Sembajwe, G., Hopcia, K., Stoddard, A. M., Kenwood, C., . . . Buxton, O. M. (2014). Work–family conflict, psychological distress, and sleep deficiency among patient care workers. *Workplace Health & Safety, 62,* 282–291.

Karasek, R., & Theorell, T. (1990). *Healthy work: Stress, productivity, and the reconstruction of working life.* New York, NY: Basic Books.

Kim, S. S., Okechukwu, C. A., Buxton, O. M., Dennerlein, J. T., Boden, L. I., Hashimoto, D. M., & Sorensen, G. (2013). Association between work-family conflict and musculoskeletal pain among hospital patient care workers. *American Journal of Industrial Medicine, 56,* 488–495. http://dx.doi.org/10.1002/ajim.22120

Kim, S. S., Okechukwu, C. A., Dennerlein, J. T., Boden, L. I., Hopcia, K., Hashimoto, D. M., & Sorensen, G. (2014). Association between perceived inadequate staffing and musculoskeletal pain among hospital patient care workers. *International Archives of Occupational and Environmental Health, 87,* 323–330. http://dx.doi.org/10.1007/s00420-013-0864-y

Krieger, N. (2010). Workers are people too: Societal aspects of occupational health disparities—An ecosocial perspective. *American Journal of Industrial Medicine, 53*, 104–115. http://dx.doi.org/10.1002/ajim.20759

Krieger, N., Chen, J. T., Waterman, P. D., Hartman, C., Stoddard, A. M., Quinn, M. M., . . . Barbeau, E. M. (2008). The inverse hazard law: Blood pressure, sexual harassment, racial discrimination, workplace abuse and occupational exposures in U.S. low-income Black, White and Latino workers. *Social Science & Medicine, 67*, 1970–1981. http://dx.doi.org/10.1016/j.socscimed.2008.09.039

LaMontagne, A. D., Barbeau, E., Youngstrom, R. A., Lewiton, M., Stoddard, A. M., McLellan, D., . . . Sorensen, G. (2004). Assessing and intervening on OSH programmes: Effectiveness evaluation of the Wellworks-2 intervention in 15 manufacturing worksites. *Occupational and Environmental Medicine, 61*, 651–660. http://dx.doi.org/10.1136/oem.2003.011718

LaMontagne, A. D., Martin, A., Page, K. M., Reavley, N. J., Noblet, A. J., Milner, A. J., . . . Smith, P. M. (2014). Workplace mental health: Developing an integrated intervention approach. *BMC Psychiatry, 14*, 131. http://dx.doi.org/10.1186/1471-244X-14-131

Lax, M. B. (2016). The perils of integrating wellness and safety and health and the possibility of a worker-oriented alternative. *New Solutions, 26*, 11–39. http://dx.doi.org/10.1177/1048291116629489

Levy, B. S., Wegman, D. H., Baron, S. L., & Sokas, R. K. (Eds.). (2006). *Occupational and environmental health: Recognizing and preventing disease and injury* (5th ed.). Philadelphia, PA: Lippincott Williams & Wilkins.

Lipscomb, J., Trinkoff, A., Brady, B., & Geiger-Brown, J. (2004). Health care system changes and reported musculoskeletal disorders among registered nurses. *American Journal of Public Health, 94*, 1431–1435. http://dx.doi.org/10.2105/AJPH.94.8.1431

Lipscomb, J. A., Trinkoff, A. M., Geiger-Brown, J., & Brady, B. (2002). Work-schedule characteristics and reported musculoskeletal disorders of registered nurses. *Scandinavian Journal of Work, Environment & Health, 28*, 394–401. http://dx.doi.org/10.5271/sjweh.691

Loeppke, R. R., Hohn, T., Baase, C., Bunn, W. B., Burton, W. N., Eisenberg, B. S., . . . Siuba, J. (2015). Integrating health and safety in the workplace: How closely aligning health and safety strategies can yield measurable benefits. *Journal of Occupational and Environmental Medicine, 57*, 585–597. http://dx.doi.org/10.1097/JOM.0000000000000467

Macfarlane, G. J., Pallewatte, N., Paudyal, P., Blyth, F. M., Coggon, D., Crombez, G., . . . van der Windt, D. (2009). Evaluation of work-related psychosocial factors and regional musculoskeletal pain: Results from a EULAR Task Force. *Annals of the Rheumatic Diseases, 68*, 885–891. http://dx.doi.org/10.1136/ard.2008.090829

McLellan, D., Moore, W., Nagler, E., & Sorensen, G. (2017). *Implementing an integrated approach: Weaving worker health, safety, and well-being into the fabric of your organization.* Boston, MA: Dana-Farber Cancer Institute. Retrieved from http://centerforworkhealth.sph.harvard.edu/sites/default/files/10.12.17_Guidelines_Screen_post.pdf

McLellan, D. L., Cabán-Martinez, A. J., Nelson, C. C., Pronk, N. P., Katz, J. N., Allen, J. D., . . . Sorensen, G. (2015). Organizational characteristics influence implementation of worksite health protection and promotion programs: Evidence from smaller businesses. *Journal of Occupational and Environmental Medicine, 57*, 1009–1016. http://dx.doi.org/10.1097/JOM.0000000000000517

McLellan, D., Pronk, N., & Pember, M. (2015, November). *The feasibility and acceptability of disseminating integrated health promotion and health protection interventions through a vendor in small- to medium-sized businesses.* Poster presented at the annual meeting of the American Public Health Association, Chicago, IL.

McLellan, R. K. (2016). Total Worker Health: A promising approach to a safer and healthier workforce. *Annals of Internal Medicine, 165*, 294–295. http://dx.doi.org/10.7326/M16-0965

Mellor, N., & Webster, J. (2013). Enablers and challenges in implementing a comprehensive workplace health and well-being approach. *International Journal of Workplace Health Management, 6*, 129–142. http://dx.doi.org/10.1108/IJWHM-08-2011-0018

Montano, D., Hoven, H., & Siegrist, J. (2014). Effects of organisational-level interventions at work on employees' health: A systematic review. *BMC Public Health, 14*, 135. http://dx.doi.org/10.1186/1471-2458-14-135

National Institute for Occupational Safety and Health. (n.d.). *Total Worker Health.* Retrieved from https://www.cdc.gov/niosh/twh/totalhealth.html

National Institute for Occupational Safety and Health. (2008). *Expanding our understanding of the psychosocial work environment: A compendium of measures of discrimination, harassment and work–family issues.* Retrieved from http://www.cdc.gov/niosh/docs/2008-104/pdfs/2008-104.pdf

National Institute for Occupational Safety and Health. (2012). *Research compendium: The NIOSH Total Worker Health™ Program: Seminal research papers 2012.* Retrieved from http://www.cdc.gov/niosh/docs/2012-146/pdfs/2012-146.pdf

National Institute for Occupational Safety and Health. (2016). Hierarchy of controls applied to *Total Worker Health.* Retrieved from https://www.cdc.gov/niosh/twh/letsgetstarted.html

Nelson, C. C., Wagner, G. R., Cabán-Martinez, A. J., Buxton, O. M., Kenwood, C. T., Sabbath, E. L., . . . Sorensen, G. (2014). Physical activity and body mass index: The contribution of age and workplace characteristics. *American Journal of Preventive Medicine, 46*(3, Suppl. 1), S42–S51. http://dx.doi.org/10.1016/j.amepre.2013.10.035

Nishitani, N., & Sakakibara, H. (2010). Job stress factors, stress response, and social support in association with insomnia of Japanese male workers. *Industrial Health, 48*, 178–184. http://dx.doi.org/10.2486/indhealth.48.178

Occupational Safety and Health Administration. (2008). *OSHA fact sheet: Effective workplace safety and health management systems.* Retrieved from https://www.daviecountync.gov/DocumentCenter/View/5294/6B-OSHA-Fact-Sheet-Effective-Workplace-Safety-and-Health-Management-Systems

Okechukwu, C. A., Krieger, N., Sorensen, G., Li, Y., & Barbeau, E. M. (2009). MassBuilt: Effectiveness of an apprenticeship site-based smoking cessation intervention for unionized building trades workers. *Cancer Causes & Control, 20*, 887–894. http://dx.doi.org/10.1007/s10552-009-9324-0

Olson, R., Anger, W. K., Elliot, D. L., Wipfli, B., & Gray, M. (2009). A new health promotion model for lone workers: Results of the Safety & Health Involvement For Truckers (SHIFT) pilot study. *Journal of Occupational and Environmental Medicine, 51*, 1233–1246. http://dx.doi.org/10.1097/JOM.0b013e3181c1dc7a

Pronk, N. P. (2013). Integrated worker health protection and promotion programs: Overview and perspectives on health and economic outcomes. *Journal of Occupational and Environmental Medicine, 55*(12, Suppl.), S30–S37. http://dx.doi.org/10.1097/JOM.0000000000000031

Pronk, N. P., Katz, A. S., Lowry, M., & Payfer, J. R. (2012). Reducing occupational sitting time and improving worker health: The Take-a-Stand Project, 2011. *Preventing Chronic Disease, 9*, E154. http://dx.doi.org/10.5888/pcd9.110323

Pronk, N. P., McLellan, D. L., McGrail, M. P., Olson, S. M., McKinney, Z. J., Katz, J. N., . . . Sorensen, G. (2016). Measurement tools for integrated worker health protection and promotion: Lessons learned from the SafeWell Project. *Journal of Occupational and Environmental Medicine, 58*, 651–658.

Punnett, L., Cherniack, M., Henning, R., Morse, T., & Faghri, P. (2009). A conceptual framework for integrating workplace health promotion and occupational ergonomics programs. *Public Health Reports, 124*(Suppl. 1), 16–25. http://dx.doi.org/10.1177/00333549091244S103

Reme, S. E., Dennerlein, J. T., Hashimoto, D., & Sorensen, G. (2012). Musculoskeletal pain and psychological distress in hospital patient care workers. *Journal of Occupational Rehabilitation, 22*, 503–510. http://dx.doi.org/10.1007/s10926-012-9361-5

Rivilis, I., Van Eerd, D., Cullen, K., Cole, D. C., Irvin, E., Tyson, J., & Mahood, Q. (2008). Effectiveness of participatory ergonomic interventions on health outcomes: A systematic review. *Applied Ergonomics, 39*, 342–358. http://dx.doi.org/10.1016/j.apergo.2007.08.006

Rohlman, D. S., Parish, M., Elliot, D. L., Montgomery, D., & Hanson, G. (2013). Characterizing the needs of a young working population: Making the case for total worker health in an emerging workforce. *Journal of Occupational and Environmental Medicine, 55*(12, Suppl.), S69–S72. http://dx.doi.org/10.1097/JOM.0000000000000039

Sabbath, E. L., Hurtado, D. A., Okechukwu, C. A., Tamers, S. L., Nelson, C., Kim, S. S., . . . Sorenson, G. (2014). Occupational injury among hospital patient-care workers: What is the association with workplace verbal abuse? *American Journal of Industrial Medicine, 57*, 222–232. http://dx.doi.org/10.1002/ajim.22271

Schulte, P. A., Pandalai, S., Wulsin, V., & Chun, H. (2012). Interaction of occupational and personal risk factors in workforce health and safety. *American Journal of Public Health, 102*, 434–448. http://dx.doi.org/10.2105/AJPH.2011.300249

Shaw, W. S., Robertson, M. M., McLellan, R. K., Verma, S., & Pransky, G. (2006). A controlled case study of supervisor training to optimize response to injury in the food processing industry. *Work, 26*, 107–114.

Siegrist, J. (1996). Adverse health effects of high-effort/low-reward conditions. *Journal of Occupational Health Psychology, 1*, 27–41. http://dx.doi.org/10.1037/1076-8998.1.1.27

Sorensen, G., Barbeau, E., Stoddard, A. M., Hunt, M. K., Kaphingst, K., & Wallace, L. (2005). Promoting behavior change among working-class, multiethnic workers: Results of the healthy directions—small business study. *American Journal of Public Health, 95*, 1389–1395. http://dx.doi.org/10.2105/AJPH.2004.038745

Sorensen, G., Emmons, K., Hunt, M. K., Barbeau, E., Goldman, R., Peterson, K., . . . Berkman, L. (2003). Model for incorporating social context in health behavior interventions: Applications for cancer prevention for working-class, multiethnic populations. *Preventive Medicine, 37*, 188–197. http://dx.doi.org/10.1016/S0091-7435(03)00111-7

Sorensen, G., Landsbergis, P., Hammer, L., Amick, B. C., III, Linnan, L., Yancey, A., . . . Workshop Working Group on Worksite Chronic Disease Prevention. (2011). Preventing chronic disease in the workplace: A workshop report and recommendations. *American Journal of Public Health, 101*(Suppl. 1), S196–S207. http://dx.doi.org/10.2105/AJPH.2010.300075

Sorensen, G., McLellan, D., Dennerlein, J., Pronk, N., Allen, J. D., Boden, L. I., . . . Wagner, G. R. (2013). Integration of health protection and health promotion: Rationale, indicators, and metrics. *Journal of Occupational and Environmental Medicine, 55*(12, Suppl.), S12–S18.

Sorensen, G., McLellan, D. L., Sabbath, E. L., Dennerlein, J. T., Nagler, E. M., Hurtado, D. A., . . . Wagner, G. R. (2016). Integrating worksite health protection and health promotion: A conceptual model for intervention and research. *Preventive Medicine, 91*, 188–196. http://dx.doi.org/10.1016/j.ypmed.2016.08.005

Sorensen, G., Nagler, E. M., Hashimoto, D., Dennerlein, J. T., Theron, J. V., Stoddard, A. M., . . . Wagner, G. (2016). Implementing an integrated health protection/health promotion intervention in the hospital setting: Lessons learned from the Be Well, Work Well Study. *Journal of Occupational and Environmental Medicine, 58*, 185–194. http://dx.doi.org/10.1097/JOM.0000000000000592

Sorensen, G., Stoddard, A., LaMontagne, A., Emmons, K., Hunt, M., Youngstrom, R., . . . Christiani, D. (2002). A comprehensive worksite cancer prevention intervention: Behavior change results from a randomized controlled trial (United States). *Cancer Causes & Control, 13*, 493–502. http://dx.doi.org/10.1023/A:1016385001695

Sorensen, G., Stoddard, A. M., Stoffel, S., Buxton, O., Sembajwe, G., Hashimoto, D., . . . Hopcia, K. (2011). The role of the work context in multiple wellness outcomes for hospital patient care workers. *Journal of Occupational and Environmental Medicine, 53,* 899–910. http://dx.doi.org/10.1097/JOM.0b013e318226a74a

Stokols, D. (1996). Translating social ecological theory into guidelines for community health promotion. *American Journal of Health Promotion, 10,* 282–298. http://dx.doi.org/10.4278/0890-1171-10.4.282

Tullar, J. M., Brewer, S., Amick, B. C., III, Irvin, E., Mahood, Q., Pompeii, L. A., . . . Evanoff, B. (2010). Occupational safety and health interventions to reduce musculoskeletal symptoms in the health care sector. *Journal of Occupational Rehabilitation, 20,* 199–219. http://dx.doi.org/10.1007/s10926-010-9231-y

Tveito, T. H., Sembajwe, G., Boden, L. I., Dennerlein, J. T., Wagner, G. R., Kenwood, C., . . . Sorensen, G. (2014). Impact of organizational policies and practices on workplace injuries in a hospital setting. *Journal of Occupational and Environmental Medicine, 56,* 802–808. http://dx.doi.org/10.1097/JOM.0000000000000189

Umukoro, P. E., Arias, O., Stoffel, S. D., Hopcia, K., Sorensen, G., & Dennerlein, J. T. (2013). Physical activity at work contributes little to patient care workers' weekly totals. *Journal of Occupational and Environmental Medicine, 55*(12, Suppl.), S63–S68.

Velazquez, V., Baker, R., Dewey, R., Andrews, K., & Stock, L. (2010). *The whole worker: Guidelines for integrating occupational health and safety with workplace wellness programs.* Oakland, CA: Commission on Health and Safety and Workers' Compensation. Retrieved from http://www.dir.ca.gov/chswc/WOSHTEP/Publications/WOSHTEP_TheWholeWorker.pdf

6

A Participatory Framework for Integrated Interventions

Martin G. Cherniack and Laura Punnett

The *Total Worker Health*® paradigm poses an alternative to traditional workplace health promotion by recognizing the contribution of the organizational and psychosocial work environment to chronic conditions such as heart disease and diabetes. The literature on mechanisms includes endocrinological and other physiological pathways, whereas newer evidence on behaviorally mediated effects is growing steadily (e.g., Chandola et al., 2008). Specific features of the work environment—from work scheduling to supervisor–employee relations—can act as either barriers to or facilitators of healthy behaviors. For example, low decision latitude at work is associated with obesity (Brunner, Chandola, & Marmot, 2007), alcohol consumption (Head, Stansfeld, & Siegrist, 2004), smoking, and reduced aerobic exercise during leisure time (Brisson, Larocque, Moisan, Vézina, & Dagenais, 2000). Having

This research was funded by the National Institute for Occupational Safety and Health (NIOSH) Grant U19 OH008857. This chapter is solely the responsibility of the authors and does not represent the official views of NIOSH. We thank Suzanne Nobrega for editorial review and Neha Sahasrabudhe for formatting assistance. The work described here represents the efforts of multiple investigators, including Alicia Dugan, Jeff Dussetschleger, Mazen el Ghaziri, Pouran Faghri, Marian Flum, Robert Henning, Raj Kotejoshyer, Suzanne Nobrega, Michelle Robertson, Nicholas Warren, and Yuan Zhang. Many students at the University of Massachusetts and University of Connecticut provided excellent assistance in data collection, coding, management, and analysis. Finally, we express our deep respect for the workers who participated in these projects.

http://dx.doi.org/10.1037/0000149-007
Total Worker Health, H. L. Hudson, J. A. S. Nigam, S. L. Sauter, L. C. Chosewood, A. L. Schill, and J. Howard (Editors)
Copyright © 2019 by the American Psychological Association. All rights reserved.

few decision-making opportunities is a notable feature of low-wage, low-status jobs, suggesting that work organization is thus also one mechanism of socioeconomic disparities in health.

A separate organizational issue, also remediable, is the increasing use of extended shift schedules. The relationship of overtime work with clinical fatigue has been strongly established for driving crashes (National Center on Sleep Disorders Research, National Heart, Lung, and Blood Institute, and National Highway Traffic Safety Administration Expert Panel on Driver Fatigue and Sleepiness, 1998) as well as with occupational injuries of other types (Dembe, Erickson, Delbos, & Banks, 2005; Vegso et al., 2007; Wagstaff & Sigstad Lie, 2011). The American College of Environmental and Occupational Medicine (Lerman et al., 2012) criticized the extensive use of overtime to compensate for short-staffing, noting its growing distribution and the strong association with absenteeism due to fatigue and health issues. Overtime work is strongly implicated in cardiovascular morbidity, with elevated risk of incident coronary heart disease (Virtanen et al., 2010) and nonfatal myocardial infarction (Hayashi, Kobayashi, Yamaoka, & Yano, 1996). There is also a marked association between overtime and depression (Virtanen, Stansfeld, Fuhrer, Ferrie, & Kivimäki, 2012).

In contrast, a health-promoting organizational environment at work can provide time, space, and material and social supports for enhancing choices such as smoking cessation, healthy diet, leisure-time exercise, and improved work–family balance. This approach forms the basis for an integrated programmatic approach to health, safety, and well-being in the workplace that emphasizes creating health-conducive conditions of work. (Throughout this chapter, *integration* refers to the *Total Worker Health* [TWH] goal of simultaneously addressing both work and nonwork root causes for a broad range of worker health and well-being outcomes.)

WORKER PARTICIPATION AS A CORE ELEMENT OF THE TWH PROGRAM

At the Center for the Promotion of Health in the New England Workplace (CPH-NEW), one of the first two National Institute for Occupational Safety and Health Centers of Excellence for *Total Worker Health*®, recognition of the particular importance of decision latitude for chronic disease risks has led to a focus on programs that increase opportunities for participation in decision-making by frontline workers. The direct involvement of workers in the planning and design of interventions can benefit group and individual self-efficacy. This is consistent with the concept of "sense of coherence" (Antonovsky, 1987), an internal resource for overcoming stress and an intermediate variable on the causal pathway from participatory activities to effective decision-making. Sense of coherence has been extended by other investigators to examine engagement in multiple settings (residential, educational, clinical, and occupational) and evaluate its role in reducing burnout and other adverse outcomes (Bauer & Jenny, 2007; Kähönen, Näätänen, Tolvanen, & Salmela-Aro, 2012). Engaging workers in the design of interventions is also expected to contribute to program reach, effectiveness, and sustainability because employees can inform program design with firsthand information about obstacles to their own and colleagues' health and well-being.

As practiced at CPH-NEW, participation to increase worker decision-making is not a single intervention but a gradual process that builds incrementally, with learning on the part of the workers as well as the researchers (Hugentobler, Israel, & Schurman, 1992; Nielsen, 2013). Although the process invites consideration of risk factors originating both in and outside work, changes may address either of these or both at a given point in time. We consider that a selected intervention meets the TWH criterion when it is selected after consideration of root causes in both domains, which is one step in an ongoing process of continuous evaluation and improvement (Henning et al., 2009; von Thiele Schwarz, Augustsson, Hasson, & Stenfors-Hayes, 2015).

CPH-NEW researchers have developed a structured process to support worker participation in problem selection, investigation, and intervention for the TWH approach. Next, we describe some historical background for workers becoming stakeholders in workplace interventions. We then provide examples of our implementation strategy, offer preliminary evidence of program success, and discuss some of the challenges to this approach.[1]

PARTICIPATORY ACTION RESEARCH

One precedent for effecting change in a formally under-represented population is found in participatory action research (PAR) and its application to community-based participatory research (CBPR; Horowitz, Robinson, & Seifer, 2009; Minkler & Wallerstein, 2011). At its core, CBPR requires the engagement of all key parties—administrators, employers, workers, and investigators—in the multiple stages of planning, development, implementation, and project evaluation. The underlying principle of self-determination is coupled with a pragmatic understanding that improvements in workplace culture and individual worker health and well-being will ultimately stall without this commitment (Birken & Linnan, 2006).

Although we take PAR as the most general form of participatory decision-making in research, the translation from community-based participation into the workplace is not a simple adaptation. The workplace is inherently hierarchical, and confidentiality, subordination, and access to resources are not equally distributed. For these reasons, the introduction of participatory formats for improving workforce health requires development of structured processes for

---

[1]The National Labor Relations Act of 1935 may limit the form and structure of employee involvement in worker-management teams, committees, or groups. Employers should seek legal assistance if they are unsure of their responsibilities or obligations under the National Labor Relations Act.

effecting change within the existing organizational system while seeking ways to increase worker decision latitude and autonomy (Henning et al., 2009). Iterative trials and evaluations of these interventions—whether successful or not—produce empirical learning for each setting; generalizability to other contexts must be assessed for each in turn.

PARTICIPATORY ERGONOMICS

The most developed background experience for participatory interventions in the workplace comes from participatory ergonomics (PE). PE has been an accepted approach to the prevention of work-related musculoskeletal diseases for more than 2 decades; it was used first in manufacturing (Smith, 1994) and then extended to other sectors (e.g., Haines, Wilson, Vink, & Koningsveld, 2002; Haukka et al., 2008; Hignett, Wilson, & Morris, 2005; Punnett et al., 2013). Haims and Carayon (1998) recognized the empirical nature of these interventions and attempted to compose a methodologic intervention scheme by inserting the expert and participant-guided methodology of action research. Their prescribed stages were (a) training of the workforce by ergonomics professionals; (b) goal-setting by an ergonomics committee, with researcher facilitation; (c) workforce surveying, led by the committee; (d) worksite ergonomic evaluations by the committee; and (e) systems planning with expert assistance. Although useful, a more defined and translatable protocol is required for scale-up and generalized implementation, as also noted by Nielsen and Abildgaard (2013). This necessitates a series of well-designed field projects for iterative elaboration and refinement of that protocol.

In both its macro- and microergonomic formulations, PE addresses workplace organization. *Macroergonomics* refers to the analysis and design of workplace systems; microergonomics refers to job-level interface between the individual and the machine or work process. There are also some opportunities for broader health interventions. However, what PE traditionally does not broach are individual health issues, such as sleep, body weight, and family relationships. For application to the TWH program, the PE process must be expanded to include factors outside the workplace. Our own experience through CPH-NEW has underlined both its applicability and its limitations. Although it offers a platform to compose a more integrated work and health perspective, there has often been reluctance to address certain relevant issues, such as work scheduling, which are generally seen as managerial prerogatives.

OTHER WORKPLACE PARTICIPATORY PROCESSES

Other workplace participatory schemes are in use internationally; these take a variety of forms and produce varied outcomes, depending on such cultural, economic, and policy factors as workforce unionization and health care systems.

Optimizing Productivity in the United States

In the U.S. automobile industry, workforce participation in production processes and attention to quality of work life coincided with the decline of unionization (Rinehart, 1984). One newer development has been the inclusion of workers and their families in preventive health services (Yen, Edington, McDonald, Hirschland, & Edington, 2001). However, the potential benefit of cooperative decision-making about personal health matters is tempered by caution, especially if participatory health activities are run parallel to a "lean" process, which often leads to workforce downsizing, exacerbates job stress, and even encourages substance misuse (Cherniack, 2015; Landsbergis, Cahill, & Schnall, 1999).

An inherent problem with "high-performance" work systems that engage the workforce in team practices and decision processes for production efficiencies is the potential cost in quality of work life, and in some circumstances an intrusion into personal and family time (Gordon & Whelan-Berry, 2004). Bringsén, Andersson, Ejlertsson, and Troein (2012) observed that the approach falls short of being salutogenic (health supporting) when the objective is limited to goals such as rewards and teamwork. An orientation toward team processes and work culture has implicit omissions, perhaps most exemplified in the "California Corporation," a term used for work practices in the Silicon Valley electronics industry, in which teamwork and innovation occur at a cost to home life (Carnoy, 2009). Participatory goals may be achieved, but if work hazards are discounted and if the iron necessities of production are off-limits to modification, then worker and family well-being will be sacrificed.

Work Councils in Northern Europe

Northern European attention to the role of work stress preceded programs in the United States. The first steps in enhancing workplace participatory control came through the passage of more stringent health and safety legislation; the Swedish 1976 Co-Determination Act opened the way for the unions to negotiate agreements about the organization of work (Gourevitch et al., 1984). In Denmark and Sweden, the two most documented societies for workforce participation, there has been modest but positive evidence for improvement in quality of work (Gallie, 2003).

The German Works Constitution Act provides for the rights of employees to elect representatives to works councils (*Betriebsräte*). In principle, the Works Constitution Act provides for workforce participation in company planning, policies, and operations, including limited rights to information and consultation (FitzRoy & Kraft, 1993). Effective councils have redirected resources to health protection in the immediate environment (Askildsen, Jirjahn, & Smith, 2006). There appears to be limited drag on productivity, at least in larger firms (Addison, Schnabel, & Wagner, 2001). Overall, however, the *Betriebsräte* approach has had less pertinence to workforce health.

A more explicit example of integration comes from German "health circles," which have coincidently addressed both work organization and individual risk factors for cardiovascular disease (Aust & Ducki, 2004). They exist in mature industries with larger workforces, where there is already an established history of work councils and quality councils. The German health circle concept follows recognition that health-related issues are left unaddressed in quality circles invested in productivity and working conditions. The necessarily higher level of mutual trust in health circles is more difficult to achieve than what is required to discuss optimizing productivity (Brandenburg & Slesina, 1994).

EFFECTS OF THE HEALTH CARE SYSTEM ON WORKPLACE PARTICIPATORY PROCESSES

Robust national health or national health insurance systems, such as in much of Europe, have tended to encourage national workplace health programs because the costs of chronic disease, including early exit from the labor force, are borne societally instead of by individuals' employers (Downey & Sharp, 2007). The United States differs from its European peer countries by financing health care at the level of the individual firm; employer-sponsored health promotion has followed. This effect distinguishes TWH concepts of integration from the holism that is emphasized by Scandinavian investigators, who articulate the concepts of *intersectorality* and *equitability* as social rather than firm-specific goals (Lindström & Eriksson, 2009; Ringsberg & Borup, 2011). Nonetheless, health costs may have substantial societal impact in countries with a robust social safety net. This motivates public health efforts in those countries to seek effective workplace health promotion strategies, including integration with occupational health services.

The weaker federal mechanisms in the United States for unemployment support, education and retraining, and health care affordability outside of work cede a substantial role to the states and to employers. Costs of medical care weigh more heavily on the firm, motivating attention to individual behavior and nonoccupational disease. Further, when workplace health promotion programs are incentivized for the individual and focus primarily on group health insurance cost reduction or productivity, the consequences may be perceived coercion, increased socioeconomic health disparities, and dissociation of work from chronic disease and well-being by inserting an individual focus (Cherniack, 2015).

Separate from the form of the health care system, the increasing evolution of nonstandard work arrangements such as large-scale subcontracting is likely to marginalize workplace-based implementation of TWH concepts over time. The combined effects of all of these forces argue for a more comprehensive public health view of how to integrate occupational protection with extraoccupational measures to promote well-being (Baron et al., 2014; see also Chapter 11, this volume).

EVOLUTION AND APPLICATION OF THE PARTICIPATORY PROCESS FOR THE TWH PROGRAM: CASE STUDIES

Using evidence from prior PE programs, and recognizing that a tailored approach would be needed to fit a participatory program model within standard organizational structures in the United States, CPH-NEW researchers developed an approach for adapting PE methods to provide salutogenic benefits, in line with TWH goals. This structured process for root-cause analysis and intervention planning is now termed the CPH-NEW Healthy Workplace Participatory Program (HWPP). The program comprises a protocol for convening and training a committee of workers to assess and prioritize workforce health and safety problems; conduct root cause analysis, considering both work and nonwork contributing factors; brainstorm solutions and criteria for determining their success; make a formal presentation to management regarding strengths and weaknesses of the alternatives; and evaluate the selected intervention to determine whether it met the initial goals set by the committee (Dugan et al., 2016; Nobrega et al., 2017; Robertson, Henning, Warren, Nobrega, & Dove-Steinkamp, 2015). The cycle of steps is pursued iteratively; as one problem is determined to be resolved adequately, a new one is selected. The core instrument that guides these cycles is the Intervention Design and Analysis Scorecard (IDEAS) Tool, publicly disseminated online long with numerous TWH training and evaluation materials (University of Massachusetts Lowell, n.d.).

Used in the context of worker or labor-management team formation, the HWPP provides a structure for obtaining input from frontline workers, middle managers, and upper level managers about the causes of unsafe work, poor health, and/or lack of well-being within the workforce and for engaging these groups to collaborate on remedies. To qualify as a TWH strategy, it is not necessary that each specific *intervention* includes both work and nonwork components. Instead, integration is achieved by explicitly encouraging participants to consider the broad scope of possible risk factors, both within and outside work, and their interactions in each *cycle* of problem definition and solution. HWPP also meets the TWH definition through the nature of the program process itself by working to enhance workers' skills, confidence, and opportunities to take part in health-related decision-making within the workplace.

The formal HWPP was developed initially from the experiences of implementing a participatory, integrated team process in the nursing home sector (Case 1) and then formally designated and tested in a diverse set of workplaces (Case 2). More extensive experiences came with HWPP use in an intervention study to improve the health of public sector corrections officers (Cases 3, 4, and 5). Where there was labor union representation, the bargaining units were engaged, minimally in Case 2 but in the latter three cases as full partners with the investigators and managers.

The following cases collectively illustrate the value of the participatory process for eliciting workers' experiences and self-education to inform development of integrated interventions that are meaningful and acceptable to them and to engage them in postproject sustainability. The cases also reflect the need for a structured process to maintain worker participation and for ongoing evaluations to support the program's continuous improvement and autocorrection while engagement is still being established. Health-related outcomes reported here include changes in work environment, self-efficacy, and personal health behaviors. Long-term changes in disease risk might be inferred, if the interventions were to remain in place, but could not be documented within the available study periods of these projects.

Case 1: The Health-Promoting Nursing Home

The first CPH-NEW health care study, "Promoting Physical and Mental Health of Caregivers through Transdisciplinary Intervention" (ProCare), featured a participatory intervention team process in three skilled nursing facilities (SNFs). The teams brainstormed the features of an "ideal nursing home" for both residents and staff. They selected specific goals for improved worker health and well-being and developed solutions to the potential obstacles. The investigators facilitated the discussions, ensured circulation of minutes and agendas, and met with the on-site team coordinators between meetings.

The three teams demonstrated enthusiastic uptake of the "integration" paradigm and achieved initial successes in improving the health environment in their workplaces (Zhang et al., 2016). Each team independently selected lack of healthy food options at work as its first priority, and together they were able to obtain healthier food choices in vending machines. In one facility the kitchen agreed to provide soups, salads, and sandwiches at reduced cost to employees. One team initiated the creation of a community garden, providing fresh produce, teamwork, physical activity, and an outdoor experience that could be shared with some residents. Other accomplishments included securing a quiet break room for staff relaxation and recovery, ergonomics training, nutrition, and weight loss programs. The participatory process had high participant acceptance and engagement; team members reported positive attention to organizational issues such as teamwork, respect, communication, and locus of decision-making.

Compared with three control SNFs with active corporate wellness programs but no worker involvement in program development, staff at the participatory sites were more aware of and likely to participate in activities such as exercise and nutrition/weight loss programs. More staff members in the participatory sites (28% vs. 16% in control SNFs) reported opportunities for decision-making. Both managers and employees cited the importance of factors such as employee program ownership, empowerment, and skill building, all of which are promising for long-term sustainability.

However, although proof of concept was demonstrated, over the longer term the scheduled reduction of investigator facilitation was followed by incorporation of the teams into other, existing activities and erosion of staff participation in project planning. The dilution of the health mission was aggravated by administrator changes, not uncommon within SNF middle management.

The loss of administrative memory resulted in loss of managerial participation and material support for program development, such as allocation of limited but important financial resources and provision of time release for program participation (Zhang, Flum, West, & Punnett, 2015).

Process evaluations identified other significant but modifiable challenges to long-term sustainability. These included communication barriers, especially between units, shifts, and levels of the managerial hierarchy; dependence on highly motivated individuals at both the facility and regional levels, but without rewards for champions' or administrators' efforts; and corporate shifts in demonstrated commitment to employee health promotion efforts. Another barrier was the differences between managers' and front-line workers' perceptions of the SNF environment (Zhang et al., 2011). These observations led to refinement of the CPH-NEW criteria for organizational readiness for change (Zhang et al., 2015).

The disappointing inability of the employer to recognize the contrast in effectiveness between the facilitated workplace health promotion program and the more generic corporate-sponsored program indicates an important limitation in management culture. "Data-driven" language pervaded company operational principles, and the organization's priorities included several potentially related concerns, including costs of employee disability, employee turnover, and resident outcomes. However, periodic and episodic shifting of priorities, in contrast to following evidence for their intersections, posed a cultural (rather than a financial) barrier to sustaining and strengthening this initiative to improve worker health.

Case 2: Initial Field Trials of the HWPP

Four employers were recruited from a group of organizations completing a worksite wellness capacity-building program. Employers were offered an opportunity to expand program scope and sustainability by addressing root causes of health issues—including both work organization and nonoccupational factors—and transferring problem-solving skills to people within the organization (Nobrega et al., 2017). The four organizations that volunteered were (a) a real estate management firm, (b) a human services nonprofit agency, (c) a state government human resources office, and (d) a public sector correctional institution. Each study site designated an internal program champion responsible for implementation, a design team (DT) of six to eight employees to prioritize problems and develop intervention proposals, and a managerial-level steering committee (SC) to select DT proposals to be implemented and provide overall program oversight and resources. A study investigator served as dedicated facilitator for each DT.

The HWPP was effective for engaging front-line employees. All four sites were able to implement the process and completed at least one complete cycle, that is, they implemented at least one intervention. The goal of identifying both occupational and nonoccupational risk factors was readily adopted by most DT and SC members. Thus the "integration" concept—the key feature of the TWH approach—was successfully presented and taken up as definitional. Because HWPP is a participatory process, the desired health goals selected by the DT and SC members in each organization varied. Certain activities were initiated during the 2-year program:

- Education of apartment renters to reduce unnecessary work orders; better wireless phone service to reduce missed calls; better management of work orders—*to reduce stress from high workload and poor communication.* (Site A)

- Uniforms made of looser, more breathable fabric—*to reduce overheating and physical discomfort during physical exertion.* (Site A)

- Procurement policy to support purchasing of ergonomic equipment; provision of computer workstation adjustment information; training of ergonomic champions; walking breaks—*to reduce physical discomfort and associated stress.* (Sites B and C)

- Health fair with information responding to staff health concerns—*to address sleep disorders, overweight, mental health, and injury risk.* (Site D)

The funded study period was not long enough to complete quantitative evaluation at any site. However, multiple benefits were documented by participating workers, especially development of a more organized understanding of causes and outcomes of the selected problems; the ability to identify root causes; and the skills to compare possible solutions to find the best fit between the possible interventions and the organization's workforce, company culture, and budget. Other benefits included improved communication among personnel at different levels of the organization and ability to develop a common understanding of workplace obstacles to health, safety, and well-being. All of these represent foundational achievements for a sustainable program.

Baseline facilitators of program success included a preestablished priority on health and safety, a strong culture of quality and continuous improvement, relatively good communication channels, and consistent upper management support. Challenges to program success included the time required to accomplish the entire process, especially the first time through the cycle. (The research team responded during the study by reducing the start-up time line and other measures to facilitate a faster intervention process.) Other factors that impeded timely progress were cited as change-resistant management, highly bureaucratic decision/approval processes, and high staff turnover (including layoffs and retirements).

Connecticut Department of Corrections Interventions

In 2006, CPH-NEW responded to a request from union leaders in a state corrections system for help in addressing serious health problems experienced by correctional officers (COs) and supervisors. Among COs in early career, 38% were prehypertensive or hypertensive and 78% were overweight or obese (Cherniack et al., 2016). There was also elevated prevalence of depression, work–family time conflicts, and sleep disturbances. Survey and demographic data were consistent with external evidence that nearly one in four correctional officers fit the criteria for posttraumatic stress disorder (Spinaris, Denhof, & Kellaway, 2012). Correctional officers suffer from suicide rates significantly higher than rates in the general population and other related occupations such as police officers (Stack & Tsoudis, 1997).

Health Improvement Through Employee Control (HITEC) began by comparing a program that engaged correctional officers in the participatory design of workplace interventions and a conventional program in which health promotion interventions were introduced in a top-down manner by health professionals. Reflecting sustained labor and management engagement and input, the research design and intervention protocols evolved steadily over the course of 10 years. The following examples illustrate the later use of the IDEAS Tool to concretize participatory action in integrated interventions at different stages of this evolving partnership. Because decision-making that involves organizational change or investment was beyond the authority of the COs themselves, over time two steering committees were created, at the facility and state (system-wide) levels, to oversee intervention selection and eventual implementation.

Case 3: Indoor Air Quality

Indoor air quality rarely presents as a one-dimensional issue. Particular exigencies in corrections include the concentration of many people in a confined space and the age of many facilities with obsolete temperature and humidity controls. In Department of Corrections (DOC) facilities, concerns over tuberculosis and other infectious diseases among the inmates, and popular press attention to mold exposure, inspired COs' concern about microbial contamination. In addition, there were prevalent suspicions that ambient temperature and humidity were only regulated during daytime work hours, the result being poor air quality. These concerns were resolved through the IDEAS process that followed.

In this project, one site was organized around an ongoing CO DT, and the second site featured labor-management Kaizen Effectiveness Teams (Dugan et al., 2016). The DT's work was augmented by consultative air quality assessment services from the state of Connecticut. In addition, the facility heating, ventilation, and air conditioning maintenance engineers attended selected DT meetings to clarify the operating features of the ventilation systems. The DT was assisted by the researchers to maximize their use of available resources, including content training, from the state Department of Public Health. They were also assisted in making cost estimates of different remediations to present a menu of choices to the facility SC.

The DT members made notable and relatively sophisticated adaptations in their approach to the problem over time. These involved considerable revision of accepted assumptions, such as the putative inattention of maintenance staff during second and third shifts and the prominence of microbial hazards, following recognition that a large portion of discomfort and complaints were caused by large temperature shifts. Measured results were thus accepted in place of unsubstantiated perception. These process outcomes strengthened the DT's capacity and self-efficacy for the longer term.

A variety of maintenance and related practices were overhauled within the facility. The DT enlisted the investigators' assistance in preparing and administering a pre– and post–indoor air quality survey, which showed dramatic perceived improvements. Eventually, the state of Connecticut's response exceeded the best case projection of the DT by accepting their third and most costly priority, that is, complete replacement of the old and problematic facility heating, ventilation, and air conditioning system. The level of detail and step-wide process initiated by the DT consistently surprised administrators and engendered credibility for the DT and the entire PAR process. Together, it appeared that these factors created a climate where a substantial investment became possible.

Case 4: Work and Sleep

This project was initiated by the DOC Supervisors' Union as a self-contained derivative of the original HITEC intervention with COs. Supervisors perceived some of their problems as arising in their system-wide distribution with small numbers in separate locations; as a consequence, they established their own DT and followed the cycle of steps as just described. They began with the administration of their own survey, developed with researcher assistance, to evaluate and prioritize threats to their well-being. They identified issues of hypertension, job stress, lack of exercise, high caloric intake, work–family conflict, and drug and alcohol use as causatively overlapping. The most approachable core factor appeared to be high overtime and extended work hours, leading to disturbed and inadequate sleep, as well as exacerbating some of the other problems.

In brainstorming possible intervention strategies, the DT delineated three distinct areas: (a) personal and internal factors, such as exercise and relaxation techniques; (b) external and environmental factors, such as driving hours, lighting at work, and wind-down periods; and (c) work organizational factors, particularly long work hours and frequent overtime. Ideas selected to address the personal and environmental interventions were low in cost, using existing in-house resources. Development of a Sleep Hygiene Checklist and a supervisor-specific sleep app for mobile devices, offering bedtime prompts and relaxation exercises, were the main project outputs to support behavior change. There was also an extensive train-the-trainers program to enhance intervention effectiveness.

Managing overtime hours through reorganization and sharing among employees was recognized as a more complex and multistage issue, in part because of fiscal issues and in part because of divisions within the membership around the core issue of overtime income versus health (see the preceding discussion of the evidence on this point). It remains under ongoing discussion by the bargaining unit leadership at this time.

Case 5: Peer-to-Peer Mentoring of New Officers

Arising from the HWPP process, the COs themselves eventually proposed and created a longer term program for integrated health and work mentoring between experienced and new officers. The rationale grew out of discussion of the baseline HITEC findings that adverse health patterns in COs were established within the first 3 years of employment (Cherniack et al., 2016). Veteran officers (mentors) were paired with new officers (protégés or mentees) to form relationships outside of the supervisory command. Regular informal meetings provided opportunities for new officers to discuss problems and to receive support and guidance from experienced officers. Training of mentors in health and well-being topics was conducted originally by the study team and subsequently by staff from the DOC training academy.

In 2014 to 2015, 105 mentors and 183 mentees were enrolled. Baseline and 12-month health evaluations were augmented by focus groups and surveys to assess the quality of the mentor–mentee relationship. Mentored cadets experienced a beneficial effect on blood pressure levels after 1 year when compared to a control group of new, nonmentored recruits. Controlling for baseline values, there was an increasing trend among mentees in *health improvement intentions* ($p = .081$, $n = 172$). *Mentorship quality* predicted a trend-level improvement in *organizational health climate* ($p = .097$, $n = 64$). Of interest, the mentors themselves became more aware of their own health challenges, the work and nonwork contributing factors, and potential impact on job performance.

CHALLENGES AND CONCLUSION

Our observations of PAR in corrections and in health care show that success depends upon a variety of factors, including participation of workers and supervisors, leadership, continuity and timing, resilience, and financial circumstances (Dugan et al., 2016; Zhang et al., 2016). Specifically in HITEC, the key factor in integrated program success was resilience: the capacity to regroup after project denial, wait out leadership and staff changes, and maintain functional continuity through failed interventions and reduced workforce participation (Dugan et al., 2016). Another enabling factor here was active attendance by bargaining unit leadership. The elements recognized as key to program resilience—a steering committee with an extended time line focus, a history of CO and supervisor cooperative success, and the authority to execute consensual actions—were developed through patience on all sides, commitment to compromise, ability both to surrender and to accept responsibility and authority, and the articulation of shared goals through the experience of participatory action. The generalizability of these experiences and program components to other sectors, and proof that they can be sustained and scaled up, remain to be evaluated.

Experiences in the first two case studies, in particular, showed that new research design strategies and study tools were required to manage the participatory process in a way that supported meaningful research evaluation. The predominant health outcomes of interest, involving metabolic, mental health and cardiovascular conditions, evolve over a longer time period than typical study funding periods. Other challenges included balancing active participant planning with protection of fixed research methods and hypotheses, confronting the tension between stopping with positive early results and building a sustainable and a continuous improvement process, and imposing evaluation measures for interventions where process change is as important as health outcomes.

To incorporate worker participation in decision-making within a workplace, management and labor must engage in a cooperative effort, where this may not be the norm to date. Further, the construct of "fidelity" to the research design may conflict with active participant planning after the study begins, and process evaluations may be more salient than effectiveness outcomes, especially in the earlier cycles of problem definition and attempted solutions, before much common history has been established.

The successes and failures of HITEC and ProCare occurred in work environments that are challenging to TWH-type integrated interventions. The 24–7 provision of custodial care can mitigate against attention to workers, even though their well-being may impact others. Both projects have demonstrated that in two populations usually thought to be resistant to self-care and workplace engagement, there can be extraordinary levels of workforce involvement and innovation when important obstacles are recognized and addressed. In addition, for cultural change to take hold, programmatic interventions require a perspective that exceeds the life span of current key employers and managers, let alone an annual budget. Sustainability may well require long-term professional engagement in a format similar to that typical of other services such as environmental controls, environmental testing, or accounting.

REFERENCES

Addison, J. T., Schnabel, C., & Wagner, J. (2001). Works councils in Germany: Their effects on establishment performance. *Oxford Economic Papers, 53,* 659–694. http://dx.doi.org/10.1093/oep/53.4.659

Antonovsky, A. (1987). *Unraveling the mystery of health: How people manage stress and stay well.* San Francisco, CA: Jossey-Bass.

Askildsen, J. E., Jirjahn, U., & Smith, S. C. (2006). Works councils and environmental investment: Theory and evidence from German panel data. *Journal of Economic Behavior & Organization, 60,* 346–372. http://dx.doi.org/10.1016/j.jebo.2004.01.006

Aust, B., & Ducki, A. (2004). Comprehensive health promotion interventions at the workplace: Experiences with health circles in Germany. *Journal of Occupational Health Psychology, 9,* 258–270. http://dx.doi.org/10.1037/1076-8998.9.3.258

Baron, S. L., Beard, S., Davis, L. K., Delp, L., Forst, L., Kidd-Taylor, A., . . . Welch, L. S. (2014). Promoting integrated approaches to reducing health inequities among low-income workers: Applying a social ecological framework. *American Journal of Industrial Medicine, 57,* 539–556. http://dx.doi.org/10.1002/ajim.22174

Bauer, G., & Jenny, G. (2007). Development, implementation and dissemination of occupational health management (OHM): Putting salutogenesis into practice. In J. Houdmont & S. McIntyre (Eds.), *Occupational health psychology: European perspectives on research education and practice* (pp. 219–250). Dordrecht, the Netherlands: Springer.

Birken, B. E., & Linnan, L. A. (2006). Implementation challenges in worksite health promotion programs. *North Carolina Medical Journal, 67,* 438–441.

Brandenburg, U., & Slesina, W. (1994). Health promotion circles: A new approach to health promotion at worksite. *Homeostasis in Health and Disease, 35,* 43–48.

Bringsén, A., Andersson, H. I., Ejlertsson, G., & Troein, M. (2012). Exploring workplace related health resources from a salutogenic perspective: Results from a focus group study among healthcare workers in Sweden. *Work, 42,* 403–414.

Brisson, C., Larocque, B., Moisan, J., Vézina, M., & Dagenais, G. R. (2000). Psychosocial factors at work, smoking, sedentary behavior, and body mass index: A prevalence study among 6995 white collar workers. *Journal of Occupational and Environmental Medicine, 42,* 40–46. http://dx.doi.org/10.1097/00043764-200001000-00011

Brunner, E. J., Chandola, T., & Marmot, M. G. (2007). Prospective effect of job strain on general and central obesity in the Whitehall II Study. *American Journal of Epidemiology, 165,* 828–837. http://dx.doi.org/10.1093/aje/kwk058

Carnoy, M. (2009). *Sustaining the new economy: Work, family, and community in the information age.* Cambridge, MA: Harvard University Press.

Chandola, T., Britton, A., Brunner, E., Hemingway, H., Malik, M., Kumari, M., . . . Marmot, M. (2008). Work stress and coronary heart disease: What are the mechanisms? *European Heart Journal, 29,* 640–648. http://dx.doi.org/10.1093/eurheartj/ehm584

Cherniack, M. (2015). The productivity dilemma in workplace health promotion. *The Scientific World Journal, 2015,* 937063. http://dx.doi.org/10.1155/2015/937063

Cherniack, M., Dussetschleger, J., Dugan, A., Farr, D., Namazi, S., El Ghaziri, M., & Henning, R. (2016). Participatory action research in corrections: The HITEC 2 program. *Applied Ergonomics Pt A, 53,* 169–180. http://dx.doi.org/10.1016/j.apergo.2015.09.011

Dembe, A. E., Erickson, J. B., Delbos, R. G., & Banks, S. M. (2005). The impact of overtime and long work hours on occupational injuries and illnesses: New evidence from the United States. *Occupational and Environmental Medicine, 62,* 588–597. http://dx.doi.org/10.1136/oem.2004.016667

Downey, A. M., & Sharp, D. J. (2007). Why do managers allocate resources to workplace health promotion programmes in countries with national health coverage? *Health Promotion International, 22,* 102–111. http://dx.doi.org/10.1093/heapro/dam002

Dugan, A. G., Farr, D. A., Namazi, S., Henning, R. A., Wallace, K. N., El Ghaziri, M., . . . Cherniack, M. G. (2016). Process evaluation of two participatory approaches: Implementing total worker health® interventions in a correctional workforce. *American Journal of Industrial Medicine, 59,* 897–918. http://dx.doi.org/10.1002/ajim.22593

FitzRoy, F. R., & Kraft, K. (1993). Economic effects of codetermination. *The Scandinavian Journal of Economics, 95,* 365–375. http://dx.doi.org/10.2307/3440362

Gallie, D. (2003). The quality of working life: Is Scandinavia different? *European Sociological Review, 19,* 61–79. http://dx.doi.org/10.1093/esr/19.1.61

Gordon, J. R., & Whelan-Berry, K. S. (2004). It takes two to tango: An empirical study of perceived spousal/partner support for working women. *Women in Management Review, 19,* 260–273. http://dx.doi.org/10.1108/09649420410545980

Gourevitch, P., Martin, A., Ross, G., Bornstein, S., Markovits, A., & Allen, C. (1984). *Unions and economic crisis: Britain, West Germany and Sweden.* London, England: George Allen Unwin.

Haims, M. C., & Carayon, P. (1998). Theory and practice for the implementation of 'in-house,' continuous improvement participatory ergonomic programs. *Applied Ergonomics, 29,* 461–472. http://dx.doi.org/10.1016/S0003-6870(98)00012-X

Haines, H., Wilson, J. R., Vink, P., & Koningsveld, E. (2002). Validating a framework for participatory ergonomics (the PEF). *Ergonomics, 45,* 309–327. http://dx.doi.org/10.1080/00140130210123516

Haukka, E., Leino-Arjas, P., Viikari-Juntura, E., Takala, E. P., Malmivaara, A., Hopsu, L., . . . Riihimäki, H. (2008). A randomised controlled trial on whether a participatory ergonomics intervention could prevent musculoskeletal disorders. *Occupational and Environmental Medicine, 65,* 849–856. http://dx.doi.org/10.1136/oem.2007.034579

Hayashi, T., Kobayashi, Y., Yamaoka, K., & Yano, E. (1996). Effect of overtime work on 24-hour ambulatory blood pressure. *Journal of Occupational and Environmental Medicine, 38,* 1007–1011. http://dx.doi.org/10.1097/00043764-199610000-00010

Head, J., Stansfeld, S. A., & Siegrist, J. (2004). The psychosocial work environment and alcohol dependence: A prospective study. *Occupational and Environmental Medicine, 61,* 219–224. http://dx.doi.org/10.1136/oem.2002.005256

Henning, R., Warren, N., Robertson, M., Faghri, P., Cherniack, M., & the CPH-NEW Research Team. (2009). Workplace health protection and promotion through participatory ergonomics: An integrated approach. *Public Health Reports, 124*(Suppl. 1), 26–35. http://dx.doi.org/10.1177/00333549091244S104

Hignett, S., Wilson, J. R., & Morris, W. (2005). Finding ergonomic solutions—Participatory approaches. *Occupational Medicine, 55,* 200–207. http://dx.doi.org/10.1093/occmed/kqi084

Horowitz, C. R., Robinson, M., & Seifer, S. (2009). Community-based participatory research from the margin to the mainstream: Are researchers prepared? *Circulation, 119,* 2633–2642. http://dx.doi.org/10.1161/CIRCULATIONAHA.107.729863

Hugentobler, M. K., Israel, B. A., & Schurman, S. J. (1992). An action research approach to workplace health: Integrating methods. *Health Education Quarterly, 19,* 55–76. http://dx.doi.org/10.1177/109019819201900105

Kähönen, K., Näätänen, P., Tolvanen, A., & Salmela-Aro, K. (2012). Development of sense of coherence during two group interventions. *Scandinavian Journal of Psychology, 53,* 523–527. http://dx.doi.org/10.1111/sjop.12020

Landsbergis, P. A., Cahill, J., & Schnall, P. (1999). The impact of lean production and related new systems of work organization on worker health. *Journal of Occupational Health Psychology, 4,* 108–130. http://dx.doi.org/10.1037/1076-8998.4.2.108

Lerman, S. E., Eskin, E., Flower, D. J., George, E. C., Gerson, B., Hartenbaum, N., . . . American College of Occupational and Environmental Medicine Presidential Task Force on Fatigue Risk Management. (2012). Fatigue risk management in the workplace. *Journal of Occupational and Environmental Medicine, 54,* 231–258. http://dx.doi.org/10.1097/JOM.0b013e318247a3b0

Lindström, B., & Eriksson, M. (2009). The salutogenic approach to the making of HiAP/healthy public policy: Illustrated by a case study. *Global Health Promotion, 16,* 17–28. http://dx.doi.org/10.1177/1757975908100747

Minkler, M., & Wallerstein, N. (Eds.). (2011). *Community-based participatory research for health: From process to outcomes.* New York, NY: Wiley and Sons.

National Center on Sleep Disorders Research, National Heart, Lung, and Blood Institute, and National Highway Traffic Safety Administration Expert Panel on Driver Fatigue and Sleepiness. (1998). *Drowsy driving and automobile crashes* (Report No. DOT HS 808 707). Washington, DC: U.S. Department of Health & Human Services. Retrieved from https://www.nhtsa.gov/staticfiles/nti/pdf/808707.pdf

National Labor Relations Act, 29 U.S.C., § 151-169 (1935). Retrieved from https://www.nlrb.gov/resources/national-labor-relations-act-nlra

Nielsen, K. (2013). How can we make organizational interventions work? Employees and line managers as actively crafting interventions. *Human Relations, 66,* 1029–1050. http://dx.doi.org/10.1177/0018726713477164

Nielsen, K., & Abildgaard, J. S. (2013). Organizational interventions: A research-based framework for the evaluation of both process and effects. *Work and Stress, 27,* 278–297. http://dx.doi.org/10.1080/02678373.2013.812358

Nobrega, S., Kernan, L., Plaku-Alakbarova, B., Robertson, M., Warren, N., Henning, R., & the CPH-NEW Research Team. (2017). Field tests of a participatory ergonomics toolkit for Total Worker Health. *Applied Ergonomics, 60,* 366–379. http://dx.doi.org/10.1016/j.apergo.2016.12.007

Punnett, L., Warren, N., Henning, R., Nobrega, S., Cherniack, M., & the CPH-NEW Research Team. (2013). Participatory ergonomics as a model for integrated programs to prevent chronic disease. *Journal of Occupational and Environmental Medicine, 55*(Suppl.), S19–S24. http://dx.doi.org/10.1097/JOM.0000000000000040

Rinehart, J. (1984). Appropriating workers' knowledge: Quality control circles at a General Motors plant. *Studies in Political Economy, 14,* 75–97. http://dx.doi.org/10.1080/19187033.1984.11675633

Ringsberg, K. C., & Borup, I. (2011). The role of health promotion in the transition of the Nordic welfare states. *Scandinavian Journal of Public Health, 39*(6, Suppl.), 4–5. http://dx.doi.org/10.1177/1403494810395841

Robertson, M., Henning, R., Warren, N., Nobrega, S., & Dove-Steinkamp, M. (2015). Participatory design of integrated safety and health interventions in the workplace: A case study using the Intervention Design and Analysis Scorecard (IDEAS) Tool. *International Journal of Human Factors and Ergonomics, 3,* 303–326. http://dx.doi.org/10.1504/IJHFE.2015.073008

Smith, M. J. (1994). Employee participation and preventing occupational diseases caused by new technologies. In G. E. Bradley & H. W. Hendrick (Eds.), *Human factors in organizational design and management I* (pp. 719–724). Amsterdam, the Netherlands: Elsevier.

Spinaris, C. G., Denhof, M. D., & Kellaway, J. A. (2012). *Posttraumatic stress disorder in United States corrections professionals: Prevalence and impact on health and functioning.* Retrieved from the Desert Waters Correctional Outreach website: http://desertwaters.com/wp-content/uploads/2013/09/PTSD_Prev_in_Corrections_09-03-131.pdf

Stack, S. J., & Tsoudis, O. (1997). Suicide risk among correctional officers: A logistic regression analysis. *Archives of Suicide Research, 3,* 183–186. http://dx.doi.org/10.1080/13811119708258270

University of Massachusetts Lowell. (n.d.). *Healthy Workplace Participatory Program.* Retrieved from http://www.uml.edu/Research/CPH-NEW/Healthy-Work-Participatory-Program

Vegso, S., Cantley, L., Slade, M., Taiwo, O., Sircar, K., Rabinowitz, P., . . . Cullen, M. R. (2007). Extended work hours and risk of acute occupational injury: A case-crossover study of workers in manufacturing. *American Journal of Industrial Medicine, 50,* 597–603. http://dx.doi.org/10.1002/ajim.20486

Virtanen, M., Ferrie, J. E., Singh-Manoux, A., Shipley, M. J., Vahtera, J., Marmot, M. G., & Kivimäki, M. (2010). Overtime work and incident coronary heart disease: The Whitehall II prospective cohort study. *European Heart Journal, 31,* 1737–1744. http://dx.doi.org/10.1093/eurheartj/ehq124

Virtanen, M., Stansfeld, S. A., Fuhrer, R., Ferrie, J. E., & Kivimäki, M. (2012). Overtime work as a predictor of major depressive episode: A 5-year follow-up of the Whitehall II study. *PLoS ONE, 7,* e30719. http://dx.doi.org/10.1371/journal.pone.0030719

von Thiele Schwarz, U., Augustsson, H., Hasson, H., & Stenfors-Hayes, T. (2015). Promoting employee health by integrating health protection, health promotion, and continuous improvement: A longitudinal quasi-experimental intervention study. *Journal of Occupational and Environmental Medicine, 57,* 217–225. http://dx.doi.org/10.1097/JOM.0000000000000344

Wagstaff, A. S., & Sigstad Lie, J. A. (2011). Shift and night work and long working hours—A systematic review of safety implications. *Scandinavian Journal of Work, Environment & Health, 37,* 173–185. http://dx.doi.org/10.5271/sjweh.3146

Yen, L., Edington, M. P., McDonald, T., Hirschland, D., & Edington, D. W. (2001). Changes in health risks among the participants in the United Auto Workers—General Motors LifeSteps Health Promotion Program. *American Journal of Health Promotion, 16,* 7–15. http://dx.doi.org/10.4278/0890-1171-16.1.7

Zhang, Y., Flum, M., Kotejoshyer, R., Fleishman, J., Henning, R., & Punnett, L. (2016). Workplace participatory occupational health/health promotion program: Facilitators and barriers observed in three nursing homes. *Journal of Gerontological Nursing, 42*(6), 34–42. http://dx.doi.org/10.3928/00989134-20160308-03

Zhang, Y., Flum, M., Nobrega, S., Blais, L., Qamili, S., & Punnett, L. (2011). Work organization and health issues in long-term care centers: Comparison of perceptions between caregivers and management. *Journal of Gerontological Nursing, 37,* 32–40. http://dx.doi.org/10.3928/00989134-20110106-01

Zhang, Y., Flum, M., West, C., & Punnett, L. (2015). Assessing organizational readiness for a participatory occupational health/health promotion intervention in skilled nursing facilities. *Health Promotion Practice, 16,* 724–732. http://dx.doi.org/10.1177/1524839915573945

II

ORGANIZATIONAL APPROACHES TO *TOTAL WORKER HEALTH*® INTERVENTIONS

7

Occupational Safety, Health, and Well-Being Programs in Small Midwest Enterprises

Shelly Campo, Kevin M. Kelly, and Diane S. Rohlman

Many researchers now recognize that aspects of the workplace (scheduling, shift work, physically demanding work, chemical exposures) not only increase the risk of injury and illness but also impact health behaviors (smoking, physical activity) and health outcomes (sleep disorders and fatigue, obesity, musculoskeletal disorders; Zhang, Flum, West, & Punnett, 2015). In turn, ill health and chronic conditions can impact performance at work, increasing risk for injury, absenteeism, and reduced productivity (Goetzel et al., 2004). Programs that expand the traditional occupational safety and health focus of protecting workers from work-specific safety and health hazards to include the promotion of health and well-being have been shown to be more effective than programs addressing these separately (Anger et al., 2015; Sorensen et al., 2013). The National Institute for Occupational Safety and Health's (NIOSH's) *Total Worker Health®* approach, defined as policies, programs, and practices that integrate protection from work-related safety and health hazards with promotion of injury and illness prevention efforts to advance worker well-being, specifically meets this need (NIOSH, n.d.). Understanding employers' safety and health prevention practices is a necessary step to prioritize interventions. This chapter reports on a survey of employers' current practices in the Midwest and compares the results to a

We thank Dr. James Merchant. This research was supported by Centers for Disease Control and Prevention/National Institute for Occupational Safety and Health Cooperative Agreement No. U19OH008858 to the Healthier Workforce Center.

http://dx.doi.org/10.1037/0000149-008
Total Worker Health, H. L. Hudson, J. A. S. Nigam, S. L. Sauter, L. C. Chosewood, A. L. Schill, and J. Howard (Editors)
Copyright © 2019 by the American Psychological Association. All rights reserved.

single state survey conducted several years before that also examined work-place programs to determine changes in the adoption of programs, policies, and practices.

WORKFORCE HEALTH STATUS IN THE U.S. MIDWESTERN STATES

There is a critical need for *Total Worker Health* (TWH) programs in the Midwest. The states in this region (Federal Region VII: Iowa, Kansas, Nebraska, and Missouri) suffer disproportionately from higher burdens of occupational injury and illness, as well as high rates of unhealthy behaviors compared to other regions of the country. Together, these four states consistently show alarmingly high rates of occupational fatalities (ranging from 4.2 to 6.0 per 100,000 workers), well exceeding the national rate of 3.8 per 100,000 workers in 2014 (United Health Foundation, 2015). Major occupations within the region include construction and agriculture, two of the most hazardous employment sectors. These industries also include many small employers.

In addition, smoking, binge drinking, and obesity are at higher rates than national averages (Hymel et al., 2011; United Health Foundation, 2015). Missouri is one of 10 states with the highest tobacco use. Iowa and Nebraska both have adult binge drinking rates exceeding 20% (Centers for Disease Control and Prevention [CDC], 2015), fewer than 20% of adults in this region meet physical activity guidelines, and all four states have higher-than-national-average obesity rates (CDC, 2014). Moreover, this region is predominantly rural, based on U.S. Department of Agriculture classifications. Rural populations have significant health disparities, including increasing gaps in life expectancy (Singh & Siahpush, 2014). For example, a survey conducted of Iowa workers in 2010 found that self-reported general health status for rural employees was poorer than their urban counterparts (Merchant, Kelly, Burmeister, & Lozier, 2014). At the same time, out-of-pocket expenses and employee contributions to monthly health care premiums are higher for rural employees compared with urban employees (Merchant et al., 2014). Employers in the Midwest need these TWH programs, practices, and policies to address the health and safety needs of the region.

Injuries and illnesses, along with chronic diseases, exert an enormous burden on society in terms of human suffering, disability, and years of life lost, as well as financial cost. Leigh (2011) estimated that in 2007 the total medical costs from all fatal and nonfatal occupational injuries and illnesses in the United States were $250 billion in both direct and indirect costs. Furthermore, injured workers have lower income and wages than they would if the injury had not occurred (Seabury et al., 2014). Occupational injuries and illnesses remain a public health threat to the workforce and a major threat to the economy (Bureau of Labor Statistics, 2015). The high rates of injury, unhealthy behavior, and financial costs indicate that there is a significant burden in the region and a need to develop, evaluate, and implement TWH programs to reduce these burdens.

TWH NEEDS IN SMALL BUSINESSES

Most workers are employed in small businesses (Bowen, Morara, & Mureithi, 2009). These organizations typically do not have programs addressing worker health promotion (Pronk, 2013). In addition, occupational injury and illness rates are higher among small businesses (Cunningham, Sinclair, & Schulte, 2014). Although smaller employers are typically cognizant of the traditional hazards in the workplace that put workers at risk of injury or illness (e.g., chemical exposure, repetitive motion, machinery), they often fail to consider the impact of the work environment or organization on long-term health outcomes or lifestyle behaviors (e.g., obesity, cardiovascular disease, loss of sleep; Linnan et al., 2008). In addition, small firms are more financially precarious (Antonsson, 1997; Lamm, 1997) and have owners with multiple responsibilities, including the safety and health of employees, despite a lack of expertise (Cahalin et al., 2015; Champoux & Brun, 2003). As a result, smaller employers may use less effective methods of hazard control (Antonsson, 1997; Gardner, Cross, Fonteyn, Carlopio, & Shikdar, 1999) and have fewer occupational safety and health programs compared to their larger counterparts (Linnan et al., 2008). In addition, employees working for small enterprises in the Midwest pay more for health care than employees who work for larger enterprises. Their employers respond to premium increases by raising deductible levels and copays, therefore increasing the burden on the workforce (Merchant et al., 2014). Finally, even though evidence supports the benefits of integrated programs, very little evidence exists for its benefits to small employers (Pronk, 2013).

Integration of safety and health activities in small enterprises may actually be quite different from integration of safety and health activities in larger enterprises. For example, the safety and health activities of microbusinesses (i.e., fewer than 10 employees) are likely to be integrated by default because an individual employee is likely to have several roles and often these roles are overlapping with other employees. The CEO of a small business may also be the safety officer, as well as manage employee benefits and offer wellness programs. Consequently, current measures of integration that specifically ask about people working together on committees or pooling resources (Sorensen et al., 2013; Williams et al., 2016) may not be appropriate in a smaller setting, where integration may occur by default and without any intention to improve safety and health outcomes.

IOWA STATEWIDE SURVEY AND CASE STUDIES OF SMALL EMPLOYERS

Historically, Iowa's occupational fatality rates have exceeded national averages (U.S. Department of Labor, Bureau of Labor Statistics, 2016), demonstrating a need to investigate the health and safety programs among Iowa employers. The current study builds upon work previously conducted by the Healthier Workforce Center of the Midwest. Statewide surveys and focus groups of Iowa employers (Merchant et al., 2014; Merchant, Lind, Kelly, & Hall, 2013) identi-fied the health and safety practices and needs of workplaces and examined their burden on employers and employees and the corresponding impact on rising health care costs; productivity; and, most important, worker health and well-being.

These surveys and focus groups were based on the Institute of Medicine's (IOM's) employee total health management model (henceforth IOM model), which describes the components of a comprehensive approach to employee health, making the case that organizational safety and health programs, poli-cies, and practices must be integrated to be effective and sustainable. The IOM model includes components such as occupational and environmental health, disease and case management, absence management, behavioral health, health advocacy, primary care centers, health insurance, and wellness (IOM, 2005). In 2013, Merchant et al. translated the IOM model into a 12-item questionnaire to conduct a statewide survey among employers of all sizes and to provide esti-mates of the adoption of IOM components among these employers. Data were collected from 1,206 employers through web-based questionnaires with a tele-phone follow-up. Of these employers, 1,115 employed up to 250 employees, representing all major employment sectors. More than half were located in rural counties, and 55% of companies had nine or fewer employees. Many more components were adopted by employers with 50 or more employees.

The most common components adopted by employers included workers' compensation insurance, an occupational safety and health program, and the provision of health or medical information at the worksite. It is not surprising that workers' compensation was most frequently implemented, because Iowa requires employers to purchase workers' compensation insurance unless they are self-insured or receive an exemption. Fewer employers offer additional health promotion initiatives, including chronic disease management, behav-ioral health or wellness programs, and health screenings/health risk assess-ments. In addition, the smaller the business, the less likely they will offer these components.

These findings were echoed during a series of case studies subsequently conducted with small Midwest employers (Rohlman, Campo, Hall, Robinson, & Kelly, 2018). Qualitative findings indicated that small employers, although emotionally invested in the health and safety of their workers, are limited by small budgets, time, and expertise to implement a TWH program. For the TWH approach to be adopted in an organization, NIOSH identified four key areas needed. The NIOSH (2008) Essential Elements of Effective Workplace Programs and Policies for Improving Worker Health and Wellbeing (henceforth Essential Elements) include four overarching categories: organizational culture and leadership, program design, program implementation and resources, and program evaluation. In small businesses, the inclusion of the Essential Elements categories may be a good indicator of the adoption of TWH approach. In spite of these limitations, employers that had adopted integrated programs, policies, and practices addressed all of the Essential Elements overarching TWH categories (NIOSH, 2008). Program adoption in all of these cases included overwhelming support from upper-level management.

Both the surveys and case studies had limitations, suggesting the need for more research. Although the survey used a large, random statewide sample of predominantly small employers for which little research is available, the generalizability of these results is limited because the focus was on a single state at one specific point in time. Furthermore, the measurement of adoption ("Do you currently offer") or planned adoption ("Do you plan to offer in the next 12 months") for each IOM model component does not capture the full range of adoption stages an employer may be experiencing. The stages of change model provides a broader spectrum of behaviors that are more reflective of the change process (Prochaska & DiClemente, 1983). This widely used model of behavior change suggests that change is a process and not instantaneous in most cases (Prochaska & DiClemente, 1983). The model suggests that individuals and organizations move through five stages in their decision making about whether to adopt a new behavior or program: precontemplation, contemplation, preparation, action, and maintenance. In precontemplation, there is no thought given to and no intention to make any changes. In contemplation, thought and motivation for change grow, and there may be an action taken in the next 6 months. In preparation, there is an intention to make a change in the next 30 days, and steps are being taken to implement changes. In action, change has occurred but has yet to become part of regular activities and culture. In maintenance, changes that typically takes 6 months or more have become routinized. The progression is not always linear; as barriers are encountered, the stage may regress. Depending on the stage of change, different messages and information need to be provided (Slater, 1999). For example, an organization in precontemplation would have to learn what the TWH approach is and why they should implement a TWH program or activity, whereas an organization in preparation would need low-cost solutions and easy implementation ideas to facilitate action. There is a difference between an organization that is considering change but is unable to implement because of limited resources and an organization that is actively preparing to implement a change.

In addition, integration of safety and health activities is a focus of the TWH definition and program, and moreover, it is important to explicitly evaluate the degree to which small employers implement the NIOSH (2008) Essential Elements. No effort to date has explicitly asked if employers have heard of the concept of TWH and, if so, how they would define it in order to benchmark the awareness of NIOSH's branding efforts. Finally, the earlier surveys were conducted prior to the implementation of the 2010 Patient Protection and Affordable Care Act (ACA) that has specific provisions for employers to encourage them to more directly address the prevention of illness and injury (U.S. Centers for Medicare & Medicaid Services, 2017), which may have impacted adoption of safety and health programs, policies, and practices in the last several years.

SURVEY OF SMALL EMPLOYERS IN THE MIDWEST

To address the limitations of the previous studies, a regional survey was conducted to assess current levels of adoption and integration among small employers in Federal Region VII (Iowa, Kansas, Missouri, and Nebraska). The aims of the 72-item survey that was designed to expand and replicate the Merchant et al. (2013) survey were as follows:

- Ascertain the degree to which employers are aware of the TWH concept.

- Describe *leadership commitment* to programs addressing safety and wellness (Essential Element Category 1). "Wellness" was used because it is the term used in the IOM and the 2011 TWH definition. Furthermore, it is the term that employers are familiar with and was the term used in the prior Iowa survey (Merchant et al., 2013).

- Evaluate if there is involvement across departments and level of the organization in *designing* safety and wellness policies and programs (Essential Element Category 2).

- Characterize the degree of adoption and/or *implementation* (Stage of Change from precontemplation to maintenance) of safety and wellness programs (Essential Element Category 3).

- Estimate the prevalence of *evaluation* practices across safety and wellness programs (Essential Element Category 4).

Between November 2016 and March 2017, we conducted a mixed mode (web and telephone) survey of small businesses. The randomly stratified sample was selected from Dun & Bradstreet's comprehensive database of employers in the four-state region. Businesses across all industries were eligible to participate. Business size (fewer than 250 employees) and location (state) were the only factors considered during sample selection. Recruitment letters were sent to small businesses inviting them to complete an online survey. Those who did not respond within 6 days were then contacted by telephone. Of the 3,456 businesses contacted by mail, 337 (9.7%) completed the online survey. Follow-up phone calls to nonrespondents resulted in 108 additional businesses agreeing to participate. An initial evaluation of these respondents revealed a number of employers who reported full-time employees in excess of 249, a combination of full-time and part-time or temporary employees fewer than 10, or no full-time employees. Removing those respondents from the sample resulted in 356 organizations (115 in Iowa, 82 in Kansas, 72 in Missouri, and 87 in Nebraska) that completed the survey (75.6% completed online). The number of full-time workers employed by these organizations ranged from two to 245, with a mean of 76.3 (± 54.6) employees, a median of 66, and a mode of 100. Of the respondents, 17% identified themselves as the owner or an executive officer of the business, 34% as a manager, 36% as human resources personnel, 2% as safety officers or personnel, and 11% other positions.

Employers' Awareness of the TWH Program

When asked directly if they had ever heard about the TWH concept, the overwhelming response was "no" (92%). Brand awareness varied a little by state, with the highest recognition in Iowa (9.6%) and Nebraska (8.0%) and the lowest in Kansas (7.3%) and Missouri (5.6%). These results strongly suggest that brand awareness for the TWH concept among small employers in the region remains low; they have never heard of the concept. It is important to note that the two states with the highest brand awareness have had a NIOSH TWH Center of Excellence (Healthier Workforce Center at the University of Iowa) since 2006 and that Nebraska has had a TWH Affiliate organization since 2016 (the Nebraska Safety Council). The centers and affiliates are selected by NIOSH, and part of their charge is to promote the TWH brand.

Leadership Commitment to Safety and Wellness Programs (Essential Element Category 1)

Sixty-four percent of respondents indicated that top management was supportive of safety programs and of wellness programs. Respondents believed that top management was more supportive of safety programs (86.8%) than wellness programs (69.4%). Respondents from Nebraska were most likely to believe that they had leadership support for both wellness (71.3%) and safety (93.1%) programs. Lowest leadership support was reported in Missouri for wellness programs (67.1%) and in Kansas for safety programs (79.3%).

Designing Safety and Wellness Policies and Programs (Essential Element Category 2)

Employee engagement across departments in the design of programs and policies is considered essential for TWH. Integration is demonstrated because about half or more of surveyed businesses include employees across departments and level of the organization in the design and development of safety and wellness programs and policies (see Table 7.1).

Adoption and Implementation of Safety and Wellness Programs (Essential Element Category 3)

Overall, 82.8% of respondents have at least one safety program and 68.2% have at least one wellness program. Less than 10% report having neither a safety nor

TABLE 7.1. Employee Involvement Across Departments and Levels in Design of Programs and Policies

	Iowa %	Kansas %	Missouri %	Nebraska %
Safety programs	67.0	64.6	67.1	70.9
Safety policies	69.9	63.4	80.0	75.0
Wellness programs	44.5	45.7	52.9	55.3
Wellness policies	49.1	49.4	58.0	60.0

a wellness program. Approximately 56% have at least one safety and at least one wellness program (at least one of each). To have integrated programs, employers must have programs addressing both safety and wellness. This indicates that 44% of the small employers in the sample do not have the foundation on which to build a TWH program.

The stage of change of having safety and wellness programs was overwhelmingly bimodal (see Table 7.2). Nearly all employers either were not even thinking about safety or wellness programs or policies (precontemplation) or had been implementing safety or wellness programs and policies for more than 6 months (maintenance). Almost none were contemplating, preparing to adopt (within the next 30 days), or had recently adopted (within 6 months) these programs or policies. In terms of safety, worksite safety programs and disaster preparedness were the most likely to be in the maintenance stage, and ergonomics and industrial hygiene programs were the most likely to be in the precontemplation stage. Workplaces that reported having various safety programs also tended to report that these were required programs in their workplace, including worksite safety programs (61%), industrial hygiene (65%), environmental exposure control (73%), and disaster preparedness (61%). In terms of wellness, behavioral health programs were in the maintenance stage for about half of the respondents, whereas chronic disease programs hovered at about 20%. These results did not vary widely by state.

There were some significant changes in the reporting of safety and wellness program adoption in Iowa from surveys conducted in 2012 (Merchant et al.,

TABLE 7.2. Wellness and Safety Program Adoption by Stage of Change

	Precontemplation %	Contemplation %	Preparation %	Action %	Maintenance %
Wellness program	53.6	4.5	0.3	0	41.6
Behavioral health programs	46.1	1.1	0	2.5	50.3
Chronic disease program	80.7	0.6	0	0.6	18.1
Worksite safety program	21.1	0.9	0.6	9.3	68.1
Disaster preparedness program	25.4	1.4	0	0.3	72.9
Industrial hygiene programs	76.4	0.8	0.6	1.1	21.5
Environmental exposure control program	53.7	0.9	0	1.4	44.0
Ergonomics program	80.8	1.7	0.3	4.5	12.7

TABLE 7.3. Changes in Safety and Wellness Program Adoption in Iowa Between 2011 and 2017

	2012 Survey[a]: % Yes	2017 Survey Iowa Only: % Yes	*p*
Wellness programs	18.4	28.3	< .0136
Chronic disease management program	12.4	8.8	.2813
Behavioral health program	19.6	51.3	< .0001
Occupational safety program	49.3	81.6	< .0001

[a]Data from Merchant, Lind, Kelly, and Hall (2013).

2013) and 2017. These adjustments included significant increases in the rates of adoption in wellness programs, behavioral health programs, and occupational safety programs (see Table 7.3). These changes may be been due to the implementation of the ACA between the two data collections. The ACA has specific provisions for employers to encourage them to more directly address the prevention of illness and injury (U.S. Centers for Medicare & Medicaid Services, 2017).

Evaluation Practices Across Safety and Wellness Programs (Essential Element Category 4)

Overall, we saw varying levels of the use of evaluation metrics, ranging from 23% to 69% (see Table 7.4). The two most frequently used metrics to evaluate wellness programs were health risk assessments (53.6%), which are not recommended for use in businesses with fewer than 50 employees due to confidentiality concerns, and program participation rates (51.9%). In terms of safety, not surprisingly, workplace injury rates were used by more than two thirds of employers. Injury rates may also not be as meaningful for smaller employers. For example, one workplace injury in a microbusiness with fewer than

TABLE 7.4. Evaluation Metrics Used in Safety and Wellness Programs

	Safety %	Wellness %
Formative		
Suggestion box	31.5	34.8
Process		
Participant satisfaction data	26.7	42.1
Program participation rates	28.9	51.9
Participation evaluation data (i.e., contacted, opted out, withdrew)	23.9	32.3
Formative, process, or outcome		
Health care utilization and cost data	29.4	48.1
Workplace injury rates	69.7	49.4
Sick day use and frequency	29.5	39.6
Health risk assessments	31.8	53.6

10 employees would have a very different impact on injury rates compared with a larger employer with 250 employees.

The TWH concept emphasizes the need for integration of safety, health, and well-being components, including the sharing and use of data across organizational units to develop and evaluate programming. We saw evidence of integration among survey respondents, for example, the use of health risk assessments to evaluate safety programs and the use of workplace injury rates to evaluate wellness programs. Considering safety data when designing health programs and health data when designing safety programs can be an indicator that businesses understand that safety, health, and well-being are linked.

DISCUSSION AND FUTURE DIRECTIONS

The current survey data indicate that small enterprises in the Midwest are engaging in some of the NIOSH (2008) Essential Elements categories but not all. In the area of management support, top managers are perceived as supporting both safety and health. However, the actual adoption of safety and health programs and variations among them indicate the need to continue to educate top management about the benefits of adopting new programs.

In Iowa, we saw a significant rise in the reporting of the adoption of programs addressing safety, wellness, and behavioral health in a 6-year period (2011–2017). However, continued change in Iowa and throughout the region is highly unlikely given that almost no employers reported being in the contemplation, preparation, or recent action stage for the adoption of any of the safety or wellness programs. The implication is that for those employers who have not already adopted and are not even considering it (precontemplation), interventions should start with convincing management of the vital need and the benefits of safety and wellness programs, policies, and practices in workplaces to protect worker health and safety and to promote worker well-being. Slater (1999) suggested that message strategies used to persuade audiences in the precontemplation stage need to increase the sense of severity, sense of susceptibility, efficacy of the recommended behavior (in this case, the adoption of the TWH concept), and to focus on the use of exemplars to influence audiences. Examples of this approach were developed by the Healthier Workforce Center of the Midwest in the form of short videos featuring small employers who have adopted integrated programs using the NIOSH (2008) Essential Elements (http://www.hwcmw.org).

For those enterprises that have already adopted programs for more than 6 months (maintenance), different interventions are needed. The TWH approach moves beyond mere adoption of both safety and wellness programs to emphasize the need to integrate these efforts. Some of our adopters may need interventions to encourage new or further integration. Although we found little brand awareness when we asked specifically about "TWH," we did see evidence of integration among some of our respondents in the design, implementation, and evaluation of programs. For example, the use of injury data in the planning of wellness programs and the use of health risk assessment data in the planning of safety programs may indicate that these organizations see the interrelationship of safety and health, which is a foundation of building TWH programs. It is unknown whether this evidence of integration was an intentional effort on the part of employers or an artifact of the size of the employer. Among smaller employers the same organizational members may need to take on responsibility for multiple, qualitatively different prevention activities and that the convergence of these activities within the same individual may account for the coordination among programs.

Although we see a disconnect between TWH awareness and behavior among small businesses, this may not matter. Past behavior is well known to be the largest contributor to future behavior. Among employers already implementing integrated safety and health programs, the focus should be on the reinforcement of continued behavior to ensure maintenance of these activities, particularly as businesses may grow in size and employee roles become more specialized (e.g., an employee's position becomes dedicated to safety). It is important to maintain the integration that has been established and the recognition that this integration is beneficial. For small enterprises, it may be particularly important to emphasize that they are already engaging in a TWH approach and that the TWH concept is not something new.

Recognizing the need for resources and tools for employers to facilitate the implementation of TWH programs, policies, and practices, the NIOSH (2008) Essential Elements were updated in the form of a workbook for employers, *Fundamentals of Total Worker Health® Approaches: Essential Elements for Advancing Worker Safety, Health, and Well-Being* (hereafter TWH Fundamentals; NIOSH, 2016). The TWH Fundamentals include five defining elements. The scope of the first essential element was broadened in the TWH Fundamentals to recognize that support for safety and health needs to occur at all levels, not just top management. The second TWH Fundamental, a new component, requires the need to eliminate or reduce safety or health hazards in the workplace rather than focusing on changing workers' behaviors. The third TWH Fundamental reinforces the need for worker engagement throughout design and implementation. The fourth TWH Fundamental component emphasizes the need to protect the confidentiality and privacy of workers. This is particularly challenging in small workplaces. The final TWH Fundamental component is integration. Unfortunately, although evaluation is discussed in sections of the document, the emphasis on the critical need for evaluation at all stages of implementation has been muted. There is still a need for more specific, quick, and easy-to-use tools for employers to conduct formative, process, and outcome evaluation. Future studies are also needed to assess the effectiveness of this new workbook among employers of all sizes.

CONCLUSION

Although the majority of employers in the United States and in our region consist of small businesses, they have received less attention from occupational safety and health and TWH practitioners. Characterized by higher injury rates;

limited financial resources; and expertise in health protection, health promotion, and worker well-being, these enterprises have greater needs than their larger counterparts. Although we saw evidence that many safety and wellness programs and policies had been adopted, there is clearly room for growth and a need to ascertain whether the adopted programs are effective.

Conveying information to managers, particularly in small businesses, about evidence-based programs is an important component of the NIOSH TWH approach. Unfortunately, information products intended for managers are often merely abbreviated versions of scientific reports, materials developed for larger organizations, or suggestions requiring significant financial investment that leave small businesses at a loss as to how to improve their day-to-day operations and the safety and health of their valued workers. In addition, managers in small businesses are often inundated with information from wellness program vendors who claim to have the programs and expertise to improve employee health and well-being but lack evidence-based findings. This recent study indicates that some small employers are showing signs of adopting elements of the TWH approach but that there is clear need to continue to target this vital audience.

REFERENCES

Anger, W. K., Elliot, D. L., Bodner, T., Olson, R., Rohlman, D. S., Truxillo, D. M., . . . Montgomery, D. (2015). Effectiveness of total worker health interventions. *Journal of Occupational Health Psychology, 20,* 226–247. http://dx.doi.org/10.1037/a0038340

Antonsson, A.-B. (1997). Small companies. In D. Brune, G. Gerhardson, G. W. Crockford, & D. D'Auria (Eds.), *The workplace* (Vol. 2, Pt. 5.3, pp. 466–477). Geneva, Switzerland: International Labour Office.

Bowen, M., Morara, M., & Mureithi, S. (2009). Management of business challenges among small and micro enterprises in Nairobi–Kenya. *KCA Journal of Business Management, 2,* 16–31. http://dx.doi.org/10.4314/kjbm.v2i1.44408

Bureau of Labor Statistics. (2015). *Injuries, illnesses, and fatalities: Customized industry injury and illness rate tool.* Retrieved from http://www.bls.gov/iif/

Cahalin, L. P., Kaminsky, L., Lavie, C. J., Briggs, P., Cahalin, B. L., Myers, J., . . . Arena, R. (2015). Development and implementation of worksite health and wellness programs: A focus on non-communicable disease. *Progress in Cardiovascular Diseases, 58,* 94–101. http://dx.doi.org/10.1016/j.pcad.2015.04.001

Centers for Disease Control and Prevention. (2014). Nutrition, physical activity and obesity: Data, trends and maps, BRFSS. Retrieved from https://nccd.cdc.gov/NPAO_DTM/IndicatorSummary.aspx?category=28&indicator=29

Centers for Disease Control and Prevention. (2015). Prevalence of binge drinking among U.S. adults, 2015. Retrieved from https://www.cdc.gov/alcohol/data-stats.htm

Champoux, D., & Brun, J. P. (2003). Occupational health and safety management in small size enterprises: An overview of the situation and avenues for intervention and research. *Safety Science, 41,* 301–318. http://dx.doi.org/10.1016/S0925-7535(02)00043-7

Cunningham, T. R., Sinclair, R., & Schulte, P. (2014). Better understanding the small business construct to advance research on delivering workplace health and safety. *Small Enterprise Research, 21,* 148–160. http://dx.doi.org/10.1080/13215906.2014.11082084

Gardner, D., Cross, J. A., Fonteyn, P. N., Carlopio, J., & Shikdar, A. (1999). Mechanical equipment injuries in small manufacturing businesses. *Safety Science, 33,* 1–12. http://dx.doi.org/10.1016/S0925-7535(99)00019-3

Goetzel, R. Z., Long, S. R., Ozminkowski, R. J., Hawkins, K., Wang, S., & Lynch, W. (2004). Health, absence, disability, and presenteeism cost estimates of certain physical and mental health conditions affecting U.S. employers. *Journal of Occupational and Environmental Medicine, 46*, 398–412. http://dx.doi.org/10.1097/01.jom.0000121151.40413.bd

Hymel, P. A., Loeppke, R. R., Baase, C. M., Burton, W. N., Hartenbaum, N. P., Hudson, T. W., . . . Larson, P. W. (2011). Workplace health protection and promotion: A new pathway for a healthier—and safer—workforce. *Journal of Occupational and Environmental Medicine, 53*, 695–702. http://dx.doi.org/10.1097/JOM.0b013e31822005d0

Institute of Medicine. (2005). *Integrating employee health: A model program for NASA*. Washington, DC: National Academies Press.

Lamm, F. (1997). Small businesses and OH&S advisors. *Safety Science, 25*, 153–161. http://dx.doi.org/10.1016/S0925-7535(97)00013-1

Leigh, J. P. (2011). Economic burden of occupational injury and illness in the United States. *Milbank Quarterly, 89*, 728–772. http://dx.doi.org/10.1111/j.1468-0009.2011.00648.x

Linnan, L., Bowling, M., Childress, J., Lindsay, G., Blakey, C., Pronk, S., . . . Royall, P. (2008). Results of the 2004 national worksite health promotion survey. *American Journal of Public Health, 98*, 1503–1509. http://dx.doi.org/10.2105/AJPH.2006.100313

Merchant, J. A., Kelly, K. M., Burmeister, L. F., & Lozier, M. (2014). *Iowans speak out on their health: The rural–urban divide*. Iowa City: University of Iowa, College of Public Health. Retrieved from http://www.public-health.uiowa.edu/hwcmw/wp-content/uploads/2014/05/Full-Report-Appendices-7-14-11.pdf

Merchant, J. A., Lind, D. P., Kelly, K. M., & Hall, J. L. (2013). An employee total health management–based survey of Iowa employers. *Journal of Occupational and Environmental Medicine, 55*, S73–S77. http://dx.doi.org/10.1097/JOM.0000000000000045

National Institute for Occupational Safety and Health. (n.d.). *Total Worker Health®*. Retrieved from https://www.cdc.gov/niosh/twh/totalhealth.html

National Institute for Occupational Safety and Health. (2008). *Essential elements of effective workplace programs and policies for improving worker health and wellbeing*. Retrieved from https://www.cdc.gov/niosh/docs/2010-140/pdfs/2010-140.pdf

National Institute for Occupational Safety and Health. (2016). *Fundamentals of Total Worker Health® approaches: Essential elements for advancing worker safety, health, and well-being* (DHHS [NIOSH] Publication No. 2017-112). Washington, DC: U.S. Department of Health and Human Services.

Patient Protection and Affordable Care Act, 42 U.S.C. § 18001 et seq. (2010).

Prochaska, J. O., & DiClemente, C. C. (1983). Stages and processes of self-change of smoking: Toward an integrative model of change. *Journal of Consulting and Clinical Psychology, 51*, 390–395. http://dx.doi.org/10.1037/0022-006X.51.3.390

Pronk, N. P. (2013). Integrated worker health protection and promotion programs: Overview and perspectives on health and economic outcomes. *Journal of Occupational and Environmental Medicine, 55*, S30–S37. http://dx.doi.org/10.1097/JOM.0000000000000031

Rohlman, D. S., Campo, S., Hall, J., Robinson, E. L., & Kelly, K. M. (2018). What could *Total Worker Health* look like in small enterprises. *Annals of Work Exposures and Health, 62*(Suppl. 1), S34–S41. http://dx.doi.org/10.1093/annweh/wxy008

Seabury, S. A., Lakdawalla, D. N., Walter, D., Hayes, J., Gustafson, T., Shrestha, A., & Goldman, D. P. (2014). Patient outcomes and cost effects of Medicaid formulary restrictions on antidepressants. *Forum for Health Economics & Policy, 17*, 153–168. http://dx.doi.org/10.1515/fhep-2014-0016

Singh, G. K., & Siahpush, M. (2014). Widening rural–urban disparities in life expectancy, U.S., 1969–2009. *American Journal of Preventive Medicine, 46*, e19–e29. http://dx.doi.org/10.1016/j.amepre.2013.10.017

Slater, M. D. (1999). Integrating application of media effects, persuasion, and behavior change theories to communication campaigns: A stages-of-change framework. *Health Communication, 11*, 335–354. http://dx.doi.org/10.1207/S15327027HC1104_2

Sorensen, G., McLellan, D., Dennerlein, J. T., Pronk, N. P., Allen, J. D., Boden, L. I., . . . Wagner, G. R. (2013). Integration of health protection and health promotion: Rationale, indicators, and metrics. *Journal of Occupational and Environmental Medicine, 55,* S12. http://dx.doi.org/10.1097/JOM.0000000000000032

United Health Foundation. (2015). United Health Foundation's America's Health Rankings. Retrieved from https://www.americashealthrankings.org/explore/annual/measure/Overall/state/ALL?edition-year=2015

U.S. Centers for Medicare & Medicaid Services. (2017). *How the Affordable Care Act affects small businesses.* Retrieved from https://www.healthcare.gov/small-businesses/health-care-law-and-businesses/how-aca-affects-businesses/

U.S. Department of Labor, Bureau of Labor Statistics. (2016, December 16). *National census of fatal occupational injuries in 2015* (USDL-16-2304) [Press release]. Retrieved from https://www.bls.gov/news.release/archives/cfoi_12162016.pdf

Williams, J. A., Schult, T. M., Nelson, C. C., Cabán-Martinez, A. J., Katz, J. N., Wagner, G. R., . . . McLellan, D. L. (2016). Validation and dimensionality of the integration of health protection and health promotion score: Evidence from the PULSE Small Business and VA Medical Center surveys. *Journal of Occupational and Environmental Medicine, 58,* 499–504. http://dx.doi.org/10.1097/JOM.0000000000000732

Zhang, Y., Flum, M., West, C., & Punnett, L. (2015). Assessing organizational readiness for a participatory occupational health/health promotion intervention in skilled nursing facilities. *Health Promotion Practice, 16,* 724–732. http://dx.doi.org/10.1177/1524839915573945

8

Creating and Sustaining Integrated Prevention Approaches in a Large Health Care Organization

Robert K. McLellan

Large organizations have the resources to build a comprehensive set of programs, policies, and services in an environment that protects and promotes the health, safety, and well-being of their workforce. Thresholds for defining a large business range from 500 to 1,500 employees depending on the industry sector, with other discriminatory criteria that include revenue (All of Small Business, 2014). The primary challenge for the practitioner in these establishments becomes how to create a sustainable *Total Worker Health*® approach in a mature organization with an ingrained culture that has treated occupational and personal health and safety as separate concerns. Success depends on committed leadership with a clear, shared vision in a supportive culture aligned with the mission and goals of the business.

With reference to relevant literature, this chapter portrays the experience of Dartmouth-Hitchcock (D-H), an academic medical center, as a model for creating a comprehensive and effective *Total Worker Health* (TWH) program in a large organization. As used in this context, a *TWH practitioner* refers to the person that led this initiative, which in this case was an occupational physician in charge of employee health. However, professionals with other backgrounds relevant to employee health, safety, and well-being may well serve this role so long as they are grounded in the key elements of an effective TWH program as outlined by the National Institute for Occupational Safety and Health (NIOSH; 2016a):

- Demonstrate leadership commitment to worker safety and health at all levels of the organization.

http://dx.doi.org/10.1037/0000149-009
Total Worker Health, H. L. Hudson, J. A. S. Nigam, S. L. Sauter, L. C. Chosewood, A. L. Schill, and J. Howard (Editors)
Copyright © 2019 by the American Psychological Association. All rights reserved.

- Design work to eliminate or reduce safety and health hazards and promote worker well-being.
- Promote and support worker engagement throughout program design and implementation.
- Ensure confidentiality and privacy of workers.
- Integrate relevant systems to advance worker well-being.

The TWH practitioner's overall function is to embed a TWH approach in organizational operations and strategies to advance worker well-being and thereby promote business success.

The chapter begins with a consideration of how the culture of the organization and its mission, vision, and values shape the focus and sustainability of a TWH program. The next section introduces an approach to building and integrating a team with a common vision and measurable goals. The chapter then explores employee engagement and the creation of a supportive environment along with a suite of programs and services to achieve TWH goals. After a discussion of data collection and program evaluation and improvement, the chapter concludes with a review of obstacles encountered in developing the program.

ORGANIZATIONAL CULTURE: WHAT MATTERS?

Organizations exist for a purpose. They have a vision, mission, and goals with annual operating plans that in large businesses align with a formally constructed strategy. Creating a *new* approach to advancing the health, safety, and well-being of the workforce requires organizational change. The TWH practitioner's first role, then, is as an anthropologist. What matters to the leaders and staff of the organization? What are the shared beliefs and values that underlie the operations, programs, and policies of the employer? What priority does the organization currently place on health and safety?

D-H is a health system with more than 9,000 employees anchored by an academic campus in New Hampshire, with multiple outpatient clinics and affiliated hospitals throughout New Hampshire and Vermont (D-H, 2017a). With reference to NIOSH's document "Essential Elements of Effective Workplace Programs and Policies for Improving Worker Health and Well-Being," the author interviewed key informants about D-H's culture (NIOSH, 2008). This process, when combined with an employee survey, created a picture of the organization's health and safety culture and its programmatic strengths and gaps. Although there was consensus on the overall mission, vision, and values of the organization, respondents varied widely in reports of how well they felt that the institution had supported the health, safety, and well-being of their work group.

BUILDING SUSTAINABILITY

Although a senior leader may champion the launch of a TWH program, the program cannot survive dependent on a leader, a fad, or temporary budget opportunities. To endure, the approach must become more than a program;

it must align with the vision and mission of the organization and be embedded in its operational plan as a strategy for business success. Accordingly, the vision and mission developed for the TWH program at D-H as outlined next telegraphs that its work helps meet the institution's goals by defining its workforce as a population to be served, substituting "workforce" for population in the D-H vision and mission statement.

Vision: Achieve the healthiest workforce possible.

Mission: Create an engaging culture to advance workforce health, safety, and well-being through research, education, clinical practice, and community partnership.

Senior leaders quickly grasped that if D-H was to improve the health of populations, there was no better place to start than with its workforce. As well, D-H, like many businesses, had struggled with health care costs rising more rapidly than inflation. As a business imperative, D-H leadership recognized the need to approach the health of its workforce in a more intentional manner.

CREATING A TEAM AND ALIGNING EFFORT

Named Live Well/Work Well (LWWW) to reflect its comprehensive and integrated approach, the program created a new organizational structure that brought together all employer-owned employee health and safety services and personnel under one umbrella, with one budget and reporting structure. These personnel included occupational and primary care professionals (physicians, associate providers, nurses, psychologists, occupational therapist, safety and industrial hygiene personnel, social workers, care coordinators, health coaches, and administrative staff). This approach may not be feasible or even desirable for all businesses. In the end, the organizational chart is less important than creating a set of integrated tactics to achieve a common set of goals.

Creating a multidisciplinary group is not sufficient to build a team that provides integrated services. LWWW leadership presented managers of existing programs (Occupational Medicine, Environmental Health and Safety, Employee Assistance Program, Workability, Employee Primary Care, Care Coordination, Health Improvement Program) with emerging evidence of effective synergies created through TWH strategies (Anger et al., 2015). Team building proceeded with presentations to teach all LWWW staff the vocabulary and activities of each discipline. Next, LWWW leadership introduced employee and organizational issues that challenged the different groups to consider how they could collaborate to bring integrated solutions. Later, the staff presented scenarios for which they had worked together to address employee or organizational concerns. LWWW now creates its annual operating plan with overarching goals and the expectation that each discipline will develop tactics collectively to achieve them.

LWWW established a steering committee composed of the managers of each of the disciplines within LWWW to facilitate collaborative decision-making. Leadership then combined the existing separate safety, wellness, and environmental sustainability committees in a new group named Partners in Health,

Environment, Wellness and Safety. This new committee included staff outside of LWWW such as representatives of high occupational risk departments, the environmental sustainability program, and institutional communications. Partners in Health, Environment, Wellness and Safety seeks to identify and support integrated approaches to solve recurrent occupational health and safety problems through a participative process. Another committee was established to incorporate decision-making about benefit design and health plan management decisions with LWWW operations.

SETTING MEASURABLE GOALS

To create a sustainable and effective TWH initiative, leadership should set measurable, consensual goals at the outset. Program developers must define effectiveness in ways that meet the expectations of its stakeholders. Often, business leaders expect a favorable return on investment (ROI) when initiating new programs or purchasing new equipment. When ROI considerations are paramount in decisions about the initial or continued investment in a TWH program, stakeholders often look for the economic returns to be greater than, or at least "worth," the investment. However, conducting a formal ROI analysis of TWH programs requires considerable expertise and data collection beyond the capacity of most employers (Goetzel et al., 2014). For many employers, a value on investment analysis might be a more practical and meaningful tool. A value on investment analysis asks the question of how much the organization is willing to invest to achieve a particular nonfinancial goal. For example, some employers may more highly value qualitative assessments such as how well the program aligns with its mission, enhances its reputation, and promotes employee engagement and loyalty (Abraham & White, 2017).

The launch of LWWW committed D-H to a journey toward the healthiest, safest, and highest performing workforce possible, but how would success be measured? LWWW sets annual injury reduction targets for Occupational Safety and Health Administration (OSHA) incident rates and workers' compensation claims to mark progress toward a vision of zero harm. The program also seeks opportunities for preventive interventions by tracking leading indicators, such as nonrecordable reports of injury, near misses, and hazardous conditions. LWWW monitors personal health status with biometrics, lifestyle risks, disease burden, care gaps, and cost. However, the World Health Organization (2006) defined *health* as "not merely the absence of disease and infirmity" (p. 1) This broader concept of health extends to employee well-being that may be a major determinant of productivity and engagement, arguably more important to employers than ideal biometrics (Schulte et al., 2015). Well-being brings into focus the social determinants of health such as economic and job security, meaningful work, justice, equity and adequate resources, and time to perform work. In alignment with this more comprehensive definition of health, LWWW supports multiple dimensions of individual well-being: lifestyle, intellectual, emotional, occupational, financial, environmental, and spiritual.

TABLE 8.1. Live Well/Work Well Program Evaluation Measures

Health risks	Work environment
Lifestyle risks	Culture of health
Burnout	Job hazards
Perceived health and quality of work life	Access to healthy food and physical activity
Biometrics	Job engagement

Health outcomes	Occupational health and safety
Disease burden	Reports of near misses
Prevention/Disease management care	Reports of injury
Gaps	OSHA recordable injuries and illnesses rate
Social function	OSHA Days Away, Restricted, or Transferred rate
	Workers' compensation claims

Business outcomes	Program delivery
Total group health-care costs	Participation in assessments and programs
Workers' compensation costs	Engagement in programs
Disability costs	Program satisfaction
Presenteeism	
Employee turnover	

Note. OSHA – Occupational Safety and Health Administration.

Table 8.1 outlines metrics that D-H currently uses. Several published score-cards assess the extent to which an organization has implemented a TWH approach and advanced the health, safety, and well-being of its employees (Centers for Disease Control and Prevention, 2016; NIOSH, 2016b).

ENGAGING EMPLOYEES

In a recent survey, 58% of employers ranked employee engagement as the biggest obstacle to the success of their health initiatives (Willis Towers Watson, 2010). An organization can generate quick successes with targeted health promotion and protection initiatives, especially when combined with financial incentives (NIOSH, 2016c). Accordingly, many employers turn to financial incentives or disincentives to motivate healthy behaviors or achieve a specific health outcome ("Companies Are Spending," 2015). Without this external motivation, on average only about 20% of employees participate in employer-sponsored health programs (Mattke, Schnyer, & Van Busum, 2012). When D-H provided a $200 incentive in 2010, health risk assessment (HRA) participation rose from 10.5% the previous year to 60.5%. In subsequent years, D-H increased the wellness reward to $300. However, to achieve the full reward, participants were expected to participate in health-promoting activities as well as to complete an HRA. In 2016, rather than providing financial inducements, D-H offered employees free activity trackers and remote medical sensing devices for those with certain chronic diseases to self-manage their health and activity.

Whether financial incentives drive long-term behavioral change or improvement in medical outcomes remains unproven ("Companies Are Spending,"

2015). Although reasonable, well-designed programs can use incentives, and the Affordable Care Act (Patient Protection and Affordable Care Act, 2010) supports their use, many legal and ethical pitfalls exist. Legal constraints have been established, and several lawsuits have alleged that certain incentive programs are discriminatory or invade privacy (Plump & Ketchen, 2016; Regulations Under the American With Disabilities Act, 2016). Moreover, some authors have argued that ROI from incentive programs relies on shifting costs to the sickest and most socioeconomically disadvantaged (Horwitz, Kelly, & DiNardo, 2013). In recognition of these considerations, LWWW emphasizes creating a supportive culture through its programs, services, and environmental interventions as its main strategy to engage employees in advancing health, safety, and well-being.

CREATING WORKING CONDITIONS THAT ADVANCE HEALTH, SAFETY, AND WELL-BEING

As illustrated by the Hierarchy of Controls Applied to NIOSH TWH, employers should prioritize interventions that eliminate hazards and create working conditions supportive of health and safety over efforts to encourage personal safe and healthy behavior (NIOSH, 2016a). As outlined next, LWWW strives to influence many aspects of working conditions to create a culture of health and safety.

Physical Environment

In addition to providing a safe work environment, large organizations can use their facilities and grounds to promote physical activity. Some companies construct elaborate on-site health clubs for its staff. LWWW provides smaller exercise areas throughout its campus and uses attributes of its built and natural environment to encourage physical activity. One LWWW program promotes the use of stairwells rather than elevators through inspirational signage and wall murals (Community Preventive Services Task Force, 2016). Indoor and outdoor self-directed scavenger hunts encourage staff to walk to solve puzzles for small rewards. Mapped inside and outside walks are promoted, and employee gardens provide staff the opportunity to be physically active while growing healthy vegetables they can harvest for their consumption.

Nutritional Environment

Backed by a new nutrition policy, dietary services have increased the nutritional value and quality of the food served in the main cafeteria. The dining room manager replaced unhealthy food choices like trans fats, sugar-sweetened beverages, and fried foods with healthy, locally sourced, and tastefully prepared produce, fish, and healthy grains along with point-of-sale iconography that makes it easy to identify healthy choices. D-H requires vending machine and other on-site food vendors to comply with the organization's nutrition policy.

Communications and the Information Environment

At the outset, program leadership communicated the foundational premise of the TWH approach: The safety and health of a workforce are inextricably linked and profoundly influenced by both the work environment and the employer's programs, policies, and services. The D-H TWH program uses the moniker "Live Well/Work Well" to telegraph the relationship between work and health. To emphasize its alignment with the D-H culture, LWWW adapted iconography and marketing phrasing already used by D-H for communicating its strategy and values. For example, when D-H began a new communications campaign, it asked the community to "imagine a health system that focuses on health, not just health care" (D-H, 2015b). LWWW responded by using similar graphics with the phrase "Imagine a healthy and safe place to work and live."

Product quality underlies the reputation and success of any company. For health care organizations, the primary "product" is high-value (safe and effective at reasonable cost), compassionate health care. Since its launch, LWWW has partnered with the D-H patient safety and experience departments to broadcast the interaction between employee and patient safety. All organizations can emphasize that the well-being of their workforce influences the quality and cost of production and might well determine business and stock market success (Fabius et al., 2016).

Social Environment and the Organization of Work

The sustainability and overall effectiveness of a TWH program depend on top leadership commitment and leadership alignment at all levels (Goetzel et al., 2014; NIOSH, 2008). As evidence of its commitment, D-H leadership communication now incorporates the term "quadruple aim" to emphasize not only the importance of compassionate, high-quality, reasonable-cost care but also the well-being of caregivers (Bodenheimer & Sinsky, 2014). In the words of D-H's chief quality and value officer, George Blike (personal communication, May 24, 2017), "We recognize that before we can provide the highest-quality patient care, we have to assure the safety and well-being of our staff."

Social connection plays a potent role in guiding the health behavior of individuals within a group (Andersson & Christakis, 2016; Christakis & Fowler, 2008). D-H uses group challenges, a network of more than 130 health champions, and social media technology to leverage the influence of social networks to promote healthy behaviors. LWWW has also designed group activities that integrate job training with healthy and safe work. For example, LWWW health coaches and safety personnel worked with the housekeeping department to engage all of its staff in a series of competitive, physically active team games that trained personnel how to perform their job correctly and safely.

Workplace culture can support or undermine employee involvement in health initiatives (Goetzel et al., 2014). A study of the D-H workforce found that the psychosocial attributes of a work group strongly influenced employee participation rates in HRA and biometric screening that varied from 10% to

83% between groups (R. K. McLellan et al., 2009). Work unit characteristics that correlated with employee participation included perceptions of job safety, whether supervisors cared about employees' well-being, pay fairness, comfort expressing a grievance, liking coworkers, and having happy coworkers. Partly in response to these findings, D-H launched a 9-month training program to provide frontline leaders the skills and direction to create a supportive culture of health and safety in their work groups. A Canadian standard for advancing psychological health and safety in the workplace helps guide this initiative (Bureau de Normalization du Québec & CSA Group, 2013). Participants in the training assess their teams in 13 domains that influence psychological safety, including civility/respect, workload management, psychological support, involvement/influence, and recognition/reward. The team then uses a collaborative approach to address those areas where there are opportunities for improvement.

D-H recently adopted an organizational framework to address the professional burnout and emotional distress driven by the organization of health care work and the inherent challenge in caring for humans at times of personal crisis (Swensen & Shanafelt, 2017). Using this framework, LWWW collaborates with other departments to create programming in six major areas: providing participative management training for leaders, designing organizational systems such as work schedules and technology, building social community, removing sources of frustration and inefficiency, reducing preventable patient harm, and supporting health care providers whose patients have suffered adverse events.

D-H has created numerous other policies and procedures shown to foster healthy and safe working conditions (Barbosa et al., 2015; Ducatman & McLellan, 2000). Examples of these policies include a ban on tobacco use on campus, a drug-free workplace, safe patient handling and disruptive patient procedures, and paid family leave (through the short-term disability benefit). Lactation rooms and flexible scheduling permit mothers to breastfeed while working.

Community Environment

Emerging evidence makes a business case for employers to engage in promoting community health (Institute of Medicine, 2015). For example, companies hire employees from their local communities to which they return after work. A healthier and safer community helps support a healthy and safe workforce. In response, large organizations increasingly reach beyond their four walls to cooperate with other businesses and agencies to create healthy communities (Oziransky, Yach, Tsu-Yu, Luterek, & Stevens, 2015). One D-H hospital serves as the backbone of a collaborative that has developed an initiative to create the "Healthiest Community by 2020" (Healthy Monadnock, 2016). As a component of its population health programs, D-H has also created a network of 162 citizen representatives who work with D-H to inspire and advance healthier communities across New Hampshire and Vermont through education, advocacy, and philanthropy (see http://www.partnersforcommunitywellness.org/).

PROVIDING COMPREHENSIVE SERVICES

In addition to creating safe and supportive working conditions, a TWH initiative offers services to address the breadth and interrelatedness of the health and safety needs of a company's workforce. At least one type of wellness program is offered by 98% of firms with 200 or more workers offer (Henry J. Kaiser Family Foundation, Health Educational and Research Trust, 2014). One third of employers (33%) with more than 5,000 employees offer general medical worksite clinics, whereas 16% of employers with 500 to 4,999 employees offer these clinics (Mercer, 2018). Otherwise and for smaller sites, big employers contract with community occupational health providers overseen by corporate medical directors. D-H provides a suite of on-site services that include an occupational health clinic (staffed by physicians, associate providers, and nurses), safety and industrial hygiene, ergonomic consultation, a workability program to prevent and manage work disability, health coaching and programming, and an employee assistance program to manage psychological distress. Some employers add day care, dental care, chiropractic, and rehabilitation therapy. D-H, along with 29% of other large organizations (more than 5,000 employees), includes employee-dedicated primary care in its on- or near-site services to facilitate easy access to care, reduce time away from work, improve outcomes at lower cost, and promote employee satisfaction (Umland, 2015). As well, some employers have fully in-sourced their workers' compensation claims management system to promote the integration of safety professionals, adjusters, and selected medical and nursing providers (Bernacki & Tsai, 2003).

An entire complement of services need not be created in-house. Rather, incorporating community agencies and external vendors along with internal resources becomes part of the overall strategy. Such services often include HRAs, biometric screening, wellness services, engagement surveys, administration of health plan and benefit claim transactions, health clubs, social assistance, and a range of medical services covered by the health plan but not feasible to provide on-site.

COLLECTING AND USING WORKFORCE HEALTH, SAFETY, AND WELL-BEING DATA

D-H gathers data about the health, safety, and well-being of its workforce using five general approaches: observation, administrative data sets, biometric screening, biosensing technology, and questionnaires. Data become useful only when analyzed in ways that inform programming and allow monitoring of the effectiveness of these programs. In contrast to occupational health data, the collection and use of personal health data raise many legal and privacy concerns.

Observation

Safety and industrial hygiene professionals identify occupational hazards through observation and measurement. Examples of occupational safety audit and compliance assessment forms, including the approach used by D-H, can be found in the SafeWell Practice Guidelines (D. McLellan, Harden, Markkanen, & Sorensen, 2012). Several audit tools assess the extent to which the work environment may promote healthy behaviors. Examples of instruments used by LWWW include the Environmental Assessment Tool and Checklist of Health Promotion Environments at Worksites (DeJoy et al., 2008; Oldenburg, Sallis, Harris, & Owen, 2002). Other instruments, like some found in the SafeWell Practice Guidelines, combine hazard identification with an assessment of the health-promoting aspects of the workplace (D. McLellan et al., 2012).

Administrative Data

Several administrative data sets provide descriptive information about the health and safety of the workforce. These include safety metrics (OSHA total recordable incident rate, OSHA "Days Away, Restrictions and Transfers" rate, reports of injury, and near misses), insurance claims (workers' compensation, group health, disability, electronic medical records), and human resource metrics (absenteeism, retention, wages). Personnel software, payroll systems, and time clocks supplemented by manual entry serve as sources for most human resource measures.

Biometric Screening

To obtain information about lifestyle risk factors and to guide their employees toward healthier lifestyles and needed medical care, employers conduct biometric screening, which may include weight, height, waist circumference, blood pressure, and blood tests for lipids and blood sugar. The United States Preventive Services Task Force does not recommend routine annual biometric screening of all adults, though given the prevalence of risk factors in the workplace and workforce turnover, most workers fall within U.S. Preventive Services Task Force periodic screening criteria (American Diabetes Association, 2009; U.S. Preventive Services Task Force, 2017). Nonetheless, annual screening of the entire workforce will not identify new biometric concerns in many employees. As a consequence, D-H has reduced screening frequency to about once every 3 years but has left open the option for interested individuals to obtain more frequent assessment through personal health coaching.

Biosensing Technologies

According to the Health Enhancement Research Organization's 2015 Wearables in Wellness survey, 46% of employers offer fitness trackers as a component of their wellness program with the expectation that they will motivate behavioral change as well as collect aggregate data (Pallarito, 2016). D-H offered its employees a free, but taxable, wearable device. Thirty percent of eligible employees obtained the tool and enrolled in the program. Just 30% of those participants remained actively engaged after the first few months. The cumulative experience of many employers is that partial rather than full subsidization of activity trackers promotes better use, at least for the short run (Pallarito, 2016). Whether wearable technologies promote long-term behavioral change or the achievement of lifestyle goals remains uncertain; in fact, some studies have demonstrated a negative effect (Jakicic et al., 2016).

D-H also offered remote medical sensing devices, such as blood pressure cuffs and electronic scales, to members of its health plan to support medication compliance and monitor disease status measures. A continuously available pool of nurses and health coaches monitored the data and reached out to these patients as needed. When compared with a matched group of D-H health plan members, the chronically ill patients enrolled in this program used $255 less health care per member per month (PMPM), which represented a 36% reduction in the total cost of their care and a 56% reduction in hospital admissions.

Questionnaires

Surveys, focus groups, and personal interviews collect information about health, work culture, and job engagement. Biannually, D-H deploys an engagement survey to all employees to better understand individual worker's perceptions about working conditions in several domains, including supervision, pay and rewards, empowerment, operating efficiency, adequacy and safety of working environment (physical and social), professional development, burnout, and patient care. In 2017, LWWW initiated a separate annual survey on physician burnout that explored drivers and solutions. HRAs serve as a gateway to most employers' health promotion programs. They have evolved beyond a means to gather aggregate health information to link employees with tailored online or telephonic health coaching. Increasingly, HRA vendors gamify their offerings to increase engagement. In 2016, as a trial, LWWW decided to replace the usual 20- to 30-minute annual HRA with an approach that delivered one to two questions to enrolled employees every few days via a text message to their cell phone. Unfortunately, only 21% of these employees answered at least one HRA question delivered in this manner. Based on this poor experience, LWWW has decided to return to a more traditional annual HRA questionnaire.

Data Warehousing and Analysis

Large employers may maintain data warehouses or contract with vendors to store and analyze data. Analysis of these data can reveal correlations between aspects of workforce health, safety, and productivity that can inform effective interventions. D-H maintains a data warehouse that ingests employees' health claims, survey results, biometrics, employee safety metrics, human resource measures, and patient safety (quality) metrics. The D-H Analytics Institute provides monthly reports on these data and offers custom analyses.

Legal and Privacy Concerns

OSHA and state workers' compensation statutes require business establishments to collect and report individuals' occupational illnesses and injuries. However, several national and state laws constrain employers' right to gather and use personal health data. These include the Health Insurance Portability and Accountability Act of 1996, the ADA Amendments Act of 2008, and the Genetic Information Nondiscrimination Act of 2008. LWWW complies with these legal firewalls to protect health information based on the role its personnel serve. For example, an LWWW occupational health clinician performing an employer mandated preplacement examination is acting as an agent of the employer, documents in an occupational health record, and may not access the examinee's personal health record without consent. An LWWW primary care clinician serves as a treating provider and routinely accesses and documents in the personal medical records of the patient being treated. LWWW managers review deidentified HRA and group health claims data, but the LWWW medical director of the health plan acting in a role supporting D-H self-insured health plan operations may view identified personal health claim information. As employers begin to use wearable and even implantable technologies to track employee work and personal behaviors, employees have raised concerns about their privacy beyond that protected by existing law. Nonetheless, in a recent survey, 56% of respondents said that they would use employer-provided wearable technology to improve their well-being at work (PwC, 2015). From an employer's perspective, the collection of activity data, such as poor sleep, also raises the possibility of liability for employee accidents when activity data could potentially have predicted an accident.

EXAMPLES OF INTEGRATED INTERVENTIONS AT THE INDIVIDUAL, TEAM, AND ORGANIZATIONAL LEVELS

Epidemiologic data associate the incidence and severity of workers' compensation claims with chronic disease and health risks (Jinnett, Schwatka, Tenney, Brockbank, & Newman, 2017). The observation that occupational and personal risks interact and cluster in certain job types and work environments serves as a basis for designing many D-H TWH initiatives. (Miranda, Gore, Boyer, Nobrega, & Punnett, 2015; Schulte, Pandalai, Wulsin, & Chun, 2012). The rising prevalence of chronic disease in the workforce and its influence on workability has prompted additional programming to address this interaction of work and health.

Individual-Level Integrated Interventions

LWWW has several approaches to address the bidirectional relationship between work and health for individual employees. To integrate health promotion and disease management with the care of work-related injury, D-H occupational health providers screen employees with occupational injuries for personal risk factors and comorbidities. The clinicians refer workers to LWWW services appropriate to their need. Workers' compensation adjusters servicing D-H claims see pop-up screens about LWWW services on their computers and are encouraged to refer workers as necessary. Another large health care employer, the University of California in Los Angeles, launched a structured health improvement program called Work Strong to lower lifestyle risk in employees with repeated workers compensation claims. Since 2012, those participating in the voluntary lifestyle change program have had 29% lower workers' compensation costs compared with nonparticipants (T. W. Warner, personal communication, July 12, 2016).

Slips, trips, and falls remain among the most common work-related injuries at D-H. Older employees are more likely to have one of these injuries, either at work or home, and with more severe consequences than their younger colleagues (Enix, Flaherty, Sudkamp, & Schulz, 2011). As of 2016, D-H had 1,389 employees older than 60. In response to these data, LWWW built an evidence-based program demonstrated to reduce fall risk to offer proactively to our older employees (Huang, Feng, Li, & Lv, 2017).

Because about 40% of working adults report a chronic health condition that impairs their ability to work, LWWW collaborated with Liberty Mutual's Center for Disability Research to design an intervention to help chronically ill employees cope with work (Shaw et al., 2014). Investigators recruited D-H employees with symptoms of chronic disease for research that provided the intervention group with five 2-hour workshop sessions. The sessions provided chronic illness and pain self-management techniques with a focus on workplace problems commonly encountered by chronically ill workers. Those workers participating in the intervention reported significantly more work engagement than those in the control group (Besen, Tveito, McLellan, & Shaw, 2017).

Team-Level Interventions

Because occupational and personal health risk cluster, surveillance of occupational injury data point to work teams for whom integrated interventions may have the greatest impact. Safety personnel identify high occupational risk departments. If in addition to a poor safety record the work group has another concerning indicator, such as a low culture of health index, low percentile nursing quality, or low percentile patient satisfaction, the group is invited to partner with an LWWW Safety, Wellness Action Team intervention. After reviewing the concerning metrics with the work group leadership, the Safety, Wellness Action Team facilitates a semistructured focus group with representatives of front-line staff to get their ideas about why the team is experiencing extraordinary safety and performance problems. Typically, these sessions identify opportunities for health promotion, psychosocial interventions, and changes in work organization, as well as safety measures. All work unit staff then receive surveys to characterize the local health and safety culture and self-scored tools to assess their personal well-being. Staff is reminded of supportive LWWW resources for individual needs. LWWW personnel then collaborate with work unit staff to design interventions that target identified issues. Interventions usually combine safety initiatives along with other programming such as behavioral health, chaplaincy, health promotion, resiliency building, supervisor training, or environmental interventions.

Organizational-Level Integrated Interventions

Most companies highly value product and service quality. Integrating employee safety and health with organizational quality initiatives can substantially advance TWH efforts. Since the publication of *Crossing the Quality Chasm* and with pressure from accrediting organizations, health systems have competed to improve their quality of care (Committee on Quality of Health Care in America, 2001). D-H, like most health care organizations, has created an extensive infrastructure tasked with patient safety. Leveraging this infrastructure greatly multiplies the resources available to protect employees. In practice, this means that the D-H quality scoreboard now includes employee with patient safety. Every morning, staff gather in a safety huddle to review both patient and employee safety incidents that occurred in the prior 24 hours and devise corrective actions. Employee safety issues discussed include stress, disruptive behavior, and staffing, as well as musculoskeletal injuries or hazards. Resources devoted to investigating the root causes of serious patient events are now used for employee accidents as well. Moreover, when leaders talk about a commitment to "zero patient harm," in the same breath they also pledge "zero employee harm" (G. Blike, personal communication, May 24, 2017). Moreover, D-H has mandated that all employees attend a 4-hour workshop to help promote a culture that draws the connections between employee and patient safety. In brief, building on evidence collected by the Joint Commission (2012), D-H has incorporated the concept that patient experience, safety, and outcomes are inextricably linked with employee health, safety, and well-being.

OSHA (2016) published a monograph that explores the opportunities that the sustainability movement presents for advancing the health and safety of workers. Health Care Without Harm (https://noharm.org/) provides leadership and programming for the health care industry that integrates environmental sustainability with community and workforce health. As a Healthier Hospitals program (http://www.healthierhospitals.org/) participant, D-H commits to meeting specific goals for leaner energy, less waste, safer chemicals, healthier food, and smarter purchasing as part of its effort to "create a sustainable health system, to improve the lives of the people and communities we serve, for generations to come" (D-H, 2015a, p. ii).

EVALUATING RESULTS

The value of employer-sponsored health and safety initiatives begins with the extent to which the program reinforces the vision, mission, values, and business strategy of an organization. LWWW serves as a potent symbol of the D-H commitment to its vision to "achieve the healthiest population possible" (D-H, 2017b). LWWW can proudly point to the regional and national recognition that its employee health program has received for its innovative approach and successes. The program was one of the first TWH Affiliates and has earned several awards, including the American Heart Association's Fit-Friendly Worksite Award and the New Hampshire Governor's Council on Physical Activity and Health Outstanding Achievement Award, and it received recognition by Health Care Without Harm's (2016) Healthy Food in Health Care initiative.

Demonstration of value also depends on quantifiable evidence of effectiveness. By most, but not all criteria, D-H employee safety and workers' compensation experience are exemplary. In the last employee engagement survey, 85% of staff felt that D-H was very good or excellent in protecting their health and safety. Reports of all injuries fell 10% over the last year compared to the prior year. With medical costs contained and a successful workability program, the workers' compensation experience modification rate has been steadily dropping from 0.7 in 2014 to 0.56 in 2016, almost half the rate of like employers. The most current OSHA metrics also document successes. The Days Away, Restrictions, and Transfers rate is 22% of the national rate for hospitals, and the Total Recordable Incident Rate is 60% of the national hospital rate.

Scorecards that document progress toward a healthy work environment have improved over time, earning D-H awards and positive publicity. In addition to making progress in creating a fit-friendly campus, changes in nutritional policies in the cafeteria have led to some very specific remarkable results. For example, after eliminating the sale of sugar-sweetened beverages in the cafeteria, the cafeteria sold 4,754,184 less sugar-sweetened beverage calories, compared with the same 4 months of the prior year.

Over a 3-year period, HRA participants reported a steady improvement in their lifestyle scores (0–100, with 100 being best) with the aggregate summary score rising from 77 to 82. This engaged cohort of employees also experienced a steady decline in its PMPM health claim expenses. Almost 400 health plan members with chronic disease used a vendor's remote medical sensors and experienced a 36% reduction in their total cost of care. Total PMPM health claim costs (employee as subscriber, employer, and administrative expenses) for the entire health plan membership have risen by just 5% over the past 3 years. Over the last year, the total PMPM health claim costs have decreased 3% compared with the 4.07% increase in the national unadjusted health care inflation rate for 2016 (YCharts, 2018).

CHALLENGES

Building a TWH program requires surmounting many challenges. Some are likely to be universal, such as obtaining senior leadership commitment, demonstrating value, building an integrated team, aligning leadership throughout an organization, addressing the differing needs of a diverse workforce, engaging frontline workers in participatory program design, earning the trust of employees that their confidentiality will be protected, and overcoming the inertia for organizational change. Large organizations can present labyrinthine bureaucracies that slow decision-making and program implementation. As well, they frequently have multiple facilities situated far from one another. Particularly problematic for a TWH program is recognizing its scope of authority as it identifies conditions of work that impact health and safety. Although LWWW can advise, management maintains the prerogative over important considerations such as pay, scheduling, and staffing. LWWW periodically needs to revisit the same obstacles as leadership and staff change, and institutional priorities evolve. Each organization will also have hurdles unique to its culture and industry. For example, the D-H workforce is exposed to shift work, long shifts, and emotionally demanding work in a very hazardous industry. Administrative staff not only has safer work than their clinical colleagues, but they also have more flexibility during their workdays to participate in health promotional activities. The ethos of clinicians has been that care for the patient always comes first. Only recently has evidence begun to make the point that employee health and safety provides the necessary foundation for superior patient care. In an era of high levels of professional burnout and increasing concerns about financial sustainability, engaging clinicians who are driven to work ever harder with employer-sponsored programming becomes more challenging.

CONCLUSION

Large organizations usually have a panoply of services, programs, and personnel that can serve as the building blocks for a comprehensive program to advance the health, safety, and well-being of their workforce. However, creating a sustainable, integrated approach to prevention requires alignment with the organization's vision, mission, and goals, embedding the tactics in business operations and addressing the interrelatedness of factors relevant to the health and safety of a company's workforce. At the outset, TWH practitioners should define measurable goals that are valuable to the business and its many stakeholders. Successful methods will include organizational, team-based, and individual integrated interventions. Building a supportive environment and aligning leadership at all levels will more reliably engage employees in achieving organizational goals over the long run than financial incentives and disincentives.

REFERENCES

Abraham, J., & White, K. M. (2017). Tracking the changing landscape of corporate wellness companies. *Health Affairs, 36,* 222–228. http://dx.doi.org/10.1377/hlthaff.2016.1138

The ADA Amendments Act of 2008, Pub. L. No. 110-325, 122 Stat. 3553 (2009).

All of Small Business. (2014). *Summary of size standards by industry.* Retrieved from https://allofsmallbusiness.com/summary-size-standards-industry-sector/

American Diabetes Association. (2009). Diagnosis and classification of diabetes mellitus. *Diabetes Care, 32*(Suppl. 1), S62–S67. http://dx.doi.org/10.2337/dc09-S062

Andersson, M. A., & Christakis, N. A. (2016). Desire for weight loss, weight-related social contact, and body mass outcomes. *Obesity, 24,* 1434–1437. http://dx.doi.org/10.1002/oby.21512

Anger, W. K., Elliot, D. L., Bodner, T., Olson, R., Rohlman, D. S., Truxillo, D. M., . . . Montgomery, D. (2015). Effectiveness of total worker health interventions. *Journal of Occupational Health Psychology, 20,* 226–247. http://dx.doi.org/10.1037/a0038340

Barbosa, C., Bray, J. W., Dowd, W. N., Mills, M. J., Moen, P., Wipfli, B., . . . Kelly, E. L. (2015). Return on investment of a work-family intervention: Evidence from the work, family, and health network. *Journal of Occupational and Environmental Medicine, 57,* 943–951. http://dx.doi.org/10.1097/JOM.0000000000000520

Bernacki, E. J., & Tsai, S. P. (2003). Ten years' experience using an integrated workers' compensation management system to control workers' compensation costs. *Journal of Occupational and Environmental Medicine, 45,* 508–516. http://dx.doi.org/10.1097/01.jom.0000063629.37065.0c

Besen, E., Tveito, T. H., McLellan, R. K., & Shaw, W. S. (2017, June). *Short-term outcomes from the MANAGE AT WORK trial: A self-management group intervention to overcome work-place challenges associated with chronic physical health conditions.* Poster presented at the 12th International Conference on Occupational Stress and Health, Minneapolis, MN.

Bodenheimer, T., & Sinsky, C. (2014). From triple to quadruple aim: Care of the patient requires care of the provider. *Annals of Family Medicine, 12,* 573–576. http://dx.doi.org/10.1370/afm.1713

Bureau de Normalization du Québec, & CSA Group. (2013, January). *Psychological health and safety in the workplace—Prevention, promotion, and guidance to staged implementation* (No. CAN/CSA-Z1003-13/BNQ9700-803/2013). Mississauga, Ontario, Canada: CSA Group.

Centers for Disease Control and Prevention. (2016). HRQOL concepts. Retrieved from https://www.cdc.gov/hrqol/concept.htm

Christakis, N. A., & Fowler, J. H. (2008). The collective dynamics of smoking in a large social network. *New England Journal of Medicine, 358,* 2249–2258. http://dx.doi.org/10.1056/NEJMsa0706154

Committee on Quality of Health Care in America. (2001). *Crossing the quality chasm: A new health system for the 21st century.* Washington, DC: Institute of Medicine, National Academies Press.

Community Preventive Services Task Force. (2016). The guide to community preventive services. Retrieved from http://www.thecommunityguide.org/

Companies are spending more on corporate wellness programs but employees are leaving millions on the table. (2015, March 26). Retrieved from https://www.businesswire.com/news/home/20150326005585/en/Companies-Spending-Corporate-Wellness-Programs-Employees-Leaving

Dartmouth-Hitchcock. (2015a, Fall). *Imagine.* Retrieved from https://www.dartmouth-hitchcock.org/documents/pdf/ImagineMagazine-fall-2015.pdf

Dartmouth-Hitchcock. (2015b). *Your Stay at Dartmouth-Hitchcock* [Patient handbook, p. 4]. Retrieved from https://www.dartmouth-hitchcock.org/documents/pdf/patient_handbook_2015.web.pdf

Dartmouth-Hitchcock. (2017a). *Dartmouth-Hitchcock facts.* Retrieved from http://www.dartmouth-hitchcock.org/about_dh/dh-facts.html

Dartmouth-Hitchcock. (2017b). *Mission, vision, and values.* Retrieved from http://www.dartmouth-hitchcock.org/about_dh/mission_vision_values.html

DeJoy, D. M., Wilson, M. G., Goetzel, R. Z., Ozminkowski, R. J., Wang, S., Baker, K. M., . . . Tully, K. J. (2008). Development of the Environmental Assessment Tool (EAT) to measure organizational physical and social support for worksite obesity prevention programs. *Journal of Occupational and Environmental Medicine, 50,* 126–137. http://dx.doi.org/10.1097/JOM.0b013e318161b42a

Ducatman, A. M., & McLellan, R. K. (2000). Epidemiologic basis for an occupational and environmental policy on environmental tobacco smoke. *Journal of Occupational and Environmental Medicine, 42,* 1137–1141. http://dx.doi.org/10.1097/00043764-200012000-00003

Enix, D., Flaherty, J., Sudkamp, K., & Schulz, J. (2011). Balance problems in the geriatric patient. *Topics in Integrative Health Care, 2*(1).

Fabius, R., Loeppke, R. R., Hohn, T., Fabius, D., Eisenberg, B., Konicki, D. L., & Larson, P. (2016). Tracking the market performance of companies that integrate a culture of health and safety: An assessment of corporate health achievement award applicants. *Journal of Occupational and Environmental Medicine, 58,* 3–8. http://dx.doi.org/10.1097/JOM.0000000000000638

Genetic Information Nondiscrimination Act of 2008, Pub. L. No. 110-233, 122 Stat. 881 (2008).

Goetzel, R. Z., Henke, R. M., Tabrizi, M., Pelletier, K. R., Loeppke, R., Ballard, D. W., . . . Metz, R. D. (2014). Do workplace health promotion (wellness) programs work? *Journal of Occupational and Environmental Medicine, 56,* 927–934. http://dx.doi.org/10.1097/JOM.0000000000000276

Health Care Without Harm. (2016). *Healthy food in health care.* Retrieved from https://noharm-uscanada.org/healthyfoodinhealthcare

Health Insurance Portability and Accountability Act of 1996, Pub. L. No. 104-91, 110 Stat. 1936 (1996).

Healthy Monadnock. (2016). *Vision and goals.* Retrieved from https://healthymonadnock.org/mission-statement/

Henry J. Kaiser Family Foundation, Health Educational and Research Trust. (2014). *2014 employer health benefits survey.* Retrieved from http://kff.org/health-costs/report/2014-employer-health-benefits-survey/

Horwitz, J. R., Kelly, B. D., & DiNardo, J. E. (2013). Wellness incentives in the workplace: Cost savings through cost shifting to unhealthy workers. *Health Affairs, 32,* 468–476. http://dx.doi.org/10.1377/hlthaff.2012.0683

Huang, Z. G., Feng, Y. H., Li, Y. H., & Lv, C. S. (2017). Systematic review and meta-analysis: Tai Chi for preventing falls in older adults. *BMJ Open, 7*(2), e013661-2016-013661. http://dx.doi.org/10.1136/bmjopen-2016-013661

Institute of Medicine. (2015). *Business engagement in building healthy communities: Workshop summary.* Washington, DC: National Academies Press. http://dx.doi.org/10.17226/19003

Jakicic, J. M., Davis, K. K., Rogers, R. J., King, W. C., Marcus, M. D., Helsel, D., . . . Belle, S. H. (2016). Effect of wearable technology combined with a lifestyle intervention on long-term weight loss: The IDEA randomized clinical trial. *JAMA, 316,* 1161–1171. http://dx.doi.org/10.1001/jama.2016.12858

Jinnett, K., Schwatka, N., Tenney, L., Brockbank, C. V., & Newman, L. S. (2017). Chronic conditions, workplace safety, and job demands contribute to absenteeism and job performance. *Health Affairs, 36,* 237–244. http://dx.doi.org/10.1377/hlthaff.2016.1151

The Joint Commission. (2012). *Improving patient and worker safety: Opportunities for synergy, collaboration, and innovation.* Oakbrook Terrace, IL: Author.

Mattke, S., Schnyer, C., & Van Busum, K. R. (2012). A review of the U.S. workplace wellness market. *RAND Health Quarterly, 2*(4), 7. Retrieved from https://www.rand.org/pubs/periodicals/health-quarterly/issues/v2/n4/07.html

McLellan, D., Harden, E., Markkanen, P., & Sorensen, G. (2012). *Safewell practice guidelines: An integrated approach to worker health* (Ver. 2.0). Boston, MA: Harvard School of Public Health Centre for Work Health and Well-Being.

McLellan, R. K., Mackenzie, T. A., Tilton, P. A., Dietrich, A. J., Comi, R. J., & Feng, Y. Y. (2009). Impact of workplace sociocultural attributes on participation in health assessments. *Journal of Occupational and Environmental Medicine, 51,* 797–803. http://dx.doi.org/10.1097/JOM.0b013e3181a4b9e8

Mercer. (2018). *2018 Worksite Medical Clinics Survey*. Retrieved from https://www.mercer.us/what-we-do/health-and-benefits/strategy-and-transformation/mercer-worksite-clinic-survey.html

Miranda, H., Gore, R. J., Boyer, J., Nobrega, S., & Punnett, L. (2015). Health behaviors and overweigh in nursing home employees: Contributions of workplace stressors and implications for worksite health promotion. *Scientific World Journal, 2015*, 915359.

National Institute for Occupational Safety and Health. (2008). *Essential elements of effective workplace programs and policies for improving workplace health and wellbeing* (DHHS [NIOSH] Publication No. 2010-140). Washington, DC: U.S. Department of Health and Human Services. Retrieved from https://www.cdc.gov/niosh/docs/2010-140/pdfs/2010-140.pdf

National Institute for Occupational Safety and Health. (2016a). *Fundamentals of Total Worker Health® approaches: Essential elements for advancing worker safety, health, and well-being* (DHHS [NIOSH] Publication No. 2017-112). Washington, DC: U.S. Department of Health and Human Services. Retrieved from https://www.cdc.gov/niosh/docs/2017-112/pdfs/2017_112.pdf

National Institute for Occupational Safety and Health. (2016b). *Total worker health: Planning, assessment, and evaluation resources*. Retrieved from https://www.cdc.gov/niosh/twh/tools.html

National Institute for Occupational Safety and Health. (2016c). *Total worker health: Simple steps to get started*. Retrieved from https://www.cdc.gov/niosh/twh/steps.html

Occupational Safety and Health Administration. (2016, December). *Sustainability in the workplace: A new approach for advancing worker safety and health* (OSHA 3409). Retrieved from https://www.osha.gov/sustainability/docs/OSHA_sustainability_paper.pdf

Oldenburg, B., Sallis, J. F., Harris, D., & Owen, N. (2002). Checklist of Health Promotion Environments at Worksites (CHEW): Development and measurement characteristics. *American Journal of Health Promotion, 16*(5), 288–299. http://dx.doi.org/10.4278/0890-1171-16.5.288

Oziransky, V., Yach, D., Tsu-Yu, T., Luterek, A., & Stevens, D. (2015). *Beyond the four walls: Why community is critical to workforce health*. Retrieved from the Robert Wood Johnson Foundation website: https://www.rwjf.org/en/library/research/2015/07/beyond-the-four-walls--why-community-is-critical-to-workforce-he.html

Pallarito, K. (2016). *Wearables for wellness fit right in*. Retrieved from http://www.businessinsurance.com/article/00010101/NEWS03/305229995/Wearables-for-wellness-fit-right-in

Patient Protection and Affordable Care Act, 42 U.S.C. § 18001 et seq. (2010).

Plump, C. M., & Ketchen, D. J., Jr. (2016). New legal pitfalls surrounding wellness programs and their implications for financial risk. *Business Horizons, 59*, 267–272. http://dx.doi.org/10.1016/j.bushor.2016.02.002

PwC. (2015). *Half of people would use a workplace smartwatch—PwC research* [Press release]. Retrieved from http://pwc.blogs.com/press_room/2015/04/half-of-people-would-use-a-workplace-smartwatch-pwc-research.html

Regulations Under the Americans With Disabilities Act, 29 C.F.R. § 1630 (2016).

Schulte, P. A., Guerin, R. J., Schill, A. L., Bhattacharya, A., Cunningham, T. R., Pandalai, S. P., . . . Stephenson, C. M. (2015). Considerations for incorporating "well-being" in public policy for workers and workplaces. *American Journal of Public Health, 105*, e31–e44. http://dx.doi.org/10.2105/AJPH.2015.302616

Schulte, P. A., Pandalai, S., Wulsin, V., & Chun, H. (2012). Interaction of occupational and personal risk factors in workforce health and safety. *American Journal of Public Health, 102*, 434–448. http://dx.doi.org/10.2105/AJPH.2011.300249

Shaw, W. S., Besen, E., Pransky, G., Boot, C. R., Nicholas, M. K., McLellan, R. K., & Tveito, T. H. (2014). Manage at work: A randomized, controlled trial of a self-management group intervention to overcome workplace challenges associated with chronic physical health conditions. *BMC Public Health, 14*, 515-2458-14-515. http://dx.doi.org/10.1186/1471-2458-14-515

Swensen, S. J., & Shanafelt, T. (2017). An organizational framework to reduce professional burnout and bring back joy in practice. *Joint Commission Journal on Quality and Patient Safety, 43*, 308–313. http://dx.doi.org/10.1016/j.jcjq.2017.01.007

Umland, B. (2015). *Employers launch worksite clinics despite ACA uncertainty.* Retrieved from http://ushealthnews.mercer.com/article/444/employers-launch-worksite-clinics-despite-aca-uncertainty

U.S. Preventive Services Task Force. (2017). USPSTF A and B recommendations. Retrieved from https://www.uspreventiveservicestaskforce.org/Page/Name/uspstf-a-and-b-recommendations/

Willis Towers Watson. (2010, February). *2010 health care cost survey.* Retrieved from https://www.towerswatson.com/en-US/Insights/IC-Types/Survey-Research-Results/2010/02/2010-Health-Care-Cost-Survey

World Health Organization. (2006). *Constitution of the world health organization* (45th ed., Basic Documents Suppl.). New York, NY: Author.

YCharts. (2018). U.S. health care inflation rate. Retrieved from https://ycharts.com/indicators/us_health_care_inflation_rate

Total Worker Health®
Approaches in Small- to
Medium-Sized Enterprises

Lee S. Newman and Liliana Tenney

This chapter focuses on the unique needs and challenges facing small and medium enterprises (SMEs) and their employees in addressing occupational health, safety, and well-being. In 2013, 56.8 million U.S. workers representing 48% of the total workforce were employed by *small businesses*, defined by the U.S. Small Business Administration as having fewer than 500 employees, and with the vast majority (98%) having fewer than 100 employees. Small enterprises employ a disproportionate number of workers in every high-risk industry sector, including accommodation and food services, wholesale trade, construction, agriculture, forestry, fishing, and transportation. These workers bear a greater burden of occupational fatalities, illnesses, and injuries (Sinclair, Cunningham, & Schulte, 2013). They also have comparable and sometimes higher than average rates of chronic health conditions and unhealthy behaviors (Newman et al., 2015; Schwatka et al., 2017). Unfortunately, SMEs generally do not offer the same level of health protection, health promotion, employee benefits, and wages found in larger enterprises (Anger et al., 2015; McCoy, Stinson, Scott, Tenney, & Newman, 2014; Pronk, 2013). Research has confirmed that there is low adherence to traditional occupational safety and health best practices by small companies as well as a low degree of adoption of work organization/benefits best practices and health promotion programs (Linnan et al., 2008) despite the observation that 93% of surveyed small business owners have reported that their employees' health is important to their

http://dx.doi.org/10.1037/0000149-010
Total Worker Health, H. L. Hudson, J. A. S. Nigam, S. L. Sauter, L. C. Chosewood, A. L. Schill, and J. Howard (Editors)
Copyright © 2019 by the American Psychological Association. All rights reserved.

bottom line (National Small Business Association, 2012). Our research affirms the link between workers' chronic health conditions, past work-related injuries, and SME productivity (Jinnett, Schwatka, Tenney, Brockbank, & Newman, 2017), yet SME engagement in preventive policies, programs, and practices remains low (Sinclair et al., 2013).

From an integrated *Total Worker Health®* perspective, our understanding of the barriers to adoption and the effectiveness and sustainability of *Total Worker Health* (TWH) programs in small business is extremely limited (Bradley, Grossman, Hubbard, Ortega, & Curry, 2016; Feltner et al., 2016; Institute of Medicine, 2014). Most TWH intervention studies have been conducted in large enterprises and offer little evidence to support the generalization of results to the small business setting (Institute of Medicine, 2014). This chapter summarizes the relevant research and provides examples from research and practice experience in designing and testing SME interventions conducted at the Center for Health, Work & Environment at the Colorado School of Public Health. The authors use Health Links, a signature program of the center that they cofounded and oversee, to provide case studies that illustrate how research can inform practice and suggest a systematic approach to developing sustainable, scalable TWH solutions in SMEs. This chapter aims to help describe the specialty of "the TWH practitioner" as the person who can assess, design, and implement TWH strategies that meet the needs of the workplace and individual workers. In addition, the chapter identifies areas for future research to address the substantial gaps in knowledge of what works in SMEs.

LOOKING BEYOND THE NUMBERS

The challenge of understanding the needs and solutions for SMEs starts with an examination of what SMEs are and how they may differ from large enterprises. Even the way that we have defined small business—as fewer than 500 employees—ignores the wide range of business size within that group (i.e., from fewer than 50 to fewer than 100 employees) that may attribute to differences in the way the TWH program is implemented. As Cunningham, Sinclair, and Schulte (2014) pointed out, imprecision in the definition of small business and an overreliance on employee number to define an SME interfere with our ability to understand how to foster meaningful improvements in occupational safety, health, and well-being. The current work of the National Institute for Occupational Safety and Health (NIOSH) small business assistance and outreach program (Cunningham et al., 2014; Sinclair et al., 2013) highlights that although company size and annual revenue are convenient metrics, they set arbitrary cutoffs that may miss the importance of contextual factors. As discussed in the case studies that follow, the context in which a business operates is probably even more important in SMEs than for larger organizations, which are better resourced and more self-sufficient. Several lines of evidence have suggested that contextual factors influence well-being and the effectiveness of workplace interventions that seek to improve worker well-being and traditional workplace safety (Harris, Hannon, Beresford, Linnan, & McLellan, 2014). Smaller businesses may require greater assistance from external organizations, such as government, insurance agencies, chambers of commerce, peers, and other businesses in their community to address occupational safety and health regulations, to gain access to consultation services and technical assistance, and to find social support and recognition for improving practices (Harris et al., 2014; Hasle & Limborg, 2006; Sinclair et al., 2013).

Characteristics that need to be considered include business structure; age maturity of the enterprise; organization of work; wages; provision of employee benefits, including health care; characteristics of the workforce, including reliance on seasonal, part-time, and/or subcontract workers; management and leadership; social environment or culture of the organization; access to financial and other resources; and support in the business community, including intermediary organizations (Cunningham et al., 2014; Harris et al., 2014). Unfortunately, remarkably few studies have identified or examined these and other contextual factors affecting our understanding of SMEs (Feltner et al., 2016). From a practical standpoint, it has been our observation that the multibillion-dollar, for-profit health promotion industry typically has ignored SMEs or has approached implementation in SMEs with scaled-down versions of services developed for larger firms. There is little evidence suggesting that "small businesses are just little big businesses" (Institute of Medicine, 2014, p. 37). And, in our experience, a scaled-down big business approach fails to capitalize on some of the unique strengths of SMEs, which we discuss later.

BARRIERS AND FACILITATORS TO ADOPTION

Although these lines of reasoning would seem to suggest that SMEs would be ready to see the potential benefits and advance an agenda of workplace safety, health, and well-being, uptake has been poor (Linnan et al., 2008; McCoy et al., 2014; National Small Business Association, 2012). This result led us to start critically examining some of the obstacles, especially those related to adoption of interventions as suggested by the work of Glasgow, Vogt, and Boles (1999), who defined *adoption* as the "proportion and representativeness" of settings (p. 1323), such as the workplace that adopts a policy or program. In a 2014 systematic review of research examining the barriers to adoption of worksite wellness programs by SMEs (McCoy et al., 2014), we found only one rigorously designed study. In 2008, 24% of large U.S. businesses offered all elements of a comprehensive program as defined by HealthyPeople 2020 (Office of Disease Prevention and Health Promotion, n.d.), whereas only 4.6% of small worksites offered those components (Linnan et al., 2008). Linnan et al. (2008) identified major barriers, including lack of employee interest, lack of staff resources, limited funding, low participation on the part of high-risk employees, and lack of management support. This research literature continues to be populated by qualitative, descriptive studies of low rigor that have suggested a laundry list of potential barriers, including direct costs, lack of facility space to carry out programs, perceived lack of expertise, high cost of third-party services, lack of local service providers, low likelihood of return on investment (ROI), concern about employee privacy, and concern that management seems paternalistic (McCoy et al., 2014).

Since the time of this review, several new studies have been published and provide additional insights. In a study of 218 Australian worksites with fewer than 20 employees, Taylor, Pilkington, Montgomerie, and Feist (2016) found that smaller employers that embraced health promotion ranked employee morale and work–life balance as the most important reason for providing programs, whereas larger businesses emphasized work-related injury prevention. In a survey of human resources managers in 117 U.S. businesses with fewer than 750 employees, McLellan et al. (2015) observed that top leadership support proved important for occupational safety and health policies and programs, but having accompanying resources, such as dedicated budgets, staff, and standing committees, were even more strongly related to implementation, especially for worksite health promotion. Williams et al. (2015) conducted a web-based survey of human resources managers in small to medium employers (fewer than750 employees) and provided descriptive evidence that even in SMEs that have embraced health promotion, many fall short in organizational leadership and commitment, coordination between health protection and promotion, processes for training and accountability, coordination of management and employee engagement strategies, use of incentives and benefits, integrated evaluation and surveillance, and development of comprehensive program content. In our longitudinal study of 260 small businesses that adopted a health promotion program (Newman et al., 2015), employers reported lack of program expertise, uncertain ROI, and privacy concerns as leading reasons for reticence.

From an integrated TWH perspective, the barriers to adoption and the effectiveness and sustainability of the TWH program in SMEs remain poorly understood. In addition, few of the published TWH interventions use models of organizational change management or other theoretical frameworks, thus limiting understanding of how to effect change, generalize, scale, and maintain TWH solutions (Anger et al., 2015; Bradley et al., 2016). For example, factors important for transformational change, such as organizational safety climate and health climate, are moderators in the adoption of workplace safety and health practices; however, little is known about the role of climate in SMEs (Clarke, 2010; Cunningham et al., 2014).

UNIQUE OPPORTUNITIES FOR HIGH IMPACT

The introduction of interventions in small workplaces is a unique opportunity to have a high impact on worker safety and health because of high burden and high need. Consider the public health case for addressing health protection and other prevention efforts that advance the safety, health, and well-being of workers in SMEs. With nearly 6 million small workplaces employing more than half of the nation's private sector employees, according to the U.S. Census Bureau (n.d.), any interventions that prove to be scalable will have potential to reach and impact large numbers of individuals, including many lower wage employees who are at increased risk for chronic diseases as well as for occupational illnesses, injuries, and fatalities.

However, this public health message is unlikely to resonate with small business owners and operators. What is needed is a better appreciation of what the value proposition is from the small business owner's perspective. The opportunity lies in finding that message and marketing it effectively as a business opportunity—a subject that has received little attention from the academic community—to hone the right message and get it across in a way that resonates with business leaders.

In the examples that follow, when interventions succeed, it is in part because SMEs have been offered a clear and compelling rationale that helps them understand why it is good for their business. That message may be shaped around ROI or, more often, around the *value* on investment (VOI) specific to the motivations driven by personal moral convictions rather than business drivers. Although much more needs to be done to research the messaging that works best, qualitatively, business owners have reported that they want happier, healthier, more productive employees, and that they want to be able to compete for the best recruits when they are hiring (National Small Business Association, 2012). They are seeking ways of reducing absenteeism and of reducing presenteeism. Consistent with this line of thought, in our recently published study of the relationship between workplace safety and chronic conditions in SME employees, we observed substantial impacts on productivity in terms of absenteeism and presenteeism (Jinnett et al., 2017). The absence or loss of even a single employee can produce substantial operational, cultural, and financial consequences.

To understand how to best reach SMEs, it is necessary to first identify and understand one's target audience. Interventions and SME engagement are most successful when SME leadership possesses a higher degree of health and safety literacy, understands how the workplace can impact worker health and safety, and is both committed and visible in leading the TWH program. Thus, leadership engagement in fostering TWH programs presents an opportunity in SMEs where the majority of firms are owner managed and where investment and control lie with the same person. Whereas larger organizations may be more likely to consult with specialists, such as organizational/industrial psychologists and other occupational health and safety professionals, SMEs more realistically need to become TWH generalists to serve their own organizations. Facets of the organization that appear to contribute to success include companies that show a high degree of cross-department collaboration, have close-knit employees, and show a greater sense of culture and connectedness between management and employees. Communication that comes from respected community members, peers, and customers is particularly powerful. SMEs are accustomed to establishing collaborative relationships with external vendors, insurance agents and insurers, local chambers of commerce, and existing public health infrastructure (McPeck, Ryan, & Chapman, 2009), suggesting an untapped opportunity for achieving potentially greater reach and impact than might be achievable in large business and is in keeping with the socio-ecological framework (Harris et al., 2014). Examples of successful interventions that consider SME in situ follow.

In an interesting analysis of the challenges and opportunities, Harris et al. (2014) suggested that inroads will be made in smaller workplaces if TWH practitioners gain a better understanding of the small enterprise's context, readiness, and capacity. They also suggested that one must consider contextual challenges, including economics (e.g., low profit-margins) and high employee turnover rates (that may dampen the enthusiasm for underwriting health promotion for chronic illnesses but raise enthusiasm for short-term benefits like influenza vaccinations and injury prevention). The researchers described the *readiness challenge*, meaning that the beliefs of individual decision makers regarding the relevance and feasibility of such programs impact adoption. In addition, they suggested that because SMEs have limited internal capacity to implement programs, they need help in identifying TWH issues and addressing logistical challenges. Our own research across a wide range of industries has shown that when these barriers are mitigated, smaller enterprises are eager to engage (Newman et al., 2015; Schwatka et al., 2017).

Extrinsic motivators that help drive SMEs to invest in worker health, safety, and well-being also have been attributed to businesses' interest in addressing their environment and social impacts. All businesses, large and small, have come under increasing pressure to engage in corporate social responsibility (CSR). Businesses are driven by the desire to be sustainable, have a more engaged workforce, build relationships, attract new customers, and increase profits (Vives, 2006). Businesses focused on CSR redefine success by building company values that prioritize a triple bottom line that measures company performance on people, planet, and profits (Jenkins, 2009). SMEs are well positioned to not only contribute to significant community impact through CSR and TWH practices but align the two for creating better business systems that lead to benefits, such as greater competitive advantage (Jenkins, 2009). The next section provides a framework to engage businesses and proposes ways to overcome many of the unique challenges SMEs face. The section also illustrates ways in which SMEs are well positioned to take advantage of the TWH approach.

HOW TO ENGAGE SMALL- AND MEDIUM-SIZED ENTERPRISES USING A *TOTAL WORKER HEALTH* FRAMEWORK

Conventional approaches to engaging businesses to adopt and implement health promotion and health protection have been based on a one-size-fits-all model adapted from what has worked in large businesses (Newman et al.,

2015). The TWH program is recognized as a useful approach to improving worker safety, health, and well-being in the work environment. However, the question of how best to command the attention of SMEs, how to assess their TWH practices, and how to disseminate the evidence to them effectively often leaves both researchers and practitioners puzzled. Anger et al. (2015) published a literature review to identify the effectiveness of TWH interventions and concluded that there is a need to learn how to improve dissemination of best practices. In 2003, Schulte et al. identified special dissemination challenges: a need for information among a changing workforce, new and young workers, small businesses, and workers with difficulty in understanding or reading English. Sinclair et al. (2013) used the diffusion of innovation model to incorporate intermediary organizations, such as trade associations, to reach small employers and found that there are opinion leader organizations and individual influences within intermediaries who are key to decisions and actions about occupational safety and health programming. As we aim to reach these decision makers, it is important to remember that the same motivational pressures that engage SMEs in TWH practices may not be the same for large companies.

Use Approachable Assessment Tools and Messaging

SMEs stand to benefit from a process that starts by measuring benchmarks through approachable assessment tools. Many tools have been developed to assess organizational activities for health promotion, safety, well-being, and integration. Businesses that are in various stages of readiness to change learn not only what they currently are doing right but where they can improve their impact. When these assessments are coupled and followed up with technical assistance that can be customized based on the needs of the unique business and its workforce, actionable recommendations and organizational-level changes occur (Pronk et al., 2016).

We have identified the importance of designing programs that are readily understood and that have a low barrier to adoption. In 2017, Thompson, Schwatka, Tenney, and Newman (2018) used qualitative methods involving a series of focus groups with SME decision makers and employees to understand how to improve TWH adoption, implementation, and messaging. Participants expressed the importance of assessment and benchmarking health and safety to identify tailored recommendations. When it came to the format of assessments, they expressed concern about the difficulty and challenges of completing extensive forms favored by academics. Some of the reasons they cited included the forms are too long, the information they asked for was not accessible to them, and the information requested required input from multiple people in their organization. They thought that networking through local chambers of commerce and business organizations, conference attendance and sponsorship, and social media (e.g., Facebook; blogs; local and national radio, such as National Public Radio; Google searches) were important and appropriate methods to get the TWH message out to businesses. They agreed that partnering with insurance carriers, insurance agents, and other businesses that service SME provides a good way to foster SME engagement. Interestingly, in those focus groups, Thompson et al. (2018) found that people's perceptions of health, safety, and well-being often differ sometimes in substantial ways. In general, wellness and safety were viewed as distinct from one another, with *wellness* being defined as a benefit and *safety* perceived as a requirement. Interestingly, the major drivers that participants cited for investing time and money into TWH activities, such as employee benefits, safety programs, and health promotion activities, did not revolve around business threat or cost burden. SME owners expressed the importance of improving employee motivation, productivity, and overall happiness. The findings confirmed the importance of focusing on VOI versus ROI to motivate SMEs (Ozminkowski et al., 2016).

This formative research led us to develop strategies that had a defined target audience, used clear and concise messaging, were interactive, and used key metrics to evaluate intervention effectiveness. Our dissemination to SMEs was guided by the following three core principles: (a) increase TWH knowledge and practice through research translation, communication, and outreach; (b) build capacity for the TWH program in communities through training and education, and strategic partnerships; and (c) engage in activities aimed at increasing adoption and implementation of TWH best practices, policies, and programs with input from both employers and their employees.

Overall, engaging SMEs depends largely on how they receive the information and their stage of readiness to change (Cunningham et al., 2014). Practitioners may benefit from a mixed methods approach to develop key messaging for the business opportunity for SMEs; articulating clear calls to action—that is, simple steps toward adopting and implementing the TWH program—and designing and implementing strategies to incorporate TWH training, communications, and programs into existing business programs. These strategies are based on understanding key factors, including the organizational structure, characteristics of the business, organization of work itself, and other contextual elements that are essential in defining the target audience: *what* employers and *who* from the organization you should be talking to. In addition, developing a strategic outreach and marketing plan should consider industry, size, geographic location, and workforce demographics.

Build Capacity Through Local Partnerships

Local community coalitions are starting to form across the country and are catalyzing around the concepts of the TWH approach and fostering "healthy businesses." In our community-based work, we have found ourselves both observing and helping to foster a supportive social context for change. These groups, as illustrated in Figure 9.1, include business organizations, offices of economic development, chambers of commerce, county public health, health care organizations, and safety and health promotion professionals, and our local TWH trainers. The following questions can help local coalitions and

FIGURE 9.1. Partnership Model for Engaging Small and Medium Enterprises (SMEs)

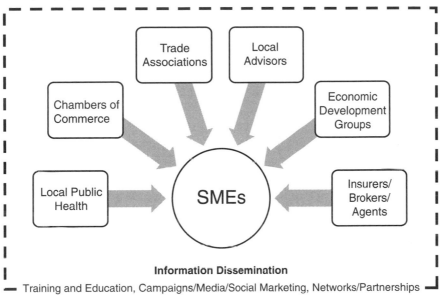

Information Dissemination
Training and Education, Campaigns/Media/Social Marketing, Networks/Partnerships

community groups to set goals for SME engagement with their local target audiences, increase reach, and promote broader commitment in the business community around health and safety:

- What words will make sense to, and resonate with, SMEs? Researchers and TWH practitioners frequently use terms that are jargon to anyone outside of the field, such as "total worker health," "health promotion," "health protection," "dissemination," and "needs assessment." Break through the language barrier.

- How can you build and coordinate regional and local capacity to deliver TWH information, education, and training that is relevant to the needs of SMEs? Employers favor local, in-person advising and information exchange.

- How can you provide TWH trainings and education for owners, managers, and employees in SMEs?

- How can you communicate effectively through website content, social media, success stories, media and channel partners, and stakeholder groups?

- How can you coordinate and collaborate across partners to disseminate best practices, benefits, and case studies to SME influencers, managers, and employees?

- How can you apply innovative dissemination approaches to provide science-based TWH information that will reach a geographically dispersed audience, especially when the workforce may include precarious workers?

- How can you create culturally and context-sensitive approaches for applying the TWH approach?

- How will you monitor and evaluate your goals and objectives on an ongoing basis?

Groups that have established relationships with SMEs, such as insurance brokers, can succeed by incorporating TWH messaging into service lines, benefit packages, and existing communications (Sinclair et al., 2013). For early stage or struggling small employers, it is critical to find ways to leverage these channels so that the TWH program is not adding to information clutter or being construed as a distraction from more urgent business priorities. The Health Links model, described in the next section, works closely with both community-level and employer-level stakeholder groups to improve health, safety, and well-being.

THE HEALTH LINKS MODEL

In 2012, we developed Health Links, a TWH intervention for small business (Schwatka et al., 2018). The program was designed by conducting focus groups and key informant interviews with business leaders, small business owners, managers, employees, chambers of commerce, insurers, brokers, offices of economic development, marketing and advertising consultants, public health officials, experts from occupational health and safety, health promotion practitioners, NIOSH Centers of Excellence for *Total Worker Health*, and other stakeholders. We determined that the intervention must (a) be based on best available evidence, (b) accommodate the needs of many different types of small businesses and workforces, (c) be feasible for small businesses to access and adopt (e.g., inexpensive, not resource/time intensive), (d) be scalable, (e) apply basic principles of organizational change management, and (f) generate metrics so that the program could be evaluated in five domains using the RE-AIM model: reach, effectiveness, adoption, implementation, and maintenance of the intervention (Glasgow et al., 1999).

The result was the creation and launch of Health Links, a mentoring program that champions health and safety at work. The comprehensive certification and advising program uses evidence-based strategies to help organizations and their team members achieve total worker health. A cornerstone of the intervention is the Health Links healthy business certification that was developed by adapting constructs from Centers of Excellence for *Total Worker Health* (Harvard School of Public Health, Center for Work, Health, & Well-Being, 2012), the Centers for Disease Control (2016) Worksite Health ScoreCard, and the World Health Organization healthy workplace framework and model (Burton & World Health Organization, 2010). The Health Links team hired a professional advertising firm to help create an intuitive, professional-grade website with a look and feel that would appeal to businesses. The website hosts an online assessment tool that is short, is written with as little jargon as possible, explains key terms, provides feedback, and collects data on key measures. Questions in the assessment were selected that would be relevant and generalizable to businesses in all sectors and of all sizes.

The assessment is an online questionnaire that measures an organization's health and safety culture based on six benchmarks: organizational supports, workplace assessments, health policies and programs, safety policies and programs, engagement, and evaluation. The assessment includes questions that map to major health and safety areas, from stress management to return-to-work programs. Results of the questionnaire were used to determine whether a business is recognized as a certified healthy business or as a *kick-start business* for organizations that are at early stages of adoption but aspire to become certified. Certified healthy businesses may fall into one of three certification levels: certified, partner, or leader.

On completion of the online Health Links assessment, employers are provided with a report card identifying areas in which they can improve across the benchmarks. Employers are then offered two on-site advising sessions conducted by a trained TWH advisor. The advisors, who are based in each geographic region, received training from members of the Health Links faculty and staff. The local advisor network was developed to scale reach and implementation and was based on feedback from businesses that the personal touch of having in-person, local, trusted technical assistance is important to SMEs. During the advising sessions, each advisor goes through the business's assessment and report card to collaborate with the business to target tailored evidence-based strategies and establish an action plan. Advisors remain available to provide ongoing follow-up to answer questions and support reassessment every year. To measure employer TWH activities, the online assessment and advising sessions evaluate how organizations are implementing TWH practices. Participation in Health Links qualifies businesses for both local and statewide recognition, opportunities to connect with local business–public health coalitions that have made the TWH program a regional priority, and local providers of services that can enhance the ability of a business to achieve its goals for improving safety, health, and well-being (Schwatka et al., 2018).

After 3 years of engaging businesses, the authors of this chapter observed a high level of interest from both rural and urban business communities. It's evident that Health Links also can result in a Trojan horse effect whereby businesses that start with more emphasis on one TWH element (e.g., "health promotion/wellness") subsequently adopt other elements that we introduce at the same time (e.g., safety policies, programs, practices). Preliminary data (Schwatka et al., 2018) have suggested that this intervention helps SMEs not only adopt TWH programming elements but also maintain these changes over the long term because these SMEs continue to engage with their local Health Links community and resources. Dissemination through local channel partners emphasizes the importance of such intermediary organizations to deliver and reinforce TWH interventions to small businesses, as has been reported in the literature (Sinclair et al., 2013).

As of 2016, the authors of this chapter have gained experience with more than 500 businesses through Health Links across a range of geographic locations, business sizes, and industries. Our preliminary data have suggested that although there seems to be an agreement between the quantity of health promotion and health protection activities (measured by number and type of policies and programs), there is significant variation. Some organizations may display predominantly more safety than health promotion behaviors or vice versa. We have observed that most certified businesses are starting the TWH program because they are interested in improving the health of their employees and their families, improving employee morale, enhancing productivity, and increasing employee retention. The majority of businesses have reported that their leadership (i.e., owner or managers) participates in TWH activities, has coordinated health and wellness activities with safety, and has promoted health and safety of off-site workers.

TOTAL WORKER HEALTH IN PRACTICE

In working with SMEs, Health Links has evaluated the short- and long-term outcomes related to goals set to help businesses adopt and implement TWH best practices. This process has largely been based on applying the RE-AIM framework (Glasgow et al., 1999), developed to translate research into practice, to help with dissemination and to help programs apply to real-world settings. The application of RE-AIM has ensured a consistent approach to focus on reach, effectiveness, adoption, implementation, and maintenance. Short-term outcomes have included (a) increased reach to small- and medium-sized businesses, and to underserved groups; (b) increased adoption and implementation of TWH best practices in SMEs; (c) increased knowledge, positive attitudes, and behaviors among employers around TWH best practices; (d) increased TWH capacity at the local level; and (e) changes in organizational behavior. Long-term impacts have included maintenance of TWH best practices in SMEs, safer and healthier workplaces, and strategic partnerships that lead to increased capacity for the TWH approach.

Two examples illustrate how SMEs that engaged through Health Links have taken steps to adopt and implement health and safety practices.

Example 1: A Construction Company

U.S. Engineering, a Colorado-based construction company with 586 employees, has incorporated health and safety into its mission and value statement:

> The mission of our company wellness program is to improve the lives of our team members and their families by supporting a culture of mental, emotional, and physical well-being. As a mechanical contractor, we help build hospitals, schools, and a variety of other facilities in our community. So every morning when we go to work, we remember why we strive to be the best at what we do, because we are making lives and communities better and strengthening the place we call home. The health and safety of our employees is important because our people

are key to achieving this mission. And as a construction company, safety is not just one of our priorities, it's one of our core values. Looking out for one another is at the heart of what safety means for our organization. (Health Links, n.d.b)

The company has taken several steps to incorporating health and safety components into the workplace, including the following:

- Hired a safety director who runs the partners in safety program, which encourages and holds employees responsible for taking an active role in safety on the job; carries out the "Believe in Zero"[1] philosophy, which sets values to keep workers safe and healthy every day; runs safety training classes; and offers monthly safety meetings.

- Surveyed employees to address health and wellness needs to form a seven-member wellness steering committee, wrote a mission statement, branded the program, solicited ideas, and communicated a clear and consistent message.

- Offers and promotes strong health insurance benefits, an employee assistance program, an in-house exercise facility, water stations, and team sponsorships for community events.

- Takes an integrated approach to tracking and reviewing data, including medical claims, absenteeism, turnover (i.e., employee retention), safety records (e.g., injuries, illnesses, experience modification rate), and employee participation and feedback surveys.

In this example, the business has coordinated, and, in some instances, integrated internal and external TWH activities into core business activities and the company's overall core values. The company has been successful in adopting and implementing the TWH program by focusing on core areas of leadership commitment, employee feedback, frequent and consistent messaging, and evaluation. These efforts have allowed leaders to adapt and maintain health and safety as a business priority.

Example 2: A Rural Health Clinic

Mountain Family Health Centers is a small health clinic with 13 employees and is located in rural Colorado. The center engaged with Health Links to assess and benchmark, and to learn what first steps to take to improve health and safety in the workplace. As a result, the center stressed the importance of having broad representation to provide feedback and gain employee buy-in, and provided a list of tips:

- Gain leadership support by having a clear plan of action.

- Collaboration is key.

- Start a committee made of representatives from across the organization.

---

[1] Believe in Zero is a campaign the company implements to strive toward zero injuries or fatal accidents.

- [Workplace health and safety] is a living and breathing plan that should evolve. Communicate clearly and often to staff about any changes and successes. (Health Links, n.d.a)

For this small business, the priority for TWH program adoption and implementation was to set goals and define a process that allowed it to successfully convince leadership that employee health and safety was significant to how the business functions every day. This theme is common to every business regardless of size. What this case illustrates is how integrating the TWH approach can be presented to SMEs as low-cost, low-demand ways as simple as incorporating communication into existing staff meetings using informal methods, such as team-huddles to gather feedback, and presenting small successes through managers. Importantly, the business recognized the value of involving its workforce in decision making, itself an important factor in reducing workplace stress.

Through the Health Links experience of implementing the TWH program into practice—even though many participating businesses have been identified as early adopters—we learned that SMEs are willing to engage. The needs of businesses may vary, which requires programs be approachable and adaptable to SMEs. Because the business case for SMEs is largely focused on the VOI, strategies should address the impact of the TWH approach on employee morale, recruitment, and retention, and, overall, the influence that establishing a healthy company culture can have on workers, their families, and even the larger community. Importantly, local partnerships are essential to reaching and disseminating information to SMEs. Although not all businesses are addressing safety as their number one priority, the Health Links program has helped introduce safety to many SMEs by way of engaging them first around health and wellness. It has been critical to broadening the definitions of wellness and safety to reach SMEs and have them embrace the TWH approach through the lens of being a "healthy business." Doing so has allowed them to self-define what the TWH program means to them and their workers, and to take a more all-inclusive approach to improving overall employee well-being that is best suited their organization and employee needs. Key stakeholders within individual SMEs have included the owner, middle managers, and the employees themselves. Each needs to be involved in defining the values, goals, and strategies for the TWH approach, and making sure everyone in the businesses is aware of the commitment to health and safety. Maintenance and sustainability of the TWH program depends on commitment from owners and managers, retention of wellness champions within the organization, and an established health and safety culture that is set before adopting and implementing new TWH activities.

RESEARCH GAPS AND SPECIAL CHALLENGES

More research needs to be conducted to understand how engaging SMEs is related to the context and characteristics of the organization, including the culture that often is set by the values, behaviors, and attitudes of the owner and leadership teams. Future research also is needed to determine if engagement with SMEs through assessments, consultation, and training will result in sustained changes in organizational behavior and, ultimately, in improved worker health, safety, well-being, and productivity (Bradley et al., 2016). As one of NIOSH's Centers of Excellence for *Total Worker Health*, the Center of Health, Work & Environment at the Colorado School of Public Health has designed a longitudinal, prospective, randomized controlled study to test these hypotheses. Importantly, that study also will examine how social networks and communications impact outcomes at the organizational level (Center for Health, Work & Environment, 2017). It is critical to improve not only the access to TWH information but to conduct research on dissemination, adoption, and how businesses use the information. There is a need to develop a business opportunity model specific to SME that presents the tangible benefits around worker productivity, recruitment, retention, and organizational reputation in the community.

The TWH program has the potential to be a useful approach to improving safety, health, and well-being in the SME environment. However, more outreach and dissemination are needed to increase awareness, knowledge, and adoption of best practices (Cunningham et al., 2014; Schulte et al., 2003). It also is important to design programs that are feasible to understand and adopt. We need skilled TWH practitioners in businesses, in the occupational safety and health field, and at the community level that have both competency in TWH fundamentals as well as experience consulting with small enterprises to help businesses adopt and implement the TWH program. More development also is needed to define TWH competencies and address new workforce training and education. Despite the challenges inherent in conducting research in the SME setting, studies are needed to improve quantitative and qualitative understanding of the TWH program in SMEs.

REFERENCES

Anger, W. K., Elliot, D. L., Bodner, T., Olson, R., Rohlman, D. S., Truxillo, D. M., . . . Montgomery, D. (2015). Effectiveness of *Total Worker Health* interventions. *Journal of Occupational Health Psychology, 20,* 226–247. http://dx.doi.org/10.1037/a0038340

Bradley, C. J., Grossman, D. C., Hubbard, R. A., Ortega, A. N., & Curry, S. J. (2016). Integrated interventions for improving total worker health: A panel report from the National Institutes of Health Pathways to Prevention workshop: *Total Worker Health*—What's work got to do with it? *Annals of Internal Medicine, 165,* 279–283. http://dx.doi.org/10.7326/M16-0740

Burton, J., & World Health Organization. (2010). *WHO healthy workplace framework and model: Background and supporting literature and practices.* Retrieved from http://apps.who.int/iris/bitstream/handle/10665/113144/9789241500241_eng.pdf?sequence=1&isAllowed=y

Center for Health, Work & Environment. (2017). Small + safe + well (SSWell) [Study]. Retrieved from http://www.ucdenver.edu/academics/colleges/PublicHealth/research/centers/CHWE/Research/Pages/SSWell.aspx

Centers for Disease Control. (2016). Worksite Health ScoreCard. Retrieved from http://www.cdc.gov/dhdsp/pubs/worksite_scorecard.htm

Clarke, S. (2010). An integrative model of safety climate: Linking psychological climate and work attitudes to individual safety outcomes using meta-analysis. *Journal of*

Occupational and Organizational Psychology, 83, 553–578. http://dx.doi.org/10.1348/096317909X452122

Cunningham, T. R., Sinclair, R., & Schulte, P. (2014). Better understanding the small business construct to advance research on delivering workplace health and safety. *Small Enterprise Research, 21,* 148–160. http://dx.doi.org/10.1080/13215906.2014.11082084

Feltner, C., Peterson, K., Palmieri Weber, R., Cluff, L., Coker-Schwimmer, E., Viswanathan, M., & Lohr, K. N. (2016). The effectiveness of *Total Worker Health* interventions: A systematic review for a National Institutes of Health Pathways to Prevention workshop. *Annals of Internal Medicine, 165,* 262–269. http://dx.doi.org/10.7326/M16-0626

Glasgow, R. E., Vogt, T. M., & Boles, S. M. (1999). Evaluating the public health impact of health promotion interventions: The RE-AIM framework. *American Journal of Public Health, 8,* 1322–1327. http://dx.doi.org/10.2105/AJPH.89.9.1322

Harris, J. R., Hannon, P. A., Beresford, S. A., Linnan, L. A., & McLellan, D. L. (2014). Health promotion in smaller workplaces in the United States. *Annual Review of Public Health, 35,* 327–342. http://dx.doi.org/10.1146/annurev-publhealth-032013-182416

Harvard School of Public Health, Center for Work, Health, & Well-Being. (2012). *SafeWell practice guidelines: An integrated approach to worker health.* Retrieved from http://centerforworkhealth.sph.harvard.edu/sites/default/files/safewell_guidelines/SafeWellPracticeGuidelines_Complete.pdf

Hasle, P., & Limborg, H. J. (2006). A review of the literature on preventive occupational health and safety activities in small enterprises. *Industrial Health, 44,* 6–12. http://dx.doi.org/10.2486/indhealth.44.6

Health Links. (n.d.a). Success stories: Mountain Family Health Centers/Glenwood Springs, CO [Interview]. Retrieved from https://www.healthlinkscertified.org/what-we-do/success-stories/mountain-family-health-centers

Health Links. (n.d.b). Success stories: U.S. Engineering Company/Westminster, CO [Interview]. Retrieved from https://www.healthlinkscertified.org/what-we-do/success-stories/us-engineering

Institute of Medicine. (2014). *Promising and best practices in Total Worker Health: Workshop summary.* Washington, DC: The National Academies Press.

Jenkins, H. (2009). A "business opportunity" model of corporate social responsibility for small-and medium-sized enterprises. *Business Ethics: A European Review, 18,* 21–36. http://dx.doi.org/10.1111/j.1467-8608.2009.01546.x

Jinnett, K., Schwatka, N., Tenney, L., Brockbank, C. V. S., & Newman, L. S. (2017). Chronic conditions, workplace safety, and job demands contribute to absenteeism and job performance. *Health Affairs, 36,* 237–244. http://dx.doi.org/10.1377/hlthaff.2016.1151

Linnan, L., Bowling, M., Childress, J., Lindsay, G., Blakey, C., Pronk, S., . . . Royall, P. (2008). Results of the 2004 national worksite health promotion survey. *American Journal of Public Health, 98,* 1503–1509. http://dx.doi.org/10.2105/AJPH.2006.100313

McCoy, K., Stinson, K., Scott, K., Tenney, L., & Newman, L. S. (2014). Health promotion in small business: A systematic review of factors influencing adoption and effectiveness of worksite wellness programs. *Journal of Occupational and Environmental Medicine, 56,* 579–587. http://dx.doi.org/10.1097%2FJOM.0000000000000171

McLellan, D. L., Cabán-Martinez, A. J., Nelson, C. C., Pronk, N. P., Katz, J. N., Allen, J. D., . . . Sorensen, G. (2015). Organizational characteristics influence implementation of worksite health protection and promotion programs: Evidence from smaller businesses. *Journal of Occupational & Environmental Medicine, 57,* 1009–1016. http://dx.doi.org/10.1097/JOM.0000000000000517

McPeck, W., Ryan, M., & Chapman, L. S. (2009). Bringing wellness to the small employer. *American Journal of Health Promotion, 23,* 1–12. http://dx.doi.org/10.4278%2Fajhp.23.5.tahp

National Small Business Association. (2012). *Workplace wellness programs in small business: Impacting the bottom line.* Retrieved from http://www.nsba.biz/wp-content/uploads/2012/09/wellness-survey-v3.pdf

Newman, L. S., Stinson, K. E., Metcalf, D., Fang, H., Brockbank, C., Jinnett, K., . . . Goetzel, R. Z. (2015). Implementation of a worksite wellness program targeting small businesses: The Pinnacol Assurance health risk management study. *Journal of Occupational & Environmental Medicine, 57,* 14–21. http://dx.doi.org/10.1097/JOM.0000000000000279

Office of Disease Prevention and Health Promotion. (n.d.). *HealthyPeople 2020.* Retrieved from https://www.healthypeople.gov/

Ozminkowski, R. J., Serxner, S., Marlo, K., Kichlu, R., Ratelis, E., & Van de Meulebroecke, J. (2016). Beyond ROI: Using value of investment to measure employee health and wellness. *Population Health Management, 19,* 227–229. http://dx.doi.org/10.1089/pop.2015.0160

Pronk, N. P. (2013). Integrated worker health protection and promotion programs: Overview and perspectives on health and economic outcomes. *Journal of Occupational & Environmental Medicine, 55,* S30–S37. http://dx.doi.org/10.1097/JOM.0000000000000031

Pronk, N. P., McLellan, D. L., McGrail, M. P., Olson, S. M., McKinney, Z. J., Katz, J. N., . . . Sorensen, G. (2016). Measurement tools for integrated worker health protection and promotion: Lessons learned from the SafeWell project. *Journal of Occupational & Environmental Medicine, 58,* 651–658. http://dx.doi.org/10.1097/JOM.0000000000000752

Schulte, P. A., Okun, A., Stephenson, C. M., Colligan, M., Ahlers, H., Gjessing, C., . . . Sweeney, M. H. (2003). Information dissemination and use: Critical components in occupational safety and health. *American Journal of Industrial Medicine, 44,* 515–531. http://dx.doi.org/10.1002/ajim.10295

Schwatka, N. V., Atherly, A., Dally, M. J., Fang, H., vS Brockbank, C., Tenney, L., . . . Newman, L. S. (2017). Health risk factors as predictors of workers' compensation claim occurrence and cost. *Occupational & Environmental Medicine, 74,* 14–23. http://dx.doi.org/10.1136/oemed-2015-103334

Schwatka, N. V., Tenney, L., Dally, M. J., Scott, J., Brown, C. E., Weitzenkamp, D., . . . Newman, L. S. (2018). Small business *Total Worker Health:* A conceptual and methodological approach to facilitating organizational change. *Occupational Health Science, 2,* 25–41. http://dx.doi.org/10.1007/s41542-018-0013-9

Sinclair, R. C., Cunningham, T. R., & Schulte, P. A. (2013). A model for occupational safety and health intervention diffusion to small businesses. *American Journal of Industrial Medicine, 56,* 1442–1451. http://dx.doi.org/10.1002/ajim.22263

Taylor, A. W., Pilkington, R., Montgomerie, A., & Feist, H. (2016). The role of business size in assessing the uptake of health promoting workplace initiatives in Australia. *BMC Public Health, 16,* 353. http://dx.doi.org/10.1186/s12889-016-3011-3

Thompson, J., Schwatka, N. V., Tenney, L., & Newman, L. S. (2018). *Total Worker Health:* A small business leader perspective. *International Journal of Environmental Research and Public Health, 15,* 2416. http://dx.doi.org/10.3390/ijerph15112416

U.S. Census Bureau. (n.d.). Annual survey of entrepreneurs (ASE). Retrieved from https://www.census.gov/programs-surveys/ase/data/tables.html

Vives, A. (2006). Social and environmental responsibility in small and medium enterprises in Latin America. *Journal of Corporate Citizenship, 2006,* 39–50. http://dx.doi.org/10.9774/GLEAF.4700.2006.sp.00006

Williams, J. A., Nelson, C. C., Cabán-Martinez, A. J., Katz, J. N., Wagner, G. R., Pronk, N. P., . . . McLellan, D. L. (2015). Validation of a new metric for assessing the integration of health protection and health promotion in a sample of small and medium size employer groups. *Journal of Occupational and Environmental Medicine, 57,* 1017–1021. http://dx.doi.org/10.1097/JOM.0000000000000521

10

A Labor–Management Approach to Addressing Health Risks in the Unionized Construction Sector

Jamie F. Becker and Scott P. Schneider

In a multiemployer industry such as construction in which employment may be temporary and people can work for multiple employers during the course of a year, it can be difficult to address health and safety risks and their potential long-term impact on organizations, workers, and their families. These conditions also can make it easy to assign blame to workers for illnesses and injuries they report. Joint labor–management efforts, however, can successfully overcome these problems. The Laborers' Health & Safety Fund of North America (LHSFNA), a joint labor–management trust fund, was founded in 1988 by the Laborers' International Union of North America (LIUNA). The LHSFNA conducts research, develops policy, provides technical support, and disseminates information to LIUNA members, health and welfare funds, and LIUNA's signatory employers. In addition, the LHSFNA encourages *Total Worker Health*® best practices on behalf of LIUNA entities and signatory contractors.

This chapter first focuses on the challenges to implementing a *Total Worker Health* (TWH) approach in the multiemployer industry of construction. Many of these challenges also can exist in other industries—like construction—in which people may work for several different employers during the course of a year. Additional industries include trucking, manufacturing, arts and entertainment, service industries, mining, and communication. We then provide several examples of how the LHSFNA, a joint labor–management organization built around the common interests of LIUNA members and their signatory employers, has

http://dx.doi.org/10.1037/0000149-011
Total Worker Health, H. L. Hudson, J. A. S. Nigam, S. L. Sauter, L. C. Chosewood, A. L. Schill, and J. Howard (Editors)
Copyright © 2019 by the American Psychological Association. All rights reserved.

addressed the TWH approach within the unionized multiemployer construction sector. We describe both large- and small-scale initiatives.

CHALLENGES OF THE CONSTRUCTION INDUSTRY IN RELATION TO *TOTAL WORKER HEALTH*

The inherent nature of the construction industry—multiple employers, shorter term relationships with workers, and the long-term nature of chronic health symptoms—can make collecting data that demonstrates the impact of TWH interventions particularly challenging. It also is challenging to measure the impact of advocacy efforts, yet we know it is important that both labor and management continue to have a seat at the table and make their voices heard.

Safety Hazards

The characteristics that set the construction industry apart from many other industries also contribute to why a TWH program can be difficult to implement in construction. Construction is one of the most dangerous industries in the United States. According to the U.S. Department of Labor, Bureau of Labor Statistics ([BLS], 2016a), out of 4,836 worker fatalities in private industry in 2015, 937 (19.4%) were in construction. The leading causes of private sector worker deaths (excluding highway collisions) in the construction industry were falling, being struck by or in between an object, and being electrocuted (Center for Construction Research and Training [CPWR], 2013). These "fatal four" were responsible for more than two thirds of construction worker deaths in 2015 (BLS, 2016b). Through its TWH program, the National Institute for Occupational Safety and Health ([NIOSH], 2015) of the Centers for Disease Control and Prevention encourages employers to adopt "policies, programs and practices that integrate protection from work-related safety and health hazards with promotion of injury and illness prevention efforts to advance worker well-being." However, when efforts need to be taken on a daily basis to keep workers safe from serious accidents, injuries, and even death, discussing less immediate aspects of safety and health, such as would be described under a comprehensive TWH approach, can be challenging.

Chronic Health Conditions

Because workers employed in construction may work for several employers during the course of a year, it can be difficult to address chronic health and safety risks, and their potential long-term impact. Many of the occupational health risks construction workers face often do not manifest into physical or chronic health conditions until years after exposure.

According to the Partnership to Fight Chronic Disease and the U.S. Workplace Wellness Alliance (2009), "almost 80 percent of workers have at least one chronic condition . . . [and] 55% of workers have more than one chronic condition" (p. 5). In addition to the safety hazards associated with construction, there are numerous health hazards. Exposure to asbestos, silica, noise, concrete, welding fumes, ergonomic risks, sun exposure, and many other work-related exposures can impair the health of construction workers. Many of the health risks construction workers face can take years of chemical and environmental exposure before they result in chronic health conditions.

In addition, the workforce as a whole is aging, which carries with it the greater likelihood of chronic health conditions in general. The average construction worker is almost 42 years old (Dong, Wang, Ringen, & Sokas, 2017). The industry as a whole and industry trade groups in particular see the need to address chronic health conditions to help keep workers healthy and ensure they have longer, more productive careers.

In the following information (emphasis shown is from the original source material), CPWR (2008) provides evidence about occupational diseases and disease risks associated with construction:

- **Lung cancer deaths are 50% higher** among construction workers than the U.S. population, even when adjusted for smoking.

- Construction workers are **twice as likely to have chronic obstructive lung diseases**, such as chronic bronchitis and emphysema, as the rest of [the U.S. population].

- Construction workers are **five times as likely to have cancer** of the lung lining, mesothelioma, and 33 times as likely to have asbestosis. . . .

- [Of 2,600 construction workers at Department of Energy facilities examined between 1996 and 2001], **5% had asbestosis** and **25% had scarring of the lung lining** from asbestos exposure [(Dement et al., 2003)].

- Construction workers breathe dust (containing silica, asbestos and other particulates), welding fumes (containing heavy metals) and toxic gases.

- 30–40% of construction workers suffer musculoskeletal disorders and **chronic pain.**

- 50% of construction workers have noise-induced **hearing loss.**

- Construction workers account for 17% of workers with elevated blood lead levels, which is disproportionately high because construction is only 8% of the workforce. . . .

- When welding, 75% of boilermakers, 15% of ironworkers and 7% of pipe-fitters exceed the accepted 8-hour level for manganese exposure. . . .

According to Ringen, Dong, Goldenhar, and Cain (2018; Ringen, Englund, Welch, Weeks, & Seegal, 1995), factors that can increase the safety and health risk of construction workers include the following:

- changing worksite environments and conditions;
- multiple contractors and subcontractors;

- constantly changing relationships with other work groups;
- exposures to health hazards, both from their own work and nearby activities;
- inconsistent work and possible financial insecurity;
- paid sick leave is usually not provided to construction workers;
- long hours, often combined with long commutes;
- physically demanding work leading to overuse injuries and working while in pain;
- production pressure and peer pressure to work under tight deadlines;
- traveling away from home or being on the road for extended periods;
- synergistic effect of occupational exposures with tobacco use; and
- not feeling free to speak up about safety or other jobsite concerns.

In addition to workplace exposures and conditions, construction workers are at an increased risk for other chronic health conditions due to higher levels of smoking, obesity, diabetes, and high blood pressure (CPWR, 2013). Although there may be a natural inclination to look at a worker's lifestyle off the job as a contributor to these risk factors, the structure of the industry is often the ultimate cause of many of the chronic conditions seen in this population. People's work lives can influence and constrain their ability to make positive choices for their health. Work has an impact on sleep, mental health, the ability to eat healthy meals, time to exercise, the ability to follow medical recommendations and other health-related factors.

Construction work by its very nature requires a TWH approach. A construction worker who works six 10-hour shifts in a week, drives 1 to 2 hours each way to work, and perhaps works a night shift, rarely seeing his or her family, has little time to think about eating proper meals, getting exercise, and stopping smoking. Having no paid sick leave means going to work even when injured, thus aggravating chronic conditions. Work has a dramatic impact on both occupational health and nonoccupational factors, which are difficult to untangle, thus making a TWH approach essential.

JOINT LABOR–MANAGEMENT HEALTH AND WELFARE FUNDS

Employer-sponsored insurance is by far the most common source of health coverage in the United States. An estimated 147 million people under age 65 are covered by such plans (Kaiser Family Foundation & Health Research and Educational Trust, 2015). Unionization greatly improves the likelihood of receiving employment-based health insurance. Among construction workers who were union members, 81% had health insurance through employment compared with 34% among nonunion workers (CPWR, 2013).

Contributions to cover health insurance in the union sector are negotiated into collective bargaining agreements, and employers typically pay into a multi-employer fund. A *multiemployer plan* is a collectively bargained plan maintained by more than one employer—usually within the same or related industries—and a labor union. If the multiemployer plan is a *Taft-Hartley plan*, the plan sponsor is a joint board of trustees consisting of equal representation from labor and management; these trustees are responsible for the overall operation and administration of the plan (International Foundation of Employee Benefit Plans, 2014).

Multiemployer plans offer portability: Participants retain coverage if they switch employment from one contributing employer to another within the same plan. But whether someone works for a particular contributing employer for 5 days or 5 months, the state of that person's health can eventually affect the cost of employer-provided health care benefits as well as on-the-job performance due to physical limitations, absenteeism, or both. In the long term, both employers and workers will be impacted by the toll that health conditions— serious or minor, short term or chronic—can take on health care utilization.

Both the unions and their signatory employers have incentives to invest in workers' safety and health over the long term. Although employers may not see the direct or immediate impact of preventing or addressing long-term health and safety risks, they will see the benefits over time. A reduction in absenteeism and employees who are able to work without physical restrictions can have a direct impact on an employer's bottom line.

BENEFITS OF JOINT LABOR–MANAGEMENT PLANS TO *TOTAL WORKER HEALTH* EFFORTS

The LHSFNA is uniquely positioned to address the TWH program due to the LHSFNA's makeup as a joint labor–management partnership. Safe worksites lead to greater productivity, lower insurance costs, and increased profitability (Fabius et al., 2013). Healthy laborers incur fewer health care costs, and large pools of laborers and other workers help control health insurance premiums. The LHSFNA helps contractors realize the human and financial benefits of health and safety while also providing a forum in which to address common health and safety concerns.

At its core, the LHSFNA practices TWH policies by design and as an inherent result of addressing certain health and safety issues in a comprehensive manner. Staff members of the LHSFNA work together on many issues about which there is an overlap between occupational safety and health and health promotion. Examples include skin cancer and heat stress prevention, noise exposure and hearing loss prevention, and back injury prevention, as well as addressing the various aspects of the current opioid epidemic and its impact on worksite safety and health.

The goals of approaching health and safety in this fashion are to help prevent injury and illness on and off the worksite so that members will have a long, productive career and enjoy retirement; reduce health care costs for laborers' health and welfare funds; reduce workers' compensation costs; and help signatory contractors to be more competitive.

Following are descriptive examples of health and safety issues that the LHSFNA has been able to address from occupational and nonoccupational perspectives. The success of these interventions can be quantified (in terms of the number of requests for services and so on), but it is difficult to demonstrate their ultimate impact on injuries and illnesses. The value of these examples is to show that there are multiple ways to contribute to the TWH approach. The LHSFNA has achieved this goal within the multiemployer environment by positioning itself as a valuable resource to labor and management interests, and finding ways to create incentives for positive actions on both sides.

Prevention of Skin Cancer and Heat Stress

Overexposure to the sun is the leading cause of skin cancer. More than 5.4 million cases of nonmelanoma skin cancer are diagnosed in more than 3.3 million people in the United States every year (Rogers, Weinstock, Feldman, & Coldiron, 2015). Outdoor workers exposed to sunlight have an increased risk of skin cancer and other types of cancer (e.g., lip, stomach, leukemia, lymphoma; Peters, Koehoorn, Demers, Nicol, & Kalia, 2016). Spending much of their time outdoors puts laborers at risk for overexposure to the sun's harmful ultraviolet rays, which are proven to cause premature skin aging and skin cancer. In addition, specific occupational factors, including exposure to radiation, coal tar, pitch, creosote, and arsenic, may contribute to skin cancer. There is also opportunity for nonoccupational sun exposure during yard work, outdoor recreation, and other outdoor activities.

Working outdoors also puts construction laborers at high risk of heat stress, which occurs when high temperatures or workloads do not allow the body to cool off fast enough. Heat stress can lead to dehydration, muscle cramps, and heat exhaustion, and to heat stroke, which can be fatal. In addition to these serious risks, heat stress can also lead to decreased job performance and increased risk of injury (Lucas, Epstein, & Kjellstrom, 2014).

Workers at greater risk of heat stress include those who are 65 years of age or older, are overweight, have heart disease or high blood pressure, or take medications affected by extreme heat (NIOSH, 2017). According to the Occupational Safety and Health Administration (OSHA; 2016a), heat stress can be prevented by allowing workers to acclimatize to the heat and by providing them with water, rest, and shade. In addition, it is recommended for employers to plan for emergencies, train workers to recognize and prevent heat stress, and monitor workers for signs of illness.

For almost 20 years, the LHSFNA has been educating members and raising awareness about the dangers of skin cancer through its sun sense program, which kicks off annually in May to align with Skin Cancer Prevention Month. The goal of the program is to encourage members to take steps on and off the job to protect themselves from the sun so that they may prevent skin cancer and lessen the impact of sun exposure. The campaign helps create awareness through a hands-on component and a more traditional educational component. The LHSFNA makes branded samples of sunblock; lip balm with sun protection factor, or SPF; and hard hat neck protectors available free to LIUNA affiliates, who then distribute them to LIUNA members. The direct educational components include various worker-friendly publications that provide information on the causes and risk factors for skin cancer, steps to take to prevent skin cancer, and how to conduct a skin cancer self-exam for early detection. Materials include posters, a toolbox talk, a bookmark, and publications with infographics. Wearing sunscreen along with sunglasses, hats, and other protective clothing can help prevent overexposure, but the key is for workers to make these practices daily habits year round.

Interest in the LHSFNA's sun sense program continues to increase each year. To capitalize on this success, the LHSFNA expanded the program in 2015 to include heat stress. Now known as *sun sense plus*, the program includes information designed to increase awareness and prevention efforts related to heat stress. In addition to developing posters and a brochure to address heat stress awareness and prevention, the program made branded neck-cooling cloths with instructions in English and Spanish available for distribution to various LIUNA entities, including district councils, local unions, training centers, and signatory contractors. Years of experience running the sun sense campaign showed that people tended to associate sun exposure with high temperatures, so it was a natural fit to add a heat stress component to a campaign that already was visible and successful.

The LHSFNA's sun sense plus program begins each year when a memorandum describing the program, an order form, and a page with product visuals and descriptions are mailed to LIUNA district councils, local unions, and training centers. In 2017, the LHSFNA introduced online product ordering for the sun sense plus program; that feature has been well received. The LHSFNA is aiming for all campaign product ordering to be done online, hopefully within a year or two. Now the goal of the campaign is to educate and create awareness among members and employers regarding skin cancer and heat stress prevention.

Noise Exposure and Hearing Loss Prevention

Hearing loss is one of the most common occupational hazards: Approximately 22 million workers are exposed annually to hazardous levels of occupational noise (Tak, Davis, & Calvert, 2009). Noise-induced hearing loss is preventable but is permanent and irreversible once hearing damage occurs (Murphy & Tak, 2009). Hazardous noise exposures are cumulative. Every exposure—even a few seconds at a time—contributes to potential hearing loss (Schulz, 2014). According to Tak et al. (2009), workers in the mining sector, followed by those in construction and manufacturing, are most likely to suffer from hearing impairment. A NIOSH (2016) study determined that a 25-year-old construction worker has the hearing ability of a 50-year-old who has not been exposed to occupational noise. OSHA (2016b) estimated that $242 million is spent annually on workers' compensation for hearing loss disability. Although potential noise exposures can happen off the job, studies have shown that occupational exposure is much more significant than nonoccupational exposure; a possible exception is hunting-related gunshot-noise exposure (Neitzel, Seixas,

Goldman, & Daniell, 2004). Workers can get 8 hours of exposure every day on the job, whereas their nonoccupational exposure tends to be much less.

To address hearing loss prevention, the LHSFNA spearheaded the development of an American National Standards Institute (ANSI) standard on hearing loss prevention in the construction industry. This consensus standard was developed to address an inadequate OSHA standard that had exempted construction workers from needing hearing protection when exposed to harmful levels of noise throughout their workday. The standard is task based and recommends the use of hearing protection whenever any task-related noise exposure exceeds 85 decibels, even for a short period. It also recommends that employers buy quieter equipment and implement other noise-control strategies (ANSI & American Society of Safety Engineers [ASSE], 2013).

The LHSFNA also hosted a National Conference on Preventing Hearing Loss in Construction, which was cosponsored by OSHA and NIOSH. The conference included a powerful address from LIUNA Apprenticeship Coordinator Bill Duke (LHSFNA, 2000), who discussed how he developed hearing loss from construction noise and described its impact on his life. That recorded address has since been used in LIUNA training programs. The LHSFNA assisted the LIUNA Training and Education Fund in developing its hearing protection course and sent hearing protection to LIUNA training centers for use in training or during classes. The LHSFNA staff also helped OSHA revise its noise website and create an OSHA booklet specifically about noise in construction (OSHA, 2011). Staff members of the LHSFNA have also actively assisted organizations, such as the American Industrial Hygiene Association (AIHA) noise committee, thus helping to position the LHSFNA as a leader in the field.

The LHSFNA maintains several publications on noise and construction that include task-based exposure information for employers and hearing loss prevention tips for employees. All of the LHSFNA's training and educational materials recognize the potential for nonoccupational exposures and urge hearing loss prevention efforts off the job. Hearing loss prevention on the job emphasizes reducing noise exposure as much as possible by implementing job controls and by supplementing these controls with hearing protection. For off-the-job exposures, hearing protection is the more common solution.

Hearing protection is difficult in construction because workers are often concerned about missing warning signals that may be vital to their safety. According to Neitzel and Seixas (2005), this may be one reason hearing protectors are not used as much as they should be in this industry. The LHSFNA has addressed this concern by stressing noise-control solutions and the availability of new hearing protectors that make communication easier, such as electronic earmuffs and flat attenuation plugs that protect hearing, while allowing for better communication and warning workers to avoid *overprotection* (i.e., too much attenuation).

Back Injury Prevention

Back injuries are the leading occupational injury for construction laborers (BLS, 2016c). Work-related back injuries and illnesses are often caused by repeated exposure to activities, such as lifting and carrying materials, sudden movements, whole body vibration, bending or twisting, repetitive and forceful hand activity, and working in a cramped space for long periods (OSHA, 2017).

Occupational risk can be reduced by planning the work beforehand and using mechanical equipment to move materials and other means, such as setting a weight limit for manual handling or requiring two-person lifts. "Proper" lifting usually is impossible in construction because few materials are in small, convenient sizes that workers can lift between knee and shoulder height. Moreover, nonoccupational risk factors, such as aging, obesity, and poor physical condition, can contribute to back pain and back injuries (Dong, Wang, & Largay, 2015). Nonoccupational risk is primarily addressed through education and technique.

The LHSFNA has developed educational materials that stress the importance of "working smarter, not harder." Materials widely distributed by the LHSFNA discuss the prevention of sprains and strains, focusing on how to change the work to fit the worker rather than changing the worker to fit the task. The LHSFNA also has produced educational materials on back injury prevention and on methods for selecting better—from an ergonomic perspective—hand tools. The LHSFNA also has worked with the LIUNA Training and Education Fund on back injury prevention training materials for laborers.

Staff of the LHSFNA also has helped develop an ANSI standard to prevent musculoskeletal disorders by reducing occupational risk (ANSI & ASSE, 2007). Although previous attempts to create consensus ergonomics have failed, the LHSFNA has played a key role in development by working closely with industry stakeholders to create a standard that garnered the support of all parties involved. With no federal ergonomics standard and few state rules, this ANSI standard is the only national guide that details how employers can prevent these injuries, which are so notable in construction. Staff members of the LHSFNA are also active on professional committees, such as the AIHA ergonomics committee, and have coauthored an AIHA report that critiques the use of preemployment physicals to prevent ergonomic injuries (Deist, Schneider, & Prodans, 2015). Getting a national association to support a strong critique of these physicals will help protect construction workers from becoming victims of employment discrimination and is one example of how participating in committees and working groups furthers TWH initiatives and goals.

Chronic Pain and the Opioid Epidemic

A significant number of people are affected by chronic pain nationwide. At least 100 million American adults—more than the total affected by heart disease, cancer, and diabetes combined—are affected by chronic pain (Tsang et al., 2008). According to Portenoy, Ugarte, Fuller, and Haas (2004), "about one-third of people who report pain indicate that their pain is 'disabling,' defined as both severe and having a high impact on functions of daily life" (pp. 317–318).

Chronic pain and the role of prescription narcotic painkillers to treat it have recently been thrust into the public spotlight. Many communities within the United States are currently facing an opiate addiction epidemic. Prescription opioids treat moderate to severe pain and are often prescribed after a surgery or injury, or for pain associated with serious health conditions, such as cancer. In 2014, opioids were involved in 61% of U.S. drug overdose deaths. The epidemic has led to a similar increase in heroin usage and overdoses because prescription opioids are often a gateway to heroin abuse (Rudd, Aleshire, Zibbell, & Gladden, 2016).

Work is a major contributing factor to chronic pain. The BLS (2016d) reported that in 2015, more than 324,700 workers lost time at work because of musculoskeletal sprains, strains, or tears, whereas another 136,000 lost work time due to soreness or pain. The LHSFNA is encouraging stakeholders to look beyond treating pain and examine the root causes of pain and how to modify or change them. Methods to prevent pain from occurring in the first place include ergonomics programs, injury and illness prevention programs, and an increased focus on fitting the job to the worker.

In addition to addressing work-related issues that are contributing to pain, construction employers are now finding a need to address the health, safety, and economic factors associated with the use of opioids to treat pain. Some of the challenges relating to employee opiate use surround what information an employer is legally able to obtain about an employee's use of prescription drugs. Drug-free workplace programs (DFWPs) that include drug testing are a common component to a comprehensive safety program. However, addressing prescription drug abuse and nonmedical use in DFWPs can be challenging, given that prescription drugs are legal.

The LHSFNA recommends comprehensive training for employees and supervisors that focuses on health and safety issues related to alcohol and all drugs, including prescription drugs. It also recommends that supervisors be trained to recognize the signs and symptoms of being under the influence of alcohol and drugs, including opiates. The supervisor's job does not include diagnosing whether an employee is high or intoxicated; rather, his or her job is to recognize and observe when someone is exhibiting unsafe and concerning behavior, and to then address the behavior to prevent an accident, injury, or both.

The LHSFNA has provided assistance and support around DFWP issues on behalf of LIUNA entities. Recently, the LHSFNA has been able to tailor that support to address opioid-specific issues. The DFWP services provided by the LHSFNA include reviewing and editing existing DFWP policies, helping to develop new policies, developing and conducting employee and supervisor training, developing related educational materials and posters, submitting comments on pertinent legislative issues, and addressing related mental health and treatment issues and topics. The LHSFNA also consults LIUNA health and welfare funds on mental health and substance use disorder benefit best practices, and provides request for proposal assistance when LIUNA health and welfare funds establish a member assistance program or seek new vendors.

As a result of the opioid epidemic, the LHSFNA has increased its efforts in several areas related to drug-free workplaces to specifically address opioid use and abuse efforts. In addition to focusing on DFWP policy language related to prescription drugs, the LHSFNA is tailoring employee and supervisory trainings to emphasize prescription drugs, especially pain medication, as well as heroin. The LHSFNA has joined the Facing Addiction Action Network, developed educational information on opioid abuse, emphasized the importance of mental health assistance and rehabilitation when working with LIUNA health and welfare funds, and worked closely with pharmacy benefit managers when opportunities arise to address opioid-related issues.

CONCLUSION

The TWH field is young and growing. Researchers, businesses, labor representatives, and federal agencies will need to continue to work together to find best practices that optimize the safety and health of U.S. workers while recognizing that there is not a one-size-fits-all approach to the TWH program. Different kinds of workplaces and jobs must be considered when deciding which programs, policies, and interventions to implement.

For a TWH approach to succeed, safety must be a priority, and workers cannot be blamed for working conditions that preclude them from making safe and healthy choices, and safe behaviors at work. To achieve this goal, labor and management must have an equal seat at the table and be given the opportunity to hear and understand the concerns, priorities, and goals of each side as they relate to the TWH approach.

The LHSFNA will continue to focus its efforts involving the TWH program and the unique characteristics of the construction industry that affect the context of the TWH approach. Areas of focus in the future will likely include chronic pain, mental health, the aging workforce, automation, avoidance of blaming the worker, and assurance that workers will have their voices heard.

REFERENCES

American National Standards Institute, & American Society of Safety Engineers. (2007). *ANSI/ASSE A10.40-2007 (R2013) Reduction of musculoskeletal problems in construction.* Des Plaines, IL: American National Standards Institute.

American National Standards Institute, & American Society of Safety Engineers. (2013). *ANSI/ASSE A10.46-2013 Hearing loss prevention for construction and demolition workers.* Des Plaines, IL: American National Standards Institute.

Bureau of Labor Statistics. (2016a). *Census of fatal occupational injuries: Table A-9. Fatal occupational injuries by event or exposure for all fatal injuries and major private industry sector, all United States, 2015.* Retrieved from https://www.bls.gov/iif/oshwc/cfoi/cftb0303.xlsx

Bureau of Labor Statistics. (2016b). *Census of fatal occupational injuries summary, 2015* (USDL-16-2304) [Press release]. Retrieved from https://www.bls.gov/news.release/cfoi.nr0.htm

Bureau of Labor Statistics. (2016c). *Table R2. Number of nonfatal occupational injuries and illnesses involving days away from work by industry and selected parts of body affected by injury or illness, private industry, 2015.* Retrieved from https://www.bls.gov/iif/oshwc/osh/case/ostb4754.pdf

Bureau of Labor Statistics. (2016d). *Table R49. Number of nonfatal occupational injuries and illnesses involving days away from work by nature of injury or illness and industry sector, private industry, 2015*. Retrieved from https://www.bls.gov/iif/oshwc/osh/case/ostb4801.pdf

Center for Construction Research and Training. (2008). *Occupational disease among construction workers*. Retrieved from http://www.cpwr.com/sites/default/files/research/OccupationalDiseaseAmongWorkers.pdf

Center for Construction Research and Training. (2013). *The construction chart book: The U.S. construction industry and its workers* (5th ed.). Silver Spring, MD: Author.

Deist, B., Schneider, S., & Prodans, R. (2015). *Application and limitations of functional capacity evaluations in managing work-related musculoskeletal disorder risks/hazards* (American Industrial Hygiene Association Position Paper). Retrieved from https://www.aiha.org/government-affairs/PositionStatements/Application%20and%20Limitations%20of%20Functional%20Capacity%20Evaluations_Final_2018.pdf

Dement, J. M., Welch, L., Bingham, E., Cameron, B., Rice, C., Quinn, P., & Ringen, K. (2003). Surveillance of respiratory diseases among construction and trade workers at Department of Energy nuclear sites. *American Journal of Industrial Medicine, 43,* 559–573. http://dx.doi.org/10.1002/ajim.10226

Dong, X. S., Wang, X., & Largay, J. A. (2015). Occupational and non-occupational factors associated with work-related injuries among construction workers in the USA. *International Journal of Occupational and Environmental Health, 21,* 142–150. http://dx.doi.org/10.1179/2049396714Y.0000000107

Dong, X. S., Wang, X., Ringen, K., & Sokas, R. (2017). Baby boomers in the United States: Factors associated with working longer and delaying retirement. *American Journal of Industrial Medicine, 60,* 315–328. http://dx.doi.org/10.1002/ajim.22694

Fabius, R., Thayer, R. D., Konicki, D. L., Yarborough, C. M., Peterson, K. W., Isaac, F., . . . Dreger, M. (2013). The link between workforce health and safety and the health of the bottom line: Tracking market performance of companies that nurture a "culture of health." *Journal of Occupational and Environmental Medicine, 55,* 993–1000. http://dx.doi.org/10.1097/JOM.0b013e3182a6bb75

International Foundation of Employee Benefit Plans. (2014). *What is a multiemployer plan?* Retrieved from https://www.ifebp.org/News/FeaturedTopics/Multiemployer/Pages/default.aspx

Kaiser Family Foundation, & Health Research and Educational Trust. (2015). *Employer health benefits 2015 summary of findings*. Retrieved from http://files.kff.org/attachment/summary-of-findings-2015-employer-health-benefits-survey

Laborers' Health & Safety Fund of North America. (Producer). (2000). *Bill Duke discusses hearing loss among Laborers* [DVD]. Available from Laborers' Health & Safety Fund of North America, 905 16th Street NW, Washington, DC 20006.

Lucas, R. A., Epstein, Y., & Kjellstrom, T. (2014). Excessive occupational heat exposure: A significant ergonomic challenge and health risk for current and future workers. *Extreme Physiology & Medicine, 3,* Article 14. http://dx.doi.org/10.1186/2046-7648-3-14

Murphy, W., & Tak, S. (2009, November 24). NIOSH science blog: Workplace hearing loss [Blog post]. Retrieved from https://blogs.cdc.gov/niosh-science-blog/2009/11/24/hearing/

National Institute for Occupational Safety and Health. (2015, November 13). *Total Worker Health*. Retrieved from https://www.cdc.gov/niosh/twh/totalhealth.html

National Institute for Occupational Safety and Health. (2016, October 20). *Noise and hearing loss prevention facts and statistics*. Retrieved from https://www.cdc.gov/niosh/topics/noise/chart-50yrold.html

National Institute for Occupational Safety and Health. (2017, June 5). *Heat stress*. Retrieved from https://www.cdc.gov/niosh/topics/heatstress/

Neitzel, R., & Seixas, N. (2005). The effectiveness of hearing protection among construction workers. *Journal of Occupational and Environmental Hygiene, 2,* 227–238. http://dx.doi.org/10.1080/15459620590932154

Neitzel, R., Seixas, N., Goldman, B., & Daniell, W. (2004). Contributions of non-occupational activities to total noise exposure of construction workers. *Annals of Occupational Hygiene, 48*, 463–473.

Occupational Safety and Health Administration. (2011). *OSHA pocket guide—Worker safety series: Protecting yourself from noise in construction* (OSHA Publication No. 3498-12N). Retrieved from https://www.osha.gov/Publications/3498noise-in-construction-pocket-guide.pdf

Occupational Safety and Health Administration. (2016a). *Occupational heat exposure prevention*. Retrieved from https://www.osha.gov/SLTC/heatstress/prevention.html

Occupational Safety and Health Administration. (2016b). *Occupational noise exposure*. Retrieved from https://www.osha.gov/SLTC/noisehearingconservation/index.html

Occupational Safety and Health Administration. (Ed.). (2017). Section VII: Chapter 1. Back disorders and injuries. *OSHA Technical Manual*. Retrieved from https://www.osha.gov/dts/osta/otm/otm_vii/otm_vii_1.html#6

Partnership to Fight Chronic Disease and U.S. Workplace Wellness Alliance. (2009). *The burden of chronic disease on business and U.S. competitiveness: Excerpt from the 2009 almanac of chronic disease*. Retrieved from http://www.prevent.org/data/files/News/pfcdalmanac_excerpt.pdf

Peters, C. E., Koehoorn, M. W., Demers, P. A., Nicol, A. M., & Kalia, S. (2016). Outdoor workers' use of sun protection at work and leisure. *Safety and Health at Work, 7*, 208–212. http://dx.doi.org/10.1016/j.shaw.2016.01.006

Portenoy, R. K., Ugarte, C., Fuller, I., & Haas, G. (2004). Population-based survey of pain in the United States: Differences among White, African American, and Hispanic subjects. *Journal of Pain, 5*, 317–328. http://dx.doi.org/10.1016/j.jpain.2004.05.005

Ringen, K., Dong, X. S., Goldenhar, L. M., & Cain, C. T. (2018). Construction safety and health in the USA: Lessons from a decade of turmoil. *Annals of Work Exposures and Health, 62*, S25–S33. http://dx.doi.org/10.1093/annweh/wxy069

Ringen, K., Englund, A., Welch, L., Weeks, J. L., & Seegal, J. L. (Eds.). (1995). *Construction safety and health: Vol. 10. Occupational medicine: State of the art reviews*. Philadelphia, PA: Hanley & Belfus.

Rogers, H. W., Weinstock, M. A., Feldman, S. R., & Coldiron, B. M. (2015). Incidence estimate of nonmelanoma skin cancer (keratinocyte carcinomas) in the US population, 2012. *JAMA Dermatology, 151*, 1081–1086. http://dx.doi.org/10.1001/jamadermatol.2015.1187

Rudd, R. A., Aleshire, N., Zibbell, J. E., & Gladden, R. M. (2016, January 1). Increases in drug and opioid overdose deaths—United States, 2000–2014. *CDC Morbidity and Mortality Weekly Report, 64*, 1378–1382. Retrieved from https://www.cdc.gov/mmwr/pdf/wk/mm6450.pdf

Schulz, T. (2014, June 17). Off-the-job safety: Protecting your hearing at home and play [Blog post]. Retrieved from http://ehstoday.com/hearing-protection/job-safety-protecting-your-hearing-home-and-play

Tak, S., Davis, R. R., & Calvert, G. M. (2009). Exposure to hazardous workplace noise and use of hearing protection devices among US workers—NHANES, 1999–2004. *American Journal of Industrial Medicine, 52*, 358–371. http://dx.doi.org/10.1002/ajim.20690

Tsang, A., Von Korff, M., Lee, S., Alonso, J., Karam, E., Angermeyer, M. C., . . . Watanabe, M. (2008). Common chronic pain conditions in developed and developing countries: Gender and age differences and comorbidity with depression-anxiety disorders. *Journal of Pain, 9*, 883–891. http://dx.doi.org/10.1016/j.jpain.2008.05.005

11

Community Health Programs

Promising Practices and Opportunities for Expanding Total Worker Health®

Sherry Baron, Emma K. Tsui, Isabel Cuervo, and Nadia Islam

The *Total Worker Health®* concept has evolved to include a broad range of organizational policies, practices, and programs that influence working conditions and the health, safety, and well-being of workers (National Institute for Occupational Safety and Health [NIOSH], 2016c; Sorensen et al., 2016). Beyond the factors directly related to the work environment, the *Total Worker Health* (TWH) vision aims to include programs that consider the needs of workers and families in the context of their community (NIOSH, 2016c). Achieving this vision will necessitate collaboration with a broader group of stakeholders and researchers, including those who focus on promoting the health of broader communities as well as workers. In this chapter, we first discuss recent changes in the structure of work in the United States and how those changes influence the need to expand the reach of TWH programs beyond the worksite. Next, we provide a brief history of the evolution of community health that demonstrates the synergy between community health and TWH approaches. We then describe specific approaches and activities from community health practice that support the TWH mission.

This chapter was funded in part through the Prevention Research Center Workplace Health Research Network by the Centers for Disease Control and Prevention grant number 3U48 DP005008-0151 SIP 14-031.

http://dx.doi.org/10.1037/0000149-012
Total Worker Health, H. L. Hudson, J. A. S. Nigam, S. L. Sauter, L. C. Chosewood, A. L. Schill, and J. Howard (Editors)
Copyright © 2019 by the American Psychological Association. All rights reserved.

THE CHANGING STRUCTURE OF WORK IN THE UNITED STATES

The changing structure of the workplace is an important dynamic that is pushing the need for a more expansive TWH vision. Many workers are currently underserved by workplace health programs, especially low-wage, often non-unionized and immigrant workers, as well as those employed in small companies or scattered in small numbers across multiple sites or who work in temporary jobs irrespective of the company size (Linnan et al., 2008). Yet, health surveillance data have suggested that these workers could benefit most from integrated and effective TWH programs (Steege, Baron, Marsh, Menéndez, & Myers, 2014). For example, workers who are low-income, African American, Hispanic, and are an immigrant, and those with less than a high school education are more likely to work in a job with a work-related injury and illness rate twice the national average (Baron et al., 2014). Income level and race are also associated with decreased overall life expectancy (Williams, Mohammed, Leavell, & Collins, 2010) and increased risk of chronic disease (Sommer et al., 2015).

According to Fusaro and Shaefer (2016), in 2013, 30% of all wage and salary workers (an estimated 36 million workers) earned less than $13.50 per hour, the wage that brings a family of three to 125% of the poverty threshold, and a third of those workers lacked health coverage during the previous year. Hammerback et al. (2015), in a qualitative study, found that low-wage workers were interested in having access to workplace health promotion programs and thought their employers would benefit through increased worker productivity and morale, although most had never participated in a program and believed their employer would never prioritize employee health. Common low-wage occupations, such as construction laborers and domestic, child care, and home health workers, require frequently changing worksites or work in solitary conditions, making the implementation of worksite-based programs even more challenging (Baron et al., 2014). Low-wage workers are also more likely to be employed by small businesses (Acs & Nichols, 2007), and small businesses in general are less likely to provide workplace health programs (Claxton et al., 2016). Harris, Hannon, Beresford, Linnan, and McLellan (2014) reviewed the landscape of workplace health programs in small businesses and found few successful models. Challenges include financial instability, high employee turnover, and limited capacity given resource constraints.

Changes in the economy, especially since the economic recession of 2008, have caused an increasing proportion of workers to be employed in temporary or nonstandard work arrangements. David Weil (2014), former director of the Wage and Hours Division of the U.S. Department of Labor, described the current workplace as *fissured:* Employers increasingly use contractors and subcontractors for hiring, evaluation, pay, supervision, training, and coordination of workers. L. F. Katz and Krueger (2016) estimated that in 2015, 15.8% of workers in the United States were employed in *alternative work arrangements*, defined as temporary help workers, on-call workers, contract workers, or independent contractors—a 50% increase since 2005. By employing workers in nonstandard jobs, companies decrease labor costs, reduce employment during periods of low production, and avoid providing workers with benefits, such as health insurance and pensions (Howard, 2017). These attributes that make temporary workers attractive to employers can also make temporary work more hazardous. Temporary workers are often unclear about who is responsible for their safety and health at the workplace, the agency that is their legal employer, or the person at the worksite who directly supervises their work (Howard, 2017). Temporary work is associated with work-related injuries and mental health problems, and these adverse health outcomes have been attributed to higher workloads, longer working hours, decreased training, and poor workplace communication (Benach et al., 2014; Howard, 2017; Landsbergis, Grzywacz, & LaMontagne, 2014).

EXPANSION OF *TOTAL WORKER HEALTH* PROGRAMS BEYOND THE WORKSITE

Given the current structure and composition of workplaces in the Unites States, a more expansive vision is needed not only for the scope but also for the reach of TWH programs. A challenge is developing innovative approaches and intervention programs that overcome the barriers to including low-wage workers and those employed in temporary jobs or by small businesses. Intervening at the worksite has been the dominant TWH approach and has obvious advantages for accessing workers, supervisors, and employers and investigating and eliminating hazards from the production process. However, limiting TWH programs to the worksite will likely mean that an important portion of the working population is excluded and could potentially lead to broadening rather than reducing health disparities associated with work. To conceptualize an alternative approach, we have drawn on interdisciplinary environmental social sciences theories about the role of place in the dynamic interrelationship between humans and the physical environment (Gieseking, Mangold, Katz, Low, & Saegert, 2014). As an example, the worker embodies the effects of his or her workplace as he or she occupies multiple spaces, whether in the worksite, in family spaces, or within broader community spaces. This approach can be applied to the work environment to reframe the concept of the workplace to encompass the entire experience of work and all of the values, attitudes, behaviors, and health risks that arise based on the work experience, whether at work, at home, or in the community. Benach et al. (2014), in reviewing the health impact of precarious employment, echoed this notion: "Some of the most important consequences of precarious employment are situated outside the productive sphere and relate to the social and material consequences of precariousness" (p. 242).

The impact of the work environment on other spaces in a worker's life is not a new concept, especially as it applies to the stress that workers experience in balancing work and home commitments (Sorensen et al., 2011).

Some employers, especially those employing professional and other white-collar workers, have implemented new policies to reduce work–family stress, including on-site child care, flexible working hours, and telecommuting policies. The impact of these programs on worker and family health as it applies to a broader range of workers and worksites, such as low-wage, temporary workers or small businesses, is an understudied area of research (Kelly et al., 2014). Irrespective of wage level or type of worker, previous studies have not extended the concept of work–family stress to include both positive and negative impacts of the workplace environment as workers interface in broader community spaces.

COMMUNITY HEALTH THEORY AND PRACTICE

A brief history of the evolution of community health as a public health discipline provides a context for how it aligns with the TWH mission and how community health practitioners are important collaborators in the development of more comprehensive programs to promote worker health. Initially, the community health discipline was primarily focused on health behaviors and actions of individuals, and had some sense of a shared community identity. Over time, it has evolved to emphasize health promotion via changes to social and physical environments. For many community health practitioners today individual-, community-, and population-level approaches are seen as reinforcing elements of multilevel public health programs (Braveman, Egerter, & Williams, 2011).

The 1970s shaped the field of contemporary community health in two important ways. First, Marc LaLonde (1974), Canada's minister of National Health and Welfare, issued a groundbreaking report, *A New Perspective on the Health of Canadians*, which altered the landscape by making the case that gains in population health status and reduction of health care costs could best be achieved by preventive actions taken outside of the health care system. In 1979, not long after the publication of the LaLonde report, the U.S. Department of Health and Human Services issued its first *Healthy People* report, thus beginning the national public health process of goal-setting and benchmarking that continues to the present. Each subsequent decade, the *Healthy People* report tells a story of a shift from a focus on individual health behavior change to an increasing interest in the environments that shape health and the social and political conditions that influence health now known as the *social determinants of health* (SDOH) framework (U.S. Department of Health and Human Services, 2010).

An SDOH framework focuses on a range of factors, including socioeconomic status, race, and ethnicity as well as racism, discrimination, social structure, social position, housing, transportation, political environment, cultural beliefs, and norms. It recognizes the contextual factors that impact risk and protective factors from individual, family, neighborhood, community, systems, and environmental or institutional levels. It argues that these economic and social determinants have a more significant impact on population health than personal behaviors or access to medical care (Braveman et al., 2011). Addressing and understanding the impact of SDOH has been operationalized through the application of the social ecological framework (SEF).

The SEF examines the ways in which multiple levels of influence can impact health outcomes, including at the individual, interpersonal, institutional, community, and policy levels of influence (Baron et al., 2014; Green, Richard, & Potvin, 1996). In a worker context, the SEF is particularly relevant for understanding how one major social determinant—employment and work—is impacted by other domains of influence and also is consistent with the current TWH approach (NIOSH, 2016a), as shown in Figure 11.1. For example, factors at the individual level include behaviors and their immediate precursors, such as lack of knowledge about how to use workplace protective equipment or which foods have the highest nutritional value. At the interpersonal level, a lack of coworker, supervisor, or family support for healthy choices or practices may compromise health. Conversely, membership in labor unions or community-based organizations may provide information and other supports. At the institutional level, worksites can be redesigned to reduce exposures and improve the organization of work to reduce workplace stressors. Healthy design of schools, housing, and transportation systems also create safer and healthier community environments and commuting experiences. Community-level interventions, such as construction permitting and safety requirements, and high employment standards for those working in community-funded programs or projects, can reduce or even eliminate work hazards. Community initiatives improve leisure time activities through the quality and accessibility of parks and recreational facilities. Policies contribute to reducing workplace and community hazards through exposure standards and enforcement programs, and improve worker well-being through living wage and paid leave laws.

Community health practitioners now fully embrace the SDOH and SEF approaches, recognizing that individual-level interventions alone will not solve current challenges in promoting the health of communities. Hortensia Amaro (2014), associate editor of the *American Journal of Public Health*, wrote: "A nagging frustration with the negative impacts of toxic environments on individual-level intervention effects has led me to a new focus on place-based interventions" (p. 964). She went on to define *place-based interventions* as those "which address contextual factors that shape major public health problems," which includes "revisiting the important roles of social capital, collective efficacy, community organizing, and empowerment of community residents as agents of change for improving community conditions that impact health" (p. 964). This more comprehensive approach to community health promotion overlaps with many of the underlying goals, approaches, and issues captured in the TWH framework. Next, we describe some of the major approaches community health practitioners use to address the SDOH and how these can stimulate ideas for ongoing collaborations as part of TWH programs.

FIGURE 11.1. Social Ecological Framework as Applied to Total Worker Health and Community Health

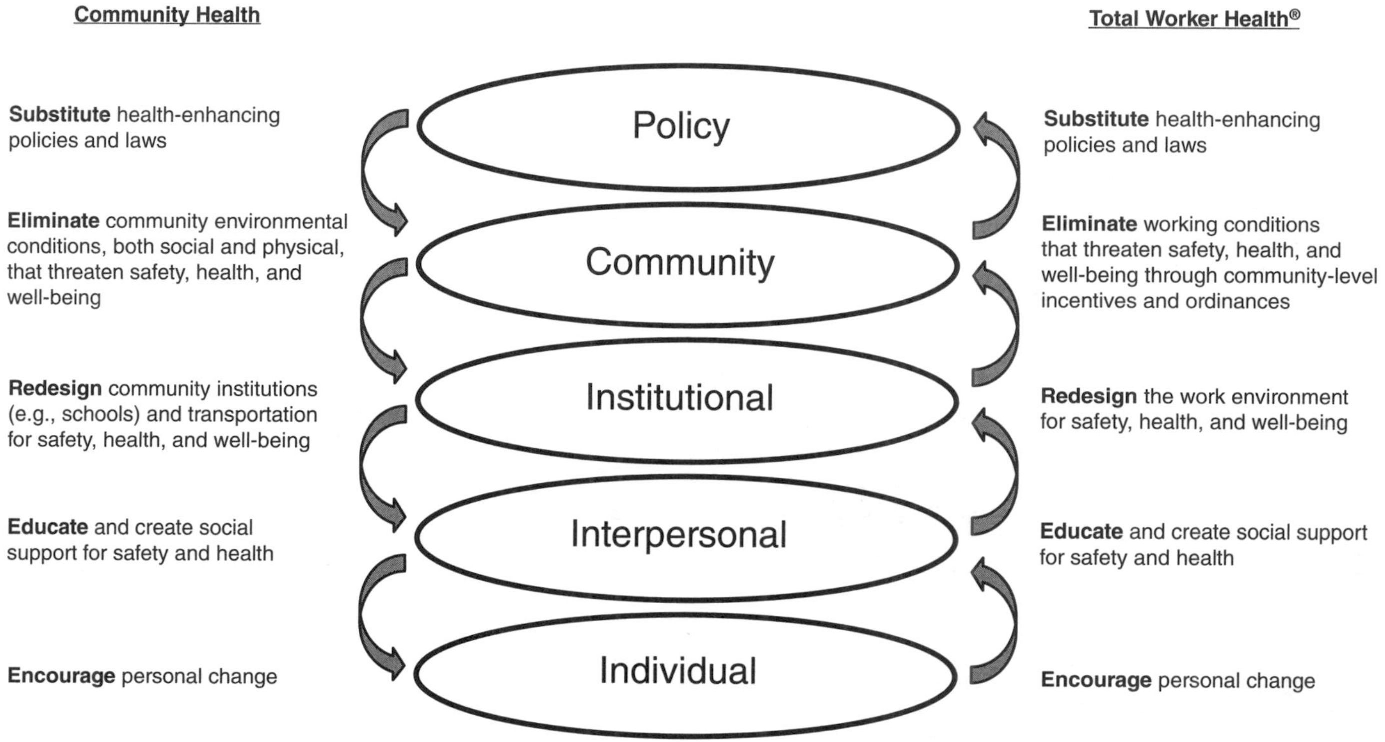

<u>Community Health</u>

Substitute health-enhancing policies and laws

Eliminate community environmental conditions, both social and physical, that threaten safety, health, and well-being

Redesign community institutions (e.g., schools) and transportation for safety, health, and well-being

Educate and create social support for safety and health

Encourage personal change

<u>Total Worker Health®</u>

Substitute health-enhancing policies and laws

Eliminate working conditions that threaten safety, health, and well-being through community-level incentives and ordinances

Redesign the work environment for safety, health, and well-being

Educate and create social support for safety and health

Encourage personal change

Policy

Community

Institutional

Interpersonal

Individual

The National Institute for Occupational Safety and Health (NIOSH) hierarchy of controls as applied to *Total Worker Health* (NIOSH, 2016b) can be adapted to the social ecological framework shown here and demonstrates the parallels between the Total Worker Health approach and community health approaches.

COMMUNITY-BASED PARTICIPATORY RESEARCH

Engagement of appropriate stakeholders across all stages of a project is an essential principle for intervention research using the SEF and SDOH approaches. A community-based participatory research (CBPR) framework provides a practical approach for this type of engagement. *Community-based participatory research* is defined as "a collaborative approach to research that equitably involves all partners in the research process and recognizes the unique strengths that each brings" (D. L. Katz, 2004, p. 1). Unlike "traditional" health research, CBPR calls for the active and equal partnership of community stakeholders throughout the research process, including selecting health concerns and research questions, determining study design, recruiting participants, designing instruments, implementing research or interventions, and disseminating findings. Overall, CBPR (a) promotes active collaboration and participation at every stage of research, (b) facilitates colearning, (c) ensures research or interventions are community driven, (d) disseminates results in useful ways for community stakeholders, (e) ensures research and intervention strategies are culturally appropriate, and (f) defines community as a unit of identity. If done well, CBPR promotes benefits, such as increased trust between researchers and communities, enhanced quantity and quality of collected data, and stronger infrastructure building and sustainability (Israel, Schulz, Parker, & Becker, 1998). The CBPR framework suggests that researchers' knowledge (e.g., research design, measurement tools, data analysis) works in concert with community stakeholders' knowledge (e.g., cultural norms and values, community dynamics, organizational politics) to ensure the successful development and implementation of research and interventions. Thus, social determinants and CBPR approaches allow us to use a contextualized approach to addressing the health of workers—one that engages both community and policy stakeholders, integrates traditional health promotion and prevention efforts with occupational safety and workplace health initiatives, and enhances worker and community involvement in the design and implementation of programs. TWH approaches can be informed by CBPR principles and strategies that emphasize the importance of worker involvement in all aspects of the research process, including identifying the research questions, documenting workplace and community risks and assets, disseminating findings, and generating action-oriented policy and programs that marry occupational and community health issues. Table 11.1 provides a more detailed description of these strategies.

Although not as well developed in occupational health research, the CBPR approach has much in common with well-established principles and approaches for occupational safety and health intervention programs. Worker participation through joint worker (or union) and management safety and health committees is associated with improved workplace safety (Punnett et al., 2013). Reviews of TWH research have underscored the importance of worker participation in successful programs (Bradley, Grossman, Hubbard, Ortega, & Curry, 2016). The Center for the Promotion of Health in the New England Workplace,

TABLE 11.1. *Total Worker Health®* **Approaches and Alignment With Community-Based Participatory Research Principles and Strategies**

CBPR principle	Strategy	TWH approaches
Collaborative, equitable partnership in all phases of research	Engagement that spans identifying priorities, to design, to intervention development and implementation, to evaluation, to dissemination	Workers are engaged in all phases of the research project from identifying the research question, developing methods, analyzing findings, and disseminating findings to policymakers, employers, or other change agents
Community is the unit of identity	Research is focused on the community	Community identity can be informed by both occupation and other dimensions, such race or ethnicity, or geography
CBPR builds on strengths and resources of community	Research builds on community assets and moves away from a deficit model	Workers can identify key assets in the community in the form of persons (e.g., worker leaders), institutions (e.g., worker centers and or community-based organizations), and processes and policies that can be leveraged
CBPR fosters colearning and capacity building	Efforts are incorporated to build capacity of all partners to engage in research through orientation and training about research methods for community partners and also training that orients academic researchers to be better partners and listeners for the local knowledge and expertise of community partners in the research endeavor	Worker and researcher training opportunities are built into the research process (e.g., workers engaged in data collection and analysis methods; workers provide training to researchers on workplace context)
Balance between knowledge generation and benefit for community partners	At the outset is a genuine process for identifying the expectations and goals of the research to be conducted and eliciting the practical benefits for community partners in engaging in this research	TWH approaches are designed to be action oriented; research is designed to produce policy or programmatic solutions rather than simply identify risk factors
CBPR focuses on problems of local relevance	Communities are engaged in determining the priorities	Because TWH approaches marry occupational and community health issues, workers can identify and explore issues that span both work and community settings

TABLE 11.1. (continued)

CBPR principle	Strategy	TWH approaches
CBPR disseminates results to all partners and involves them in wider dissemination of results	Results are disseminated in multiple vehicles and strategies, peer-reviewed articles, newspaper articles, policy briefs, monographs, and community forums	TWH study findings are used for action-oriented purposes and disseminated accordingly (e.g., at city council hearings, to health department leaders)
CBPR involves a long-term process and commitment to sustainability	*Sustainability* is defined as an ongoing goal to strive toward in the development of research activities	In building both worker and researcher capacity through the CBPR process and through the establishment of equitable partnerships, TWH approaches build a sustainable platform for addressing health issues on an ongoing basis

Note. CBPR = community-based participatory research; TWH = *Total Worker Health.*

a TWH center of excellence, has designed a toolkit that assists workplaces in developing participatory programs and emphasizes the central role of worker participation in developing TWH programs—both to make the program meet their specific needs and because the process of participation itself promotes health (Nobrega et al., 2017). One of the newest TWH centers of excellence founded in 2016, the Center for Healthy Work at the University of Illinois, Chicago, will be using CBPR to explore community-level approaches for improving residents' health at work. They will develop community-based interventions that expand residents' access to healthy jobs, including drawing on their previous experience using trained community health workers (CHWs) as promoters of occupational safety (Baron et al., 2014).

The San Francisco Chinatown restaurant worker health and safety study is another example of CBPR being applied to addressing the impact of work-related stressors on a community level. It was a community–university–health department collaboration that used an SEF approach and included University of California, Berkeley, and University of California, San Francisco, researchers; a community-based organization in San Francisco's Chinatown; and the San Francisco Department of Public Health (Chang et al., 2013). The project partners undertook extensive efforts to facilitate equitable participation among its members, particularly with its immigrant worker partners. Findings from the study documented gaps in safety and health, including inadequate ventilation and lighting as well as labor policies, such as inadequate posting of minimum wage and paid sick leave notification (Chang et al., 2013). The research effort ultimately ended with groundbreaking policy change addressing wage theft at the city level (Minkler et al., 2014). This research, with one isolated group of low-wage and precarious workers, led directly to a law that benefits other low-wage workers throughout their community.

STATE AND LOCAL HEALTH DEPARTMENTS

State and local health departments form a core part of the community health infrastructure by tracking injuries and illnesses, channeling government funding for programs, and coordinating efforts across communities. They are key partners with the federal government to achieve *Healthy People* objectives. Public health agencies are in a position to intervene at multiple levels of the SEF by shaping policy and promoting systems change at the workplace and in the community as well as by offering individually focused education and preventive services, and assuring access to care. NIOSH has supported state health departments to develop occupational health surveillance and targeted intervention programs. The state and local public health infrastructure can provide many points of access to reach underserved worker groups with information about health and safety risks, and with strategies to control hazards, provide occupational health services, and provide information about legal rights. These efforts can also open communication with communities through which health departments not only provide occupational health and safety information and services but also collect information from community members about their work and other life experiences that influence health (Baron et al., 2014).

Integrating occupational health concerns into strategic public health planning can set the stage for future actions and resource allocation. For example, recently, 21 states in a coordinated effort with NIOSH added questions to identify respondents' occupation as part of the *behavioral risk factor surveillance system*, an annual telephone survey that collects state data from residents regarding their health-related risk behaviors, chronic health conditions, and use of preventive services. These data generated rates by occupation group for the American Heart Association's metrics of cardiovascular health behaviors or modifiable factors that can improve cardiovascular disease outcomes (Shockey, Sussell, & Odom, 2016). The TWH research findings, such as those by Miranda, Gore, Boyer, Nobrega, and Punnett (2015), have documented links between cardiovascular health behaviors and modifiable working conditions. State and local health departments can use this information to expand current efforts, such as in Massachusetts, where interventions to reduce workplace stress are part of the statewide strategic plan to address cardiovascular disease (Baron et al., 2014).

COMMUNITY-BASED PRIMARY CARE

Primary care practitioners, particularly those providing care to poor populations through community health centers (currently called federally qualified health centers), have a long history of advocating for their patients' health and other needs, such as food access, affordable and safe housing, and civil rights. These centers pride themselves on providing accessible health care that is affordable, culturally competent, and located close to where their patients live and work (DeVoe et al., 2016). Community clinics have played a central role in community health practice for more than 50 years; however, new advances made possible by electronic health records (EHRs) have created opportunities for better integration of SDOH approaches into the primary care encounter. Although training for primary care practitioners emphasizes attention to the social factors that influence health, research has suggested that primary care practitioners sometimes underestimate patients' social needs and that creating standardized systems for obtaining this information leads to greater action (DeVoe et al., 2016).

To promote greater standardization, the Institute of Medicine (2014) recommended the routine collection of 11 SDOH domains within the EHR, including individual-level factors, such as physical activity and alcohol and tobacco use, as well as economic and community-level determinants, such as census tract median income, financial resource strain, and social connections or isolation. Health informatics researchers, such as Behforouz, Drain, and Rhatigan (2014), have called for expanding the social history to go beyond asking patients their occupation to also asking about hours of work, job stresses, and concerns about work. Using new tools within the EHR, such as clinical decision support, to identify work exposures that might affect health can facilitate integration and coordination among primary care, public health, and community services that might assist patients in addressing work issues. NIOSH researchers in collaboration with occupational health clinicians and health informatics researchers have investigated how the development of these types of EHR clinical decision support tools could improve the way primary care practitioners approach patients' work-related concerns. Initial feedback from primary care providers is that they perceived these tools as valuable because the tools provided useful information and standardization of care, and were considered technically feasible (Baron, Filios, Marovich, Chase, & Ash, 2017).

COMMUNITY HEALTH WORKERS

CHWs, also called lay community health liaisons and health promoters, for example, are generally members of the same communities that they serve and are seen as trusted sources to provide health support services. Employed by community health centers, hospitals, and community-based organizations, they, as part of a multidisciplinary health care team, contribute to the prevention and management of chronic disease and help bridge the health equity gap in hard-to-reach populations (Brownstein, Andrews, Wall, & Mukhtar, 2015). The roles of CHWs include improving outreach to educate underserved community members about common health conditions; promoting healthy behaviors; identifying and referring community-based resources, including primary care practitioners; and organizing communities to improve environmental conditions (Lopez et al., 2017). The CHW and health promoter model has been used in a variety of intervention programs, including those that deliver workplace safety and health education in community settings for hard-to-reach workers in precarious jobs, such as farmworkers, poultry processing workers, and construction day laborers (Baron et al., 2014).

Although these examples demonstrate how CHWs could be valuable members of multidisciplinary TWH teams to address work issues in a community context, most CHW training programs include little or no information about the role of work on their patients' health. To address this gap and to promote improved integration with community health practitioners and researchers, researchers from Queens College, City University of New York, recently designed a training module for CHWs, in partnership with the community-based organization Make the Road New York, as part of their 3-month CHW training program (Baron et al., 2018). Funded in part as a program of the National Institute of Environmental Health Sciences' environmental career worker training program, these CHWs respond to disasters, perform home visits, make health assessments, provide counseling and case management services, and help conduct research to assess the health needs of families and communities. The module, titled "Working With Workers: Talking About Workplace Safety and Health" (Baron et al., 2018), provides CHWs basic knowledge, including how to start a conversation about workplace exposures, how to identify workplace hazards, how workplace exposures contribute to disease, health and safety rights of workers, and action planning.

One major goal of this CHW training is to generate mechanisms for community and worker empowerment by guiding CHWs to create better informed action plans for their clients so that workers can potentially better address their health-related issues. Pushing the link between individual and community health in community-based settings, CHWs can facilitate organizational activities that promote community empowerment. For example, occupational safety and health peer training to support the individual health of construction laborers in the New York City and the New Jersey metropolitan area was found to strengthen community resilience, a key component of community health (Cuervo, Leopold, & Baron, 2017). Similarly, in a TWH intervention project, Olson et al. (2016) found that peer-led monthly meetings with scripted training activities promoted a greater sense of peer social support for home care workers who work in isolated settings.

PROMOTION OF TRANSDISCIPLINARY AND CROSS-SECTOR RESEARCH TO INTEGRATE COMMUNITY AND OCCUPATIONAL HEALTH

In summary, an SDOH approach to promoting workers' health provides a holistic lens for conceptualizing programs and policies to address the structural factors that influence workers' lives. It also provides a common language for communication among occupational safety and health and community health researchers and practitioners. With this common understanding, the SEF provides a framework to develop multilevel programs that address influences on the health and well-being of workers and their families in the context of their worksites as well as in their family and community spaces.

To date, examples of truly integrative public health programs that address the complex interplay among factors at work, at home, and in the broader community are limited. However, community and other public health researchers and practitioners increasingly recognize that solving complex problems requires cross-sector and transdisciplinary collaborations, and many governmental and foundation funders are now encouraging or requiring such collaborations. Researchers studying the "science of team science" have tried to capture the most essential elements that produce effective transdisciplinary collaborations (Stokols, Hall, Taylor, & Moser, 2008). More recently, Flood, Minkler, Lavery, Estrada, and Falbe (2015) proposed the collective impact model as a guide to developing large-scale, social change-oriented health-promotion programs that require cross-sector collaborations. Recommendations to create strong transdisciplinary and cross-sector collaborations, whether as part of team science or through the collective impact model, share certain attributes, including developing a common integrated conceptual framework and goals, using common terminology and metrics, developing robust and open communication systems, recognizing and deemphasizing power or status differentials among collaborators, and having sufficient funding to support a collaboration infrastructure. Using these guides, the TWH approach can be one vehicle that brings together transdisciplinary and cross-sector occupational and community health researchers and stakeholders to create a more integrated vision for workers' health that meets the needs of a workforce having an increasingly limited connection to a single worksite or employer.

REFERENCES

Acs, G., & Nichols, A. (2007, September 11). *Low-income workers and their employers: Characteristics and challenges* [Report]. Retrieved from http://www.urban.org/UploadedPDF/411532_low_income_workers.pdf

Amaro, H. (2014). The action is upstream: Place-based approaches for achieving population health and health equity [Editor's Choice]. *American Journal of Public Health, 104*, 964. http://dx.doi.org/10.2105/AJPH.2014.302032

Baron, S. L., Beard, S., Davis, L. K., Delp, L., Forst, L., Kidd-Taylor, A., . . . Welch, L. S. (2014). Promoting integrated approaches to reducing health inequities among low-income workers: Applying a social ecological framework. *American Journal of Industrial Medicine, 57*, 539–556. http://dx.doi.org/10.1002/ajim.22174

Baron, S., Cuervo, I., Arias, L., Palaguachi, D., Gallardo, J., & Olivera, J. (2018). *Working with workers: Talking about workplace safety and health—A training module for community health workers*. Retrieved from http://commonercenter.org/communityhealthworkers.html

Baron, S., Filios, M. S., Marovich, S., Chase, D., & Ash, J. S. (2017). Recognition of the relationship between patients' work and health: A qualitative evaluation of the need for clinical decision support (CDS) for worker health in five primary case practices. *Journal of Occupational and Environmental Medicine, 59*, e245–e250. http://dx.doi.org/10.1097/JOM.0000000000001183

Behforouz, H. L., Drain, P. K., & Rhatigan, J. J. (2014). Rethinking the social history. *New England Journal of Medicine, 371*, 1277–1279. http://dx.doi.org/10.1056/NEJMp1404846

Benach, J., Vives, A., Amable, M., Vanroelen, C., Tarafa, G., & Muntaner, C. (2014). Precarious employment: Understanding an emerging social determinant of health.

*AnnualReviewofPublicHealth,35,*229–253.http://dx.doi.org/10.1146/annurev-publhealth-032013-182500

Bradley, C. J., Grossman, D. C., Hubbard, R. A., Ortega, A. N., & Curry, S. J. (2016). Integrated interventions for improving Total Worker Health: A panel report from the National Institutes of Health Pathways to Prevention workshop: Total Worker Health—What's work got to do with it? *Annals of Internal Medicine, 165,* 279–283.

Braveman, P., Egerter, S., & Williams, D. R. (2011). The social determinants of health: Coming of age. *Annual Review of Public Health, 32,* 381–398. http://dx.doi.org/10.1146/annurev-publhealth-031210-101218

Brownstein, J. N., Andrews, T., Wall, H., & Mukhtar, Q. (2015). *Addressing chronic disease through community health workers: A policy and systems-level approach* (2nd ed.). Atlanta, GA: Centers for Disease Control & Prevention. Retrieved from http://www.cdc.gov/dhdsp/docs/chw_brief.pdf

Chang, C., Minkler, M., Salvatore, A. L., Lee, P. T., Gaydos, M., & Liu, S. S. (2013). Studying and addressing urban immigrant restaurant worker health and safety in San Francisco's Chinatown district: A CBPR case study. *Journal of Urban Health, 90,* 1026–1040. http://dx.doi.org/10.1007/s11524-013-9804-0

Claxton, G., Rae, M., Long, M., Damico, A., Whitmore, H., & Foster, G. (2016). Health benefits in 2016: Family premiums rose modestly, and offer rates remained stable. *Health Affairs, 35,* 1908–1917. http://dx.doi.org/10.1377/hlthaff.2016.0951

Cuervo, I., Leopold, L., & Baron, S. (2017). Promoting community preparedness and resilience: Latino immigrant community-driven project following Hurricane Sandy. *American Journal of Public Health, 107,* S161–S164. http://dx.doi.org/10.2105/AJPH.2017.304053

DeVoe, J. E., Bazemore, A. W., Cottrell, E. K., Likumahuwa-Ackman, S., Grandmont, J., Spach, N., & Gold, R. (2016). Perspectives in primary care: A conceptual framework and path for integrating social determinants of health into primary care practice. *Annals of Family Medicine, 14,* 104–108. http://dx.doi.org/10.1370/afm.1903

Flood, J., Minkler, M., Lavery, S. H., Estrada, J., & Falbe, J. (2015). The collective impact model and its potential for health promotion: Overview and case study of a healthy retail initiative in San Francisco. *Health Education & Behavior, 42* 654–668. http://dx.doi.org/10.1177/1090198115577372

Fusaro, V. A., & Shaefer, H. L. (2016, October). How should we define "low-wage" work? An analysis using the Current Population Survey. *Monthly Labor Review,* U.S. Bureau of Labor Statistics. http://dx.doi.org/10.21916/mlr.2016.44

Gieseking, J. J., Mangold, W., Katz, C., Low, S., & Saegert, S. (Eds.). (2014). *The people, place, and space reader.* New York, NY: Routledge. http://dx.doi.org/10.4324/9781315816852

Green, L. W., Richard, L., & Potvin, L. (1996). Ecological foundations of health promotion. *American Journal of Health Promotion, 10,* 270–281. http://dx.doi.org/10.4278/0890-1171-10.4.270

Hammerback, K., Hannon, P. A., Harris, J. R., Clegg-Thorp, C., Kohn, M., & Parrish, A. (2015). Perspectives on workplace health promotion among employees in low-wage industries. *American Journal of Health Promotion, 29,* 384–392. http://dx.doi.org/10.4278/ajhp.130924-QUAL-495

Harris, J. R., Hannon, P. A., Beresford, S. A., Linnan, L. A., & McLellan, D. L. (2014). Health promotion in smaller workplaces in the United States. *Annual Review of Public Health, 35,* 327–342. http://dx.doi.org/10.1146/annurev-publhealth-032013-182416

Howard, J. (2017). Nonstandard work arrangements and worker health and safety. *American Journal of Industrial Medicine, 60,* 1–10. http://dx.doi.org/10.1002/ajim.22669

Institute of Medicine. (2014). *Capturing social and behavioral domains and measures in electronic health records: Phase 2.* Washington, DC: The National Academies Press.

Israel, B. A., Schulz, A. J., Parker, E. A., & Becker, A. B. (1998). Review of community-based research: Assessing partnership approaches to improve public health. *Annual*

Review of Public Health, 19, 173–202. http://dx.doi.org/10.1146/annurev.publhealth. 19.1.173

Katz, D. L. (2004). Representing your community in community-based participatory research: Differences made and measured. *Preventing Chronic Disease, 1*, A12.

Katz, L. F., & Krueger, A. B. (2016). *The rise and nature of alternative work arrangements in the United States, 1995–2015* [NBER Working Paper No. 22667]. Retrieved from https://www.nber.org/papers/w22667

Kelly, E. L., Moen, P., Oakes, J. M., Fan, W., Okechukwu, C., Davis, K. D., . . . Casper, L. (2014). Changing work and work–family conflict: Evidence from the Work, Family, and Health Network. *American Sociological Review, 79*, 485–516. http://dx.doi.org/ 10.1177/0003122414531435

LaLonde, M. (1974). *A new perspective on the health of Canadians: A working document.* Retrieved from http://www.phac-aspc.gc.ca/ph-sp/pube-pubf/perintrod-eng.php

Landsbergis, P. A., Grzywacz, J. G., & LaMontagne, A. D. (2014). Work organization, job insecurity, and occupational health disparities. *American Journal of Industrial Medicine, 57*, 495–515. http://dx.doi.org/10.1002/ajim.22126

Linnan, L., Bowling, M., Childress, J., Lindsay, G., Blakey, C., Pronk, S., . . . Royall, P. (2008). Results of the 2004 national worksite health promotion survey. *American Journal of Public Health, 98*, 1503–1509. http://dx.doi.org/10.2105/AJPH.2006.100313

Lopez, P. M., Islam, N., Feinberg, A., Myers, C., Seidl, L., Drackett, E., . . . Thorpe, L. E. (2017). A place-based community health worker program. Feasibility and early outcomes, New York City, 2015. *American Journal of Preventive Medicine, 52*, S284–S289.

Minkler, M., Salvatore, A. L., Chang, C., Gaydos, M., Liu, S. S., Lee, P. T., . . . Krause, N. (2014). Wage theft as a neglected public health problem: An overview and case study from San Francisco's Chinatown District. *American Journal of Public Health, 104*, 1010–1020. http://dx.doi.org/10.2105/AJPH.2013.301813

Miranda, H., Gore, R. J., Boyer, J., Nobrega, S., & Punnett, L. (2015). Health behaviors and overweight in nursing home employees: Contribution of workplace stressors and implications for worksite health promotion. *Scientific World Journal, 2015*, 915359. http://dx.doi.org/10.1155/2015/915359

National Institute for Occupational Safety and Health. (2016a). *Fundamentals of total worker health approaches: Essential elements for advancing worker safety, health, and well-being, December, 2016* [DHHS (NIOSH) Publication No. 2017-112]. Cincinnati, OH: U.S. Department of Health and Human Services, Centers for Disease Control and Prevention, National Institute for Occupational Safety and Health.

National Institute for Occupational Safety and Health. (2016b). Hierarchy of controls applied to *Total Worker Health*. Retrieved from https://www.cdc.gov/niosh/twh/ letsgetstarted.html

National Institute for Occupational Safety and Health. (2016c). National occupational research agenda (NORA)/national *Total Worker Health®* agenda (2016–2026): A national agenda to advance *Total Worker Health®* research, practice, policy, and capacity, April 2016 [DHHS (NIOSH) Publication No. 2016-114]. Cincinnati, OH: U.S. Department of Health and Human Services, Centers for Disease Control and Prevention, National Institute for Occupational Safety and Health.

Nobrega, S., Kernan, L., Plaku-Alakbarova, B., Robertson, M., Warren, N., & Henning, R. (2017). Field tests of a participatory ergonomics toolkit for Total Worker Health. *Applied Ergonomics, 60*, 366–379. http://dx.doi.org/10.1016/j.apergo.2016.12.007

Olson, R., Thompson, S. V., Elliot, D. L., Hess, J. A., Rhoten, K. L., Parker, K. N., . . . Marino, M. (2016). Safety and health support for home care workers: The COMPASS randomized controlled trial. *American Journal of Public Health, 106*, 1823–1832.

Punnett, L., Warren, N., Henning, R., Nobrega, S., Cherniack, M., & the CPH-NEW Research Team. (2013). Participatory ergonomics as a model for integrated programs to prevent chronic disease. *Journal of Occupational and Environmental Medicine, 55*, S19–S24. http://dx.doi.org/10.1097/JOM.0000000000000040

Shockey, T. M., Sussell, A. L., & Odom, E. C. (2016). Cardiovascular health status by occupational group—21 states, 2013. *Morbidity and Mortality Weekly Report, 65*, 793–798. http://dx.doi.org/10.15585/mmwr.mm6531a1

Sommer, I., Griebler, U., Mahlknecht, P., Thaler, K., Bouskill, K., Gartlehner, G., & Mendis, S. (2015). Socioeconomic inequalities in non-communicable diseases and their risk factors: An overview of systematic reviews. *BMC Public Health, 15*, 914–927. http://dx.doi.org/10.1186/s12889-015-2227-y

Sorensen, G., Landsbergis, P., Hammer, L., Amick, B. C., Linnan, L., Yancey, A., . . . Workshop Working Group on Worksite Chronic Disease Prevention. (2011). Preventing chronic disease in the workplace: A workshop report and recommendations. *American Journal of Public Health, 101*, S196–S207. http://dx.doi.org/10.2105/AJPH.2010.300075

Sorensen, G., McLellan, D. L., Sabbath, E. L., Dennerlein, J. T., Nagler, E. M., Hurtado, D. A., . . . Wagner, G. R. (2016). Integrating worksite health protection and health promotion: A conceptual model for intervention and research. *Preventive Medicine, 91*, 188–196. http://dx.doi.org/10.1016/j.ypmed.2016.08.005

Steege, A. L., Baron, S. L., Marsh, S. M., Menéndez, C. C., & Myers, J. R. (2014). Examining occupational health and safety disparities using national data: A cause for continuing concern. *American Journal of Industrial Medicine, 57*, 527–538. http://dx.doi.org/10.1002/ajim.22297

Stokols, D., Hall, K. L., Taylor, B. K., & Moser, R. P. (2008). The science of team science: Overview of the field and introduction to the supplement. *American Journal of Preventive Medicine, 35*, S77–S89. http://dx.doi.org/10.1016/j.amepre.2008.05.002

U.S. Department of Health and Human Services. (2010, July 26). *Healthy People 2020: An opportunity to address the societal determinants of health in the United States* [Report]. Retrieved from http://www.healthypeople.gov/2010/hp2020/advisory/SocietalDeterminantsHealth.htm

Weil, D. (2014). *Fissured workplace: Why work became so bad for so many and what can be done to improve it.* Cambridge, MA: Harvard University Press. http://dx.doi.org/10.4159/9780674726123

Williams, D. R., Mohammed, S. A., Leavell, J., & Collins, C. (2010). Race, socioeconomic status, and health: Complexities, ongoing challenges, and research opportunities. *Annals of the New York Academy of Sciences, 1186*, 69–101. http://dx.doi.org/10.1111/j.1749-6632.2009.05339.x

III

A SPECTRUM OF *TOTAL WORKER HEALTH*® APPLICATIONS

12

Developing an Integrated Approach to Workplace Mental Health

Anthony D. LaMontagne, Angela Martin, Kathryn M. Page, Nicola J. Reavley, Andrew J. Noblet, Allison J. Milner, Tessa Keegel, Amanda Allisey, Alicia Papas, Katrina Witt, and Peter M. Smith

Mental health problems commonly found in the working population represent a growing concern because of potential impacts on workers (e.g., discrimination), organizations (e.g., sickness absence, lost productivity), workplace health and compensation authorities (e.g., rising job stress-related claims), and social welfare systems (e.g., rising working age disability pensions for mental disorders; Organisation for Economic Co-operation and Development, 2012). Growing awareness of this issue has been paralleled by the rapid expansion of workplace interventions to address common mental health problems in the workplace setting, particularly as a means to prevent, detect, and manage depression and anxiety (Martin, Sanderson, & Cocker, 2009; Sanderson & Andrews, 2006).

In this chapter, we first present two background premises: (a) there is a high prevalence of mental health problems and disorders in the working population, and (b) working conditions are important and modifiable risk and protective factors for these problems. Workplace interventions to address common mental health problems have evolved relatively independently along three main threads or disciplinary traditions: medicine, public health, and psychology. The remainder of the chapter presents in detail our proposition that interventions from each of these three threads need to be integrated to achieve the greatest population mental health benefits. An integrated approach would protect mental health by reducing work-related risk factors, promote mental health by developing the positive aspects of work as well as worker strengths and positive

http://dx.doi.org/10.1037/0000149-013
Total Worker Health, H. L. Hudson, J. A. S. Nigam, S. L. Sauter, L. C. Chosewood, A. L. Schill, and J. Howard (Editors)
Copyright © 2019 by the American Psychological Association. All rights reserved.

capacities, and address mental health problems among working people regardless of cause (LaMontagne, Martin, et al., 2014).

PREVALENCE OF MENTAL HEALTH PROBLEMS IN THE WORKING POPULATION

Mental health problems, both clinical (e.g., major depression, anxiety disorders) and subclinical (e.g., psychological distress), are common in the working population. In a review of its approximately 35 member states, the OECD estimated that similar proportions of working-age populations are affected by clinical mental disorders: Point prevalence estimates are 5% for severe mental disorders and another 15% for moderate mental disorders (OECD, 2012). Among those affected, persons with common mental disorders—depression, simple phobia, and generalized anxiety disorder—have the highest workforce participation rates (Sanderson & Andrews, 2006). In Australia, for example, the 2007 national survey of mental health and well-being estimated that 15% of the working population had a history of major depressive disorder (Cocker, Sanderson, & LaMontagne, 2017). Subclinical mental health problems and generalized distress also are prevalent in the working population.

Mental health problems among working people are costly to society at large and to health care systems, employers, and affected individuals and their families. Estimates of economic costs for European Union countries are 3% to 4% of gross domestic product (International Labour Office, 2000; OECD, 2012). An Australian study found the greatest costs of depression among working people were borne by employers; turnover costs figured most prominently (Cocker et al., 2017). Costing studies to date, however, have been limited in their ability to quantify costs to affected individuals and their families, particularly concerning important social costs related to stigma and discrimination.

WORKING CONDITIONS AS MODIFIABLE RISK AND PROTECTIVE FACTORS

A substantial body of research has demonstrated the links between psychosocial working conditions—or job stressors—and worker health over the past 3 decades. The demand–control model has been particularly influential. It hypothesizes that high job strain, defined by a combination of low control over how the job is done in the face of high job demands, will be harmful to health. Although first demonstrated in relation to cardiovascular disease outcomes, subsequent studies have found that job strain also predicts elevated risks of common mental disorders (Theorell et al., 2015). Numerous other job stressors, either individually or in combination, have also been shown to influence mental health (LaMontagne, Keegel, Louie, & Ostry, 2010). These stressors include job insecurity, bullying and harassment, low social support at work, organizational injustice, and effort–reward imbalance.

Unlike many historically prominent occupational exposures (e.g., asbestos) to which only a small proportion of the working population were exposed, all working people can be potentially exposed to job stressors. Even small increases in risk from such exposures can translate into substantial—and preventable—illness burdens. The population-attributable risks for job strain in relation to depression, for example, were 13% of prevalent depression among working men and 17% among working women in an Australian working population sample (LaMontagne, Keegel, Vallance, Ostry, & Wolfe, 2008). Comparable estimates were obtained in the French working population for job strain–attributable risk for common mental disorders: 10.2%–31.1% for men and 5.3%–33.6% for women (Sultan-Taieb, Lejeune, Drummond, & Niedhammer, 2011). Using a different approach, a New Zealand birth cohort study estimated that nearly half (45%) of incident cases of depression and anxiety in previously healthy young workers were attributable to job stress (Melchior et al., 2007).

Further research is needed to firmly establish causality and the magnitude of association of job stressor exposures in relation to common mental health problems. The aforementioned estimates, however, likely underestimate the proportion of mental health disorders attributable to job stressors because a comprehensive estimate would account for all relevant job stressors and the full range of associated mental health outcomes (Cocker et al., 2017). Exposure to various job stressors has been associated with burnout, anxiety disorders, alcohol dependence, suicide, and other mental health outcomes (LaMontagne et al., 2010; Milner et al., 2017).

Preventing or reducing exposure to job stressors and improving the psychosocial quality of work could prevent a substantial proportion of common mental health problems. Such improvements would benefit other health domains as well because exposure to these same job stressors also predicts elevated risks for other high-burden chronic illnesses, such as cardiovascular disease, as well as poor health behaviors (LaMontagne, 2012; Sultan-Taieb et al., 2011).

AN INTEGRATED APPROACH TO WORKPLACE MENTAL HEALTH

We propose that the optimal response for preventing and managing this large and complex burden of mental health problems in the working population is to take an integrated approach that addresses three complementary threads: (a) protecting mental health by reducing work-related risk factors, (b) promoting mental health by developing the positive aspects of work as well as worker strengths and positive capacities, and (c) addressing mental health problems among working people regardless of cause (see Figure 12.1). A précis of the rationale and the evidence base for each thread are presented in this chapter.

Thread 1: Protect Mental Health by Reducing Work-Related Risk Factors

The relevant intervention principles and evidence in this area come predominantly from the fields of public health (e.g., occupational health and safety, health promotion) and psychology (particularly organizational psychology). Like other public health interventions, job stress prevention and control

FIGURE 12.1. The Three Threads of the Integrated Approach to Workplace Mental Health

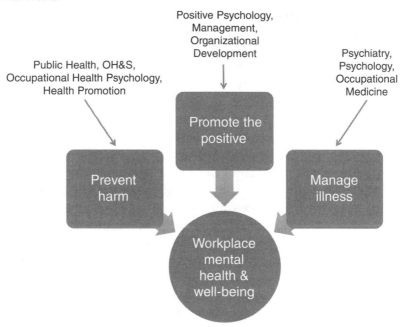

OH&S = Human Resources or Occupational Health and Safety.

interventions can be directed at the primary, secondary, or tertiary levels (LaMontagne, Keegel, & Vallance, 2007; LaMontagne, Noblet, & Landsbergis, 2012). *Primary intervention* is preventive and work directed; the aim is to minimize the incidence of work-related mental health problems by modifying the job, work environment, or both. *Secondary intervention* is generally ameliorative and worker directed, and can also prevent the progress of subclinical mental health problems to diagnosable disorders. In the current context, the aim might be to modify individuals' responses to job stressors through strategies to improve coping ability or resilience, or to modify working conditions to facilitate sustainable return to work from a mental illness. *Tertiary intervention* is reactive in that it responds to the occurrence of mental health problems; it involves the treatment of affected workers, rehabilitation, and return to work. Theoretically, tertiary (and to some extent secondary) intervention can reduce the burden of mental disorders through early detection and treatment, thus limiting severity or chronicity.

Some strategies encompass more than one level of intervention. For example, increasing worker resilience or coping capacity would be considered primary prevention if it is done before a mental health problem has occurred, and secondary if it prevents the progression of an existing problem. Most important, however, primary, secondary, and tertiary interventions are complementary; thus, all three should be combined in a comprehensive approach to both prevent and control the impacts of job stress (LaMontagne, Keegel, & Vallance, 2007). In the preventive medicine typology, this framework roughly parallels universal, selected, and indicated disease prevention (Gordon, 1983). A systems approach to job stress is both comprehensive and directed at an organization's systems in terms of policies, practices, processes, and procedures, including intervention informed by system feedback loops (LaMontagne, Keegel, & Vallance, 2007).

Systematic reviews of job stress prevention and control studies show that the most effective approaches combine interventions to reduce job stressors and strengthen workers' abilities to withstand stressors (Bambra et al., 2009; LaMontagne, Keegel, Louie, Ostry, & Landsbergis, 2007). These systematic reviews indicate *what* to do, yet the more challenging question in application to policy and practice is *how* to do it. Although the principles of intervention are broadly applicable, solutions are unique to the work context (e.g., worker socio-demographics and occupational skill levels, type of workplace, presence or absence of a union). To illustrate, strategies to improve job control for a salesclerk will differ from strategies to achieve the same for a manager, even in the same workplace. Intervention strategies need to be tailored and context appropriate (LaMontagne, Noblet, & Landsbergis, 2012), thus making the development of such interventions more involved and labor intensive than interventions for most other occupational hazards (e.g., installing a machine guard to prevent hand injuries).

Even though knowledge of solutions for various work contexts is growing, there is still a need to apply principles and develop solutions on a case-by-case basis. This need likely has contributed to the slow uptake of effective job stress prevention and control strategies in practice. Furthermore, there is a persisting disconnect between evidence-based best practice and what is currently being undertaken in the workplace setting to address mental health, that is, prevalent practice is directed more at secondary than primary intervention. In an Australian study, for example, when human resources or occupational health and safety (OH&S) staff were asked about their organization's response to job stress concerns, the most common response was to say they provided an employee assistance program (Page et al., 2013). Other barriers to the uptake of evidence-based best practice include issues of stigma similar to those concerning mental illness in general, such as a persisting view of job stress as an individual weakness (Page et al., 2013).

Job stress prevention and control strategies are distinguished by their emphasis on primary or universal prevention directed at the reduction of job stressors and the improvement of work organization. The effectiveness of job stress prevention and control interventions is supported by systematic reviews. Implementation in practice, however, has proven challenging in part because solutions need to be context specific.

Thread 2: Promote Mental Health by Developing the Positive Aspects of Work as Well as Worker Strengths and Positive Capacities

The relevant intervention principles and evidence in this area come predominantly from the rapidly developing field of *positive psychology*, which is defined as the study of "the conditions and processes that contribute to the flourishing or optimal functioning of people, groups, and institutions" (Gable & Haidt, 2005, p. 103). What distinguishes positive psychology intervention in practice is that it applies strength-based methods generally to the achievement of positive outcomes. Strength-based methods aim to identify and enhance strengths or what is being done well rather than identify and address deficits in an individual, group, or organization (Schaufeli, 2004). Strength-based approaches use methods, such as *appreciative inquiry* (asking positive questions to strengthen positive potential and facilitate change), *future search* (working toward an aspirational view of the future), and *future inquiry* (a hybrid of the two that involves all relevant stakeholders, generates respect for what has been done well, identifies a shared aspirational view of the future, and plans steps to move in that direction; Blewett & Shaw, 2013). Positive outcomes include subjective well-being, psychological capital, positive mental health, employee engagement, and positive organizational attributes (e.g., authentic leadership, supportive workplace culture, workplace social capital). *Well-being*—also referred to as subjective or psychological well-being, happiness, or life satisfaction—is more than the absence of ill-health states; it is the presence of positive feelings and functioning (Keyes, 2005). The concept also has been applied to the domain of work (Page & Vella-Brodrick, 2009). Complementing its beneficial qualities for well-being, positive mental health can protect against job stressor-related mental illness, acting as a buffer or effect modifier of the stressor—mental health relationship (Page et al., 2014). However, job stressor exposures can be detrimental to well-being as well as increase the risks of mental ill-health (LaMontagne, Milner, Krnjacki, et al., 2016).

There is a need for positive approaches at the organizational and individual levels. In addition, positive approaches would complement and align with the comprehensive or systems approach to job stress prevention described previously. Importantly, positive approaches aim to promote the positive aspects of work and worker capabilities, including well-being. Organizational-level approaches include developing positive leadership practices, optimizing the meaningfulness of work, and building a positive organizational climate (Cameron & Caza, 2004). Individual-level approaches include promoting gratitude, mindfulness, resilience, and psychological capital (Meyers, van Woerkom, & Bakker, 2013). Nevertheless, to date, positive approaches to addressing mental health in the workplace are the least commonly applied in practice compared with the other two threads of the integrated approach (Page & Vella-Brodrick, 2012).

A meta-analysis of the general literature, including 51 studies across a range of settings, concluded that well-being can be sustainably enhanced, and depressive symptoms reduced, through positive interventions (Sin & Lyubomirsky, 2009). A smaller review of 15 workplace-based positive psychology intervention studies found strong evidence of enhanced employee well-being, some evidence of alleviation of symptoms of mental health problems, and limited evidence of enhanced work performance (Meyers et al., 2013). Interventions were predominantly individual directed (e.g., promoting adult resilience and psychosocial capital), and few promoted positive organizations (e.g., strengths-based leadership coaching). None was explicitly work directed (e.g., job redesign). Both reviews found evidence of positive interventions countering ill mental health as well as promoting positive mental health and well-being.

The promise of positive approaches also is supported by established knowledge of the substantial positive influences of good quality work on mental health and well-being. In addition to the income and socioeconomic position that paid employment can provide, work can positively impact adult socialization, the development of identity, and the extension of social connections beyond family and neighborhood groups (LaMontagne et al., 2010). Furthermore, work can provide purpose and meaning, thus enhancing self-efficacy and self-esteem, both of which protect and promote mental health (LaMontagne, Martin, et al., 2014). That research on the purpose and meaning of work highlights the need for positive approaches to address eudaimonic (i.e., meaning and purpose) as well as hedonic (i.e., positive emotional or happiness) aspects of workplace well-being (Keyes, 2005).

Positive approaches provide a valuable but generally underused complement to risk-based or negatively framed approaches (e.g., OH&S). However, the evidence is limited by positive psychology's emphasis to date on the individual and the need for further evidence of effectiveness. As well as promoting well-being, positive approaches appear to protect against the ill effects of job stressor exposures. Team/group and organizational-level positive approaches are being developed and may yield greater benefits in the future than individual-level approaches alone.

Thread 3: Address Mental Health Problems Among Working People Regardless of Cause

Work in this area has expanded rapidly over the past decade and has been developed largely from an illness or medical perspective; this work emphasizes tertiary- and secondary-level interventions. Workplace programs that aim to address mental health problems or disorders commonly use psychoeducation and aim to improve mental health literacy (MHL), develop skills for early intervention, and promote help-seeking (Kitchener & Jorm, 2004). *Mental health literacy* is defined as "knowledge and beliefs about mental disorders which aid their recognition, management or prevention" (Jorm et al., 1997, p. 182). One such program with widespread international uptake is Mental Health First Aid, which seeks to improve MHL by developing knowledge and skills on how to recognize common mental disorders and providing "first aid" support until professional help can be obtained, thus increasing understanding about the causes of mental disorders, improving knowledge of the most effective treatments, and reducing stigma (Kitchener & Jorm, 2006). The effectiveness of Mental Health First Aid has been shown in various studies, including two randomized-controlled trials in workplace settings (Jorm, Kitchener, Sawyer,

Scales, & Cvetkovski, 2010; Kitchener & Jorm, 2004). In addition, there is evidence for the effectiveness of secondary and tertiary approaches to workplace suicide prevention (Milner, Page, Spencer-Thomas, & LaMontagne, 2015), particularly in specific at-risk occupations, such as protective services (Witt, Milner, Allisey, Davenport, & LaMontagne, 2017). Although MHL interventions can benefit organizations and individuals (both inside and outside of the work context), additional intervention studies and evidence synthesis are warranted.

Other strategies for addressing mental health problems in the workplace focus on organizational culture and attitudes in relation to mental illness stigma and norms around disclosure. Mental health stigma in workplaces is a pervasive challenge, just as it is in broader society. A study of 6,399 employees from 13 workplaces in the United States found that although 62% knew how to access company resources for depression care, only 29% indicated they would feel comfortable discussing the issue with their supervisor (Charbonneau et al., 2005). Unsupportive organizational culture and norms around depression disclosure are a contributing factor. Managers' and leaders' attitudes play a central role in changing these norms and are a priority target for intervention (Martin, 2010). The development and dissemination of accommodation strategies also are needed because managers, human resources professionals, and others in workplaces may be willing but unsure how to accommodate a worker with a mental health problem (compared with knowledge about physical accommodation), or may see these accommodations as too complicated to put into place (Andersen, Nielsen, & Brinkmann, 2012). Some strategies focus on the role of organizational culture as well as reduced exposure to job stressors in improving return to work from a mental illness–related absence (Reavley, Ross, Killackey, & Jorm, 2012).

Illness-focused approaches to addressing mental health problems are strongest at the tertiary and secondary, or—in preventive medicine terminology—selected and indicated levels. There is promising evidence of effectiveness, but further research is needed. Early detection and disclosure are hampered by persisting stigma and the potential for discrimination. Developing strategies to address these barriers is therefore a key priority for research, policy, and practice.

JOINING THE THREADS

A defining feature of the integrated approach is the mutually reinforcing nature of the three threads of preventing harm, promoting the positive, and addressing mental health problems. Although the protective focus of the first thread aims to identify and address factors that can undermine the mental health of employees, and therefore encourages employers to fulfill their responsibility to provide a safe and healthy working environment, the overall goal of the second thread is to complement the risk reduction approach by promoting characteristics that can strengthen individual and organizational health and maximize levels of positive well-being. To some extent, this complementarity is already apparent; for example, an understanding of the importance of job control has evolved from two sides of the same coin. Public health research has identified low job control as an important risk factor for mental health problems (Thread 1) and the promotion of autonomy (or high job control) as a common strategy in positive approaches (Thread 2). Maintaining this dual protection–promotion emphasis can benefit workplace mental health in many ways. Examples include encouraging organizations and their representatives to examine the strengths and weaknesses of their working environments, keeping a more "balanced scorecard" in relation to monitoring the performance of organizational systems, and to properly identifying and mobilizing organizational resources to build workplaces that are not just safer and fairer but are also more attractive to and engaging for employees.

The third thread can complement the first two in various ways. For example, certain knowledge and awareness aspects of MHL (Thread 3) relate directly to Threads 1 and 2. Workplace MHL strategies that we have piloted, for example, highlight that poor working conditions and job stressors are modifiable risk factors for common mental health problems and (where applicable) that there are legislated OH&S mandates to protect psychological as well as physical health (LaMontagne, Keegel, Shann, & D'Souza, 2014), thus building employee awareness of and employer commitment to the need to address working conditions (Thread 1). Workplace MHL also can highlight the protective value of resilience in relation to mental disorders, thus building motivation for and commitment to positive approaches (Thread 2). In addition, starting where organizations are receptive (e.g., MHL training) can provide the encouragement or incentives to employers (near-term improvement in MHL) needed to sustain interest and commitment to the improvement of working conditions and job quality over the longer term. Addressing MHL in this way can provide entrée into workplaces that might not otherwise conduct job stress or other work-directed interventions on their own, thus increasing the reach and uptake of integrated approaches, and potentially enhancing effectiveness.

An example of an integrated workplace mental health program in a policing context includes work-directed intervention to improve psychosocial working conditions (Thread 1) for lower ranked officers through a supportive leadership intervention for police station commanders (Thread 2) coupled with MHL training for lower ranks and station commanders (Thread 3). The supportive leadership intervention involves individual commander needs assessment and one-on-one coaching to pursue both development- and strength-based goals (LaMontagne, Milner, Allisey, et al., 2016; Page et al., 2017).

Another example of an integrated intervention is the Business in Mind program designed by Martin, Sanderson, Scott, and Brough (2009) to promote mental health in small-to-medium enterprises. Work-related risks to mental health targeted in Business in Mind are long working hours and relational psychosocial stressors. These risks have been addressed in modules on creating balance, positive relationships, and coping with stress. In relation to promoting the positive, owners or managers were encouraged to see their mental health and well-being as a business asset; this was incorporated into a module on positive growth, which drew on psychological capital intervention processes. To manage mental illness, basic MHL information was provided in a module on managing mental health. Preliminary results from this trial showed high levels of acceptability to participants and a reduction in psychological distress post-intervention, including the active control condition, which contained psycho-education material and a self-administered version using a DVD and workbook. However, participants in a telephone supported version of the intervention showed the highest reduction in distress (Martin et al., 2013).

The growing public awareness and employer receptivity to MHL intervention suggest an opportunity for articulating a notion of workplace MHL that would dovetail with an integrated approach to workplace mental health overall. Based on Jorm's earlier definition of MHL (Jorm et al., 1997), we would define *workplace MHL* as the knowledge, beliefs, and skills that aid in the prevention of mental disorders and the promotion of well-being in the workplace, and the recognition, treatment, rehabilitation, and return to work of employees affected by mental disorders. This notion of workplace MHL more clearly expresses the links between Thread 3 and the other two threads of prevention and promotion. Further work is required to continue to build the links and further integrate the threads of the integrated approach. Such work may lead to efficiencies in implementation as well as preventive synergies, such as has been realized through integrated approaches that target cancer prevention and other aspects of workplace health (see Chapter 5, this volume).

CAUTIONARY NOTES

Although an integrated approach to workplace mental health shows great promise, it is important to acknowledge potential risks and challenges. To date, there is a persisting overemphasis on individual-directed intervention in workplace health intervention policy and practice (LaMontagne, Martin, et al., 2014) that would need to be overcome to realize a genuinely integrated approach. The great uptake of workplace MHL as well as resilience-oriented positive psychology programs may be partly a reflection of this individual emphasis. For example, early MHL programs in workplace settings were largely individual-directed education and training programs, which is reflected in their evaluation to date, mainly in terms of short-term changes in individuals' knowledge, attitudes, and helping skills. In contrast, reducing job stressors and improving job quality require organizational changes, which generally require more resources and a longer period of change. In a recent integrated workplace mental health feasibility study, significant improvements in MHL were observed over 1 year, but—disappointingly—no improvements were found in job demands, job control, or workplace social support (LaMontagne, Keegel, et al., 2014). More intensive and sustained work-directed intervention, longer follow-up, or both are needed to achieve and demonstrate improvement in working conditions.

With integrated approaches also comes a risk of employers' confusing mandatory and voluntary responsibilities. Australia and many other OECD countries have a legal obligation to provide psychologically as well as physically safe working condition under OH&S law. Yet, many employers seem to embrace MHL and related programs more readily than job stress prevention. Unions and other worker advocates are understandably concerned that employer responses to mandatory requirements might be confused with or diluted by responses to voluntary programs. There is a need for improved articulation of all legal and ethical requirements relevant to workplace mental health as a component of integrated approaches, including employment, anti-discrimination, and equal opportunity as well as OH&S law (Shain, 2010). The protection of confidentiality for those who come forward to seek help from supervisors or who are returning to work from a mental illness, and antidiscrimination efforts are key considerations in integrated and other workplace mental health interventions.

To realize the greatest possible population mental health benefits, governments and other policymakers need to consider how to ensure interventions reach those workers who are most in need of them. Lower occupational status workers have the highest prevalence of mental health problems, greatest exposure to job stressors, and lowest quality jobs (LaMontagne, D'Souza, & Shann, 2012; LaMontagne, Krnjacki, Kavanagh, & Bentley, 2013). These groups typically are the least likely to receive job stress or other workplace mental health interventions. In Australia, and some other OECD countries, exceptions include blue-collar males, who have been prioritized for workplace MHL intervention by governments and nongovernmental organizations largely on the basis of their low help-seeking behaviors and high prevalence of mental health problems (LaMontagne, D'Souza, & Shann, 2012). This praiseworthy policy action could be strengthened further by the integration of interventions that reduce job stressors and improve work quality. In the absence of concerted efforts to reach priority groups, population-level implementation of integrated or other workplace mental health intervention risks the exacerbation of mental health inequalities because more advantaged groups would be more likely to experience and benefit from intervention than disadvantaged groups. The result would be widening disparities similar to those seen from population-level tobacco control and other health promotion interventions (Frohlich & Potvin, 2008).

NEXT STEPS FOR DEVELOPING INTEGRATED APPROACHES

There are various hopeful signs for the development of integrated approaches in practice, policy, and research. Receptivity is increasing among employers and other workplace stakeholders to the value of integrated approaches, and stems largely from a growing awareness of the widespread prevalence and the impact of mental health problems on productivity at work (Cocker et al., 2017) as well as from a growing recognition of the need to fulfill OH&S obligations with respect to the protection of psychological and physical health.

Integrated approaches also are developing to a varying extent in policy and practice across the OECD. For example, Canada published a National Standard for Psychological Health and Safety in the Workplace in 2013, and the World Health Organization published guidance on integrated approaches for workplace health in general in 2010 as well as specific workplace suicide prevention guidance in 2006 (see Exhibit 12.1 for these and other resources).

Although these policy and practice developments are encouraging, there is a dearth of effectiveness evaluation studies on these programs and of intervention guidance resources. Intervention research on these and other integrated approaches should be a high priority and would include the full spectrum of intervention research: development, implementation, and effectiveness. Developmental research (developing *what to do* and *how*) is a particular priority for translating integrated approaches from research to practice. Because each of the three threads has evolved relatively independently, there is a need for further improvement in the integration of strategy and guidance material, which would best be achieved through the involvement of the full range of workplace stakeholders. In an effort to develop practice-based evidence at the same time as evidence-based practice, we recently applied the Delphi consensus method

---

EXHIBIT 12.1

Developing an Integrated Approach to Workplace Mental Health: Useful Resources

- Great-West Life Centre for Mental Health in the Workplace. (n.d.). Workplace strategies for mental health. Retrieved from https://www.workplacestrategiesformentalhealth.com

- Guarding Minds @ Work. (n.d.). A workplace guide to psychological health and safety. Retrieved from http://www.guardingmindsatwork.ca

- Mental Health Commission of Canada. (2013). National Standard [of Canada for Psychological Health and Safety in the Workplace]. Retrieved from http://www.mentalhealthcommission.ca/English/national-standard

- Mental Health First Aid Australia. (2013). Guidelines for the workplace: Workplace prevention of mental health problems. Retrieved from https://mhfa.com.au/cms/guidelines#mhfaprevent

- Mental Health First Aid Australia. (2016). Guidelines for the workplace: Providing Mental Health First Aid in the workplace. Retrieved from https://mhfa.com.au/resources/mental-health-first-aid-guidelines#mhfaworkplace

- SuperFriend. (2015). *Promoting positive mental health in the Workplace: Guidelines for organisations.* Available from http://www.superfriend.com.au/supporters/research/promoting-positive-mental-health-in-the-workplace-guidelines-for-organisations

- Victorian Workplace Mental Wellbeing Collaboration. (2015). Promoting positive mental wellbeing in Victorian workplaces. Retrieved from http://leadingwellvic.com.au

- World Health Organization. (2006). *Mental health—Preventing suicide: A resource at work* [booklet]. Available from http://www.who.int/mental_health/resources/preventingsuicide/en

- World Health Organization. (2010). *Healthy workplaces: A model for action—For employers, workers, policy-makers and practitioners* [brochure]. Available from http://www.who.int/occupational_health/publications/healthy_workplaces_model.pdf

to work with industry and various stakeholder groups (e.g., managers, workers, workplace health professionals) to develop and publish on the web workplace guidelines for the prevention of mental health problems (Reavley, Ross, Martin, LaMontagne, & Jorm, 2014), the promotion of positive mental health (Davenport, Allisey, Page, LaMontagne, & Reavley, 2016), Mental Health First Aid (Bovopoulos et al., 2016), and return to work from a mental illness (Reavley et al., 2012). See Exhibit 12.1 for a list of these resources.

Implementation research also is needed to inform policy and practice to answer such research questions as: What factors facilitate or hinder implementation? What levels of support do various types and sizes of organizations need to implement integrated approaches? What is practically achievable for organizations that are implementing their own programs? Effectiveness studies are needed to assess the extent to which integrated approaches work when implemented as intended. For example, are there significant improvements in MHL, working conditions, and job quality over time? Are there improvements in mental health and well-being over time? Economic studies also will be required alongside effectiveness studies to make the business case. Although the costing studies described earlier show that there are potential savings to be made, a recent meta-analysis of 10 studies in this area found that they covered mainly screening and return-to-work interventions in isolation, and found limited evidence of positive cost-benefit ratios for screening and treatment interventions, and no favorable cost-effectiveness for return-to-work interventions (Hamberg-van Reenen, Proper, & van den Berg, 2012). It remains to be shown whether integrated approaches would yield better results.

CONCLUSION

An integrated approach to workplace mental health can expect near-term improvements in MHL to be followed by longer term improvements in working conditions and job quality—given adequate organizational commitment, support, and time to achieve organizational change. These changes, in turn, should lead to improvements in mental health and well-being. Although improvements in psychosocial and other working conditions may be more difficult to achieve than improvements in MHL, efforts should continue to be made in this regard to fulfill legal and ethical mandates to provide psychologically safe work, and to reduce the substantial burden of work-related mental health problems. Increasing awareness of work-related influences on mental health and the growing recognition of the need for "psychologically safe" work may help drive organizational efforts to improve psychosocial working conditions.

REFERENCES

Andersen, M. F., Nielsen, K. M., & Brinkmann, S. (2012). Meta-synthesis of qualitative research on return to work among employees with common mental disorders. *Scandinavian Journal of Work, Environment & Health, 38*(2), 93–104. http://dx.doi.org/10.5271/sjweh.3257

Bambra, C., Gibson, M., Sowden, A. J., Wright, K., Whitehead, M., & Petticrew, M. (2009). Working for health? Evidence from systematic reviews on the effects on health and health inequalities of organisational changes to the psychosocial work environment. *Preventive Medicine, 48,* 454–461. http://dx.doi.org/10.1016/j.ypmed.2008.12.018

Blewett, V., & Shaw, A. (2013). Future inquiry: A participatory ergonomics approach to evaluating new technology. In C. Bearman, A. Naweed, J. Dorrian, J. Rose, & D. Dawson (Eds.), *Evaluating rail technologies: A practical human factors guide* (pp. 111–125). Aldershot, England: Ashgate.

Bovopoulos, N., Jorm, A. F., Bond, K. S., LaMontagne, A. D., Reavley, N., Kelly, C. M., . . . Martin, A. (2016). Providing Mental Health First Aid in the workplace: A Delphi consensus study. *BMC Psychology, 4,* 41. http://dx.doi.org/10.1186/s40359-016-0148-x

Cameron, K. S., & Caza, A. (2004). Contributions to the discipline of positive organizational scholarship. *American Behavioral Scientist, 47,* 731–739. http://dx.doi.org/10.1177/0002764203260207

Charbonneau, A., Bruning, W., Titus-Howard, T., Ellerbeck, E., Whittle, J., Hall, S., . . . Munro, S. (2005). The community initiative on depression: Report from a multiphase work site depression intervention. *Journal of Occupational and Environmental Medicine, 47,* 60–67. http://dx.doi.org/10.1097/01.jom.0000147211.63924.87

Cocker, F., Sanderson, K., & LaMontagne, A. D. (2017). Estimating the economic benefits of eliminating job strain as a risk factor for depression. *Journal of Occupational and EnvironmentalMedicine,59,*12–17.http://dx.doi.org/10.1097/JOM.0000000000000908

Davenport, L. J., Allisey, A., Page, K., LaMontagne, A. D., & Reavley, N. (2016). How can organisations help employees thrive? The development of guidelines for promoting positive mental health at work. *International Journal of Workplace Health Management, 9,* 411–427. http://dx.doi.org/10.1108/IJWHM-01-2016-0001

Frohlich, K. L., & Potvin, L. (2008). Transcending the known in public health practice: The inequality paradox, the population approach and vulnerable populations. *American Journal of Public Health, 98,* 216–221. http://dx.doi.org/10.2105/AJPH.2007.114777

Gable, S. L., & Haidt, J. (2005). What (and why) is positive psychology? *Review of General Psychology, 9,* 103–110. http://dx.doi.org/10.1037/1089-2680.9.2.103

Gordon, R. S. (1983). An operational classification of disease prevention. *Public Health Reports, 98,* 107–109.

Hamberg-van Reenen, H. H., Proper, K. I., & van den Berg, M. (2012). Worksite mental health interventions: A systematic review of economic evaluations. *Occupational and Environmental Medicine, 69,* 837–845. http://dx.doi.org/10.1136/oemed-2012-100668

International Labour Office. (2000). *Mental health in the workplace* [Situational analysis]. Retrieved from http://www.ilo.org/wcmsp5/groups/public/@ed_emp/@ifp_skills/documents/publication/wcms_108221.pdf

Jorm, A. F., Kitchener, B. A., Sawyer, M. G., Scales, H., & Cvetkovski, S. (2010). Mental Health First Aid training for high school teachers: A cluster randomized trial. *BMC Psychiatry, 10,* 51. http://dx.doi.org/10.1186/1471-244X-10-51

Jorm, A. F., Korten, A. E., Jacomb, P. A., Christensen, H., Rodgers, B., & Pollitt, P. (1997). "Mental health literacy": A survey of the public's ability to recognise mental disorders and their beliefs about the effectiveness of treatment. *Medical Journal of Australia, 166,* 182–186.

Keyes, C. L. M. (2005). Mental illness and/or mental health? Investigating axioms of the complete state model of health. *Journal of Consulting and Clinical Psychology, 73,* 539–548. http://dx.doi.org/10.1037/0022-006X.73.3.539

Kitchener, B. A., & Jorm, A. F. (2004). Mental Health First Aid training in a workplace setting: A randomized controlled trial [ISRCTN13249129]. *BMC Psychiatry, 4,* 23. http://dx.doi.org/10.1186/1471-244X-4-23

Kitchener, B. A., & Jorm, A. F. (2006). Mental Health First Aid training: Review of evaluation studies. *Australian & New Zealand Journal of Psychiatry, 40,* 6–8. http://dx.doi.org/10.1080/j.1440-1614.2006.01735.x

LaMontagne, A. D. (2012). Invited commentary: Job strain and health behaviours—Developing a bigger picture. *American Journal of Epidemiology, 176,* 1090–1094. http://dx.doi.org/10.1093/aje/kws337

LaMontagne, A. D., D'Souza, R. M., & Shann, C. B. (2012). Socio-demographic and work setting correlates of poor mental health in a population sample of working Victorians: Application in evidence-based intervention priority setting. *International Journal of Mental Health Promotion, 14,* 109–122. http://dx.doi.org/10.1080/14623730.2012.703048

LaMontagne, A. D., Keegel, T., Louie, A. M., & Ostry, A. (2010). Job stress as a preventable upstream determinant of common mental disorders: A review for practitioners and policy-makers. *Advances in Mental Health, 9,* 17–35. http://dx.doi.org/10.5172/jamh.9.1.17

LaMontagne, A. D., Keegel, T., Louie, A. M., Ostry, A., & Landsbergis, P. A. (2007). A systematic review of the job stress intervention evaluation literature: 1990–2005. *International Journal of Occupational and Environmental Health, 13,* 268–280. http://dx.doi.org/10.1179/oeh.2007.13.3.268

LaMontagne, A. D., Keegel, T., Shann, C., & D'Souza, R. (2014). An integrated approach to workplace mental health: An Australian feasibility study. *International Journal of Mental Health Promotion, 16,* 205–215. http://dx.doi.org/10.1080/14623730.2014.931070

LaMontagne, A. D., Keegel, T., & Vallance, D. A. (2007). Protecting and promoting mental health in the workplace: Developing a systems approach to job stress. *Health Promotion Journal of Australia, 18,* 221–228. http://dx.doi.org/10.1071/HE07221

LaMontagne, A. D., Keegel, T., Vallance, D. A., Ostry, A., & Wolfe, R. (2008). Job strain—Attributable depression in a sample of working Australians: Assessing the contribution to health inequalities. *BMC Public Health, 8,* 181. http://dx.doi.org/10.1186/1471-2458-8-181

LaMontagne, A. D., Krnjacki, L., Kavanagh, A. M., & Bentley, R. (2013). Psychosocial working conditions in a representative sample of working Australians 2001–2008: An analysis of changes in inequalities over time. *Occupational and Environmental Medicine, 70,* 639–647. http://dx.doi.org/10.1136/oemed-2012-101171

LaMontagne, A. D., Martin, A., Page, K., Reavley, N. J., Noblet, A., Milner, A., . . . Smith, P. M. (2014). Workplace mental health: Developing an integrated intervention approach. *BMC Psychiatry, 14,* 131. http://dx.doi.org/10.1186/1471-244X-14-131

LaMontagne, A. D., Milner, A., Allisey, A. F., Page, K. M., Reavley, N. J., Martin, A., . . . Smith, P. M. (2016). An integrated workplace mental health intervention in a policing context: Protocol for a cluster randomised control trial. *BMC Psychiatry, 16,* 49, 1–13. http://dx.doi.org/10.1186/s12888-016-0741-9

LaMontagne, A. D., Milner, A., Krnjacki, L., Schlichthorst, M., Kavanagh, A., Page, K., & Pirkis, J. (2016). Psychosocial job quality, mental health, and subjective wellbeing: A cross-sectional analysis of the baseline wave of the Australian Longitudinal Study on Male Health. *BMC Public Health, 16*(Suppl. 3), 1049, 33–41. http://dx.doi.org/10.1186/s12889-016-3701-x

LaMontagne, A. D., Noblet, A. J., & Landsbergis, P. A. (2012). Intervention development and implementation: Understanding and addressing barriers to organizational-level interventions. In C. Biron, M. Karanika-Murray, & C. L. Cooper (Eds.), *Improving organizational interventions for stress and well-being: Addressing process and context* (pp. 21–38). London, England: Routledge/Psychology Press.

Martin, A. (2010). Individual and contextual correlates of managers' attitudes toward depressed employees (Report). *Human Resource Management, 49,* 647–668. http://dx.doi.org/10.1002/hrm.20370

Martin, A., Sanderson, K., & Cocker, F. (2009). Meta-analysis of the effects of health promotion intervention in the workplace on depression and anxiety symptoms. *Scandinavian Journal of Work, Environment & Health, 35,* 7–18. http://dx.doi.org/10.5271/sjweh.1295

Martin, A., Sanderson, K., Scott, J., & Brough, P. (2009). Promoting mental health in small-medium enterprises: An evaluation of the "Business in Mind" program. *BMC Public Health, 9,* 239–247. http://dx.doi.org/10.1186/1471-2458-9-239

Martin, A., Sanderson, K., Scott, J., Cocker, F., Dawkins, S., & Brough, P. (2013). *Business in Mind evaluation report: Interim results* [Unpublished report not for release]. Hobart, Tasmania, Australia: University of Tasmania.

Melchior, M., Caspi, A., Milne, B. J., Danese, A., Poulton, R., & Moffitt, T. E. (2007). Work stress precipitates depression and anxiety in young, working women and men. *Psychological Medicine, 37,* 1119–1129. http://dx.doi.org/10.1017/S0033291707000414

Meyers, M. C., van Woerkom, M., & Bakker, A. B. (2013). The added value of the positive: A literature review of positive psychology interventions in organizations. *European Journal of Work and Organizational Psychology, 22,* 618–632. http://dx.doi.org/10.1080/1359432X.2012.694689

Milner, A., Page, K., Spencer-Thomas, S., & LaMontagne, A. D. (2015). Workplace suicide prevention: A systematic review of published and unpublished activities. *Health Promotion International, 30,* 29–37. http://dx.doi.org/10.1093/heapro/dau085

Milner, A., Spittal, M. J., Pirkis, J., Chastang, J. F., Niedhammer, I., & LaMontagne, A. D. (2017). Low control and high demands at work as risk factors for suicide: An Australian national population-level case-control study. *Psychosomatic Medicine, 79,* 358–364. http://dx.doi.org/10.1097/PSY.0000000000000389

Organisation for Economic Co-operation and Development. (2012). *Sick on the job? Myths and realities about mental health and work.* Paris, France: Author.

Page, K. M., Allisey, A., Tchernitskaia, I., Noblet, A. J., Reavley, N., Milner, A. J., & LaMontagne, A. D. (2017). Workplace mental health: Development of an integrated intervention strategy for an Australian policing organisation. In R. Burke (Ed.), *Stress in policing: Sources, consequences and interventions* (pp. 344–357). Abingdon, England: Routledge.

Page, K. M., LaMontagne, A. D., Louie, A. M., Ostry, A. S., Shaw, A., & Shoveller, J. A. (2013). Stakeholder perceptions of job stress in an industrialized country: Implications for policy and practice. *Journal of Public Health Policy, 34,* 447–461. http://dx.doi.org/10.1057/jphp.2013.24

Page, K. M., Milner, A. J., Martin, A., Turrell, G., Giles-Corti, B., & LaMontagne, A. D. (2014). Workplace stress: What is the role of positive mental health? *Journal of Occupational and Environmental Medicine, 56,* 814–819. http://dx.doi.org/10.1097/JOM.0000000000000230

Page, K. M., & Vella-Brodrick, D. (2009). The "what," "why" and "how" of employee well-being: A new model. *Social Indicators Research, 90,* 441–458. http://dx.doi.org/10.1007/s11205-008-9270-3

Page, K. M., & Vella-Brodrick, D. A. (2012). From nonmalfeasance to beneficence: Key criteria, approaches, and ethical issues relating to positive employee health and well-being. In N. P. Reilly, M. J. Sirgy, & C. A. Gorman (Eds.), *Handbook of quality of life programs: Enhancing ethics and improving quality of life at work* (pp. 463–489). Dordrecht, The Netherlands: Springer Netherlands. http://dx.doi.org/10.1007/978-94-007-4059-4_25

Reavley, N. J., Ross, A., Killackey, E. J., & Jorm, A. F. (2012). Development of guidelines to assist organisations to support employees returning to work after an episode of anxiety, depression or a related disorder: A Delphi consensus study with Australian professionals and consumers. *BMC Psychiatry, 12,* 135. http://dx.doi.org/10.1186/1471-244X-12-135

Reavley, N. J., Ross, A., Martin, A., LaMontagne, A. D., & Jorm, A. F. (2014). Development of guidelines for workplace prevention of mental health problems: A Delphi consensus study with Australian professionals and employees. *Mental Health & Prevention, 2,* 26–34. http://dx.doi.org/10.1016/j.mhp.2014.07.002

Sanderson, K., & Andrews, G. (2006). Common mental disorders in the workforce: Recent findings from descriptive and social epidemiology. *Canadian Journal of Psychiatry, 51*, 63–75. http://dx.doi.org/10.1177/070674370605100202

Schaufeli, W. B. (2004). The future of occupational health psychology. *Applied Psychology, 53*, 502–517. http://dx.doi.org/10.1111/j.1464-0597.2004.00184.x

Shain, M. (2010). *Tracking the perfect legal storm: Converging systems create mounting pressure to create the psychologically safe workplace* [Update to Discussion Paper for the Mental Health Commission of Canada]. Retrieved from https://www.mentalhealthcommission.ca/sites/default/files/Workforce_Tracking_the_Perfect_Legal_Storm_ENG_0_1.pdf

Sin, N. L., & Lyubomirsky, S. (2009). Enhancing well-being and alleviating depressive symptoms with positive psychology interventions: A practice-friendly meta-analysis. *Journal of Clinical Psychology, 65*, 467–487. http://dx.doi.org/10.1002/jclp.20593

Sultan-Taieb, H., Lejeune, C., Drummond, A., & Niedhammer, I. (2011). Fractions of cardiovascular diseases, mental disorders, and musculoskeletal disorders attributable to job strain. *International Archives of Occupational and Environmental Health, 84*, 911–925. http://dx.doi.org/10.1007/s00420-011-0633-8

Theorell, T., Hammarstrom, A., Aronsson, G., Traskman Bendz, L., Grape, T., Hogstedt, C., . . . Hall, C. (2015). A systematic review including meta-analysis of work environment and depressive symptoms. *BMC Public Health, 15*, 738. http://dx.doi.org/10.1186/s12889-015-1954-4

Witt, K., Milner, A., Allisey, A., Davenport, L. J., & LaMontagne, A. D. (2017). Effectiveness of suicide prevention programs for emergency and protective services employees: A systematic review and meta-analysis. *American Journal of Industrial Medicine, 60*, 394–407. http://dx.doi.org/10.1002/ajim.22676

13

Productive Aging and Work

James W. Grosch, Steven Hecker, Kenneth Scott,
and Juliann C. Scholl

All would live long, but none would be old.

—BENJAMIN FRANKLIN (1705–1790)

One of society's greatest success stories over the past century has been the remarkable increase in life expectancy that has occurred in many developed countries. A child born in the United States in 1900 could expect to live to an average age of 47.3 years. By 2015, life expectancy at birth had increased to an average of 78.8 years (National Center for Health Statistics, 2017), a gain of more than 30 years. This "longevity revolution" (Butler, 2008) has produced many benefits for both individuals and society, but it also has created a number of challenges as the age structure of the population has changed. One such challenge clearly relevant to the goals of *Total Worker Health*® is how best to create a workplace that encourages workers to flourish and remain healthy and productive as they age. This chapter focuses on that challenge by briefly examining the changing age structure of the U.S. workforce, reviewing what we know about the impact of aging and emphasizing work-related outcomes in particular, and describing the concept of productive aging and basic steps that can be taken toward achieving the goal—anticipated many years ago by Benjamin Franklin—of encouraging long and healthy working

---

This chapter was authored by employees of the United States government as part of their official duty and is considered to be in the public domain. Any views expressed herein do not necessarily represent the views of the United States government, and the authors' participation in the work is not meant to serve as an official endorsement.

http://dx.doi.org/10.1037/0000149-014
Total Worker Health, H. L. Hudson, J. A. S. Nigam, S. L. Sauter, L. C. Chosewood, A. L. Schill, and J. Howard (Editors)

lives in which workers continue to make important contributions to the success of their organizations.

CHANGING DEMOGRAPHICS

Although the workforce has been gradually aging for several decades, the cumulative impact of this change in the United States and other countries has become particularly salient in recent years. Figure 13.1 presents data from the U.S. Bureau of Labor Statistics that illustrate the percentage change and anticipated change in the civilian labor force and labor force participation rate (LFPR) between 2004 and 2024 for various age groups (Toossi, 2015). During this period, the largest percentage increases in the civilian labor force are for workers 55 years and older, and the overall change for younger age groups is nearly flat. An important factor contributing to these differences is the baby boomers generation—or approximately 76 million individuals born between 1946 and 1964. Because the cohorts who preceded (i.e., Traditionalists) and followed (i.e., Generation X) the baby boomers were smaller in size and had a slower growth rate, baby boomers have had a disproportionate impact on many aspects of our society, including the workplace. With many baby boomers now beginning to retire (the oldest turned 65 in 2011), there is increasing concern that such societal programs as Social Security and Medicare will need to be

FIGURE 13.1. Percent Change and Projected Change in Civilian Labor Force and Labor Force Participation Rate, 2004–2024

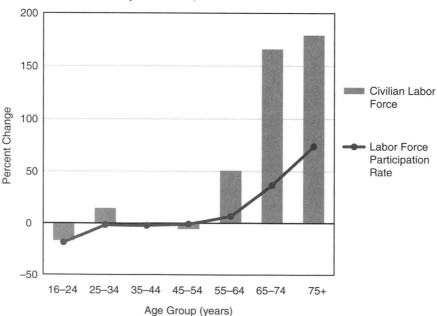

Data from tables in Toossi (2015).

restructured in to accommodate the growing number of older adults. One index reflecting this concern is called the *old-age dependency ratio*, or the population 65 years and older divided by the population aged 18 to 64. Between 2000 and 2050, this ratio is expected to increase from 20% to 37% (Colby & Ortman, 2014), which suggests a greater burden on working-age adults to help support those who are at retirement age and beyond.

The LFPR has increased and is projected to increase for workers 55 years and older but remain flat, if not slightly negative, for younger age groups (see Figure 13.1). There are many reasons why the LFPR is increasing for older workers that reflect both *pull* (i.e., positive) and *push* (i.e., negative) forces (Shultz, Morton, & Weckerle, 1998) that encourage an individual to keep working. On the pull side, older workers tend to be better educated and healthier than past generations (Lowsky, Olshansky, Bhattacharya, & Goldman, 2014; Rix, 2006), and substantial numbers have reported very good to excellent health status. In addition, the nature of work itself has changed from a manufacturing-dominated economy to one that emphasizes services and information-based activities having lower physical demands (Johnson, Mermin, & Resseger, 2007). Continuing to work also can provide a range of psychological benefits, including a sense of purpose in life and the opportunity to remain physically, mentally, and socially active.

On the push side, financial necessity is clearly a strong factor in workers' staying employed at older ages. A recent national survey of older workers reported that 44% of respondents indicated that "need the money" was the single most important reason for working or looking for work (AARP, 2014). That percentage compares with 19% of respondents who identified psychological benefits (e.g., enjoy the job, makes me feel useful) as the most important factor. For many workers, financial need is significantly reduced by participation in an employer-sponsored retirement plan. But only approximately half of all private sector workers participate in such a plan, and those who are covered have seen a gradual transition from defined benefit to defined contribution programs. Defined contribution programs do not provide a guaranteed source of income and depend on the worker's ability to contribute while working. The low level of personal savings in the United States also plays a role, particularly for workers without a pension. The Employee Benefit Research Institute (2017) estimated that only 18% of workers are "very confident" that they can retire comfortably and that fewer than half of workers have saved more than $25,000 for retirement. The need to maintain adequate health care coverage can result in staying at work and has been reported by 8% of older workers as the most important factor (AARP, 2014).

The change in the age structure of the workforce depicted in Figure 13.1 is not temporary and is expected to last well into the foreseeable future as people continue to live and work longer, and birth rates remain low. This change is also global in scope. Many countries in Europe (e.g., Italy, Germany, Sweden) and Asia (e.g., Japan, South Korea) are currently considered "older" than in the United States. There are other countries (e.g., China, Mexico) that are currently considered "younger" but are experiencing demographic trends that eventually will result in older populations than in the United States. In addition, the traditional employment relationship in many countries is changing as reflected in *gig work*, that is, the trend toward contracting with rather than employing people, and increased precariousness of employment (Weil, 2014). These changes, accompanied by an aging workforce, will create a number of challenges in the future for workers, organizations, and society.

TWO CONTRASTING VIEWS OF AGING

As interest in aging has grown, two broad perspectives on what the aging process entails have emerged. Each perspective is based on empirical support, and, collectively, both provide insight into the range of changes that may occur within an aging workforce.

Aging as Decline and Loss

Perhaps the most traditional view of aging is that of a process that involves a gradual and inevitable deterioration in function over time. Research on the biological and genetic mechanisms of senescence, for example, has posited a number of possible "pathways," including the accumulated impact of free radicals that eventually results in cellular damage, genetic mutations and failure to repair DNA damage over time, a biological clock that regulates the pace of aging through changes in the hormonal system, and a decline in the immune system that leads to increased vulnerability (Jin, 2010; Kaeberlein & Martin, 2016). These theories of aging are broadly categorized as either *nonprogrammed theories* that emphasize accumulated damage produced through environmental assault (e.g., free radicals, inadequate DNA repair) or *programmed theories* that emphasize an internal biological timetable that organisms invariably follow as they age (e.g., changes in hormones and immunity; Goldsmith, 2014). Although a consensus has yet to emerge around a single explanation of why we age, advances in this area have reinforced the view of aging as a complex process of decline that is similar perhaps to a type of universally experienced disease that eventually leads to dysfunction, disability, and death.

On the level of individual functioning, it is now well documented that nearly all physiological systems in the body show gradual decline and loss over time. A detailed description of these changes can be found elsewhere (e.g., Crawford, Graveling, Cowie, & Dixon, 2010; Johns & Weissman, 2015). However, a partial list includes sensory processes (e.g., hearing and vision), muscle strength, cardiovascular and respiratory functioning, bone health and musculoskeletal capacity, immune functioning, skin elasticity, motor processes (e.g., reaction time), and "fluid" or "working" memory (e.g., the ability to store and process new information). Although each system is different, many age-related changes begin early in life (often in the mid- to late 20s, if not younger); are not always linear or generalizable, especially in nonelderly populations; and may take place long before an individual actually notices a decline in functioning.

Collectively, these changes suggest that an aging workforce is likely to be at a disadvantage when it comes to job performance and occupational safety and health outcomes. However, at least two caveats are in order. First, the aging process is characterized by increased variability over time, and some individuals show much less decline than others (e.g., Fozard, Vercruyssen, Reynolds, Hancock, & Quilter, 1994). The reason for different rates of aging is complex but undoubtedly includes environmental and genetic factors. Second, as Peter Warr and others have pointed out, workers are at risk of being "age impaired" only when the task requirements of a job exceed a worker's ability (Warr, 1994). And for many types of jobs, an individual's physical and cognitive abilities must decline quite substantially before they are exceeded by the task requirements of work.

Aging as Development and Growth

A different view of aging has emerged from the field of lifespan development that emphasizes the dynamic and adaptive nature of the aging process. From this perspective, development and growth do not end at a given age but can continue in many forms throughout adulthood. For example, an important attribute that tends to show a positive trajectory with age is *crystalized intelligence*, which refers to knowledge and skills acquired through experience and prior learning (Cattell, 1987). Examples include verbal ability (e.g., vocabulary), domain-specific knowledge, and problem solving based on the application of accumulated knowledge. Crystalized intelligence has been found to generally increase throughout life until around age 60 (and perhaps later) and may allow individuals to compensate for normal age-related decline in fluid or working memory by supporting strategies that capitalize on existing knowledge and skills (Salthouse, 2004).

Another area that shows considerable stability, if not improvement, throughout much of the lifespan is mental health and well-being. In a large survey of Canadian adults, Akhtar-Danesh and Landeen (2007) reported that both lifetime depression and depressive episodes of 12 months or more declined consistently with age: Individuals 75 years and older had the lowest rates for both measures. An analysis of data from the health and retirement study found a consistent decline in "clinically relevant depressive symptoms" from 17.4% in respondents 51 to 54 years old to 10.4% in respondents 70 to 74 years old (Federal Interagency Forum on Aging-Related Statistics, 2016). Depressive symptoms increased slightly for individuals 75 years and older, providing some support for a *U-shape relationship*, in which the prevalence of depressive symptoms tends to be higher for the youngest and oldest age groups. What might be considered the flipside of depression, life satisfaction and subjective well-being also have been found to improve with age. Controlling for birth cohort, Sutin et al. (2013) found that well-being improved over the life course, even after taking into account health, gender, ethnicity, and education.

This increase in well-being, even as physical and cognitive functioning are declining, has been referred to as the *paradox of aging*. Explanations have focused on changes in emotion, goals, values, and motivation that occur with age (Kanfer & Ackerman, 2004). One influential theory proposed by Laura Carstensen and colleagues maintains that as people get older, their sense of the time they have left (or "time horizon") changes, and they invest greater effort into emotionally meaningful activities. The result is a shift in motivation characterized by a desire for more satisfying personal relationships and a reduced emphasis on activities that focus strictly on acquiring information (Carstensen, Fung, & Charles, 2003). Applied to the workplace, this theory suggests that as workers reach the middle and latter part of their careers and "time left" starts to dwindle, their preferences and goals are likely to gradually shift to activities that allow for greater emotional satisfaction and support of one's identity.

AGING IN THE CONTEXT OF WORK

Given the two broad views of aging outlined previously, it should come as no surprise that the impact of aging in the context of work is neither simple nor uniform in direction. Table 13.1 presents a summary of how a select group of work-related variables changes with age. Based on the current research literature, each variable is categorized as tending to worsen, improve, or have no consistent relationship with age.

Before discussing Table 13.1, a few caveats are in order. The summary is intended to characterize the overall pattern of results for each variable; there are undoubtedly exceptions that may reflect how a given construct is measured or particular features of the workplace (e.g., supervisory practices) that may overshadow the impact of age. Also, the variables in the table are broad, and

TABLE 13.1 Relationship Between Age and Selected Work and Health Measures

Tends to worsen with age	Little or no consistent relationship with age	Tends to improve with age
Fatal or severe workplace injuries (CDC, 2007a)	Core job performance (Ng & Feldman, 2008)	Nonfatal workplace injuries (CDC, 2007b)
Return to work following injury/Illness (Bureau of Labor Statistics, 2016)	Absenteeism (Hackett, 1990)	Job satisfaction (Ng & Feldman, 2010)
Chronic health conditions (e.g., arthritis, hypertension; National Institute on Aging, 2007)	Ability to learn from training (Ng & Feldman, 2008)	Counterproductive work behaviors (O'Driscoll & Roche, 2015)
Work disability (U.S. Census Bureau & U.S. Bureau of Labor Statistics, 2006)	Creativity (Ng & Feldman, 2008)	Presenteeism (Gosselin, Lemyre, & Corneil, 2013)
Work Ability (Ilmarinen, Tuomi, & Klockars, 1997)	Work-related musculoskeletal disorders (Okunribido & Wynn, 2010)	Diversity of knowledge and experience (Ng & Feldman, 2008)

Note. CDC = Centers for Disease Control and Prevention.

some subcategories may show a different association with age. For example, although nonfatal workplace injuries decline with age, a specific type of non-fatal injury—slips, trips, and falls—tends to increase and should remain a concern with an aging workforce (Layne & Pollack, 2004). Similarly, although age makes little difference in the benefit workers receive from training, research has found that other older workers may take longer to learn the same information compared with younger workers (Charness & Czaja, 2006).

For some measures, their association with age can be affected by moderator variables. For example, in an analysis of national survey data, Grosch and Pransky (2009) found that the prevalence of back pain remained fairly constant with age but declined slightly for workers 55 years and older. However, when physical demands were considered, older workers who reported being involved in repeated lifting activities at work were at much greater risk of experiencing back pain than younger workers who also reported repeated lifting. Workplace exposure (in this case, lifting) interacted with age to influence the relationship between age and musculoskeletal health.

Other caveats: The summary presented in Table 13.1 is based largely on cross-sectional studies in which workers of different ages were compared at a single point in time. This approach, in contrast to longitudinal research, which follows workers over time, has been criticized for sometimes overestimating age-related change and making it difficult to disentangle age effects from cohort, period, and healthy worker effects (Hofer & Sliwinski, 2001). Moreover, the focus in Table 13.1 is on the presence or absence of simple linear relationships, even though some studies have found evidence for curvilinear relationships with age (e.g., workers' compensation claims; Safety & Health Assessment & Research for Prevention, 2007).

Despite these issues, Table 13.1 presents a general profile of the types of change that can be expected with an aging workforce. Particularly noteworthy is that a number of consequential variables do not show a consistent relationship with age (i.e., middle column). The reasons for this pattern are undoubtedly complex, but in some cases may reflect a situation in which the losses of aging (e.g., decrease in physiological functioning) are counterbalanced by the gains (e.g., increase in crystalized intelligence). For example, although workers may experience reduced stamina and a certain degree of joint stiffening with age, they also may learn more efficient and safer strategies for doing their work so that job performance and the likelihood of musculoskeletal disorders remain relatively stable across the working life. Variables that tend to worsen with age (first column) appear to share the common thread of greater vulnerability and gradually worsening physical health that can occur with age. As a result, chronic health conditions increase in prevalence as a workforce ages, and arthritis is the most common at 48% for workers 55 years and older, followed by hypertension (43%), and diabetes (13%; National Institute on Aging, 2007). Workplace injuries, when they do occur, are more likely to be severe or fatal, to take longer to recover from, and more likely to result in disability.

Variables that tend to improve with age (third column) suggest that an aging workforce can have many important benefits for an organization that reflect underlying improvements in crystalized intelligence (e.g., fewer nonfatal injuries, diversity of knowledge) and emotional health (e.g., job satisfaction, less counterproductive behavior). Age, which is highly correlated with tenure, often is associated with more favorable working conditions, such as increased levels of autonomy and social support, which also may contribute to many of these improvements (Sauter, Streit, & Hanseman, 2009).

A complex picture emerges of the potential impact of aging within the context of work. Performance on laboratory tasks does not necessarily predict effectiveness in the workplace. This complexity has a number of important implications. First, primary prevention efforts, which focus on preventing a health or safety problem before it occurs, become paramount with an aging workforce because once a health issue surfaces, it will tend to be more severe (or fatal) and require a longer recovery period as workers age. Second, chronological age, when it plays a role, is at best a modest predictor of some health and safety outcomes, and can be overshadowed by features of the work environment, such as physical demands or work organization characteristics. The gradual, complex nature of the aging process suggests that there may be many avenues and levels of influence that can be used in advancing the safety, health, and well-being of an aging workforce. Extrapolating from Table 13.1, a basic rule of thumb should be to "minimize the losses" that may occur with aging (first column), and "maximize the gains" (third column).

PRODUCTIVE AGING AND WORK

As our knowledge of aging has increased, concepts such as *healthy aging, active aging, successful aging* and *productive aging* have been introduced to suggest that it is possible to effectively navigate the multidimensional changes that come with growing older. Although each of these concepts has a slightly different emphasis, they all advocate being proactive about age-related change and striving toward specific goals, such as avoiding disease and disability, maintaining high physical and cognitive functioning, experiencing mastery/growth, and continuing to engage with life (e.g., Martin et al., 2015; Rowe & Kahn, 1998). More recently, these concepts have been extended to the workplace and advice offered to workers and employers regarding how work-related functioning and health can be maintained or even strengthened with age. For example, Zacher (2015) proposed a comprehensive theoretical model for *successful aging at work*, which presents alternatives to traditional working life trajectories and emphasizes employees' contributions to their own successful aging at work.

In 2015, the National Institute for Occupational Safety and Health (NIOSH) established the National Center for Productive Aging and Work (NCPAW) as part of its Office for Total Worker Health. The goals of NCPAW are to advance research on productive aging through collaboration with intramural and extramural partners; expand knowledge of effective interventions and best practices; and develop a broad range of translational products and resources for workers, employers, and other stakeholders. The term *productive aging* came from the seminal work of Robert Butler and his colleagues, who developed the concept for the general population to emphasize the positive aspects of growing older and how individuals can make important contributions to their own lives, their communities and organizations, and society as a whole (Butler & Gleason, 1985). Productive aging is, in part, a counterpoint to the view of aging as basically an "accumulation of losses" and the assumption that these losses must invariably lead older adults to become disengaged, unproductive, and dependent on others. Butler emphasized that, given demographic trends, it is imperative for society to better use the skills, wisdom, and experience of older adults (Butler & Gleason, 1985). The term *productive* was defined broadly to include participation in the workforce as well as other activities that in some way benefit larger society, such as volunteer activity, family-related activities, and self-care activities that maintain independence (Bass & Caro, 2001). The relationship between good health and productive aging is understood to be bidirectional: Each directly impacts the other.

Extended to the workplace, our view of productive aging at NCPAW is that it refers to the continued ability of workers to remain engaged and make active contributions to their organizations and their own work-related skills and abilities. A safe and healthy work environment is seen as providing a necessary foundation for these contributions. Furthermore, productive aging in the context of work has four main attributes described as follows.

A Lifespan Perspective

This perspective holds that patterns of change and transition occur throughout the working life. Aging is viewed as a biopsychosocial process that involves losses and gains, and represents the product of many interacting factors inside and outside the worker. A fundamental characteristic of a lifespan perspective is *plasticity*, or the idea that an individual has the potential to change and adapt in response to his or her environment and experiences (Baltes, Lindenberger, & Staudinger, 2006; Sigelman & Rider, 2017). Although aging and eventual decline are inevitable, it also is possible for individuals, organizations, and society to manage or have some level of impact on the aging process. An important implication of this perspective is that the scope of productive aging includes all age groups of workers and is not limited to just "older workers," however that group may be defined. Prioritizing worker health and safety at all life stages is an investment that is cost effective and can reduce chronic health conditions later in life (Loeppke et al., 2013).

A Comprehensive and Integrated Approach

Given the complexity of the aging process, a multilevel, holistic strategy toward prevention and advancing worker well-being is needed. Simply focusing on a narrow range of workplace hazards or safety practices does not take full of advantages of the many pathways that play a role in how workers age and the impact of growing older.

Total Worker Health, the focus of this volume, represents one such comprehensive approach or model. Although not based primarily on aging-related research, a TWH approach prioritizes a hazard-free work environment for workers of all ages while also comprehensively addressing other workplace systems, including those relevant to the control of psychosocial hazards and exposures, the organization of work, compensation and benefits, and work–life management efforts. The emphasis of the TWH approach on integration reflects that occupational safety and health programs have traditionally been compartmentalized, have functioned independently of one another with little coordination, or both. A growing body of research, however, has indicated that workplace programs that are integrated and share common objectives are more effective than programs developed in isolation (Sorensen et al., 2013).

A related approach, more firmly anchored in aging research, is the concept of *work ability*, which refers to a worker's capacity to continue working in his or her current job given work demands and available resources (Ilmarinen, 1999). Originally developed at the Finnish Institute of Occupational Health, the concept of work ability has been the subject of extensive international research. A major premise of the model is that work ability can be maintained, if not improved, over the working life by focusing efforts on four principal factors or dimensions (Ilmarinen, 2009; Silverstein, 2008):

- *physical work environment*—for example, ergonomics programs, hygiene improvements, workstation design, changes to reduce the risk of falling, reduction of prolonged physical exertion, better delivery of visual and auditory information;

- *individual health resources*—for example, chronic disease management and monitoring, programs to promote individual health behaviors, health education and screening, return to work programs;

- *leadership and organization of work*—for example, workplace flexibility programs, job design, supervisor training, better management of working hours and shift work; and

- *professional development*—for example, supportive training methods for older workers, lifelong learning opportunities, mentoring programs, training in the use of technology.

This focus on multiple factors or levels is consistent with a TWH perspective as well as that of other models of healthy organizations, including the World Health Organization's healthy workplace framework (Burton, 2010) and the SafeWell practice guidelines (McLellan, Harden, Markkanen, & Sorensen, 2012).

Outcomes That Recognize the Priorities of Workers and Organizations

When it comes to productive aging and work, the question arises: Productive for whom? The desired outcomes for a worker may not always be the same as those for a manager or an organization. For example, *organization-centered* outcomes tend to focus on reducing health care costs, having fewer workplace injuries, and achieving lower rates of absenteeism and turnover. In comparison, *worker-centered* outcomes may emphasize maintaining or improving individual physical health, working in a safe and comfortable environment, and achieving a high level of individual well-being and the sense of making a contribution to the organization. A growing consensus among workplace experts is that changes in either of these two categories of outcomes can affect the other. Studies on worker well-being, for instance, have consistently found that improvements can lead to reduced absenteeism, higher productivity, and fewer reported workplace injuries (all organization-centered outcomes; Harter, Schmidt, & Keyes, 2002). Similarly, an organization that increases its productivity and is able to transfer knowledge to younger workers through mentoring programs may, as a result, have more resources to invest in worker well-being programs and injury prevention (Wilson, Dejoy, Vandenberg, Richardson, & McGrath, 2004).

The bidirectional nature of this relationship suggests that both categories of outcomes need to be acknowledged and prioritized in any attempt to encourage productive aging. Failure to attend to organization and worker goals may serve to undermine the programs and policies that are implemented. Focusing on both categories can contribute to a culture of health that will help sustain improvements in productive aging over time.

A Supportive Work Culture for Multigenerational Issues

Because many older workers are delaying retirement and younger workers are tending to have higher levels of education, the workforce will continue to increase in age diversity in a variety of different ways (e.g., more younger workers supervising older workers). Changing demographics have resulted in organizations in which there can be as many as five generations working together (i.e., Traditionalists, 1925–1945; baby boomers, 1946–1964; Generation X, 1965–1980; Millennials, 1981–2001; Generation Z, 2002–to be determined). A *generation* can be described as a cohort of individuals born during the same period who share a set of formative life experiences (e.g., economic and political movements, historical events) that shape attitudes, beliefs, and values.

A great deal of variability can be found within a given generation; thus, relying solely on these broad categories risks oversimplification and the creation of exaggerated stereotypes. It also can be difficult to separate the impact of generation from other changes that occur over time at work (e.g., career progression). However, that work-related values and, by extension, behaviors can vary across age cohorts has important implications for organizations when it comes to such issues as training, worker motivation, use of technology, recruitment, leadership, communication strategies, and teamwork.

In terms of productive aging, creating a supportive culture involves better understanding the generational composition of the workforce, facilitating regular discussion about generational issues, and developing a set of programs and policies that are broad enough to address the needs of all workers throughout the working life (e.g., family leave policies that appeal to both younger and older workers) and encourage positive interactions between different age cohorts (e.g., mentoring programs, age-diverse teams). A major challenge is to prevent the intergroup conflict that can sometimes accompany a multiage workforce by fostering a culture that respects and uses the unique skills, knowledge, and perspectives of workers in all age groups (Rudolph & Zacher, 2015).

GETTING STARTED: DESIGNING A WORKPLACE THAT ADVANCES PRODUCTIVE AGING

A recent national survey of human resources professionals reported that 87% expressed at least some level of awareness of the aging workforce issue. However, only 13% indicated that their organizations had actually developed or implemented a plan to change policies or practices to address this issue (Society for Human Resource Management, 2015). This discrepancy between awareness and action often is referred to as the *knowing–doing gap* (Pfeffer & Sutton, 2000) and raises an important question: Given our growing knowledge of the impact of aging on workers, what steps can organizations take to develop practical strategies for maintaining the health and productivity of workers as they age?

Unfortunately, no interventions or programs for productive aging work in all situations. The success of a particular program depends on a number of factors, including the size of the organization, the nature and complexity of the work, available resources, and readiness within the organization for change. However, it is possible to recommend a systematic planning process for productive aging that involves three distinct steps.

Conducting an Organizational Assessment

The foundation of any program or intervention should be based on a thorough understanding of the workplace issues and challenges that may be emerging as the workforce continues to age. Examining the age demographics of the workforce and how they may be changing is a starting point. How is the workforce distributed across various age groups or generations? How is that expected to change over the next 10 years as some workers become eligible for retirement? As part of this assessment, it can be helpful to consider the core types of expertise and skills that are essential to the organization's mission and whether retaining this expertise into the future represents a challenge.

Other important baseline data include a careful examination of current or potential hazards and risk factors at different levels of the work environment. This examination might involve, for example, an assessment of physical demands, ergonomic concerns, safety issues, and work organization factors. Also, collecting information on existing organizational policies, programs, and practices that support or, perhaps in some cases, unintentionally compromise worker safety and health is important. Data on the health and well-being of the workforce also can help identify priority areas through, for example, examination of sickness and injury data; workers' compensation claims; short- and long-term disability trends; and worker survey data asking about safety and health issues, including psychosocial outcomes, such as job stress, worker engagement, and the general health culture of the organization. Data for the assessment should be collected from as many relevant sources as possible, including organizational records, walk-throughs, discussion groups, and worker and management surveys.

Developing an Action Plan

Designing an intervention or program to encourage productive aging requires getting into the specifics of what will be done, by whom, and with what goals in mind. Adopting a model or theory, such as work ability, the TWH approach, or other holistic strategies, can serve as a useful guide to the different levels of change that should be considered. Figure 13.2 presents an action planning grid adapted from a training workshop on designing age-friendly workplaces that was developed by the University of Washington and is based largely on the work ability model (Silverstein, 2008; University of Washington, 2009). This grid provides an overview of the types of decisions that need to be made in developing a program or intervention for productive aging.

Typically, this grid is completed by individuals from throughout the organization who work together over several days in planning teams. A challenge is to develop goals in multiple categories that are large enough to make an impact but manageable enough to be accomplished in a reasonable amount of time. There is also growing evidence from field studies that developing several small

FIGURE 13.2. Action planning grid based on the Work Ability model

Type of Program or Intervention	Goal and How It Will Be Measured	How Will It Happen?	Who Will Ensure It Does?	When Will It Finish?	Challenges and Responses
Physical Work Environment					
Individual Health Resources					
Leadership and Work Organization					
Professional Development					

From *Designing the Age-Friendly Workplace: Participant Workbook*, by University of Washington, Seattle, 2009 (training materials based on the workbook can be found at http://www.agefriendlyworkplace.org). In the public domain.

interventions across categories (e.g., rest breaks, better illumination, simple job rotation) can cumulatively have a positive effect on a range of health and productivity outcomes (e.g., Loch, Sting, Bauer, & Mauermann, 2010).

Implementing and Evaluating Programs

Many experts on organizational interventions have noted that how an intervention or program is implemented can be as important as the content or focus of that effort (e.g., Nielsen, Taris, & Cox, 2010). When a program has the support and commitment of management, involves a transparent process in which workers are encouraged to provide input, and is adequately communicated to all stakeholders in the organization, it is much more likely to succeed. A number of resources currently exist that provide in-depth guidance with regard to the implementation process (Egan, Bambra, Petticrew, & Whitehead, 2009; NIOSH, 2016).

Although often not given as much priority, the careful evaluation of an intervention or program can provide valuable information about what works and why. A distinction often is made between evaluating the implementation process itself (e.g., reaching the intended audience, sufficient worker participation, implementing the program according to plan) and evaluating whether desired outcomes were achieved (e.g., fewer injuries, improvements in health and well-being, cost-effectiveness of a program; Cox, Karanika, Griffiths, & Houdmont, 2007). Both types of evaluation are important and provide complementary information about the success or failure of a program. In addition, it is important to choose evaluation criteria that are both short- and long-term. Early improvements may not always be sustained into the future and, conversely, programs showing few improvements at first may require a longer time horizon before they have a measurable impact.

CONCLUSION

As the age structure of many developed countries, including the United States, has changed, so too has our overall perspective on aging. Although some degree of decline and deterioration may be inevitable, there is growing evidence that the effects of aging, both positive and negative, can be moderated through efforts on many different levels. Consistent with a TWH perspective, research suggests that organizational programs most likely to succeed over the long term are those that are broad based and take a holistic view of worker safety and health. A major challenge is to further expand our knowledge of effective interventions and programs to more fully use the strengths and abilities of an aging workforce.

REFERENCES

AARP. (2014). *Staying ahead of the curve 2013: The AARP work and career survey*. Washington, DC: Author.

Akhtar-Danesh, N., & Landeen, J. (2007). Relation between depression and socio-demographic factors. *International Journal of Mental Health Systems, 1*, 4, 1–9. http://dx.doi.org/10.1186/1752-4458-1-4

Baltes, P. B., Lindenberger, U., & Staudinger, U. M. (2006). Life-span theory in developmental psychology. In R. M. Lerner (Ed.), *Handbook of child psychology: Vol. 1. Theoretical models of human development* (6th ed., pp. 569–664). New York, NY: Wiley.

Bass, S. A., & Caro, R. G. (2001). Productive aging: A conceptual framework. In N. Morrow-Howell, J. Hingerlong, & M. Sherraden (Eds.), *Productive aging: Concepts and challenges* (pp. 37–78). Baltimore, MD: Johns Hopkins University Press.

Bureau of Labor Statistics, U.S. Department of Labor. (2016). Table 5. In *Nonfatal occupational injuries and illnesses requiring days away from work, 2015* (Publication No. USDL-16-2130). Washington, DC: Author. Retrieved from https://www.bls.gov/news.release/pdf/osh2.pdf

Burton, J. (2010). *WHO healthy workplace framework and model: Background and supporting literature and practices.* Geneva, Switzerland: World Health Organization.

Butler, R. N. (2008). *The longevity revolution: The benefits and challenges of living a long life.* New York, NY: Perseus Books Group.

Butler, R. N., & Gleason, H. P. (1985). *Productive aging: Enhancing vitality in later life.* New York: Springer.

Carstensen, L. L., Fung, H. H., & Charles, S. T. (2003). Socioemotional selectivity theory and the regulation of emotion in the second half of life. *Motivation and Emotion, 27*, 103–123. http://dx.doi.org/10.1023/A:1024569803230

Cattell, R. B. (1987). *Intelligence: Its structure, growth, and action.* Amsterdam, the Netherlands: North-Holland.

Centers for Disease Control and Prevention. (2007a). Fatal occupational injuries—United States, 2005. *Morbidity and Mortality Weekly Report, 56*, 297–301.

Centers for Disease Control and Prevention. (2007b). Nonfatal occupational injuries and illnesses—United States, 2004. *Morbidity and Mortality Weekly Report, 56*, 393–397.

Charness, J., & Czaja, S. J. (2006). *Older worker training: What we know and don't know.* Washington, DC: AARP.

Colby, S. L., & Ortman, J. M. (2014, May). The baby boom cohort in the United States: 2012 to 2060—Population estimates and projections. *Current Population Reports* (pp. 25–1141). Washington, DC: U.S. Census Bureau.

Cox, T., Karanika, M., Griffiths, A., & Houdmont, J. (2007). Evaluating organizational-level work stress interventions: Beyond traditional methods. *Work & Stress, 21*, 348–362. http://dx.doi.org/10.1080/02678370701760757

Crawford, J. O., Graveling, R. A., Cowie, H. A., & Dixon, K. (2010). The health safety and health promotion needs of older workers. *Occupational Medicine, 60*, 184–192. http://dx.doi.org/10.1093/occmed/kqq028

Egan, M., Bambra, C., Petticrew, M., & Whitehead, M. (2009). Reviewing evidence on complex social interventions: Appraising implementation in systematic reviews of the health effects of organisational-level workplace interventions. *Journal of Epidemiology and Community Health, 63*, 4–11. http://dx.doi.org/10.1136/jech.2007.071233

Employee Benefit Research Institute. (2017). *The 2017 retirement confidence survey: Many workers lack retirement confidence and feel stress about retirement* [Issue Brief No. 431]. Washington, DC: Author.

Federal Interagency Forum on Aging-Related Statistics. (2016). *Older Americans 2016: Key indicators of well-being.* Washington, DC: Government Printing Office.

Fozard, J. L., Vercruyssen, M., Reynolds, S. L., Hancock, P. A., & Quilter, R. E. (1994). Age differences and changes in reaction time: The Baltimore longitudinal study of aging. *Journal of Gerontology, 49*, 179–189. http://dx.doi.org/10.1093/geronj/49.4.P179

Goldsmith, T. C. (2014). *An introduction to biological aging theory.* Crownsville, MD: Axinet Press.

Gosselin, E., Lemyre, L., & Corneil, W. (2013). Presenteeism and absenteeism: Differentiated understanding of related phenomena. *Journal of Occupational Health Psychology*, *18*(1), 75–86. http://dx.doi.org/10.1037/a0030932

Grosch, J. W., & Pransky, G. S. (2009). Safety and health issues for an aging workforce. In S. J. Czaja & J. Sharit (Eds.), *Aging and work: Issues and implications in a changing landscape* (pp. 334–358). Baltimore, MD: Johns Hopkins University Press.

Hackett, R. D. (1990). Age, tenure, and employee absenteeism. *Human Relations*, *43*, 601–619. http://dx.doi.org/10.1177/001872679004300701

Harter, J. K., Schmidt, F. L., & Keyes, C. L. (2002). Well-being in the workplace and its relationship to business outcomes: A review of the Gallup studies. In C. L. Keyes & J. Haidt (Eds.), *Flourishing: The positive person and the good life* (pp. 205–224). Washington, DC: American Psychological Association.

Hofer, S. M., & Sliwinski, M. J. (2001). Understanding ageing: An evaluation of research designs for assessing the interdependence of ageing-related changes. *Gerontology*, *47*, 341–352. http://dx.doi.org/10.1159/000052825

Ilmarinen, J. (1999). *Ageing workers in the European Union: Status and promotion of work ability, employability and employment*. Helsinki, Finland: Finnish Institute of Occupational Health, Ministry of Social Affairs and Health.

Ilmarinen, J. (2009). Aging and work: An international perspective. In S. J. Czaja & J. Sharit (Eds.), *Aging and work: Issues and implications in a changing landscape* (pp. 51–73). Baltimore, MD: Johns Hopkins University Press.

Ilmarinen, J., Tuomi, K., & Klockars, M. (1997). Changes in the work ability of active employees over an 11-year period. *Scandinavian Journal of Work, Environment & Health*, *23*(Suppl. 1), 49–57.

Jin, K. (2010). Modern biological theories of aging. *Aging and Disease*, *1*, 72–74.

Johns, D. W., & Weissman, D. N. (2015). Occupational health and safety risks for the aging worker. In A. M. Fan, G. Alexeeff, & E. Khan (Eds.), *Toxicology and risk assessment* (pp. 1087–1103). Singapore, China: Pan Stanford.

Johnson, R. W., Mermin, B. B. T., & Resseger, M. (2007). *Employment at older ages and the changing nature of work*. Washington, DC: AARP Public Policy Institute.

Kaeberlein, M. R., & Martin, G. M. (Eds.). (2016). *Handbook of the biology of aging* (8th ed.). London, England: Academic Press.

Kanfer, R., & Ackerman, P. L. (2004). Aging, adult development, and work motivation. *Academy of Management Review*, *29*, 440–458. http://dx.doi.org/10.5465/amr.2004.13670969

Layne, L. A., & Pollack, K. M. (2004). Nonfatal occupational injuries from slips, trips, and falls among older workers treated in hospital emergency departments, United States 1998. *American Journal of Industrial Medicine*, *46*, 32–41. http://dx.doi.org/10.1002/ajim.20038

Loch, C. H., Sting, F. J., Bauer, N., & Mauermann, H. (2010). How BMW is defusing the demographic time bomb. *Harvard Business Review*, *88*, 99–102. Retrieved from http://hdl.handle.net/1765/20802

Loeppke, R. R., Schill, A. L., Chosewood, L. C., Grosch, J. W., Allweiss, P., Burton, W. N., . . . Larson, P. W. (2013). Advancing workplace health protection and promotion for an aging workforce. *Journal of Occupational and Environmental Medicine*, *55*, 500–506. http://dx.doi.org/10.1097/JOM.0b013e31829613a4

Lowsky, D. J., Olshansky, S. J., Bhattacharya, J., & Goldman, D. P. (2014). Heterogeneity in healthy aging. *Journals of Gerontology: Series A*, *69*, 640–649. http://dx.doi.org/10.1093/gerona/glt162

Martin, P., Kelly, N., Kahana, B., Kahana, E., Willcox, B. J., Willcox, D. C., & Poon, L. W. (2015). Defining successful aging: A tangible or elusive concept? *Gerontologist*, *55*, 14–25. http://dx.doi.org/10.1093/geront/gnu044

McLellan, D., Harden, E., Markkanen, P., & Sorensen, G. (2012). *SafeWell practice guidelines: An integrated approach to worker health—Version 2.0*. Boston, MA: Harvard School of Public Health, Center for Work, Health and Well-being. Retrieved from http://centerforworkhealth.sph.harvard.edu/sites/default/files/safewell_guidelines/SafeWellPracticeGuidelines_Complete.pdf

National Center for Health Statistics. (2017). *Health, United States, 2016: With chartbook on long-term trends in health.* Hyattsville, MD: U.S. Department of Health and Human Services, Centers for Disease Control and Prevention, National Center for Health Statistics.

National Institute for Occupational Safety and Health. (2016). *Fundamentals of Total Worker Health® approaches: Essential elements for advancing worker safety, health, and well-being* (DHHS [NIOSH] Publication No. 2017-112). Cincinnati, OH: U.S. Department of Health and Human Services, Centers for Disease Control and Prevention, National Institute for Occupational Safety and Health. Retrieved from https://stacks.cdc.gov/view/cdc/43275

National Institute on Aging. (2007). *Growing older in America: The health and retirement study.* Bethesda, MD: National Institute on Aging, National Institutes of Health, U.S. Department of Health and Human Services.

Ng, T. W. H., & Feldman, D. C. (2008). The relationship of age to ten dimensions of job performance. *Journal of Applied Psychology, 93,* 392–423. http://dx.doi.org/10.1037/0021-9010.93.2.392

Ng, T. W. H., & Feldman, D. C. (2010). The relationships of age with job attitudes: A meta-analysis. *Personnel Psychology, 63,* 677–718. http://dx.doi.org/10.1111/j.1744-6570.2010.01184.x

Nielsen, K., Taris, T. W., & Cox, T. (2010). The future of organizational interventions: Addressing the challenges of today's organizations. *Work & Stress, 24,* 219–233. http://dx.doi.org/10.1080/02678373.2010.519176

O'Driscoll, M. P., & Roche, M. (2015). Age, organizational citizenship behaviors, and counterproductive work behaviors. In N. A. Pachana (Ed.), *Encyclopedia of geropsychology* (pp. 1–11). Singapore: Springer. http://dx.doi.org/10.1007/978-981-287-080-3_196-1

Okunribido, O., & Wynn, T. (2010). *Ageing and work-related musculoskeletal disorders: A review of the recent literature* (Health and Safety Executive Research Report No. RR799). Norwich, England: Health and Safety Executive.

Pfeffer, J., & Sutton, R. I. (2000). *The knowing–doing gap: How smart companies turn knowledge into action.* Boston, MA: Harvard Business School Press.

Rix, S. E. (2006). The aging of the American workforce. *Chicago-Kent Law Review, 81,* 593–617.

Rowe, J. W., & Kahn, R. L. (1998). *Successful aging.* New York, NY: Pantheon Books.

Rudolph, C. W., & Zacher, H. (2015). Intergenerational perceptions and conflicts in multi-age and multigenerational work environments. In L. M. Finkelstein, D. M. Truxillo, F. Fraccaroli, & R. Kanfer (Eds.), *Facing the challenges of a multi-age workforce: A use-inspired approach* (pp. 253–281). New York, NY: Routledge.

Safety & Health Assessment & Research for Prevention. (2007). *Injured at work: What workers' compensation data reveal about work-related musculoskeletal disorders (WMSDs)* (Technical Report No. 40-10b-2007). Olympia, WA: SHARP Program, Washington State Department of Labor and Industries. Retrieved from http://www.lni.wa.gov/Safety/Research/Files/InjuredAtWork.pdf

Salthouse, T. A. (2004). What and when of cognitive aging. *Current Directions in Psychological Science, 13,* 140–144. http://dx.doi.org/10.1111/j.0963-7214.2004.00293.x

Sauter, S. L., Streit, J. M., & Hanseman, D. J. (2009). Work organization and health in an aging workforce. In S. J. Czaja & J. Sharit (Eds.), *Aging and work: Issues and implications in a changing landscape* (pp. 359–393). Baltimore, MD: Johns Hopkins University Press.

Shultz, K. S., Morton, K. R., & Weckerle, J. R. (1998). The influence of push and pull factors on voluntary and involuntary early retirees' retirement decision and adjustment. *Journal of Vocational Behavior, 53,* 45–57. http://dx.doi.org/10.1006/jvbe.1997.1610

Sigelman, C. K., & Rider, E. A. (2017). *Life-span human development* (9th ed.). Boston, MA: Cengage Learning.

Silverstein, M. (2008). Meeting the challenges of an aging workforce. *American Journal of Industrial Medicine, 51,* 269–280. http://dx.doi.org/10.1002/ajim.20569

Society for Human Resource Management. (2015). *Preparing for an aging workforce.* Alexandria, VA: Author.

Sorensen, G., McLellan, D., Dennerlein, J. T., Pronk, N. P., Allen, J. D., Boden, L. I., . . . Wagner, G. R. (2013). Integration of health protection and health promotion: Rationale, indicators, and metrics. *Journal of Occupational and Environmental Medicine, 55,* S12–S18. http://dx.doi.org/10.1097/JOM.0000000000000032

Sutin, A. R., Terracciano, A., Milaneschi, Y., An, Y., Ferrucci, L., & Zonderman, A. B. (2013). The effect of birth cohort on well-being: The legacy of economic hard times. *Psychological Science, 24,* 379–385. http://dx.doi.org/10.1177/0956797612459658

Toossi, M. (2015, December). Labor force projections to 2024: The labor force is growing, but slowly. *Monthly Labor Review.* http://dx.doi.org/10.21916/mlr.2015.48

University of Washington. (2009). *Designing the age-friendly workplace: Participant workbook.* Seattle, WA: Author.

U.S. Census Bureau, & U.S. Bureau of Labor Statistics. (2006). Current population survey: Table 1. Selected characteristics of civilians 16 to 74 years old with a work disability, by educational attainment and sex: 2006. Retrieved from https://www.census.gov/data/tables/2006/demo/disability/cps-work-disability-2006.html

Warr, P. (1994). Age and employment. In H. C. Triandis, M. D. Dunnette, & L. M. Hough (Eds.), *Handbook of industrial and organizational psychology* (2nd ed., Vol. 4, pp. 480–550). Palo Alto, CA: Consulting Psychologists Press.

Weil, D. (2014). *The fissured workplace: Why work became so bad for so many and what can be done to improve it.* Cambridge, MA: Harvard University Press. http://dx.doi.org/10.4159/9780674726123

Wilson, M. G., Dejoy, D. M., Vandenberg, R. J., Richardson, H. A., & McGrath, A. L. (2004). Work characteristics and employee health and well-being: Test of a model of healthy work organization. *Journal of Occupational and Organizational Psychology, 77,* 565–588. http://dx.doi.org/10.1348/0963179042596522

Zacher, H. (2015). Successful aging at work. *Work, Aging and Retirement, 1,* 4–25. http://dx.doi.org/10.1093/workar/wau006

14

Workplace Strategies to Reduce Risks from Shift Work, Long Work Hours, and Related Fatigue Issues

Claire C. Caruso

Evidence is growing that getting adequate sleep is a basic need for life and health, and is as important as good nutrition and exercise (Luyster, Strollo, Zee, & Walsh, 2012). Healthy sleep is linked to feelings of wellness, good mental health and healthy body weight, improved safety, and the prevention of infections as well as many types of chronic illnesses (Colten & Altevogt, 2006; U.S. Department of Health and Human Services [DHHS], 2010). Three panels of sleep experts reviewed the literature, and all recommended that adults get 7 or more hours sleep each day to maintain their health and safety (Hirshkowitz et al., 2015; Mukherjee et al., 2015; Watson et al., 2015). Healthy People 2020, the science-based, 10-year national objectives for improving the health of all Americans, has three objectives for sleep health for adults: (a) increase the proportion of adults who get 7 or more hours of sleep a day, (b) increase the proportion of adults with sleep apnea symptoms who seek a medical evaluation, and (c) reduce the rate of vehicle crashes due to drowsy driving (U.S. DHHS, 2010).

This chapter gives an overview of strategies that management and safety personnel can integrate into workplace systems to reduce risks from inadequate sleep. Three types of controls are discussed to promote sleep health and an alert workforce: (a) eliminate or reduce the hazard; (b) institute policies,

This chapter was authored by an employee of the United States government as part of her official duty and is considered to be in the public domain. Any views expressed herein do not necessarily represent the views of the United States government, and the authors' participation in the work is not meant to serve as an official endorsement.

http://dx.doi.org/10.1037/0000149-015
Total Worker Health, H. L. Hudson, J. A. S. Nigam, S. L. Sauter, L. C. Chosewood, A. L. Schill, and J. Howard (Editors)

programs, and practices; and (c) educate managers and workers. Throughout the chapter, the term *manager* refers to business leaders and safety professionals who are responsible for establishing and maintaining workplace systems, and providing advice and consultation.

Both factors at work and personal factors can lead to difficulties with sleep. The percentage of American civilian workers reporting 6 or fewer hours of sleep per day (a level considered too short by sleep experts) increased from 24% in the 1980s to 30% in the 2000s (Luckhaupt, Tak, & Calvert, 2010). Certain industries show higher rates of workers' reporting they do not sleep long enough: 34% of manufacturing workers, 44% of night-shift workers in any industry, 52% of night shift health care workers, and 70% of night shift transportation workers (Centers for Disease Control and Prevention, 2012). Ricci, Chee, Lorandeau, and Berger (2007) found that 38% of the U.S. workforce had reported having low energy, poor sleep, and fatigue in the previous 2 weeks. These data indicate a large percentage of the U.S. workforce is not getting enough sleep and is fatigued on the job.

Insufficient sleep is associated with a broad range of health and safety risks, including premature death, vehicle crashes, obesity, infections, and a wide range of chronic illnesses, including cardiovascular and gastrointestinal disease, diabetes mellitus, cancer, and disturbances to mood (Durmer & Dinges, 2005; Irwin, 2015; Khanijow, Prakash, Emsellem, Borum, & Doman, 2015; Luyster et al., 2012). In its draft report on carcinogens, the National Toxicology Program (2018) concluded that persistent night-shift work that causes circadian disruption is known to be a human carcinogen. In addition, people who do not get enough sleep can show on brain function tests declines, such as in response rate, thinking, remembering, and concentration, which can affect job performance and increase the risk for making errors on the job (Goel, Rao, Durmer, & Dinges, 2009).

Shift work and long work hours are critical factors that make it difficult for workers to get enough sleep. These demanding schedules can conflict with normal human physiology, which drives people to sleep at night at consistent times day after day and drives them to be awake and active during the daytime. Night-shift and irregular work hours can lead to misalignment of sleep with circadian rhythms, which leads to trouble with falling asleep, more arousals during sleep, and early awakenings, thus leading to poorer sleep quality and shorter sleep duration. Very long shifts and not having enough time off between work shifts can make it impossible for workers to get enough sleep.

Not getting enough sleep leads to decrements in functioning and performance on the job. As a result, workers may make mistakes at work, at home, or while driving, which put themselves as well as others around them at increased risk for injuries or death. Drowsy drivers as well as their employers have been penalized when a crash has caused a death (*Marthe v. Trotter*, 1999; *State v. Scott Robb*, 2005). Therefore, in addition to possible personal injury, errors because of fatigue can have such devastating consequences as high legal fines, jail time, and lasting mental pain for those involved (Scott et al., 2014).

Immediate risks of inadequate sleep and disruption to circadian rhythms also include poor health behaviors, such as smoking, physical inactivity, and unhealthy eating patterns that lead to obesity. Long-term exposure to sleep deprivation and disruption to circadian rhythms increases risk for developing the range of chronic illnesses previously mentioned. (See National Institute for Occupational Safety and Health [NIOSH et al., 2015] for a review of the health and safety risks associated with shift work, long work hours, why these risks occur, and strategies for managers and workers to reduce these risks.)

Managers and workers share in the responsibility to reduce the risks linked to poor sleep health. Strategies for managers include improving the design of their employees' work schedules, promoting breaks during the work shift, establishing policies and systems at work to promote sleep health and alertness, fostering good coworker and supervisor relationships, and educating their workforce. Strategies for workers include allowing enough time for sleep, adopting good personal practices and behaviors to maximize sleep and alertness, and educating the important people in their lives to reduce conflicting demands from work and personal life. Workers with sleep problems or excessive work-time sleepiness can seek an assessment and treatment from a health care provider.

ELIMINATING OR REDUCING HAZARDOUS SHIFT WORK AND LONG-HOUR SCHEDULES

Night shift is linked to the most health and safety risks, followed by evening shift (Caruso, Lusk, & Gillespie, 2004; Folkard & Lombardi, 2006; NIOSH et al., 2015, Modules 2 and 3). The least risks are associated with day shifts using 8 hours of work per day. Night shifts have most of the work hours between 9.00 p.m. and 8:00 a.m.; evening shifts have most of the work hours between 2:00 p.m. and midnight; and day shifts are scheduled between 7:00 a.m. and 6:00 p.m. (McMenamin, 2007).

If possible, it is best for employers to avoid using night shifts. Some types of work and work settings may not need work carried out during the night. Due to the higher health and safety risks as well as decrements in performance associated with night shifts, managers can choose to schedule all work during the daytime hours if these hours adequately meet the needs of their operation. However, night and evening shifts cannot be avoided for critical services that are needed around the clock, such as police and fire protection, health care, transportation, communications, public utilities, and military service. Other industries require workers around the clock because their production processes and operations need to be continuous to optimize capital investment in machinery, or the manufacturing process cannot be interrupted for production reasons.

When night work is necessary, the following strategies can be used to reduce the risks. Workers will be better able to adjust to work times when they have some ability to control their schedules (Knauth & Hornberger, 2003). With some control, they can take their own physical and mental capacity for work into account as well as their social and family demands. People with a natural tendency to go to bed late and get up late will tend to have fewer difficulties working night and evening shifts because these work times fit with their natural tendencies. If given the opportunity, they may choose to work those shifts. Some organizations use self-scheduling with guidelines or limits so that workers can choose their schedules but cannot select risky patterns that put them at higher risk for fatigue. A regular, predictable schedule helps workers plan for sleep and personal responsibilities. The inability to plan is one factor that makes emergency, on call, mandatory, and unplanned overtime difficult.

Researchers cannot recommend one design for 24-hour operations that will work well in all work settings. Knauth (1998) estimated that 10,000 work-scheduling patterns are used worldwide. Schedules differ in shift start times and duration, sequence of workdays and days off, pattern of weekends off, and whether the schedule has permanent or rotating shifts. Rotating schedules can differ according to the speed and the direction of the rotation.

The *speed of shift rotation* refers to how rapidly work shift times change. With a *fast rotation*, the person works different shifts within the same week (e.g., a day shift for 2 days followed by an evening shift for the next 2 days, then a night shift for 1 day, and then 2 days off). During a *slow rotation*, the person works each shift for 2 or more weeks (e.g., 2 weeks of day shifts then 2 weeks of evening shifts). A *weekly rotation* involves working, for example, 1 week of days that is followed by 1 week of night shifts. The most difficult speed of rotation is a weekly rotation, so it is best to avoid it (Knauth & Hornberger, 2003; Monk, 2000). Concerning shift rotations, some U.S. researchers suggest slow rotations that change every 2 or more weeks because they give circadian rhythms time to adjust to the new schedule (Smith & Eastman, 2012). Some European researchers recommend the opposite: fast forward rotations (Tucker & Folkard, 2012). They reason that workers spend less time on evening and night shifts, and therefore do not experience long periods of isolation from family. Also, fast rotations do not lead to a long series of workdays misaligned with the sun's light–dark cycle. However, fast rotations do not give time for the circadian rhythms to adjust, so performance may be compromised, which is a real concern in jobs in which fatigue related errors can endanger the worker and others around them.

Another characteristic of shift rotations is the *direction of rotation*, which refers to the order of shifts worked in relation to the time of day. A *forward rotation* refers to moving from day shift to evening shift and then to night shift. A *backward rotation* means moving from night shift to evening shift and then to day shift. Forward rotations (i.e., day shift to evening shift) are easier to adjust to than backward rotations (i.e., evening shift to day shift; Knauth & Hornberger, 2003).

Most people find it difficult to adjust to night work, so experts advise using, with caution, permanent or fixed night shifts (Knauth & Hornberger, 2003). Moreover, researchers recommend that workers with permanent night shifts maintain their nighttime activity pattern on their days off from work to help their circadian system adjust to being active at night and sleeping during daylight hours (Smith & Eastman, 2012). Because of their social interests, most night workers on their time off return to a daytime activity and nighttime sleep schedule, which leads to a frequent reversal of the sleep–wake schedule that is hard on the body. If having permanent night-shift workers is essential, introduce measures that will maintain worker safety and performance from about 2:00 a.m. to 6:00 a.m. (which is the time with higher risk for sleepiness due to circadian rhythms; Wesensten, Belenky, Thorne, Kautz, & Balkin, 2004). For rotating shifts, reduce the number of consecutive night shifts scheduled to, for example, three night shifts in a row. During the evening and night, workers tolerate shorter shifts (i.e., 8 hours or less) better than longer shifts. People who work shifts that are both long and at night have the highest risks for accidents and injuries (Folkard & Lombardi, 2006).

A long series of consecutive workdays with no days off leads to fatigue, particularly when working long shifts of 12 hours or more. Experts recommend interspersing days off with workdays and avoiding scheduling many workdays together followed by 4 to 7 days off. Workers tend to tolerate five consecutive 8-hour shifts or four 10-hour shifts followed by 1 or 2 full days off. For 12-hour shifts, consider scheduling three consecutive shifts followed by 1 or 2 days off (NIOSH, Rosa, & Colligan, 1997).

Researchers discourage quick changes. Quick shift changes (e.g., an evening shift ending at 11:30 p.m. followed by a day shift beginning at 7:00 a.m. or 8:00 a.m.) give workers little time to sleep. Knauth and Hornberger (2003) recommended at least 11 hours between two work shifts. Furthermore, early start times (6:00 a.m. or earlier) tend to shorten sleep because circadian rhythms promote wakefulness a few hours before the usual bedtime (Rosa, Härmä, Pulli, Mulder, & Näsman, 1996), thus making it difficult to go to sleep early. It is best to avoid early start time, if possible.

ELIMINATING OR REDUCING RISKS LINKED TO EXTENDED WORK SHIFTS

Extended 12-hour shifts, sometimes referred to as *compressed work schedules*, allow workers to put in more hours in fewer days and have more rest days in between: for example, three to four 12-hour shifts with 3 to 4 days off each week. Although 12-hour shift systems are sometimes favored by some workers and managers, studies comparing them with 8-hour systems showed mixed results (i.e., adverse effects, no effects, or positive effects) on sleep, alertness, safety, and health factors (Knauth, 2007). Therefore, extended shifts require special consideration for a worker's needs because of the many hours worked consecutively. Knauth and Hornberger (2003) recommended that the following conditions be met for using extended shifts:

- Work is of a type suitable for long work shifts. Extended shifts may be difficult in jobs with heavy physical demands, dangerous work, fast-paced demands, or high stress.

- Work schedules are designed to minimize the buildup of fatigue.

- Adequate arrangements are in place to cover absentees.

- Overtime is not added. Shift overruns are common in some work settings, can severely reduce the opportunity for sleep, and can lead to drowsy driving.

- Adequate recovery after work is possible.

- Exposure to toxic hazards is limited. Long work hours lengthen the time of exposure to hazards in the work environment and reduce the time to recover. Prolonged exposure to noise, heat, chemicals, and other hazards could exceed established permissible exposure limits or violate other health standards.

  Employers must implement measures to monitor and limit worker exposures to health and physical hazards in the workplace as required by the Occupational Safety and Health Act of 1970. In addition, long shifts are associated with worse sleep as compared with 8-hour shifts (Knauth, 2007) and, as a result, can lead to performance decrements, including increased risk-taking behavior, such as not using personal protective equipment and driving while drowsy (Womack, Hook, Reyna, & Ramos, 2013). Also, longer exposure to physical demands increases risk for musculoskeletal injuries (Caruso & Waters, 2008).

- Sufficient breaks are provided. Folkard and Lombardi (2006) estimated that rest breaks at 2-hour intervals rather than 4- or 6-hour intervals reduce risks for accidents and errors.

USING BREAKS DURING WORK SHIFTS TO REDUCE HEALTH AND SAFETY RISKS

In general, breaks during work shifts help reduce risks. Arlinghaus et al. (2012) showed a clear dose–response relationship between rest breaks and on-the-job injuries: Longer total time on breaks was significantly related to longer time spent on work tasks without having an injury. Lombardi et al. (2014) found that after taking breaks, workers on day shift went longer without an injury than did workers on evening and night shifts. In that study, workers on evening and night shifts had poorer sleep quality and shorter sleep duration than day-shift workers, thus potentially putting them at higher risk for fatigue, errors, and injuries. Therefore, it may be especially helpful for workers on evening and night shifts to have additional breaks or longer time on breaks.

Managers can promote brief 10- to 15-minute rest breaks every 1 hour to 2 hours during work shifts and a longer break for meals. At the beginning of the shift, managers can schedule the breaks along with the other work assignments. During the shift, they can encourage workers to take their breaks and, if necessary, create a system for other workers to cover their duties while on break.

Managers also can plan enriched breaks that include activities, such as exercise or stretching, or novel or amusing diversions. If the work is physical, a break to sit and relax would be appropriate, and for sedentary work, a break to take a walk or exercise would be helpful. Research has not revealed a pattern suggesting how long the alerting effect of a rest break lasts. Several factors influence the alerting effect: how long a person has been awake, the amount of sleep debt, the time of day (circadian effect), and the amount of time spent on a task (particularly monotonous tasks).

REDUCING THE STRAIN OF FREQUENTLY RESPONDING TO E-MAILS AND PHONE CALLS AFTER THE WORK SHIFT

Having to maintain e-mail and phone contact outside of regular work hours can reduce the time available for workers to take care of personal responsibilities and sleep, and thereby increase health and safety risks (Arlinghaus & Nachreiner, 2013). Some workers may interrupt their sleep to respond to calls or participate in meetings over the Internet at night. Workers trying to meet the requests from coworkers or customers around the world may be especially exposed to these demands.

To reduce the risks and respect workers' need to relax and sleep when off from work, managers can set a work culture and expectation that after workers complete their shift, they will not carry out work tasks. With some thought and discussion, the work group may develop another way to respond to those requests. Managers can model the appropriate times for responding to e-mails and phone calls by ending e-mails and phone calls after normal business hours.

ADDRESSING PERSONAL FACTORS THAT INCREASE FATIGUE AND SLEEPINESS AT WORK

Several personal factors can lead to problems with sleep and cause sleepiness on the job, and the associated health and safety risks. This section discusses these personal factors: sleep disorders; some chronic illnesses and medications; the necessity to wake up from sleep to help family members; the need to have second jobs; and the forgoing of adequate sleep for entertainment or other social activities or obligations.

An estimated 50 million to 70 million Americans have a sleep disorder that often is not diagnosed and treated (Colten & Altevogt, 2006). The most common disorders are insomnia, sleep-disordered breathing (which includes obstructive sleep apnea), restless-legs syndrome, and narcolepsy (Kryger, Roth, & Dement, 2016). Workers can be made aware of four common symptoms of sleep disorders that occur even when spending 7 to 9 hours in bed: (a) consistently taking more than 30 minutes to fall asleep; (b) awakening several times during sleep or for long periods; (c) having to take frequent naps; and (d) often feeling sleepy, especially at inappropriate times. It may be impossible for a worker to get adequate sleep until the disorder is treated even if the worker is using the best coping strategies. Persons with untreated sleep disorders can expose themselves and people around them to significant safety risks on the job, at home, and while driving. Many treatment options are available to reduce these symptoms, increase alertness on the job, and improve quality of life. Managers can encourage workers with symptoms to see a sleep disorders specialist. The "Other Resources" section at the end of NIOSH et al. (2015) online training for nurses lists websites to find certified sleep clinics and sleep specialists.

Pain and respiratory symptoms from several chronic diseases are often more bothersome at night and interfere with getting good-quality sleep (Smolensky, Di Milia, Ohayon, & Philip, 2011). These diseases include asthma, arthritis, chronic obstructive pulmonary disease, chronic fatigue syndrome, and rhinitis. Workers can see their health care provider to explore options for better symptom control. Achieving better control of symptoms can also reduce sleep problems and excessive sleepiness on the job.

Sleepiness during work can be an unwanted side effect of certain commonly used medications, including narcotic pain medications, some antihistamines and antidepressants, and some medications used to treat insomnia (Smolensky et al., 2011). If a worker experiences excessive sleepiness or fatigue at work, the worker could see a health care provider to assess that person's medications for side effects. Sometimes the health care provider can adjust the dose or switch to another medication that is not sedating.

Certain personal responsibilities may cut into the time for sleep (McCurry, Song, & Martin, 2015; Mellor & Van Vorst, 2015). Workers who have to help an infant or sick family member at night or during the day may be unable to get enough sleep. Stress due to a family crisis or unstable work situation, such as pending layoffs, can lead to stress and insomnia. Long commutes can cut into time for sleep, especially for workers on long work shifts. Managers can provide counseling and perhaps adjust the work hours to help workers with these stressful but sometimes temporary situations.

Without knowledge about sleep health, some workers may cut into their time for sleep to spend time on entertainment or work at a second job. Managers can identify fatigued workers and explore the reasons they are not getting enough sleep. Managers can educate workers who lack knowledge about sleep health and reinforce the importance of getting enough good-quality sleep to arrive at work fit to carry out their job.

CREATING POLICIES, PROGRAMS, AND PRACTICES
TO PROMOTE SLEEP HEALTH AND MINIMIZE FATIGUE

To reduce risks, employers can establish policies, programs, and practices that promote sleep health, minimize buildup of fatigue, and maximize recovery after work. They can target several topics: work hours, what to do when a worker is too fatigued to work or drive home, services to maintain an alert workforce during emergencies requiring overtime, the use of naps during work breaks, fatigue risk management systems, and the workplace culture.

Policies can address work hours, such as setting limits on the number of hours worked per 24 hours and per 7-day period. The workplace can establish a minimum of 10 to 11 consecutive hours off from work per day so that workers may obtain 7 to 8 hours of sleep. Restrictions can be set on how much and when overtime can be worked. Managers can identify and modify policies that encourage excessive overtime, and they can establish flexible scheduling options and shorter shifts.

Policies can set procedures for a worker who is too fatigued to work. A policy could specify a backup staffing plan when a worker is unable to continue working. Managers can allow fatigued workers to request and take breaks without repercussions. Employers can establish procedures for meeting the workload when a worker is unable to work by, for example, reducing the amount of work or requesting new staff. Procedures can set forth a signal that team members can use to alert each other, such as the statement "I think this situation is not safe," and specify what follow-up actions to take.

Some workers may want to continue working when they are fatigued and may not recognize that their performance is poor. Managers can establish procedures when a fatigued worker insists on continuing work. For example, they can tell excessively fatigued workers to take the rest of the shift off to get sleep. See Part 1, Module 3, of NIOSH et al. (2015) for signs of fatigue.

Several studies report that shift work and long work hours increase the risk for drowsy driving crashes and near misses (Barger et al., 2005; Scott et al., 2007; Swanson, Drake, & Arnedt, 2012). Managers can institute several types of organizational strategies to reduce this risk. They can develop education campaigns to warn both workers and managers about drowsy driving, and that give strategies to improve alertness while driving. To develop education campaigns, managers can take content from the Module 11 in NIOSH et al. (2015) and the drowsy driving website (National Sleep Foundation, 2018). Procedures can help managers identify workers at risk and possible action steps, such as arranging transportation home for workers who are excessively fatigued after a work shift by calling a family member or taxi. Some worksites could consider arranging for rooms located close to the facility where tired workers can sleep instead of driving home.

Policies can protect a worker's time for sleep and recovery from work. For example, employers can have night and evening shift workers list the times they are not to be called. Managers can then restrict communications to workers during those times to avoid waking them when they need to sleep. Likewise, managers can schedule training, meetings, counseling, and social programs for night and evening workers at times that do not interfere with their time for sleep. Managers can protect days off so night and evening workers can recover.

To promote alertness on the job and reduce fatigue, employers can consider a policy and procedure for using naps during work breaks. The Standards of Practice Committee of the American Academy of Sleep Medicine recommends planned naps before and during the night shift for persons' having difficulty with shift work (Morgenthaler et al., 2007). The committee stated that naps are a generally accepted strategy to counteract work-time sleepiness and increase alertness on the job. The brain benefits from a brief period of actual sleep—a nap, not just a quiet period—to recover from fatigue and help restore alertness. A worker might take a short nap (about 15- to 30-minutes long) during rest breaks. A longer nap of 1 hr 30 min may be more useful to increase alertness when working long shifts of 12 hours or more during emergencies because the long nap will reduce the buildup of pressure for the body to fall asleep. Many U.S. workplaces, however, have cultural barriers to using naps on the job. Discussions may be needed to help managers and workers understand the benefits of using naps at work, and lift these barriers. To make use of naps, managers will set procedures for scheduling naps and waking workers from a nap (e.g., by an alarm or a designated person). In addition, managers will consider the level of staffing required to maintain the work while a worker is napping. Another critical element is creating a good napping environment near the work area. Furthermore, managers will build in time to allow for worker grogginess after wakening (i.e., sleep inertia) to pass before the worker carries out critical tasks. See Module 7 of NIOSH et al. (2015) online training for more information.

When overtime cannot be avoided, employers can consider providing services that reduce nonwork demands on workers so they can devote their time off to rest and sleep. Services that might be helpful include providing comfortable uniforms, laundry service for work clothes, and on-site child care. Managers can ask workers for input on what other services might be helpful. They also can work with food vendors to make healthy drinks and nutritious food available at the worksite. Sugar-rich foods, such as candy bars and donuts, can increase sleepiness, so managers can check that the foods offered in vending machines include high-fiber, good-fat, and protein-rich options (Anderson & Horne, 2006; Lowden et al., 2004). Employers also can establish procedures to avoid pressuring workers to work extra shifts. Longer shifts and shift work are associated with increased errors, which can adversely affect work products and services, and fatigued workers have made tragic errors that have led to deaths (*State v. Scott Robb*, 2005).

For workers on shift work and who long work hours, employers can encourage those workers to get regular health examinations because these work schedules are associated with a somewhat higher risk for cardiovascular, gastrointestinal, musculoskeletal, and psychological disorders; cancer; diabetes; and adverse reproductive outcomes (NIOSH et al., 2015). Employers and managers also can encourage workers with symptoms to see their health care provider promptly.

Good supervisor and coworker support can reduce some of the risks associated with shift work and long work hours (Pisarski, Lawrence, Bohle, & Brook, 2008), possibly because the positive atmosphere reduces job stress that leads to poor sleep. Therefore, managers can build a good psychological work environment that has the following characteristics:

- Managers and workers always communicate in a respectful manner and are not exposed to threats, bullying, or violence.

- Managers give workers significant control in decision making, make their roles clear, minimize time pressures, and provide the resources to get their jobs done.

- Managers provide positive feedback for a job well done.

IMPLEMENTING A FATIGUE RISK MANAGEMENT SYSTEM

Managers can establish a *fatigue risk management system*, which is a comprehensive, several-part approach that is science based and data driven, and that promotes continuous improvement (for more information, see Lerman et al., 2012). Some parts of a fatigue risk management system can be integrated into existing health and safety systems, such as incident reports.

The first part is to set up fatigue management policies, such as those discussed previously. The second part involves identifying aspects of the operation that will be vulnerable to mistakes by tired workers; collecting information about fatigue in the workforce; analyzing its risk; and instituting controls to reduce the risk, such as routinely double-checking critical tasks.

The third part is to create an anonymous, no-blame reporting system to collect the following information from workers about their incidents and near misses: the time of the incident; shift details (e.g., start time, number of hours into the shift when incident occurred); number of prior consecutive work shifts and time of those shifts; number of hours awake before the incident; number of hours of sleep in each of the previous 3 days; and normal or unusual circumstances, such as overtime because of weather emergency. Analyses of several incident reports may reveal organizational factors that managers can modify to reduce risks.

The fourth part incorporates fatigue-related factors into incident investigations to determine if fatigue was a causal factor. Data to collect include information about the worker, the work schedule, and any medical conditions or medications. See Lerman et al. (2012) for two checklists and a discussion about the types of data to consider collecting.

The fifth part is to train and provide education to workers and managers so they will understand the challenges of working shift work or long work hours, and understand the resources available to help them better cope. Training should include basic information about sleep, circadian rhythms, and fatigue; good practices to improve sleep at home and alertness on the job; and sleep disorders and the importance of identifying and treating them. Managers can schedule all staff to take this training and schedule updates periodically. The training can be part of new employee orientation. See NIOSH's (2018) work schedule topic page for links to several online training programs that are tailored for several types of workers.

The sixth part addresses sleep disorders. Workers with sleep disorders, some chronic illnesses, and certain medications may be at higher risk for work-time sleepiness and fatigue issues (Smolensky et al., 2011). Managers can encourage workers with excessive sleepiness or trouble with sleep to see their health care provider or a sleep disorders specialist for an assessment and treatment.

EDUCATING THE WORKFORCE

Lack of knowledge about sleep health is widespread across the United States (Colten & Altevogt, 2006). Sleep health is usually not taught in schools, in education and training programs for health care providers, or during health care visits, so the workplace can be a source of sleep health information. Managers can promote education and training programs and materials on topics discussed in the preceding section. The NIOSH (2018) work schedule topic page has many free resources produced by NIOSH as well as other organizations to educate workers and managers. Included are links to several online training programs and how to find a certified sleep center.

Managers and health and safety professionals can use events across the year to give short messages about sleep. For example, during the fall, health care professionals can recommend that workers make an effort to get enough good-quality sleep after receiving the flu vaccine. Several studies found that compared with participants with sleep disturbances or short sleep duration, participants who had adequate sleep after vaccination showed a higher level of antibodies that will protect them from getting the flu (Irwin, 2015). If a worker is sick with a contagious disease, managers can recommend that the worker stay home and sleep more. Getting plenty of sleep can help the person recover because sleep and the immune system work together to attack disease-causing agents. Managers also can point out to the worker that when he or she is sick, the worker will likely be more sleepy due to the disease and possibly the medications. Consequently, the worker will be at higher risk for making a mistake; therefore, it is best not to operate dangerous equipment or make critical decisions until the sleepiness has subsided.

About a week and half before the 1-hour daylight saving time changes in the fall and spring, managers can educate workers about strategies to improve their sleep and alertness, and protect themselves from the somewhat higher safety risks that occur during those weeks. The 1-hour change in time can disrupt some workers' sleep and functioning for several days. Managers can give suggestions on how to better cope with the time change. See Caruso (2016) for information that managers can share. In addition, managers can point out that others around them on the roads and at work may be having more difficulty, so workers need to be more vigilant at work, at home, and while driving.

Several other types of occasions during the year give opportunities to insert brief messages about sleep health. If the workplace holds health fairs, organizers can invite a sleep disorders specialist to distribute information about sleep and sleep disorders. During vacation season, people sometimes drive long distances to their vacation site and back home. Managers can relay that these types of long trips are a known risk factor for drowsy driving crashes and suggest that workers plan the drive wisely to protect themselves and their passengers (National Sleep Foundation, 2018).

Health and safety professionals can develop a business case for setting up systems to promote sleep health and an alert healthy workforce. Managers can gather data on sick leave, productivity, health care and workers' compensation costs, and recruitment and retention. Also, health and safety professionals can consider other positive effects: For example, alert workers are able to interact better with their customers and the public, which possibly will have positive effects on the business's image and its public relations.

Managers and health and safety professionals can promote other good health behaviors that will improve sleep and reduce fatigue. They can encourage exercise because exercising every day can improve sleep. A poll by the National Sleep Foundation (2013) found that people who exercised vigorously tended to report the best sleep; however, walking as little as 10 minutes a day helped. If the job is sedentary, managers can encourage workers to periodically get up and walk. People who sit fewer than 8 hours a day reported better sleep. People who smoke or use tobacco products have shorter sleep and sleep that is more disturbed, so employers can encourage ending the use of tobacco products (National Heart, Lung, and Blood Institute, 2011).

CONCLUSION

Sleep health is a key factor to promote a high-functioning and healthy workforce. The design of the work schedules, the culture in the workplace, and the policies, procedures, and practices all have a critical influence on sleep health and the ability of workers to be alert on the job. Overly demanding work schedules and job stress will make it difficult for workers to get enough sleep.

Health and safety professionals and managers can use the range of strategies discussed in this chapter to make their workplace a good source of sleep health information and to set up systems at work that promote sleep health. A healthy, alert, high-functioning workforce will be in everyone's interests: the manager, worker, and consumers of the organization's goods and services.

REFERENCES

Anderson, C., & Horne, J. A. (2006). A high sugar content, low caffeine drink does not alleviate sleepiness but may worsen it. *Human Psychopharmacology: Clinical & Experimental, 21*, 299–303. http://dx.doi.org/10.1002/hup.769

Arlinghaus, A., Lombardi, D. A., Courtney, T. K., Christiani, D. C., Folkard, S., & Perry, M. J. (2012). The effect of rest breaks on time to injury—A study on work-related ladder-fall injuries in the United States. *Scandinavian Journal of Work, Environment & Health, 38*, 560–567. http://dx.doi.org/10.5271/sjweh.3292

Arlinghaus, A., & Nachreiner, F. (2013). When work calls—Associations between being contacted outside of regular working hours for work-related matters and health. *Chronobiology International, 30,* 1197–1202. http://dx.doi.org/10.3109/07420528.2013.800089

Barger, L. K., Cade, B. E., Ayas, N. T., Cronin, J. W., Rosner, B., Speizer, F. E., Czeisler, C. A., & the Harvard Work Hours, Health, and Safety Group. (2005). Extended work shifts and the risk of motor vehicle crashes among interns. *New England Journal of Medicine, 352,* 125–134. http://dx.doi.org/10.1056/NEJMoa041401

Caruso, C. C. (2016, March 9). Daylight saving: Suggestions to help workers adapt to the time change [Blog post]. Retrieved from https://blogs.cdc.gov/niosh-science-blog/2016/03/09/daylight-savings/

Caruso, C. C., Lusk, S. L., & Gillespie, B. W. (2004). Relationship of work schedules to gastrointestinal diagnoses, symptoms, and medication use in auto factory workers. *American Journal of Industrial Medicine, 46,* 586–598. http://dx.doi.org/10.1002/ajim.20099

Caruso, C. C., & Waters, T. R. (2008). A review of work schedule issues and musculo-skeletal disorders with an emphasis on the healthcare sector. *Industrial Health, 46,* 523–534. http://dx.doi.org/10.2486/indhealth.46.523

Centers for Disease Control and Prevention. (2012). Short sleep duration among workers—United States, 2010. *Morbidity and Mortality Weekly Report, 61,* 281–285.

Colten, H. R., & Altevogt, B. M. (2006). *Sleep disorders and sleep deprivation: An unmet public health problem.* Washington, DC: National Academies Press.

Durmer, J. S., & Dinges, D. F. (2005). Neurocognitive consequences of sleep deprivation. *Seminars in Neurology, 25,* 117–129. http://dx.doi.org/10.1055/s-2005-867080

Folkard, S., & Lombardi, D. A. (2006). Modeling the impact of the components of long work hours on injuries and "accidents." *American Journal of Industrial Medicine, 49,* 953–963. http://dx.doi.org/10.1002/ajim.20307

Goel, N., Rao, H., Durmer, J. S., & Dinges, D. F. (2009). Neurocognitive consequences of sleep deprivation. *Seminars in Neurology, 29,* 320–339. http://dx.doi.org/10.1055/s-0029-1237117

Hirshkowitz, M., Whiton, K., Albert, S. M., Alessi, C., Bruni, O., DonCarlos, L., . . . Adams Hillard, P. J. (2015). National Sleep Foundation's sleep time duration recom-mendations: Methodology and results summary. *Sleep Health, 1,* 40–43. http://dx.doi.org/10.1016/j.sleh.2014.12.010

Irwin, M. R. (2015). Why sleep is important for health: A psychoneuroimmunology perspective. *Annual Review of Psychology, 66,* 143–172. http://dx.doi.org/10.1146/annurev-psych-010213-115205

Khanijow, V., Prakash, P., Emsellem, H. A., Borum, M. L., & Doman, D. B. (2015). Sleep dysfunction and gastrointestinal diseases. *Gastroenterology & Hepatology, 11,* 817–825.

Knauth, P. (1998). Innovative worktime arrangements. *Scandinavian Journal of Work, Environment & Health, 24,* 13–17.

Knauth, P. (2007). Extended work periods. *Industrial Health, 45,* 125–136. http://dx.doi.org/10.2486/indhealth.45.125

Knauth, P., & Hornberger, S. (2003). Preventive and compensatory measures for shift workers. *Occupational Medicine, 53,* 109–116. http://dx.doi.org/10.1093/occmed/kqg049

Kryger, M. H., Roth, T., & Dement, W. C. (Eds.). (2016). *Principles and practice of sleep med-icine* (6th ed.). St. Louis, MO: Elsevier.

Lerman, S. E., Eskin, E., Flower, D. J., George, E. C., Gerson, B., Hartenbaum, N., . . . Moore-Ede, M. (2012). Fatigue risk management in the workplace. *Journal of Occupational and Environmental Medicine, 54,* 231–258. http://dx.doi.org/10.1097/JOM.0b013e318247a3b0

Lombardi, D. A., Jin, K., Courtney, T. K., Arlinghaus, A., Folkard, S., Liang, Y., & Perry, M. J. (2014). The effects of rest breaks, work shift start time, and sleep on the onset of severe injury among workers in the People's Republic of China. *Scandinavian Journal of Work, Environment & Health, 40*, 146–155. http://dx.doi.org/10.5271/sjweh.3395

Lowden, A., Holmbäck, U., Åkerstedt, T., Forslund, J., Lennernäs, M., & Forslund, A. (2004). Performance and sleepiness during a 24 h wake in constant conditions are affected by diet. *Biological Psychology, 65*, 251–263. http://dx.doi.org/10.1016/S0301-0511(03)00114-5

Luckhaupt, S. E., Tak, S., & Calvert, G. M. (2010). The prevalence of short sleep duration by industry and occupation in the National Health Interview Survey. *Sleep, 33*, 149–159. http://dx.doi.org/10.1093/sleep/33.2.149

Luyster, F. S., Strollo, P. J., Jr., Zee, P. C., & Walsh, J. K. (2012). Sleep: A health imperative. *Sleep, 35*, 727–734. http://dx.doi.org/10.5665/sleep.1846

Marthe v. Trotter, No. MC006412, 1999 WL 318940 (Cal. Super. Ct., Los Angeles County 1999).

McCurry, S. M., Song, Y., & Martin, J. L. (2015). Sleep in caregivers: What we know and what we need to learn. *Current Opinion in Psychiatry, 28*, 497–503. http://dx.doi.org/10.1097/YCO.0000000000000205

McMenamin, T. M. (2007). A time to work: Recent trends in shift work and flexible schedules. *Monthly Labor Review, 130*(12), 3–15.

Mellor, G., & Van Vorst, S. (2015). Daytime sleepiness in men during early fatherhood: Implications for work safety. *Workplace Health & Safety, 63*, 495–501. http://dx.doi.org/10.1177/2165079915595157

Monk, T. H. (2000). What can the chronobiologist do to help the shift worker? *Journal of Biological Rhythms, 15*, 86–94. http://dx.doi.org/10.1177/074873040001500202

Morgenthaler, T. I., Lee-Chiong, T., Alessi, C., Friedman, L., Aurora, R. N., Boehlecke, B., . . . Standards of Practice Committee of the American Academy of Sleep Medicine. (2007). Practice parameters for the clinical evaluation and treatment of circadian rhythm sleep disorders. *Sleep, 30*, 1445–1459. http://dx.doi.org/10.1093/sleep/30.11.1445

Mukherjee, S., Patel, S. R., Kales, S. N., Ayas, N. T., Strohl, K. P., Gozal, D., & Malhotra, A. (2015). An official American Thoracic Society statement: The importance of healthy sleep—Recommendations and future priorities. *American Journal of Respiratory and Critical Care Medicine, 191*, 1450–1458. http://dx.doi.org/10.1164/rccm.201504-0767ST

National Heart, Lung, and Blood Institute. (2011). *Your guide to healthy sleep* (NIH Publication No. 11-5271). Washington, DC: U.S. Department of Health and Human Services, National Institutes of Health, National Heart, Lung, and Blood Institute. Retrieved from https://www.nhlbi.nih.gov/files/docs/public/sleep/healthy_sleep.pdf

National Institute for Occupational Safety and Health. (2018). *Work schedules: Shift work and long work hours.* Retrieved from https://www.cdc.gov/niosh/topics/workschedules/

National Institute for Occupational Safety and Health, Caruso, C. C., Geiger-Brown, J., Takahashi, M., Trinkoff, A., & Nakata, A. (2015). *NIOSH training for nurses on shift work and long work hours* (DHHS [NIOSH] Publication No. 2015-115). Retrieved from https://www.cdc.gov/niosh/docs/2015-115

National Institute for Occupational Safety and Health, Rosa, R. R., & Colligan, M. J. (1997). *Plain language about shiftwork* (DHHS [NIOSH] Publication No. 97-145). Cincinnati, OH: U.S. Department of Health and Human Services, Centers for Disease Control and Prevention, National Institute for Occupational Safety and Health.

National Sleep Foundation. (2013). *2013 Sleep in America® poll exercise and sleep.* Retrieved from http://sleepfoundation.org/sleep-polls-data/sleep-in-america-poll/2013-exercise-and-sleep

National Sleep Foundation. (2018). Drowsy driving [website]. Retrieved from http://drowsydriving.org

National Toxicology Program, U.S. Department of Health and Human Services. (2018). Peer review draft report on carcinogens monograph on night shift work and light at night. Retrieved from https://ntp.niehs.nih.gov/events/past/index.html?type=Peer+Review+Panels

Occupational Safety and Health Act of 1970, Pub. L. No. 91 § 596, 84 Stat. 1590 (1970).

Pisarski, A., Lawrence, S. A., Bohle, P., & Brook, C. (2008). Organizational influences on the work life conflict and health of shiftworkers. *Applied Ergonomics, 39*, 580–588. http://dx.doi.org/10.1016/j.apergo.2008.01.005

Ricci, J. A., Chee, E., Lorandeau, A. L., & Berger, J. (2007). Fatigue in the U.S. workforce: Prevalence and implications for lost productive work time. *Journal of Occupational and Environmental Medicine, 49*, 1–10. http://dx.doi.org/10.1097/01.jom.0000249782.60321.2a

Rosa, R. R., Härmä, M., Pulli, K., Mulder, M., & Näsman, O. (1996). Rescheduling a three shift system at a steel rolling mill: Effects of a one hour delay of shift starting times on sleep and alertness in younger and older workers. *Occupational & Environmental Medicine, 53*, 677–685. http://dx.doi.org/10.1136/oem.53.10.677

Scott, L. D., Arslanian-Engoren, C., & Engoren, M. C. (2014). Association of sleep and fatigue with decision regret among critical care nurses. *American Journal of Critical Care, 23*, 13–23. http://dx.doi.org/10.4037/ajcc2014191

Scott, L. D., Hwang, W. T., Rogers, A. E., Nysse, T., Dean, G. E., & Dinges, D. F. (2007). The relationship between nurse work schedules, sleep duration, and drowsy driving. *Sleep, 30*, 1801–1807. http://dx.doi.org/10.1093/sleep/30.12.1801

Smith, M. R., & Eastman, C. I. (2012). Shift work: Health, performance and safety problems, traditional countermeasures, and innovative management strategies to reduce circadian misalignment. *Nature and Science of Sleep, 4*, 111–132.

Smolensky, M. H., Di Milia, L., Ohayon, M. M., & Philip, P. (2011). Sleep disorders, medical conditions, and road accident risk. *Accident Analysis & Prevention, 43*, 533–548. http://dx.doi.org/10.1016/j.aap.2009.12.004

State v. Scott Robb, No. 04001655 (N.J. Aug. 19, 2005).

Swanson, L. M., Drake, C., & Arnedt, J. T. (2012). Employment and drowsy driving: A survey of American workers. *Behavioral Sleep Medicine, 10*, 250–257. http://dx.doi.org/10.1080/15402002.2011.624231

Tucker, P., & Folkard, S. (2012). *Working time, health and safety: A research synthesis paper* (ILO Working Papers No. 994704513402676). Geneva, Switzerland: International Labour Organization. Retrieved from https://ideas.repec.org/p/ilo/ilowps/994704513402676.html

U.S. Department of Health and Human Services. (2010). *Healthy People 2020: Sleep health.* Retrieved from Office of Disease Prevention and Health Promotion, U.S. Department of Health and Human Services website: http://www.healthypeople.gov/2020/topics-objectives/topic/sleep-health

Watson, N. F., Badr, M. S., Belenky, G., Bliwise, D. L., Buxton, O. M., Buysse, D., . . . Tasali, E. (2015). Recommended amount of sleep for a healthy adult: A joint consensus statement of the American Academy of Sleep Medicine and Sleep Research Society. *Journal of Clinical Sleep Medicine, 11*, 591–592.

Wesensten, N. J., Belenky, G., Thorne, D. R., Kautz, M. A., & Balkin, T. J. (2004). Modafinil vs. caffeine: Effects on fatigue during sleep deprivation. *Aviation, Space, and Environmental Medicine, 75*, 520–525.

Womack, S. D., Hook, J. N., Reyna, S. H., & Ramos, M. (2013). Sleep loss and risk-taking behavior: A review of the literature. *Behavioral Sleep Medicine, 11*, 343–359. http://dx.doi.org/10.1080/15402002.2012.703628

15

Reducing Work–Life Stress

The Place for Integrated Interventions

Leslie B. Hammer and MacKenna L. Perry

R esearch has tied work–life stress to a variety of outcomes that are relevant to workers, their families, and their organizations, or what Kossek (2016) referred to as the "triple bottom line." Because of its substantial impact on worker health and well-being, and its broad-reaching effects on organizations and families, work–life stress is an important target for *Total Worker Health*® interventions. Unfortunately, few work–life stress interventions have been systematically evaluated using experimental designs that allow for strong scientific conclusions about their effectiveness. Furthermore, few work–life stress interventions have been developed based on theoretically driven intervention targets. In line with the *Total Worker Health* (TWH) approach, some work–life interventions have focused on integrating a reduction in safety and health hazards with well-being promotion through the prevention of injury, illness, and stress. We believe that these TWH interventions have the most promise for reducing work–life stress. This chapter describes what we currently know about work–life interventions aimed at the reduction of stress and associated risks to the health, safety, and well-being of workers.

WORK–LIFE STRESS

Since the 1970s, it has been recognized that factors within and outside of the workplace can interact to create stress and reduce the health and well-being of workers (Kanfer, 1977). We argue that work–life stress needs to be viewed as

http://dx.doi.org/10.1037/0000149-016
Total Worker Health, H. L. Hudson, J. A. S. Nigam, S. L. Sauter, L. C. Chosewood, A. L. Schill, and J. Howard (Editors)
Copyright © 2019 by the American Psychological Association. All rights reserved.

an occupational hazard (Hammer & Sauter, 2013) and that it typically is due to a combination of work (e.g., high job demands, nonstandard work schedules) and nonwork (e.g., eldercare demands, financial insecurity) exposures. Contrary to popular belief, a recent meta-analysis demonstrated no gender differences in work–family conflict (Shockley, Shen, DeNunzio, Arvan, & Knudsen, 2017), suggesting that this is not just a woman's issue but is important for all workers. Organizational scientists are poised to make recommendations about how to mitigate these workplace exposures that contribute to work–life stress.

Work–life stress can be defined as individual's appraisal (Lazarus & Folkman, 1984) of the difficulties of integrating work and nonwork aspects of life, and it frequently is referred to as *work–life conflict* or *work–family conflict*. Work–life stress impacts numerous health and well-being outcomes, as well as work and family outcomes described later, and is consistently named as one of the most significant stressors affecting today's workforce (American Psychological Association, 2016). Furthermore, Schieman, Glavin, and Milkie (2009) found that approximately 70% of workers reported at least some interference between work and life, making work–life stress a key area of needed improvement for workers. Perceptions and severity of occupational exposures impact work–life stress; thus, TWH interventions that target such exposures have the capacity to improve the health, safety, and well-being of workers.

The influence between work and nonwork domains typically is considered bidirectional (i.e., work-to-life and life-to-work) such that one can influence the other at any given time, or both can be influenced by each other simultaneously. *Work–life conflict* occurs when a work role and a nonwork role are not fully compatible, and results in some type of physical or psychological strain (e.g., Greenhaus & Beutell, 1985). *Work–life enrichment* occurs when participation in one role benefits quality of life in the other role (e.g., Edwards & Rothbard, 2000). Research on the positive side of the work–life interface also has been referred to as *positive spillover* or *facilitation*. Another frequently used work–life term is *work–life balance*, which has been given many definitions over time (e.g., Greenhaus & Allen, 2011; Hammer & Demsky, 2014) but typically refers to harmony between work and nonwork.

Health and Well-Being Outcomes

Due to the volume of work–life research available, we focus on summary-oriented findings that illustrate the benefits of reducing work–life stress or conflict and increasing work–life enrichment. In one of the earlier meta-analyses of outcomes of work–life stress, Allen, Herst, Bruck, and Sutton (2000) found that work–life conflict was associated with increased somatic and physical symptoms, general psychological strain, burnout, and depression. In addition, Amstad, Meier, Fasel, Elfering, and Semmer (2011) found similar relationships between work–life stress and worker health and well-being outcomes. Nohe,

Meier, Sonntag, and Michel (2015) showed significant relationships between work–life stress and strain outcomes, including a work-specific strain (e.g., burnout) category and an all-inclusive strain category, which incorporated work-related strain, family-related strain (e.g., parental stress), and strain that was not specific to work or family (e.g., depression). On the enrichment side of work–life research, McNall, Nicklin, and Masuda (2010) found work–life enrichment to be associated with physical and mental health. We also know that work–life stress is related to sleep outcomes, such that increased stress is related to lower quantity and quality of sleep (Crain et al., 2014; Olson et al., 2015). Taken together, this evidence emphasizes the importance of taking a TWH perspective in the design of work–life interventions by targeting organizational- as well as individual-level factors.

Work Outcomes

Within the work domain specifically, Amstad et al. (2011) found that conflict is associated with a wide variety of work outcomes, including job and career satisfaction, organizational commitment, turnover intentions, absenteeism, performance, work stress, and organizational citizenship behaviors. Another early meta-analysis found similar evidence of associations of both directions of conflict (i.e., work-to-life and life-to-work) with job satisfaction (Kossek & Ozeki, 1998). McNall et al. (2010) determined that work–family enrichment is tied to increased job satisfaction and organizational commitment. Another study found that conflict was related to a variety of work-specific withdrawal behaviors, including interruptions and lateness (Hammer, Bauer, & Grandey, 2003). As Cullen and Hammer (2007) and others (i.e., Smith & DeJoy, 2012; Turner, Hershcovis, Reich, & Totterdell, 2014) have discovered, work–life stress also is related to workplace safety outcomes. In addition to benefitting workers, these findings provide support for organizations' investment in work–life interventions.

Family Outcomes

In the family domain, Amstad et al. (2011) found work–life conflict to be tied to lower levels of marital and family satisfaction as well as lower family-related performance and higher levels of stress. Kossek and Ozeki's (1998) meta-analysis revealed that such conflict is linked to decreased life, marital, and family satisfaction. McNall et al. (2010) found that higher work–family enrichment is associated with higher family and life satisfaction.

Beyond effects on workers' own satisfaction, performance, and stress at home, research also has examined potential benefits of decreased conflict and increased enrichment for workers' partners and families (e.g., Hammer, Allen, & Grigsby, 1997). Similar to impacts of conflict and enrichment on workers, effects may extend to other family members and also can include impact on their health, work, and home outcomes (e.g., Hammer, Cullen, Neal, Sinclair, & Shafiro, 2005). For example, in a sample of dual-earner couples, Bakker, Demerouti, and Dollard (2008) found that a worker's perceptions of conflict are indirectly related to higher home demands for his or her partner in part due to the partner's increased experience of negative social interactions with the worker. More work–family conflict for one partner led to more negative inter-actions in the relationship, which led to the partner's feeling more home demands. In turn, the partner's home demands were found to be linked to his or her own perceived conflict and exhaustion. In addition, Hammer et al. (2005) determined that work–family positive spillover is negatively related to later depressive symptoms of not only the worker but also his or her spouse. More work remains to explore possible effects of conflict and enrichment on workers' family members, and we encourage researchers to consider these effects when developing and evaluating interventions. Thus, the potential benefits of work–life stress TWH interventions are wide reaching and numer-ous, including effects on worker health and well-being, work, and family outcomes.

THEORETICAL FOUNDATIONS FOR WORK–LIFE STRESS INTERVENTIONS

Most work–life intervention research to date has focused on reduction of stress and conflict as the primary mechanism of improvement, sometimes also empha-sizing an increase in enrichment or balance (e.g., Hammer & Demsky, 2014; Hammer, Kossek, Zimmerman, & Daniels, 2007). Arguably the most promi-nent theoretical explanation of how work–life interventions can improve out-comes for workers, families, and organizations is that of increasing resources. *Conservation of resources theory* suggests that individuals strive to obtain, main-tain, and protect resources, and stress occurs when individuals experience loss of resources, threat of loss, or failure to gain expected resources (Hobfoll, 1989, 2002). According to conservation of resources theory, resources are objects, personal characteristics, conditions, or energies of value to the individual, or that serve to help the individual gain more resources. Halbesleben, Neveu, Paustian-Underdahl, and Westman (2014), though, have since redefined *resources* as anything an individual perceives to help attain his or her goals. In addition, the buffering model of social support (Cohen & Wills, 1985), job demands-control model (Karasek, 1979), and job demands-resources model (Bakker & Demerouti, 2007) address the importance of social support as a buffer of work–life stress as well as job demands and resources as critical envi-ronmental factors that impact health and well-being outcomes for workers. Thus, TWH work–life interventions often are motivated by a desire to increase employees' perceived existing and available resources, and decrease percep-tions of loss and threat to resources, thereby decreasing stress and leading to further resource gains.

TOTAL WORKER HEALTH AND WORK–LIFE STRESS INTERVENTIONS

The most recent National Occupational Research Agenda proposed for 2016–2026 identifies work–life issues as a crucial area of research (National Institute for Occupational Safety and Health [NIOSH], 2016b). The agenda specifically calls for "better management of the interface between work and life" (p. 5) and cites evaluation of work–life outcomes and opportunities for prevention as a key research output goal. However, despite growing evidence that interventions targeting job stress improve individual and organizational outcomes (e.g., LaMontagne, Keegel, Louie, Ostry, & Landsbergis, 2007), few studies have examined work–life-specific interventions, and those studies that do exist generally have lacked strong study designs (Hammer, Demsky, Kossek, & Bray, 2016). Even considering those interventions that have been empirically evaluated, Kossek, Lewis, and Hammer (2010) argued that work–life initiatives need to become more "mainstreamed" to be effective; that is, until work–life initiatives are considered essential for human resources and management teams to implement and work–life issues are central to decisions made by organizations, little systematic change to work–life stress can occur, despite its high prevalence rates.

When considering work–life stress within the context of the TWH approach, we focus on ways to prevent the negative effects of such stress on the health and well-being outcomes of workers. In particular, a body of research summarized by Hammer and Sauter (2013) has demonstrated that work–life stress has significant effects on health behaviors and resulting chronic health outcomes. The impact on health behaviors is through the negative effects of poor working conditions, which drain resources and, in turn, leave little energy left to focus on healthy behaviors. Negative health behaviors also may manifest themselves as the result of poor stress coping mechanisms, such as is found in the drinking-to-cope literature (e.g., Armeli, Todd, Conner, & Tennen, 2008). Ultimately, organizational strategies that focus on the TWH approach for work–life stress reduction are expected to be most effective, such as training supervisors how to increase support for workers' work–life stress or increasing workers' control over how, where, and when they work.

The TWH approach incorporates the reduction of work-related safety and health hazards into the development of injury- and illness-prevention strategies to help build worker health and well-being. A TWH approach prioritizes a hazard-free work environment for all workers. It also brings together aspects of work in integrated interventions that collectively address worker safety, health, and well-being. The NIOSH (2015) publication "Issues Relevant to Advancing Worker Well-Being Through Total Worker Health®" lists examples of TWH areas, most of which could be used as intervention topics, including control of physical, biological, and psychosocial hazards and exposures; organization of work; compensation and benefits; built environment supports; leadership; community supports; changing workforce demographics; policy issues; and new employment patterns. Along with this close tie between areas of TWH and work–life stress, the TWH approach can be an ideal strategy for reducing work–life stress in several key ways.

First, the TWH approach considers the occupational exposures that increase risk of disease and often interact with risk factors workers encounter or engage in outside of work. A work–life perspective offers an important lens with which to view the interaction of *job risks* and *life risks*, terms coined by Walsh, Jennings, Mangione, and Merrigan (1991) to represent occupational and personal exposures, respectively. Job risks and life risks may individually impact workers, but their combination can be far more dangerous than exposure in a single domain. For example, several studies have assessed profiles of work–life experiences and found differential effects on health, depending on combinations of positive and negative experiences. Demerouti and Geurts (2004) determined that workers with above-average negative work–life experiences in both directions (i.e., work-to-life and life-to-work) had the least favorable scores on a variety of self-reported health and well-being outcomes. Rantanen, Kinnunen, Mauno, and Tillemann (2011) found that simultaneously experiencing high levels of work-to-family conflict and family-to-work conflict is the most detrimental to well-being, regardless of the presence of positive work–life experiences (e.g., work–family enrichment). These findings illustrate how exposure to risks in the work and nonwork domains can be substantially more detrimental to worker health and well-being than exposure in a single domain, emphasizing the importance of providing a hazard-free work environment while also advancing efforts to benefit workers' health and well-being outside of work.

Second, the TWH approach is supported by the idea that those workers who are the most likely to be exposed to job risks are the ones who are also most likely to be exposed to life risks. For example, job risks associated with low-wage hourly retail work include long hours, standing and walking on concrete floors that may aggravate back injuries, and lifting and repetitive motion work that leads to musculoskeletal disorders. Frequently, these job risks also are experienced by workers who have difficulty coordinating care for children and are challenged by additional demands at home, such as single parenting and challenges in paying mortgages or rent. Work–life stress processes inherently cross work and nonwork domains, but evidence supports the idea that individuals who experience interference originating in one domain are more likely to also experience interference originating in the other domain (e.g., workers experiencing work-to-life conflict are more likely to also experience life-to-work conflict; Mesmer-Magnus & Viswesvaran, 2006). This dual exposure makes these workers particularly vulnerable to adverse health and well-being outcomes, and supports careful attention to those workers with particularly high demands in either domain. Furthermore, workers experiencing work–life stress may already be more likely to experience exposure to other risk factors, creating even further vulnerabilities. For example, meta-analytic evidence has shown that income is a significant predictor of both directions of work–life conflict (Byron, 2005), and income also is a known risk factor for a wide variety of other health and well-being problems. Overall, the interrelatedness of both directions of conflict between domains emphasizes the need for TWH work–life stress interventions because reduction of stress in one domain may reduce stress in the other domain in addition to improving many other health and well-being outcomes.

Third, the TWH approach may help increase involvement in, and benefits of, interventions, especially for high-risk workers. Although debate over the ethicality of worksite health promotion efforts has long existed (Walsh et al., 1991; Warner, 1990), workplaces provide a great deal of potential as settings to target not only job risks but life risks too (Sorensen et al., 2010). Warner (1990) argued that worksites provide a "captive audience" that may not be easily accessible beyond the workplace. Workers already spend a great deal of time interacting with work systems and are impacted by a wide spectrum of social influences that benefit participation rates—both positive (e.g., social support) and negative (e.g., unwanted pressure to change behaviors that are not, strictly speaking, job-related). Workplace interventions may encourage a climate of trust and support, but workers also may maintain skepticism about whether organizations truly have their best interests in mind when conducting work–life interventions; therefore, it is imperative that organizations focus careful attention on communication surrounding intervention implementation and evaluation (Adkins, Kelley, Bickman, & Weiss, 2011).

Another benefit of TWH interventions is that consideration of safety and health protection within the context of well-being promotion may provide added benefit to broader systems beyond the individual alone. Based on the conclusions reached during the National Institutes of Health Pathways to Prevention workshop titled "Total Worker Health®—What's Work Got to Do With It?" in 2015, Bradley, Grossman, Hubbard, Ortega, and Curry (2016) emphasized the importance of building integrated interventions that include more than individual-level behavioral risk factors alone. Experts on the panel called for attention to the work environment, specifically including work–life stress. Work–life issues provide an accessible and natural opportunity for organizations to practice integrating health protection and health promotion into a greater coordinated effort. Furthermore, if an organization successfully reduces work–life stress, many resulting outcomes will directly benefit the organization itself (Allen et al., 2000). Beyond benefit to the organization, interventions focused on the reduction of work–life stress have demonstrated potential benefits for workers' loved ones, including spouses (Eby, Casper, Lockwood, Bordeaux, & Brinley, 2005) and children (Davis et al., 2015), as well as potential benefits for the community at large (Voydanoff, 2013).

When we consider the TWH approach, it can be argued that work–life stress interventions may have some of the strongest promise, given that a key premise of the TWH approach is that risk factors from the workplace and the nonwork realm impact a worker's health, safety, and well-being. This advancement of a holistic perspective that risk factors at work and outside of work can interact and impact both health and safety on and off the job has important implications for work–life interventions. Thus, we argue that the workplace is a critical point of intervention where organizational scholars and safety and health professionals can reduce risk factors at work that can impact work–life stress, resulting in improved health and safety of workers.

CHALLENGES OF IMPLEMENTING WORK–LIFE STRESS INTERVENTIONS

It has been argued by Kelly et al. (2008) and Hammer, Demsky, et al. (2016) that intervention targets in organizations that theoretically have a high likelihood of reducing work–life stress include increasing control over when, where, and how work is done as well as increasing supervisor support for work–life integration. More recent attention has been paid to creating a culture of health and safety (Loeppke et al., 2015) that focuses on global organizational culture changes rather than any one specific target. We argue that the best way to create such a culture of health is to target those known factors that have a high probability of improving safety and health of workers, and then to conduct global assessments of culture change. It also is important to ensure that such interventions impact the triple bottom line—that is, affect workers, their families, and their workplaces (Kossek, 2016).

Conducting organizational intervention research is particularly challenging for a number of reasons (Hammer, Demsky, et al., 2016). First, intervention research that involves strong research designs that use randomized controlled trials, psychometrically sound measures, evaluations of outcomes, and statistical power to detect significant effects is costly. Employers will gauge the benefits of testing such interventions with the costs of lost time and money. The implementation of interventions that involve training or facilitated processes may add further costs. Second, less attention has been focused on how to implement such organizational TWH interventions. Examining the organizational context, including preintervention levels of risk factors and hazards as well as conducting extensive process evaluations will help to better understand how to implement such interventions (Biron, Karanika-Murray, & Cooper, 2012). Factors within the specific organizational context may have direct impacts on the effectiveness of the intervention, irrespective of the efficacy of the intervention itself, and thus must be tracked during the implementation of any intervention. This assessment of implementation fidelity (Semmer, 2006) will help to explain how contextual information (e.g., participation rates and exposure, management support, participation reaction to the intervention) impacts the success of an organizational interventions aimed at reducing health and safety risks.

EXAMPLES OF WORK–LIFE INTERVENTIONS

The remainder of the chapter reviews the few known work–life interventions that have been evaluated in the scientific literature. In the 1970s and 1980s, a line of research focused on the benefits of alternative work schedules, such as compressed work weeks, flexible work hours, and part-time work (see Hammer & Barbera, 1997, for a review). These studies, although not rigorous, tended to have cross-sectional or quasi-experimental designs, and examined the relationship between such schedule implementation on worker job satisfaction, absenteeism, turnover, and work–family conflict, demonstrating positive impacts. In their review article, Kelly et al. (2008) asked, "Do work–family initiatives reduce employees' work–family conflict and/or improve work–family enrichment?" (p. 306), and reviewed research on organizational adoption of work–life initiatives. Although adoption of initiatives involves making them available to organizational constituents, this is not the same as the deliberate implementation and evaluation of interventions.

Kelly et al. (2008) suggested that organizational scholars should start to view organizational work–life initiatives as interventions and develop them based on sound organizational theory. Furthermore, they argued that it is important to evaluate the initiatives using randomized controlled designs to enable conclusions to be drawn based on their effectiveness in improving worker, family, and organizational outcomes. They identified support for work and family and for control over work as being the two primary levers for impacting work–life outcomes for workers and, thus, argued that those levers should be the targets of any successful intervention. Furthermore, evidence clearly has demonstrated that workplace support in the form of supervisor support for work and family, such as family-supportive supervisor behaviors (FSSB; Hammer et al., 2007) and organizational support for work and family, are more effective at reducing work–family conflict than general nonspecific workplace supports (Kossek, Pichler, Bodner, & Hammer, 2011). Kelly and Moen (2007) showed the beneficial effects of control over work on work–family conflict and well-being outcomes of workers, and Hammer, Kossek, Anger, Bodner, and Zimmerman (2011) demonstrated in a randomized controlled trial the beneficial effects of FSSB training on worker job satisfaction, turnover intentions, and reports of physical health among those employees with high work–family conflict at baseline. Both are TWH organizational strategies aimed at prevention with expected effects on worker health.

The Work, Family & Health Network recently completed an extensive randomized controlled trial in two key industries: health care and information technology (https://workfamilyhealthnetwork.org/data). This effort, funded by the National Institutes for Health and the Centers for Disease Control and Prevention, is the most extensive evaluation of a work–family intervention to date. In total, more than 1,700 employees participated in this longitudinal, multiwave, multi-industry study that included spouses, children, and supervisors of the employees. This 5-year study examined how a TWH work–family intervention that included increasing control over work and increasing supervisor support for work and family within the context of work redesign led to improved health and well-being in workers, family members, and their organizations. Outcomes included improved subjective and objective measures of sleep (Crain et al., 2019; Olson et al., 2015); improved self-reported schedule control, FSSBs, and work–family conflict (Kelly et al., 2014); improved psychological health (for those with higher eldercare demands and for those who had child and elder care responsibilities; Kossek et al., 2019); reduced cigarette smoking (Hurtado et al., 2016); increased parental time with children (Davis et al., 2015), and increased children's sleep time (McHale et al., 2015). In addition, results demonstrated that the intervention protected against declines in self-reported safety compliance (for those who reported higher FSSB and higher perceived work–family climate at baseline) and declines in organizational citizenship behaviors (for those with higher control over work time; Hammer, Johnson, et al., 2016).

Data are now available for public use and can be accessed at the website just provided; also available on that site are our evidence-based workplace change tools and toolkits, and citations of published research papers. To date, six studies have demonstrated the beneficial impact of the workplace intervention known as STAR (Support.Transform.Achieve.Results; i.e., Davis et al., 2015; Hammer, Johnson, et al., 2016; Hurtado et al., 2016; Kelly et al., 2014; McHale et al., 2015; Olson et al., 2015) on worker health, safety, and well-being as well as child well-being and organizational outcomes.

Hammer and colleagues, as part of the Oregon Healthy Workforce Center, developed and evaluated the implementation of the Safety and Health Improvement Program (SHIP). That program was based on the integration of FSSB training and supervisor support for safety in combination with a team-based approach called team effectiveness process developed by Work Family Directions (Hammer, Truxillo, et al., 2015). Although no effects of the work–life stress reduction intervention were found for safety outcomes, the intervention did reduce blood pressure at the 12-month follow-up (see the Oregon Healthy Workforce Center website for SHIP and other evidence-based TWH intervention materials [https://www.ohsu.edu/ohwc]).

RECOMMENDATIONS FOR FUTURE RESEARCH AND INTERVENTIONS

Consistent with the NIOSH's *Fundamentals of Total Worker Health Approaches* (NIOSH, 2016a), we suggest that a focus on developing commitment through training leaders on the importance of support for work and family (e.g., FSSB) is a key first step in developing work–life TWH interventions. Furthermore, primary prevention interventions within the work–life field have focused on the workplace as the source of controlling and reducing such stress. Similar to the hierarchy of controls applied to the NIOSH TWH program (NIOSH, 2016a) and noted as the Defining Element 2, the primary prevention strategy suggests the first step is to eliminate the hazard in the workplace. By eliminating work–life stress through decreasing workplace demands and increasing control and support in the workplace, work–life stress interventions have the potential to improve the health, safety, and well-being of workers. Thus, taking an organizational systems-level approach to work–life stress interventions, similar to that proposed by Hammer and Zimmerman (2011), suggests that the work–family system is a mesosystem within the broader socioeconomical, legal, political, social, community, organizational, and family context. The TWH approach addresses the prevention of illness and injury from the perspective of the organizational system as well as the broader societal or national context under which we live. This approach suggests the significance of evaluating policy implementation and its effects on worker and family health and well-being. For example, with growing numbers of states and cities implementing paid sick leave and paid family leave laws, research is needed on the evaluation of such policy implementation efforts. In addition, organizational policies around work hours and schedule notification are expected to lead to reductions in work–life stress and thus have the associated beneficial outcomes for workers.

As Hammer, Cullen, and Shafiro (2006) argued, in the United States, we must rely on workplace interventions for reducing work–life stress. Unlike Europe, where appropriate parental leave and child care are nationally subsidized, we currently have little support for such paid leave at the national level, leaving many workers' needing to return to work after minimal time off following the birth or adoption of a child, to work while sick, and unable to assist aging and frail parents. Recent efforts are being made across our country to increase support for paid family leave, and progress is being made in several cities and states. As identified in the NIOSH document "Issues Relevant to Advancing Worker Well-Being Through Total Worker Health®" (NIOSH, 2015), policy issues, including family and medical leave are part of a TWH approach. The proposed national Family and Medical Insurance Leave Act (National Partnership for Women & Families, 2018) is modeled after some of the successful city and state programs that have been developed over the past few years. That act would provide up to 12 weeks of partially paid leave for family and medical needs. We see these national polices as directly supporting the TWH approach by eliminating one primary stressor workers face—loss of income—in exchange for time put toward managing work–life stress.

Future research should consider the broader national context in light of workplace work–life stress reduction interventions that include TWH practices and strategies. The combination of these larger system-level contextual factors aimed at health protection through programs, policies, and practices with the promotion of injury and illness prevention efforts to advance worker well-being demonstrates our ideal work–life stress TWH interventions. Furthermore, evaluation of the effects of such national, state, and city-level polices on work–life outcomes is needed to garner additional support both within and outside of the workplace for interventions and approaches that reduce work–life stress and result in beneficial outcomes for workers, their families, and the organizations in which they work.

REFERENCES

Adkins, J. A., Kelley, S. D., Bickman, L., & Weiss, H. M. (2011). Program evaluation: The bottom line in organizational health. In J. C. Quick & L. E. Tetrick (Eds.), *Handbook of occupational health psychology* (2nd ed., pp. 395–416). Washington, DC: American Psychological Association.

Allen, T. D., Herst, D. E. L., Bruck, C. S., & Sutton, M. (2000). Consequences associated with work-to-family conflict: A review and agenda for future research. *Journal of Occupational Health Psychology, 5,* 278–308. http://dx.doi.org/10.1037/1076-8998.5.2.278

American Psychological Association. (2016, March 10). *Stress in America: The impact of discrimination. Stress in America™ survey* [Report]. Washington, DC: Author. Retrieved from https://www.apa.org/news/press/releases/stress/2015/impact-of-discrimination.pdf

Amstad, F. T., Meier, L. L., Fasel, U., Elfering, A., & Semmer, N. K. (2011). A meta-analysis of work–family conflict and various outcomes with a special emphasis on cross-domain versus matching-domain relations. *Journal of Occupational Health Psychology, 16,* 151–169. http://dx.doi.org/10.1037/a0022170

Armeli, S., Todd, M., Conner, T. S., & Tennen, H. (2008). Drinking to cope with negative moods and the immediacy of drinking within the weekly cycle among college students. *Journal of Studies on Alcohol and Drugs, 69,* 313–322. http://dx.doi.org/10.15288/jsad.2008.69.313

Bakker, A. B., & Demerouti, E. (2007). The job demands–resources model: State of the art. *Journal of Managerial Psychology, 22,* 309–328. http://dx.doi.org/10.1108/02683940710733115

Bakker, A. B., Demerouti, E., & Dollard, M. F. (2008). How job demands affect partners' experience of exhaustion: Integrating work–family conflict and crossover theory. *Journal of Applied Psychology, 93,* 901–911. http://dx.doi.org/10.1037/0021-9010.93.4.901

Biron, C., Karanika-Murray, M., & Cooper, C. L. (2012). *Improving organizational interventions for stress and well-being: Addressing process and context* (pp. 21–38). New York, NY: Routledge.

Bradley, C. J., Grossman, D. C., Hubbard, R. A., Ortega, A. N., & Curry, S. J. (2016). Integrated interventions for improving total worker health: A panel report from the National Institutes of Health Pathways to Prevention workshop: *Total Worker Health—What's work got to do with it? Annals of Internal Medicine, 165,* 279–283. http://dx.doi.org/10.7326/M16-0740

Byron, K. (2005). A meta-analytic review of work–family conflict and its antecedents. *Journal of Vocational Behavior, 67,* 169–198. http://dx.doi.org/10.1016/j.jvb.2004.08.009

Cohen, S., & Wills, T. A. (1985). Stress, social support, and the buffering hypothesis. *Psychological Bulletin, 98,* 310–357. http://dx.doi.org/10.1037/0033-2909.98.2.310

Crain, T. L., Hammer, L. B., Bodner, T., Kossek, E. E., Moen, P., Lilienthal, R., & Buxton, O. M. (2014). Work–family conflict, family-supportive supervisor behaviors (FSSB), and sleep outcomes. *Journal of Occupational Health Psychology, 19,* 155–167. http://dx.doi.org/10.1037/a0036010

Crain, T. L., Hammer, L. B., Bodner, T., Olson, R., Kossek, E. E., Moen, P., & Buxton, O. M. (2019). Sustaining sleep: Results from the randomized controlled work, family, and health study. *Journal of Occupational Health Psychology, 24,* 180–197. http://dx.doi.org/10.1037/ocp0000122

Cullen, J. C., & Hammer, L. B. (2007). Developing and testing a theoretical model linking work—family conflict to employee safety. *Journal of Occupational Health Psychology, 12,* 266–278. http://dx.doi.org/10.1037/1076-8998.12.3.266

Davis, K. D., Lawson, K. M., Almeida, D. M., Kelly, E. L., King, R. B., Hammer, L., . . . McHale, S. M. (2015). Parents' daily time with their children: A workplace intervention. *Pediatrics, 135,* 875–882. http://dx.doi.org/10.1542/peds.2014-2057

Demerouti, E., & Geurts, S. (2004). Towards a typology of work-home interaction. *Community, Work & Family, 7,* 285–309. http://dx.doi.org/10.1080/1366880042000295727

Eby, L. T., Casper, W. J., Lockwood, A., Bordeaux, C., & Brinley, A. (2005). Work and family research in IO/OB: Content analysis and review of the literature

(1980–2002). *Journal of Vocational Behavior, 66,* 124–197. http://dx.doi.org/10.1016/j.jvb.2003.11.003

Edwards, J. R., & Rothbard, N. P. (2000). Mechanisms linking work and family: Clarifying the relationship between work and family constructs. *Academy of Management Review, 25,* 178–199. http://dx.doi.org/10.5465/amr.2000.2791609

Greenhaus, J. H., & Allen, T. D. (2011). Work–family balance: A review and extension of the literature. In J. C. Quick & L. E. Tetrick (Eds.), *Handbook of occupational health psychology* (2nd ed., pp. 165–183). Washington, DC: American Psychological Association.

Greenhaus, J. H., & Beutell, N. J. (1985). Sources of conflict between work and family roles. *Academy of Management Review, 10,* 76–88. http://dx.doi.org/10.5465/amr.1985.4277352

Halbesleben, J. R., Neveu, J. P., Paustian-Underdahl, S. C., & Westman, M. (2014). Getting to the "COR": Understanding the role of resources in conservation of resources theory. *Journal of Management, 40,* 1334–1364. http://dx.doi.org/10.1177/0149206314527130

Hammer, L., Allen, E., & Grigsby, T. (1997). Work–family conflict in dual-earner couples: Within-individual and crossover effects of work and family. *Journal of Vocational Behavior, 50,* 185–203. http://dx.doi.org/10.1006/jvbe.1996.1557

Hammer, L. B., & Barbera, K. M. (1997). Towards an integration of alternative work schedules and human resource systems: Recommendations for research and practice. *Human Resource Planning, 20,* 28–36.

Hammer, L. B., Bauer, T. N., & Grandey, A. A. (2003). Work–family conflict and work-related withdrawal behaviors. *Journal of Business and Psychology, 17,* 419–436. http://dx.doi.org/10.1023/A:1022820609967

Hammer, L. B., Cullen, J. C., Neal, M. B., Sinclair, R. R., & Shafiro, M. V. (2005). The longitudinal effects of work–family conflict and positive spillover on depressive symptoms among dual-earner couples. *Journal of Occupational Health Psychology, 10,* 138–154. http://dx.doi.org/10.1037/1076-8998.10.2.138

Hammer, L. B., Cullen, J. C., & Shafiro, M. (2006). Work–family best practices. In F. Jones, R. Burke, & M. Westman (Eds.), *Work–life balance: A psychological perspective* (pp. 261–275). East Sussex, England: Psychology Press.

Hammer, L. B., & Demsky, C. A. (2014). Introduction to work–life balance. In A. Day, E. K. Kelloway, & J. J. Hurrell (Eds.), *Workplace well-being: How to build psychologically healthy workplaces* (pp. 95–116). Hoboken, NJ: Wiley-Blackwell.

Hammer, L. B., Demsky, C., Kossek, E. E., & Bray, J. (2016). Work–family intervention research. In T. D. Allen & L. T. Eby (Eds.), *The Oxford handbook of work and family* (pp. 349–361). New York, NY: Oxford University Press. http://dx.doi.org/10.1093/oxfordhb/9780199337538.013.27

Hammer, L. B., Johnson, R. C., Crain, T. L., Bodner, T., Kossek, E. E., Davis, K. D., . . . Berkman, L. (2016). Intervention effects on safety compliance and citizenship behaviors: Evidence from the work, family, and health study. *Journal of Applied Psychology, 101,* 190–208. http://dx.doi.org/10.1037/apl0000047

Hammer, L. B., Kossek, E. E., Anger, W. K., Bodner, T., & Zimmerman, K. L. (2011). Clarifying work–family intervention processes: The roles of work–family conflict and family-supportive supervisor behaviors. *Journal of Applied Psychology, 96,* 134–150. http://dx.doi.org/10.1037/a0020927

Hammer, L. B., Kossek, E. E., Zimmerman, K., & Daniels, R. (2007). Clarifying the construct of family-supportive supervisory behaviors (FSSB): A multilevel perspective. In P. L. Perrewé & D. C. Ganster (Eds.), *Exploring the work and non-work interface: Vol. 6. Research in occupational stress and well-being* (pp. 165–204). Amsterdam, The Netherlands: Elsevier.

Hammer, L. B., & Sauter, S. (2013). Total worker health and work–life stress. *Journal of Occupational and Environmental Medicine, 55,* S25–S29. http://dx.doi.org/10.1097/JOM.0000000000000043

Hammer, L. B., Truxillo, D. M., Bodner, T., Rineer, J., Pytlovany, A. C., & Richman, A. (2015). Effects of a workplace intervention targeting psychosocial risk factors on safety and health outcomes. *BioMed Research International, 2015*, 836967. http://dx.doi.org/10.1155/2015/836967

Hammer, L. B., & Zimmerman, K. L. (2011). Quality of work life. In S. Zedeck (Ed.), *APA handbook of industrial and organizational psychology: Vol. 3. Maintaining, expanding, and contracting the organization* (pp. 399–431). Washington, DC: American Psychological Association. http://dx.doi.org/10.1037/12171-011

Hobfoll, S. E. (1989). Conservation of resources. A new attempt at conceptualizing stress. *American Psychologist, 44*, 513–524. http://dx.doi.org/10.1037/0003-066X.44.3.513

Hobfoll, S. E. (2002). Social and psychological resources and adaptation. *Review of General Psychology, 6*, 307–324. http://dx.doi.org/10.1037/1089-2680.6.4.307

Hurtado, D. A., Okechukwu, C. A., Buxton, O. M., Hammer, L., Hanson, G. C., Moen, P., . . . Berkman, L. F. (2016). Effects on cigarette consumption of a work–family supportive organisational intervention: 6-month results from the Work, Family and Health network study. *Journal of Epidemiology and Community Health, 70*, 1155–1161. http://dx.doi.org/10.1136/jech-2015-206953

Kanfer, F. H. (1977). The many faces of self-control, or behavior modification changes its focus. In R. B. Stuart (Ed.), *Behavioral self-management: Strategies, techniques, and outcome* (pp. 1–48). New York, NY: Brunner/Mazel.

Karasek, R. A. (1979). Job demands, job decision latitude, and mental strain: Implications for job design. *Administrative Science Quarterly, 24*, 285–308. http://dx.doi.org/10.2307/2392498

Kelly, E. L., Kossek, E. E., Hammer, L. B., Durham, M., Bray, J., Chermack, K., . . . Kaskubar, D. (2008). Getting there from here: Research on the effects of work–family initiatives on work–family conflict and business outcomes. *Academy of Management Annals, 2*, 305–349. http://dx.doi.org/10.5465/19416520802211610

Kelly, E. L., & Moen, P. (2007). Rethinking the clockwork of work: Why schedule control may pay off at work and at home. *Advances in Developing Human Resources, 9*, 487–506. http://dx.doi.org/10.1177/1523422307305489

Kelly, E. L., Moen, P., Oakes, J. M., Fan, W., Okechukwu, C., Davis, K. D., . . . Casper, L. M. (2014). Changing work and work–family conflict: Evidence from the Work, Family, and Health Network. *American Sociological Review, 79*, 485–516. http://dx.doi.org/10.1177/0003122414531435

Kossek, E. E. (2016). Implementing organizational work–life interventions: Toward a triple bottom line. *Community, Work & Family, 19*, 242–256. http://dx.doi.org/10.1080/13668803.2016.1135540

Kossek, E. E., Lewis, S., & Hammer, L. B. (2010). Work–life initiatives and organizational change: Overcoming mixed messages to move from the margin to the mainstream. *Human Relations, 63*, 3–19. http://dx.doi.org/10.1177/0018726709352385

Kossek, E. E., & Ozeki, C. (1998). Work–family conflict, policies, and the job–life satisfaction relationship: A review and directions for organizational behavior–human resources research. *Journal of Applied Psychology, 83*, 139–149. http://dx.doi.org/10.1037/0021-9010.83.2.139

Kossek, E. E., Pichler, S., Bodner, T., & Hammer, L. B. (2011). Workplace social support and work–family conflict: A meta-analysis clarifying the influence of general and work–family-specific supervisor and organizational support. *Personnel Psychology, 64*, 289–313. http://dx.doi.org/10.1111/j.1744-6570.2011.01211.x

Kossek, E. E., Thompson, R. J., Lawson, K. M., Bodner, T., Perrigino, M. B., Hammer, L. B., . . . Bray, J. W. (2019). Caring for the elderly at work and home: Can a randomized organizational intervention improve psychological health? *Journal of Occupational Health Psychology, 24*, 36–54. http://dx.doi.org/10.1037/ocp0000104

LaMontagne, A. D., Keegel, T., Louie, A. M., Ostry, A., & Landsbergis, P. A. (2007). A systematic review of the job-stress intervention evaluation literature, 1990–2005.

International Journal of Occupational and Environmental Health, 13, 268–280. http://dx.doi.org/10.1179/oeh.2007.13.3.268

Lazarus, R. S., & Folkman, S. (1984). *Stress, appraisal, and coping.* New York, NY: Springer.

Loeppke, R. R., Hohn, T., Baase, C., Bunn, W. B., Burton, W. N., Eisenberg, B. S., . . . Siuba, J. (2015). Integrating health and safety in the workplace: How closely aligning health and safety strategies can yield measurable benefits. *Journal of Occupational and Environmental Medicine, 57*, 585–597. http://dx.doi.org/10.1097/JOM.0000000000000467

McHale, S. M., Lawson, K. M., Davis, K. D., Casper, L., Kelly, E. L., & Buxton, O. (2015). Effects of a workplace intervention on sleep in employees' children. *Journal of Adolescent Health, 56*, 672–677. http://dx.doi.org/10.1016/j.jadohealth.2015.02.014

McNall, L. A., Nicklin, J. M., & Masuda, A. D. (2010). A meta-analytic review of the consequences associated with work–family enrichment. *Journal of Business and Psychology, 25*, 381–396. http://dx.doi.org/10.1007/s10869-009-9141-1

Mesmer-Magnus, J. R., & Viswesvaran, C. (2006). How family-friendly work environments affect work/family conflict: A meta-analytic examination. *Journal of Labor Research, 27*, 555–574. http://dx.doi.org/10.1007/s12122-006-1020-1

National Institute for Occupational Safety and Health. (2015). *Issues relevant to advancing worker well-being through Total Worker Health®.* Retrieved from https://www.cdc.gov/niosh/twh/pdfs/twh-issues-4x3_10282015_final.pdf

National Institute for Occupational Safety and Health. (2016a). *Fundamentals of Total Worker Health® approaches: Essential elements for advancing worker safety, health, and well-being* (DHHS [NIOSH] Publication No. 2017-112). Cincinnati, OH: U.S. Department of Health and Human Services, Centers for Disease Control and Prevention, National Institute for Occupational Safety and Health. Retrieved from https://stacks.cdc.gov/view/cdc/43275

National Institute for Occupational Safety and Health. (2016b). *National occupational research agenda (NORA)/national Total Worker Health® agenda (2016–2026): A national agenda to advance Total Worker Health® research, practice, policy, and capacity, April 2016* (DHHS [NIOSH] Publication No. 2016-114). Cincinnati, OH: U.S. Department of Health and Human Services, Centers for Disease Control and Prevention, National Institute for Occupational Safety and Health. Retrieved from https://www.cdc.gov/niosh/docs/2016-114/pdfs/nationaltwhagenda2016-1144-14-16.pdf

National Partnership for Women & Families. (2018). The Family and Medical Insurance Leave (FAMILY) Act [Fact sheet]. *National Partnership for Women & Families.* Retrieved from http://www.nationalpartnership.org/our-work/resources/workplace/paid-leave/family-act-fact-sheet.pdf

Nohe, C., Meier, L. L., Sonntag, K., & Michel, A. (2015). The chicken or the egg? A meta-analysis of panel studies of the relationship between work–family conflict and strain. *Journal of Applied Psychology, 100*, 522–536. http://dx.doi.org/10.1037/a0038012

Olson, R., Crain, T. L., Bodner, T., King, R., Hammer, L., Klein, L. C., . . . Buxton, O. M. (2015). A workplace intervention improves sleep: Results from the randomized, controlled work, family, and health study. *Sleep Health, 1*, 55–65. http://dx.doi.org/10.1016/j.sleh.2014.11.003

Rantanen, J., Kinnunen, U., Mauno, S., & Tillemann, K. (2011). Introducing theoretical approaches to work–life balance and testing a new typology among professionals. In S. Kaiser, M. Ringlstetter, D. R. Eikhof, & M. Pina e Cunha (Eds.), *Creating balance? International perspectives on the work-life integration of professionals* (pp. 27–46). Berlin, Germany: Springer. http://dx.doi.org/10.1007/978-3-642-16199-5_2

Schieman, S., Glavin, P., & Milkie, M. A. (2009). When work interferes with life: Work-nonwork interference and the influence of work-related demands and resources. *American Sociological Review, 74*, 966–988. http://dx.doi.org/10.1177/000312240907400606

Semmer, N. K. (2006). Job stress interventions and the organization of work. *Scandinavian Journal of Work, Environment & Health, 32,* 515–527. http://dx.doi.org/10.5271/sjweh.1056

Shockley, K. M., Shen, W., DeNunzio, M. M., Arvan, M. L., & Knudsen, E. A. (2017). Disentangling the relationship between gender and work–family conflict: An integration of theoretical perspectives using meta-analytic methods. *Journal of Applied Psychology, 102,* 1601–1635. Advance online publication. http://dx.doi.org/10.1037/apl0000246

Smith, T. D., & DeJoy, D. M. (2012). Occupational injury in America: An analysis of risk factors using data from the General Social Survey (GSS). *Journal of Safety Research, 43,* 67–74. http://dx.doi.org/10.1016/j.jsr.2011.12.002

Sorensen, G., Stoddard, A., Quintiliani, L., Ebbeling, C., Nagler, E., Yang, M., . . . Wallace, L. (2010). Tobacco use cessation and weight management among motor freight workers: Results of the gear up for health study. *Cancer Causes & Control, 21,* 2113–2122. http://dx.doi.org/10.1007/s10552-010-9630-6

Turner, N., Hershcovis, M. S., Reich, T. C., & Totterdell, P. (2014). Work–family interference, psychological distress, and workplace injuries. *Journal of Occupational and Organizational Psychology, 87,* 715–732. http://dx.doi.org/10.1111/joop.12071

Voydanoff, P. (2013). *Work, family, and community: Exploring interconnections.* New York, NY: Psychology Press.

Walsh, D. C., Jennings, S. E., Mangione, T., & Merrigan, D. M. (1991). Health promotion versus health protection? Employees' perceptions and concerns. *Journal of Public Health Policy, 12,* 148–164. http://dx.doi.org/10.2307/3342500

Warner, K. E. (1990). Wellness at the worksite. *Health Affairs, 9,* 63–79. http://dx.doi.org/10.1377/hlthaff.9.2.63

16

Integration of Workplace Prevention Programs and Organizational Effectiveness

Ron Z. Goetzel, Enid Chung Roemer, Karen B. Kent, and Katherine McCleary

Total Worker Health® is founded on the belief that an organization should have programs, policies, and environmental supports that best serve the health, safety, and well-being interests of workers (National Institute for Occupational Safety and Health [NIOSH], 2015a, 2015b). Although promoting workers' health and safety is obviously valuable in and of itself, a *Total Worker Health* (TWH) approach also is strategic from a business perspective. For one, a healthy and safe workforce may translate into cost savings for the enterprise through a reduction in unnecessary health care services use, fewer absences, lower incidence of workers' compensation claims, lower disability rates, and diminished spending on recruitment and training because of lower turnover. In addition, when good health and safety practices are the norm, employees are more committed to the organization and engaged in their work. This engagement, in turn, may result in higher worker productivity, more efficient operations, and greater competitiveness for the organization.

Traditionally, health promotion and health protection programs have been siloed and housed in different departments, thus seldom sharing data or aligning their initiatives. A TWH approach encourages synergy across organizational functions so they are complementary rather than competitive with one another. To gain traction, the TWH approach needs to expand beyond a currently narrow focus on just accident avoidance or traditional wellness programming to an

We thank Jeffrey Berko and Rachel M. Henke for their significant contributions to this chapter.

http://dx.doi.org/10.1037/0000149-017
Total Worker Health, H. L. Hudson, J. A. S. Nigam, S. L. Sauter, L. C. Chosewood, A. L. Schill, and J. Howard (Editors)
Copyright © 2019 by the American Psychological Association. All rights reserved.

expanded view in which several organizational functions and professionals must be engaged. They include human resources; rewards, compensation, and benefits; absence and disability management; workers' compensation and risk management; organizational development; occupational or environmental health and safety; operations management; public affairs; employee assistance; corporate social responsibility; facilities; and wellness. Although true integration of functions is complicated and often unnecessary, coordination and cooperation among these diverse functions are vital because, at their core, these entities are directed to achieve similar outcomes: a healthy, productive, and safe workforce.

TWH practices can be achieved by building an organization-wide culture of health and safety (COHaS), whereby leaders work in concert to establish and maintain a work environment that extends beyond simple compliance with rules and regulations, or delivering interventions through a traditional medical model. Importantly, to be successful, a TWH approach needs to be embedded within the organization's DNA—its vision, values, and day-to-day business operations—and its leaders need to be purposeful in addressing issues related to the health, safety, and well-being of employees.

In this chapter, we first explore the evolution from traditional workplace health promotion (WHP) programs to COHaS models. We emphasize the importance of building supportive cultures founded on a value on investment (VOI) paradigm in contrast to one that emphasizes only financial gains and requires a return on investment (ROI). We also describe how employers have begun to measure and evaluate VOI.

We report the results of a 2-year benchmarking study highlighting companies that built effective and sustainable COHaS programs that exemplify best practices. Then we contrast results from national surveys of employers and workers who were asked about health and safety programs at the workplace. We also illustrate the business outcomes from such initiatives as reflected by these companies' stock performance. Finally, we present a business case for expanding COHaS efforts beyond the walls of the organization and highlight efforts to improve the health of communities.

EVOLVING FROM DISEASE MANAGEMENT TO A CULTURE OF HEALTH AND SAFETY

Traditional WHP programs were established on medical models with an emphasis placed on lowering health risks, preventing diseases, and placing the onus on individuals to follow expert advice, change health habits, and adopt a healthy lifestyle. Programs urged willpower to overcome bad habits, such as tobacco use, poor diet, physical inactivity, high stress, and noncompliance with medical directives and treatments. Wellness programs often were siloed and not well integrated into other organizational functions (Hymel et al., 2011).

However, over time, WHP programs evolved into comprehensive offerings that consider the health of individuals within the context of organizational health.

At the same time, efforts to improve worker safety by addressing systemic occupational hazards were largely voluntary until the enactment of the Occupational Safety and Health Act of 1970 (Berman, 1977). This legislation set in motion requirements for companies to "own" safety, rather than blame workers for accidents. As for enforcement, states were mandated to inspect workplaces, issue citations for violations, and propose penalties—some as serious as forcing organizations to shut down dangerous worksites (Berman, 1977).

Despite similar goals of improving worker health and safety, the occupational safety and health promotion movements were organizationally separate and distinct functions. Staff had different educational backgrounds and training, were supported by often competitive funding streams within the company, and operated in adjacent regulatory environments. Unlike a traditional wellness approach that relied on personal responsibility, occupational safety was more closely aligned with a public health model that was largely systems oriented (Goetzel, Ozminkowski, Bowen, & Tabrizi, 2008). Rather than rely on individuals to make the right decisions about health, occupational health initiatives relied more heavily on laws, regulations, policies, and social marketing, and on changing the environment and norms.

In sharp contrast, health promotion was not mandated, and few rules governed its implementation. Because of its focus on the individual, health promotion was more closely aligned with the psychological perspective of behavior change (Goetzel et al., 2008) such that programs emphasized changing habits and behaviors of individuals. Only later in its evolution did program designers consider changing the environment to support individual efforts. Participation in WHP programs was voluntary, so program managers often relied on financial incentives to increase participation rates.

In 1993, DeJoy and Southern first proposed integrating health promotion and health protection as a unified strategy. The logic for integration was that companies could benefit from combining the programs, which would make them more efficient. Creating a combined WHP and occupational safety program also was consistent with employers' adoption of a human capital approach, in which workers were viewed as valuable assets that needed to be nurtured to prevent burnout (Goetzel et al., 2008). The thinking behind this approach was that complementary and synergistic programs would improve the organization's overall performance and profitability by increasing productivity and decreasing operating costs. A human capital model applied the best elements of psychological, public health, and regulatory approaches to maximize the economic and humanistic value of workers.

The TWH approach represents a further evolution of the human capital model in that it concurrently addresses individual and organizational influences on workers' health and safety, and has the ultimate aim of improving both business and employee health outcomes (Baker, Israel, & Schurman, 1996; Glanz, Sorensen, & Farmer, 1996; Pelletier, 2001).

Companies have moved away from a tunnel vision approach to health and safety. Enlightened employers no longer rely on individual decision-making to achieve a healthy workforce nor are they content with merely complying with basic regulatory requirements to assure a safe environment. The failure of such limited efforts has led to the emergence of the TWH's practices being anchored in a broader COHaS. This strategy only works when workplace leaders consistently place value on employee health, safety, and well-being, and such emphasis is sustained on several fronts.

Consistent with the idea expressed in Edgar Schein's (1990) organizational culture model, one can think of a COHaS as comprising many layers like an onion. On the surface are the physical *artifacts and symbols*—that is, the aspects of the organization that can be easily seen, such as fitness facilities and safety posters. Deeper down are *espoused values*—that is, the expressed standards, values, and rules of conduct pervasive within an organization. And, at the core are *underlying assumptions*, the deeply embedded perceptions and beliefs of workers that are taken for granted and unconsciously shape behaviors at all levels of the organization.

In practice, a COHaS is manifested in many ways. First, it involves a *physically supportive* environment (e.g., healthy food offerings; personal protective equipment; cool, shady break areas for outdoor workers). Furthermore, a COHaS extends beyond the isolated perks and programs that compose many wellness and occupational safety programs. Establishing a COHaS requires having a *psychosocially supportive* environment, which is achieved when the values and norms of an organization support employee health, safety, and well-being, starting with senior leadership and including middle managers and line workers. Table 16.1 presents the key elements of a COHaS.

ASSESSING VALUE ON INVESTMENT

Organizations adopting a COHaS understand that to compete in a global marketplace, they need to demonstrate value to their workers, customers, and outside investors. The COHaS model has required that performance metrics include broader measures of success beyond traditional ROI measures that focus on cost savings from reductions in health risks, safety incidents, medical events, and disability. For example, particular factors are relevant to organizational success and germane to building a COHaS, such as individual worker performance and contribution levels; team effectiveness; company reputation; morale, camaraderie, and job satisfaction; energy levels; and attraction and retention of top talent. However, these achievable and valuable outcomes of interest cannot be easily monetized or incorporated into an ROI calculation.

How, then, do program implementers and organizational leaders assess the "real" value of their efforts? For instance, What is the ROI from offering financial counseling or flexible work-scheduling options to employees? What about sponsoring sports teams and other social activities? And, how does one quantify

TABLE 16.1 Key Elements That Contribute to a Culture of Health and Safety

Physically supportive environment	
Healthy environment	The physical environment offers healthy options as the default, and employees have access to convenient, high-quality resources to improve health
Safe environment	Physical environmental factors (e.g., facilities, equipment, materials) are designed—or modified wherever necessary—to promote employee safety and minimize risk

Psychosocially supportive environment	
Leadership support	Many health and safety advocates are on the leadership team; leaders consistently express the importance of employee health, safety, and well-being, and these values are apparent in the way the organization is run (e.g., organizational expectations; resource allocations; staffing levels; scheduling and leave policies; how the organization evaluates, promotes and compensates workers)
Supervisor support	Managers give workers decision latitude and reasonable work goals, foster a positive work environment of teamwork and collaboration; managers provide regular opportunities for employee input on hazards and solutions, and push to implement these solutions, when appropriate
Peer support	Workers build social bonds and a sense of community; these efforts often are facilitated by employer-sponsored activities (e.g., sports teams, company picnics)

the ROI from a healthier building design that offers natural lighting, indoor plants, open stairwells, and comfortable communal spaces?

One way is by changing the framework for evaluating program success by incorporating VOI metrics that consider a disparate list of desirable outcomes, even if they cannot be easily quantified or directly attributed to an intervention. Figure 16.1 illustrates VOI metrics, which can be organized into four broad metric categories: business, health and health care, productivity, and humanistic outcomes. What follows is an illustration of how to apply this model in real-world situations.

FIGURE 16.1. Value on Investment Metrics

Business	Health & Health Care	Productivity	Humanistic Outcomes
•Performance and profitability (e.g., stock prices) •Attraction and retention of talent	•Medical claims/costs •Disability claims/costs •Employee daily health decisions at work •Safety •Health behaviors (modifiable health risks)	•Absenteeism (i.e., sick days) •Presenteeism (i.e., reduced productivity while at work due to poor health)	•Morale •Job satisfaction •Energy levels •Coworker relationships •Engagement (program participation) •Wellness program satisfaction

DEFINING, MEASURING, AND REALIZING VALUE INVESTMENT BY EMPLOYERS

Measurement of the metrics presented in Figure 16.1 requires employers to draw data from a variety of sources. Traditional sources, such as health risk assessments, workers' compensation, disability, and health insurance claim records can be supplemented with employee satisfaction surveys, turnover history, and Internet and media searches to gauge company reputation. To gain a better perspective on how companies define, measure, and realize VOI, we visited and interviewed organizations with best practice programs. Some of these organizations were manufacturing companies with a history of focusing on safety; others were primarily office environments. Regardless of their business focus, settings, or products, these companies provided substantial evidence of the benefits of shifting from siloed health and safety initiatives to a truly integrated web of programs, policies, and environmental supports that fall under the umbrella of the TWH approach.

The following vignettes illustrate the design elements and goals that underlie best practice programs, and the measures that employers use to evaluate the success of these programs.

Case Vignette: TURCK

TURCK is a small Minneapolis, Minnesota–based manufacturer in the field of industrial automation technology. Like many WHP programs, the LifeWorks@ TURCK program was developed incrementally. The program has a broad focus that includes physical, social, mental, financial, and community well-being as well as educational and professional growth. For example, the company offers an annual voluntary health risk assessment and biometric screening, group stretching and walking breaks, on-site health coaching and smoking cessation programs, free membership to fitness facilities for employees and family members, flexible scheduling options, up to 2 days of paid time off per year for volunteering, up to $100 per employee for charitable giving, tuition reimbursement, a free on-site health clinic and pharmacy, an indoor walking path, and a tiered incentive structure for participating in various WHP activities.

As a manufacturing company, TURCK is focused on protecting workers' safety. Before beginning their shifts and throughout the day, workers participate in stretching and strength-building exercises. Walkways in the plant are carefully laid out, vehicles are equipped with necessary safety features (e.g., sounds and lights to warn pedestrians), and attention is paid to temperature variation (e.g., too hot or cold) within the plant. Workers are required to wear protective equipment (e.g., helmets, safety glasses). The company also provides reimbursement for taxi services at any time when employees feel concerned about their ability to safely or legally drive (even during nonbusiness hours)—with no questions asked.

The leadership at TURCK is fully committed to the LifeWorks@TURCK program and reports that offering it is "the right thing to do" regardless of ROI. The leadership goals are to maintain an employee base that is happy and healthy, so the leadership provides the necessary tools, resources, and support to maintain and improve employee well-being. There is little interest in tracking traditional ROI metrics at TURCK; instead, the measures of success examined most often are turnover, employee satisfaction, and engagement. Since 2010, turnover rates have hovered around 1% to 4%, which is significantly below industry averages of 11% to 13%. When interviewed, employees expressed a sense of being cared for and connected to one another as well as being committed to the company that encourages such sentiments. An anonymous well-being survey found that 93% of employees reported strong agreement with the statement "I give my best effort every day," and 91% reported strong agreement with the statement "I put in extra time and effort as needed to do my work effectively." For TURCK, these are the measures that indicate program success.

Case Vignette: L.L.Bean

L.L.Bean is a major manufacturer and retailer of clothing, shoes, and outdoor equipment. Since 1982, L.L.Bean has built a comprehensive health promotion program that today reaches more than 5,000 employees, family members, and retirees. The Healthy Bean program was built on the principle that healthy people lead fuller, more active, more satisfying, and more productive lives, and are therefore better able to attend to their personal safety on the job.

According to former company president Leon Gorman, "A business is in a unique and responsible position to effectively enhance the well-being of its employees." L.L.Bean demonstrates this commitment to employees with well-articulated goals, excellent communications, visible day-to day management support, and a comprehensive set of resources to help employees improve their health. Their COHaS is further reinforced through traditions and routines like regular employee-led stretch breaks on the floor of the distribution centers and an annual Christmas Eve hike.

The company offers 12 on-site fitness centers; fitness classes; an outdoors club; regular biometric screenings; health coaching and health education, including weekly meetings with a nutritionist; Weight Watchers; smoking cessation programs; and an intensive diabetes prevention program. The working environment itself is designed to guide employees toward health improvement. For example, L.L.Bean has a tobacco-free campus; cafeterias and vending machines that promote healthier food through red-yellow-green food labeling; differential pricing for healthy versus unhealthy items; and a policy on the percentage of vending machine items that must be healthy.

To address safety, L.L.Bean trains volunteer employees (called "safety ergonomics representatives") who are tasked with evaluating the ergonomic situations of their peer workers, if requested. These assessments include the identification of potential ergonomic risk factors and modification of workstations. At individual stores, L.L.Bean has reengineered the more demanding jobs, piloted voluntary conditioning programs for employees who want to improve their fitness levels, and clearly quantified job demands so employees are better matched to the work. Many of L.L.Bean's sites have achieved the Occupational Safety and Health Agency's voluntary protection programs star status, further illustrating the company's fundamental commitment to safety in the workplace.

L.L.Bean's internal program evaluation combines traditional ROI analyses with an examination of more comprehensive VOI measures. The company routinely examines health risk, biometric, safety, disability, and health insurance claims data, and uses its findings to provide a business case for further investing in COHaS programs that direct limited resources most cost-effectively. In a recent analysis focused on avoided medical claims, the company found a positive ROI from all four evaluated program years—ranging from $1.70 to $5.30 saved for every dollar invested. L.L.Bean also has tracked employee health risks throughout the life of the program. For instance, by tracking smoking rates over time, the company has been able to show significant improvements and attribute those improvements to specific policies, most notably, big declines in years following the elimination of smoking rooms (1993) and the institution of a tobacco-free campus (2005). Moreover, in 2013, the organization's smoking rate was 6%, significantly lower than the 19% average in Maine, where the company is based.

Case Vignette: FedEx

FedEx is a leading global provider of transportation, logistics, e-commerce, and supply chain management services. With more than 200,000 employees, the company is consistently recognized for its progressive and innovative health promotion and protection policies. As company founder Fred W. Smith explained, "FedEx is built on the rock-solid foundation of employee commitment . . . with a management philosophy that prioritizes people, service, and profit, in that order."

FedEx's human capital management strategy was developed to integrate many different departments, including safety, risk management, health and wellness, disability, human resources, and operations. FedEx employees are offered a variety of programs designed to promote health and fitness; initiatives are directed at demand management (i.e., methods of forecasting, planning, and managing demand for health care services), utilization management, catastrophic case management, and disease management. Employee perks include classes on a variety of health topics, maternity education, benefit fairs, smoking cessation programs, on-site health and wellness centers, and employee assistance programs.

As stated in FedEx's mission, safety is the first consideration in all operations. FedEx's "safety above all" initiative goes beyond just reporting injury rates and requiring safety training. Safety goals are set at the corporate level and must be met each year for management to receive bonus payments. In addition, annual rewards are given to teams with the best and most improved safety records. Safety continuous improvement teams review safety practices in work areas, provide solutions to hazardous conditions, and support new hires in their adoption of safe practices.

Some of the metrics FedEx uses to assess program success include productivity loss costs, program participation, disability claims, and injury rates. The company also conducts yearly surveys to gauge opinions about the performance of managers as well as the company in general. One item asks for the level of agreement with the statement, "In my environment, we use safe work practices."

The next section further explores the role of employees' opinions in assessing COHaS programs.

ENGAGING EMPLOYEES—AND EMPLOYERS IN THE PROCESS

Recent research has identified the steps employers can take to establish VOI from COHaS programs. Developing effective cultures of health and safety generally begins with decisions made by senior leaders but also requires employee buy-in at all levels of the organization. This buy-in is especially important when organized labor constitutes a significant portion of the workforce at an organization. Union leaders need to be involved in the planning and execution of TWH programs; otherwise, they may sabotage such efforts because they believe the TWH approach is masquerading as a management initiative to save money with little or no impact on employee health and safety. In this section, we review research that has provided insights into some key elements that contribute to a sustainable and successful COHaS.

A lack of employee engagement in decision-making often is a significant contributor to program failure. To engage their workers, employers can gather input and feedback from employees about their health goals, needs, interests, and barriers, and encourage employee involvement and input in program design, implementation, and evaluation. Involving employees in program decision-making has been significantly associated with organizational commitment, mental well-being, and turnover intentions (Grawitch, Trares, & Kohler, 2007).

McCleary et al. (2017) discovered discrepancies in survey responses from employers and employees, such as between employers who say they offer WHP programs (80.6%) versus employees who report being offered them (45.0%). This discrepancy is surprising, given that program awareness is a foundational element for success. The use of strategic communications may help resolve low levels of employee awareness of TWH programs. Kent, Goetzel, Roemer, Prasad, and Freundlich (2016) described *strategic communications* as those designed to educate, motivate, market offerings, and build trust. The messages are tailored, targeted, and bidirectional, and use multiple channels with optimal timing, frequency, and placement.

McCleary et al. (2017) also found that employees do not report elements typically associated with a COHaS. For example, when employees were asked about specific elements of their work environment, fewer than half reported that their jobs allowed them to maintain good health (44.1%). Along these lines, to provide a leading indicator for future safety incidents, it would be useful to ask employees whether they feel their workplace is unsafe. Furthermore, employees indicated they would welcome health improvement support from their employers (McCleary et al., 2017). Most (59.4%) indicated that employers should play a role in improving worker health, and nearly three fourths (72.1%) thought lower insurance premiums should be offered for participation in wellness programs. Yet, only about one third (34.1%) believed their senior leaders were committed to improving the health of employees, and fewer than half (46.4%) reported that their leaders were committed to workers' health, safety, and well-being (McCleary et al., 2017).

Leadership support is another foundational element for engaging employees. One style of leadership often recommended as being particularly effective is *transformational leadership.* In contrast to a more transactional focus, these leaders appreciate the humanistic elements of the employee experience and provide a clear vision, can inspire and motivate, and show a genuine interest in the personal aspirations of workers (Bass & Riggio, 2005). A key challenge to this leadership approach, however, is the importance of gaining or improving on employees' trust.

Without trust, efforts to engage employees in health and safety activities may prove futile, particularly in unionized organizations in which union leaders and management may not agree on outcomes or methods for engagement. Trust must be built on transparency so that actions speak louder than words. Dialogue starts with the leaders' working directly with union leaders to codevelop the goals, strategies, and messaging needed to engage workers in building a COHaS. This collaboration can be accomplished by supporting health and safety committees that are empowered to offer workable suggestions about improving the work environment, both physical and social. Once ideas have been gathered, providing necessary resources and making environmental improvements can concretely demonstrate the leadership's commitment to employee health and safety.

An organization's decision to provide more support and resources (e.g., supervisor training, positive feedback, collaborative work structures, innovative problem solving) has been shown to improve levels of employee engagement (Bakker, Hakanen, Demerouti, & Xanthopoulou, 2007). Other actions by those in leadership roles include becoming visible program advocates, actively participating in health and safety programs, and encouraging open channels of communication and feedback with employees at all levels within the organization, such as sponsoring and leading wellness and safety committees, and giving employees opportunities to take ownership of designing or leading COHaS initiatives.

Ultimately, engaging the workforce requires understanding the workers' perspective. When decisions are based on financial factors alone, the range of psychosocial variables associated with VOI often are left out of the equation. Work is an integral part of a person's life, and although it may be defined differently for each person, there are health and safety elements that either motivate or inhibit full engagement in one's job. Understanding the wishes and concerns of each worker translates into personal as well as job satisfaction. Often, the result is a worker who is not only happier but also healthier and more productive.

EXPANDING BEYOND THE ORGANIZATION'S WALLS

In striving to achieve TWH practices, most businesses already understand that job-related factors, such as wages, hours of work, and stress levels, exert a major influence on workforce health and safety (NIOSH, 2015b). However, employees' health and well-being also are heavily influenced by a combination of factors that take effect before and after work (Office of Disease Prevention and Health Promotion, 2016a; Pronk, Baase, Noyce, & Stevens, 2015). The beneficial effects of internally directed TWH programs may be undercut by unhealthy community factors that influence workers and their families when employees leave the worksite. Many "upstream" drivers of death and disability are caused by unhealthy and unsafe social and environmental factors that reside outside the worksite: unhealthy food options, unsafe neighborhoods, poor schools, substandard housing, and a lack of time or space for physical activity (Office of Disease Prevention and Health Promotion, 2016b).

Improvements in employee health and safety require engaging in external activities and bringing about fundamental changes in communities where employees live, work, learn, and play (Kindig, Isham, & Siemering, 2013; Woulfe, Oliver, Zahner, & Siemering, 2010). For example, company efforts can be directed at factors in the physical environment (e.g., clean air and water, access to open space and public transit) as well as the social and economic environments of workers (e.g., employment, education, safety, and social support; McGovern, Miller, & Hughes-Cromwick, 2014; University of Wisconsin Population Health Institute & Robert Wood Johnson Foundation, 2016). Improvements in community health will make it easier for employees to focus on health and safety outside the worksite, and thereby maximize the value of TWH programs. In this way, investing in the social determinants of health can help create shared value for both businesses and their communities (Porter & Kramer, 2011; Pronk et al., 2015), and company leaders can focus on solving social problems. These investments, in turn, can present opportunities for new customers and markets, cost savings, and talent retention.

To begin to address the social determinants of health, businesses should expand their TWH programs' influence beyond compliance with health and safety regulations (NIOSH, 2015a, 2015b; Pronk et al., 2015; Webber & Mercure, 2010). Businesses should approach community health from a systematic and strategic standpoint from which they can effectively address all aspects of the social, environmental, and physical conditions of their communities (Kindig et al., 2013; NIOSH, 2015b; Pronk et al., 2015; Webber & Mercure, 2010). To address these issues simultaneously, partnerships between the business community and government agencies, the health care sector, community organizations, and community members are required (Kindig et al., 2013; Sepulveda, 2013). Multisectoral partnerships are critical to successfully address the multifaceted problems presented by the social determinants of health. Partnerships also help distribute the burden of the effort, allow for greater reach into the community, and bring diverse perspectives that allow problems to be attacked from multiple angles.

Within these partnerships, businesses are uniquely positioned to drive home the need to address social determinants of health. An obvious first step is for businesses to provide high-quality and high-paying jobs that are founded on a COHaS. In addition, businesses can create or contribute to education programming (e.g., training, mentoring), the environment (e.g., quality of air and water), the arts (e.g., museums, cultural attractions), and urban planning (e.g., healthy building designs, active commuting routes, aesthetics, areas promoting physical activity; Frumkin, 2003; Kindig et al., 2013). By leading community development efforts that promote population health and safety, businesses can establish a reputation for caring, which, in turn, enhances their brand and customer loyalty.

Recent research has illustrated employers' various levels of commitment to community health and safety, as evidenced by their motivation for participation in such initiatives (see Figure 16.2; Pronk et al., 2015). At the lowest levels

FIGURE 16.2. The Business Case Development Continuum

Compliance	Charitable	Strategic	Systemic
e.g., meeting minimal regulatory standards for worker safety	e.g., corporate giving campaigns that enhance company brand, image	e.g., core business and management systems deployed to generate health and business value	e.g., systemic solutions designed to intentionally generate population health, business value, and address social determinants of health

From "Corporate America and Community Health: Exploring the Business Case for Investment," by N. P. Pronk, C. Basse, J. Noyce, and D. E. Stevens, 2015, *Journal of Occupational and Environmental Medicine, 57*, p. 499. Copyright 2015 by American College of Occupational and Environmental Medicine. Reprinted with permission.

of participation, organizations seek to ensure that they are meeting basic regulatory requirements for workplace safety. At slightly higher levels of participation, organizations seek to enhance their image in the community as good corporate citizens that practice corporate social responsibility. At higher levels of participation, businesses seek to systematically connect their business goals with health and safety goals. And at the highest levels, businesses develop a COHaS that addresses community needs and social determinants of health as an integral part of business operations (Pronk et al., 2015). Once organizations' reasons for participating have been established, teams can move forward to determine specific approaches to address specific problems (Pronk et al., 2015).

To achieve the highest levels of the business case development continuum, employers need to recognize that the health of their businesses is tied to the health of their employees, and the health of their employees is tied to the health of their communities (National Business Group on Health, 2016; NIOSH, 2015b; Pronk et al., 2015; Sepulveda, 2013; Webber & Mercure, 2010). Maximizing benefits will require businesses to simultaneously promote corporate, social, and personal responsibility, and strike a balance between investing in individual employees' health and community social determinants of health in ways that can be sustained over time (Office of Disease Prevention and Health Promotion, 2016b).

UNDERSTANDING THAT VALUE ON INVESTMENT INCLUDES WIDELY HELD MEASURES OF BUSINESS PERFORMANCE

In a 1970 essay, noted economist Milton Friedman argued that businesses should focus only on maximizing profits for their shareholders, and nothing else. The question that arises is whether businesses that act in socially responsible ways also benefit the business owners who in a publicly traded company are its shareholders. A series of studies in 2016 addressed this issue by comparing the stock performance of companies that have exemplary health and safety programs with the performance of the average company included in the Standard and Poor's 500 stock index (S&P 500).

One such study examined the stock performance of 26 C. Everett Koop National Health Award winners (an award given annually to companies with exceptionally strong cultures of health). Researchers found that over the 14-year period tracked (2000–2014), Koop Award winners' stock values appreciated by 325% compared with the market average appreciation of 105% (Goetzel et al., 2016).

Similarly, a study that evaluated the stock performance of publicly traded companies that received high scores on the *HERO Scorecard*, an instrument used to assess a COHaS, found that high-scoring companies appreciated by 235% compared with the S&P 500 index appreciation of 159% over a 6-year simulation period (Grossmeier et al., 2016).

A third study examined the stock market performance of winners of the American College of Occupational and Environmental Medicine's Corporate

Health Achievement Award. Various stock portfolios were created that featured companies with excellent health promotion, safety, or combined TWH programs. Each portfolio outperformed the S&P 500, and the one comprising excellent health and safety programs achieved an ROI of 279% compared with the average return of 105%. Across all portfolios, and including previous studies by the researchers, the award winners achieved a cumulative return of 94% over 13 years compared with the S&P 500 cumulative return of less than 1% over the same period (Fabius et al., 2013). This growing body of evidence suggests that socially responsible companies that invest in the health and well-being of their workers can produce a higher market valuation—an affirmation of business success by Wall Street investors—when compared with other publicly traded firms.

CONCLUSION

Conventional occupational health and safety programs traditionally have focused on preventing injury and minimizing exposure to dangerous conditions in the workplace (NIOSH, 2015b). Nowadays, many employers recognize that the ultimate aims of these programs—namely, a healthy, safe, and productive workforce with associated cost savings, commitment to the organization, and increased productivity—depend on more than basic injury prevention and risk management measures. The TWH concept evolved from this line of thinking and emphasizes addressing factors that not only protect workers' safety but also promote the concept of workers' global well-being.

To be adopted by mainstream businesses, the TWH approach needs to be embedded within a holistic view of organizational health, individual health, and elements of safety. The core scaffolding for a TWH program incorporates best practices in occupational health and safety alongside evidence-based health promotion and disease prevention programs. But a TWH program also must pay attention to and collect metrics relevant to humanistic outcomes that extend beyond individual worker health and safety. For organizations, this means acting in socially responsible ways within their communities. Although it may be difficult to quantify VOI outcomes, there is growing evidence that building and sustaining a COHaS leads to attraction and retention of talent, heightened employee morale and engagement, and enhanced corporate reputation. In addition, the company's business performance, as measured by its stock price, also may be positively affected. These factors matter to customers, employees, regulators, company executives, and shareholders.

REFERENCES

Baker, E., Israel, B. A., & Schurman, S. (1996). The integrated model: Implications for worksite health promotion and occupational health and safety practice. *Health Education Quarterly, 23*, 175–190. http://dx.doi.org/10.1177/109019819602300204

Bakker, A. B., Hakanen, J. J., Demerouti, E., & Xanthopoulou, D. (2007). Job resources boost work engagement, particularly when job demands are high. *Journal of Educational Psychology, 99*, 274–284. http://dx.doi.org/10.1037/0022-0663.99.2.274

Bass, B. M., & Riggio, R. E. (2005). *Transformational leadership* (2nd ed.). Mahwah, NJ: Psychology Press.

Berman, D. M. (1977). Why work kills: A brief history of occupational safety and health in the United States. *International Journal of Health Services: Planning, Administration, Evaluation, 7*(1), 63–87.

DeJoy, D. M., & Southern, D. J. (1993). An integrative perspective on work-site health promotion. *Journal of Occupational Medicine, 35*, 1221–1230.

Fabius, R., Thayer, R. D., Konicki, D. L., Yarborough, C. M., Peterson, K. W., Isaac, F., . . . Dreger, M. (2013). The link between workforce health and safety and the health of the bottom line: Tracking market performance of companies that nurture a "culture of health." *Journal of Occupational and Environmental Medicine, 55*, 993–1000. http://dx.doi.org/10.1097/JOM.0b013e3182a6bb75

Friedman, M. (1970, September 13). The social responsibility of business is to increase its profits. *The New York Times Magazine.* Retrieved from http://link.springer.com/chapter/10.1007/978-3-540-70818-6_14#page-1

Frumkin, H. (2003). Healthy places: Exploring the evidence. *American Journal of Public Health, 93*, 1451–1456. http://dx.doi.org/10.2105/AJPH.93.9.1451

Glanz, K., Sorensen, G., & Farmer, A. (1996). The health impact of worksite nutrition and cholesterol intervention programs. *American Journal of Health Promotion, 10*, 453–470. http://dx.doi.org/10.4278/0890-1171-10.6.453

Goetzel, R. Z., Fabius, R., Fabius, D., Roemer, E. C., Thornton, N., Kelly, R. K., & Pelletier, K. R. (2016). The stock performance of C. Everett Koop award winners compared with the Standard & Poor's 500 index. *Journal of Occupational and Environmental Medicine, 58*, 9–15. http://dx.doi.org/10.1097/JOM.0000000000000632

Goetzel, R. Z., Ozminkowski, R. J., Bowen, J., & Tabrizi, M. J. (2008). Employer integration of health promotion and health protection programs. *International Journal of Workplace Health Management, 1*, 109–122. http://dx.doi.org/10.1108/17538350810893900

Grawitch, M. J., Trares, S., & Kohler, J. M. (2007). Healthy workplace practices and employee outcomes. *International Journal of Stress Management, 14*, 275–293. http://dx.doi.org/10.1037/1072-5245.14.3.275

Grossmeier, J., Fabius, R., Flynn, J. P., Noeldner, S. P., Fabius, D., Goetzel, R. Z., & Anderson, D. R. (2016). Linking workplace health promotion best practices and organizational financial performance: Tracking market performance of companies with highest scores on the HERO Scorecard. *Journal of Occupational and Environmental Medicine, 58*, 16–23. http://dx.doi.org/10.1097/JOM.0000000000000631

Hymel, P. A., Loeppke, R. R., Baase, C. M., Burton, W. N., Hartenbaum, N. P., Hudson, T. W., . . . Larson, P. W. (2011). Workplace health protection and promotion: A new pathway for a healthier—and safer—workforce. *Journal of Occupational and Environmental Medicine, 53*, 695–702. http://dx.doi.org/10.1097/JOM.0b013e31822005d0

Kent, K., Goetzel, R. Z., Roemer, E. C., Prasad, A., & Freundlich, N. (2016). Promoting healthy workplaces by building cultures of health and applying strategic communications. *Journal of Occupational and Environmental Medicine, 58*, 114–122. http://dx.doi.org/10.1097/JOM.0000000000000629

Kindig, D. A., Isham, G. J., & Siemering, K. Q. (2013). *The business role in improving health: Beyond social responsibility.* Washington, DC: Institute of Medicine. http://dx.doi.org/10.31478/201308b Retrieved from https://nam.edu/wp-content/uploads/2015/06/TheBusinessRole.pdf

McCleary, K., Goetzel, R. Z., Roemer, E. C., Berko, J., Kent, K., & Torre, H. (2017). Employer and employee opinions about workplace health promotion (wellness) programs: Results of the 2015 Harris Poll Nielsen survey. *Journal of Occupational and Environmental Medicine, 59*, 256–263. http://dx.doi.org/10.1097/JOM.0000000000000946

McGovern, L., Miller, G., & Hughes-Cromwick, P. (2014, August 21). *The relative contribution of multiple determinants to health outcomes* [Health Affairs Health Policy Brief].

Retrieved from http://healthaffairs.org/healthpolicybriefs/brief_pdfs/healthpolicybrief_123.pdf

National Business Group on Health. (2016). *Integrating wellness and occupational health and safety in the workplace*. Retrieved from https://www.businessgrouphealth.org/tools-resources/toolkits/integrating-wellness

National Institute for Occupational Safety and Health. (2015a). Total Worker Health: *History*. Retrieved from https://www.cdc.gov/niosh/twh/history.html

National Institute for Occupational Safety and Health. (2015b). *Total Worker Health: What is* Total Worker Health? Retrieved from https://www.cdc.gov/niosh/twh/totalhealth.html

Occupational Safety and Health Act of 1970, Pub. L. 91-596, 84 Stat. 1590 (1970).

Office of Disease Prevention and Health Promotion, U.S. Department of Health and Human Services. (2016a). *Determinants of health*. Retrieved from https://www.healthypeople.gov/2020/about/foundation-health-measures/Determinants-of-Health

Office of Disease Prevention and Health Promotion, U.S. Department of Health and Human Services. (2016b). *Social determinants of health*. Retrieved from https://www.healthypeople.gov/2020/topics-objectives/topic/social-determinants-of-health

Pelletier, K. R. (2001). A review and analysis of the clinical- and cost-effectiveness studies of comprehensive health promotion and disease management programs at the worksite: 1998–2000 update. *American Journal of Health Promotion, 16*, 107–116. http://dx.doi.org/10.4278/0890-1171-16.2.107

Porter, M. E., & Kramer, M. R. (2011, January 1). Creating shared value. *Harvard Business Review*. Retrieved from https://hbr.org/2011/01/the-big-idea-creating-shared-value

Pronk, N. P., Baase, C., Noyce, J., & Stevens, D. E. (2015). Corporate America and community health: Exploring the business case for investment. *Journal of Occupational and Environmental Medicine, 57*, 493–500. http://dx.doi.org/10.1097/JOM.0000000000000431

Schein, E. H. (1990). Organizational culture. *American Psychologist, 45*, 109–119. http://dx.doi.org/10.1037/0003-066X.45.2.109

Sepulveda, M.-J. (2013). From worker health to citizen health: Moving upstream. *Journal of Occupational and Environmental Medicine, 55*(12), S52–S57. http://dx.doi.org/10.1097/JOM.0000000000000033

University of Wisconsin Population Health Institute, & Robert Wood Johnson Foundation. (2016). *What and why we rank* [County health rankings model and road maps]. Retrieved from http://www.countyhealthrankings.org/our-approach

Webber, A., & Mercure, S. (2010). Improving population health: The business community imperative. *Preventing Chronic Disease, 7*, A121. Retrieved from https://www.cdc.gov/pcd/issues/2010/nov/10_0086.htm

Woulfe, J., Oliver, T. R., Zahner, S. J., & Siemering, K. Q. (2010). Multisector partnerships in population health improvement. *Preventing Chronic Disease Dialogue, 7*, A119. Retrieved from http://www.cdc.gov/pcd/issues/2010/nov/10_0104.htm

17

Future Directions and Opportunities for *Total Worker Health*

Heidi L. Hudson and Jeannie A. S. Nigam

The field of occupational safety and health (OSH) is undergoing a significant transformation as the landscape of work changes. In this concluding chapter, we highlight three cross-cutting themes—drawn from recent literature and discussions with thought leaders—that are driving a paradigm shift in the area of OSH. We begin with a discussion of how work and the workforce are changing. Next, we describe the links between work and health, and, finally, we reflect on expanding views of OSH. Collectively, these themes advocate for a *Total Worker Health*® approach that integrates health protection with broader interventions to advance worker well-being (National Institute for Occupational Safety and Health [NIOSH], 2015b). The rationale for this approach builds on prior efforts that advocate for the protection of worker well-being (see Chapter 2, this volume). We conclude with a discussion of opportunities for the *Total Worker Health* (TWH) approach to move the OSH field forward through investments in training, science, and practice, and propose a new direction for achieving well-being through work.

This chapter was authored by employees of the United States government as part of their official duty and is considered to be in the public domain. Any views expressed herein do not necessarily represent the views of the United States government, and the authors' participation in the work is not meant to serve as an official endorsement.

http://dx.doi.org/10.1037/0000149-018
Total Worker Health, H. L. Hudson, J. A. S. Nigam, S. L. Sauter, L. C. Chosewood, A. L. Schill, and J. Howard (Editors)

CHANGING WORK ARRANGEMENTS AND WORKFORCE

Such forces as globalization, economic transformation, and technological innovations present new and complex challenges for workers, employers, and societies around the world. These changes are driving profound disruptions in the design of work and how work is accomplished. As technology advances and organizations face global competitive pressure, employers may change work processes, create entirely new forms of business organizations, introduce nonstandard work arrangements, alter or discontinue employment-related benefits, and modify the types and levels of safety protections they provide to workers. Artificial intelligence, machine learning, robotization, ambient intelligence (e.g., sensors, wireless modules worn by workers), and real-time surveillance can reduce work-related hazards and raise productivity but also may create new concerns for worker safety, health, privacy, and job security. Meanwhile, the organized labor movement has waned, health and wealth disparities are growing, and more than 60% of Americans have reported that work is a significant source of stress (American Psychological Association, 2017). Altogether, these changes can have a substantial effect on the overall safety, health, well-being, and financial stability of workers, and, in turn, enterprise sustainability and national economic productivity (Deutsche Gesetzliche Unfallversicherung [DGUV], 2016; European Agency for Safety and Health at Work [EU-OSHA], 2016; Peckham, Baker, Camp, Kaufman, & Seixas, 2017).

Nonstandard employment arrangements (e.g., temporary, volunteer, contingent, part-time, on-call, direct hire, agency-supplied, contract, freelance) and new forms of work, such as on-demand and app-based, digitally supported gig work, pose an especially pertinent concern for OSH. The concern is that nonstandard work arrangements usually lack the traditional protections and benefits of traditional or standard employment, and result in a host of consequences for workers. Workers in nonstandard arrangements, especially those who are low-wage earners (Howard, 2017b), may bear more injury risk and greater job insecurity than workers in standard employment arrangements because they often are assigned hazardous tasks (and are reluctant to object), the work is generally temporary, and legal guidelines do not assign responsibility for providing physical and policy protections for workers (Benach, Vives, Amable, Vanroelen, Tarafa, & Muntaner, 2014; Howard, 2017a). In addition, these arrangements can intensify the entanglement of personal and work-related exposures and risks because many of these jobs are performed outside of traditional work settings (e.g., in one's home). Also, these jobs often are enabled by technology that has been shown to exacerbate the struggle to disconnect from work and further blur the lines between work and life (Cocorocchia, 2016).

The changing makeup of the workforce presents another challenge. Specifically, there is uncertainty regarding how to design work to support a diverse workforce comprising multiple generations, more working women, a higher proportion of older workers, and a growing number of workers with illnesses and disabilities that may limit functional ability. The aging of the workforce is of particular concern. Although *how* people age varies significantly, even under the best circumstances, aging is associated with gradual cognitive and physical decline that can potentially affect people's capacity to participate in work (see Chapter 13).

Moreover, the incidence of chronic disease (e.g., diabetes, obesity, metabolic disorder) among workers of all ages is increasing. Chronic health conditions affect about 60% of Americans (Buttorff, Ruder, & Bauman, 2017). Misuse of prescription drugs, which may be associated with chronic conditions, and the use of illicit drugs are on the rise as evidenced by the present opioid epidemic in the United States. (Mack, Jones, & Ballesteros, 2017; U.S. Department of Health and Human Services, Public Health Service, Office of the Surgeon General, 2018). In addition, some workers struggle with mental health problems (see Chapter 12). When people suffer from physical illness or psychological strain, they are unable to fully perform their work duties—a circumstance made more troubling for employers when coupled with knowledge that workers who engage in physically and cognitively challenging jobs are already at increased risk for absenteeism and presenteeism (i.e., employees' being present at work but unable to be fully engaged in the environment; Hymel et al., 2011; Jinnett, Schwatka, Tenney, Brockbank, & Newman, 2017).

As a consequence of these changes in the workforce, employment, and the nature of work, the lines between work and nonwork risks and health outcomes continue to blur—all of which begs the need for more holistic interventions that simultaneously address work and nonwork risks.

GROWING RECOGNITION OF THE LINK BETWEEN WORK, HEALTH, AND WELL-BEING

Scientific evidence on the link between work and health has demonstrated the need to address job conditions to better protect the overall health of workers. Historically, the focus has been on workplace physiochemical exposures, but multiple scientific disciplines increasingly are recognizing and becoming more aware that psychosocial factors at work can contribute to chronic health problems (e.g., cardiovascular disease, depression; Ganster & Rosen, 2013; Rehkopf, Modrek, Cantley, & Cullen, 2017; Schnall, Dobson, & Landsbergis, 2016). Of special interest is an accumulating body of evidence that has suggested that less than ideal working conditions (e.g., long work hours, lack of supervisory support, harassment, low wages, lack of access to paid sick leave) contribute to health problems that previously were not given much consideration as being work related (Ganster & Rosen, 2013; Luckhaupt, Cohen, Li, & Calvert, 2014; Miranda, Gore, Boyer, Nobrega, & Punnett, 2015; Wang, Sanderson, Dwyer, Venn, & Gall, 2018). For example, attempting to cope with stress associated with the demanding conditions of work may lead to health risk behaviors (e.g., alcohol, drug, tobacco use; unhealthy dietary behavior; inadequate physical activity; Fransson et al., 2012; Hammer & Sauter, 2013; Heikkilä et al., 2012). In turn, all of these health conditions have the potential to impair productivity (Shi, Sears, Coberley, & Pope, 2013)

Evidence also has shown that risks on the job interact with nonwork risks (e.g., genetics, age, gender, alcohol use, prescription drug use) to affect the safety, health, and well-being of workers both on and off the job (Schulte, Pandalai, Wulsin, & Chun, 2012; see Chapter 3, this volume). For example, obesity can increase the risk of osteoarthritis for workers whose jobs require frequent kneeling versus those who are not obese (Schulte et al., 2012). Similarly, obesity increases the risk of asthma, and that association is worsened for workers exposed to toxins in the workplace (Schulte et al., 2012). The effects of these exposures extend beyond the individual worker as shown by findings that work–life stress (see Chapter 15, this volume) and worker injuries (Asfaw, Pana-Cryan, Bushnell, & Sauter, 2015) may negatively affect the health of children and other family members.

BROADENING PERSPECTIVES ON WORKER HEALTH

Since the passage of the Occupational Safety and Health Act of 1970, workers' risks of being injured, sickened, or killed on the job have declined significantly. Because of the decrease in workplace-associated injuries and the improvements in working conditions, OSH is recognized as one of the 10 great achievements in public health (Centers for Disease Control and Prevention [CDC], 2011). Nonetheless, the societal burden of work-related injuries and illnesses remains substantial, and the full impact of work on health has yet to be established.

Consequently, global leaders and scholars are calling for an expanded view of worker safety and health—one that sees work as more integral to individual, population, and societal well-being (Black, 2008; DGUV, 2016; EU-OSHA, 2016; National Institute for Occupational Safety and Health [NIOSH], 2016a; Peckham et al., 2017; World Health Organization [WHO], 2010). Such an expanded approach would consider the whole lives of workers, altogether address the role of work and work conditions on the health of populations, and harness opportunities to promote and protect the health and well-being of workers and their communities locally, nationally, and globally (Peckham et al., 2017; WHO, 2010). This new perspective would confirm and expand the notion of work as a critical social determinant of health, and draw the field of OSH more closely to public health and population health.

As these fields begin to converge, it is important to reflect on how public health and population health are defined, and how they are evolving. CDC (2017) refers to *public health* as "the science and art of preventing disease, prolonging life, and promoting health through the organized efforts and informed choices of society, organizations, public and private communities, and individuals." In the past, public health efforts have focused primarily on individual risk factors (especially those associated with infectious diseases) to improve health.

More recently, emphasis has shifted to examining social and ecological determinants of health (Arora et al., 2016; Institute of Medicine [IOM], 2003). Similar to the population health model, this shift has involved increasing recognition that working conditions and employment are critical factors that shape people's social position and health status (WHO, 2019), and has been fueled in part by the rise of at-risk and vulnerable populations (e.g., older workers, young workers, foreign-born workers, minorities, temporary and contract laborers) and the need to address growing health inequities. Although definitions for this broad concept are still evolving, *population health* may be referred to as the health outcomes of a group of individuals, including the distribution of such outcomes and health determinants within the group and the policies and interventions that affect those factors (Kindig & Stoddart, 2003).

The movement toward holistic and integrated approaches that both protect and promote the safety and health of worker populations is now evident in initiatives in occupational and public health organizations around the world. In the United States, NIOSH launched the TWH program as a comprehensive and integrated approach that provides a pathway to improve worker creativity, innovation, and productivity by assuring that work and work environments are safe and health enhancing (NIOSH, 2011; see Chapter 2, this volume). Both WHO and EU-OSHA established cross-national initiatives that encourage new and holistic ways to promote worker safety and health, and to ensure sustainable work (EU-OSHA, 2016; WHO, 2016). In Britain, Black (2008) called for an expanded role for occupational health in a visionary report on work and health. Black's vision recognizes the relationship between health and work as integral to the prosperity and well-being of individuals, their families, workplaces, and wider communities. The report recommended that occupational health be brought into the mainstream of health care provisions to develop an integrated approach for worker health.

EXPANDING OCCUPATIONAL SAFETY AND HEALTH THROUGH *TOTAL WORKER HEALTH*

The TWH approach provides a pathway for broadening the scope of worker safety and health. Although the scientific evidence base is relatively new, the interest in the integrated concept of the TWH approach has gained substantial traction among leaders in workplace health and safety (Loeppke et al., 2015; NIOSH, 2015a). Private sector and industry attention toward TWH strategies also is a positive development for the field and a testament that more expansive approaches to advancing worker safety, health, and well-being are not entirely an academic enterprise (NIOSH, 2016c). Still, additional investment is needed by those who have a stake in protecting workforce and worker safety, health, and well-being to enhance the science, practice, and skills and training of professionals in a TWH program. To further these investments, leaders and scholars have recommended expanding beyond the network of traditional

OSH stakeholders interested in the intersections between work, health, and well-being as discussed next (Peckham et al., 2017; see Chapter 2, this volume).

Enhance the Scientific Evidence Supporting *Total Worker Health*

The TWH field is developing, and several sources have provided insight on needs and ways to advance the discipline (Bradley, Grossman, Hubbard, Ortega, & Curry, 2016; IOM, 2014; Loeppke et al., 2015; NIOSH, 2016a; Sorensen et al., 2011) and enhance the evidence base supporting integrated programs. Perhaps the most cited is the need for an improved understanding of the concept of integration (Bradley et al., 2016) and the adoption of a more systems-based approach that examines contextual factors at the individual, organizational, and societal levels to better understand mechanisms through which exposures at home and work affect safety, health, and well-being. In this regard, Sorensen and colleagues in Chapter 5, this volume, offer a multidimensional conceptual model for integrating workplace programs that can be used to guide both research and practice. In this approach, successful intervention designs reflect input from many disciplines (e.g., business, industry, health care, labor, academia) and organizational levels, including management, workers, and labor. However, there is a gap in the research that simultaneously examines how multiple workplace factors (e.g., physical hazards, psychological risks, the social environment) contribute to workers' overall health and well-being (Greiner, 2012; Rehkopf et al., 2017; Sauter & Hurrell, 2017).

Much consideration also has been given to the question, What to study? Researchers have cited the need to incorporate understudied populations in TWH research and practice (e.g., including populations at increased risk based on demographics, on where they live, or on what social disadvantages they have; Bradley et al., 2016); study small business and target high-risk industry sectors; examine organizational culture and its relation to the success of the TWH approach (IOM, 2014; see Chapter 1, this volume); and recognize organization of work as a distinct risk within OSH. Furthermore, because TWH interventions to date have primarily examined individual health concerns as the outcomes of interest (e.g., health behaviors), additional attention needs to be given to safety behaviors and compliance (Feltner et al., 2016), a reduction in organizational risk factors (e.g., work organization risks), improvement of work-related outcomes (e.g., occupational injury, organizational effectiveness), and an enhancement of the positive aspects of work (e.g., worker satisfaction).

There also is a need for improved research methods using more rigorous research designs as well as qualitative and mixed methods designs. As part of this effort, more attention should be given to the use of core and common measures to enable a comparison and contrast of findings and aggregation of data (Bradley et al., 2016; NIOSH, 2016a). Another recommendation is that to facilitate learning and further aid in the application and replication of findings published, research (especially applied research) should include sufficient detail on the methods, modes of measuring TWH constructs, and successes and

challenges of implementation. Tamers et al. (2018) discussed many of the fore-
going concerns and summarized expert recommendations from a workshop on
methodological considerations to improve the effectiveness of TWH research.

Apply *Total Worker Health* in Practice

Several practice-based developments are needed to advance the TWH field. For
instance, improved translation of TWH research into practice and policy is vital.
For better application of science into practice, the field needs to begin designing
and evaluating interventions for dissemination and adoption of practices and
policies. However, little has been invested into understanding the impact of
disseminating and implementing OSH information. OSH professionals can
draw from the emerging field of implementation science for insight regarding
factors that influence adoption of evidence into practice and how research can
be applied to drive policy change (Bradley et al., 2016). There is also a distinct
need to translate science around known work-related risks (e.g., work–family
conflict) and to bring awareness of those risks to other related disciplines (e.g.,
human resources) and then use that knowledge to inform practice-based
research. For best practice in this area, an agenda for dissemination and implementation research is essential (Dugan & Punnett, 2017; Schulte et al., 2017).

Several upstream developments are needed to amplify the application of the
TWH approach in practice. Fundamental but challenging to this movement is
demonstrating the value that a TWH approach brings to the long-term sustainability of the employer, industry, and society. Perhaps one of most critical developments is to inspire the gatekeepers of health—labor, health care, and public
health—to engage in new ways that bring greater visibility to the value of an
integrated approach to work and health (Black, 2008; Loeppke et al., 2015;
Sepulveda, 2013). Scholars have expressed that this high-level engagement
could stimulate more alignment of the field with long-standing and current
social movements (e.g., labor rights, worker advocacy, paid family leave), and
encourage broader collaboration among and within labor, academia, government, and industry (Peckham et al., 2017; see Chapter 11, this volume). For
example, novel solutions to access worker populations could develop with new
or better engagement with economic development, community-based, and
labor organizations. As well, new models of interventions at the levels of the
workplace, community, industry, and society could establish the results sought
for simultaneously addressing work- and non–work-related risks. Many of
these actions involve expanding the role of professionals that protect worker
safety, health, and well-being.

Expand the Professional Capacity for *Total Worker Health*

As we reshape the way we think about OSH, there is demand to transform
the capacity of the workforce that advances the safety, health, and well-being
of workers. To accomplish this change involves growing the network of

professionals who have a stake in improving worker well-being in response to the health risks and challenges facing today's workers and employers, and broadening the training and education to better respond to the burden of OSH and new challenges posed by the changing nature of work. First, we can draw from the traditional base of OSH professionals (e.g., occupational safety, industrial hygiene, occupational medicine, occupational health nursing) and expand the network to include professionals in fields such as public health, population health, positive psychology, risk management, human resources management, and organizational sciences.

Future training and education should encompass a broad concept of worker health, including work-related and nonwork exposures and risks. This concept involves an understanding of the social, political, and legal contexts affecting workers' health, and the inclusion of social sciences, management, business economics, and policy processes (Peckham et al., 2017). Because many OSH professionals traditionally are concentrated in large firms, which employ a minority of U.S. workers (IOM, 2000), practice settings (e.g., small businesses) ought to be considered in the development of training and education. In addition, the training needs to address skills and abilities to effectively communicate the value of an integrated approach to various audiences, such as industry, academia, labor, and health care (Black, 2008). Training of this nature is rapidly evolving and already taking place in academic centers, organizations, and scientific conferences across the country (NIOSH, 2016b). To aid in these important developments, NIOSH and partners from academia and industry are forming a recommended set of competencies that can serve as a framework for training and educating professionals; that framework then provides the next generation of OSH leadership to protect workers and ensure a healthier national workforce. As a result of these developments, new roles for practitioners and novel specialties are expected to emerge as a new cadre of professionals is established.

A NEW DIRECTION: USING WORK TO PROMOTE COMPREHENSIVE WELL-BEING

In this chapter, a case is made for using safe, high-quality, well-designed work as a substantive way to advance the well-being of workers and societies. As the TWH field advances through investments in science, practice, and capacity building, the opportunities to promote population health and well-being are vast. Because the TWH concept takes a lifespan perspective and emphasizes integration across multiple workplace programs that promote and protect worker health, the philosophy holds particular promise for developing and sustaining workers' well-being as their needs evolve and they continue to contribute to society through paid work during the many phases of their life (Hammer & Sauter, 2013; see Chapters 13 and 15, this volume). The aim of OSH is to protect and keep workers safe and healthy. Changing times demand that we progress beyond traditional OSH approaches. We assert that by approaching work through a broader lens, employers and their partners can work together to achieve the ultimate goal—sustained worker well-being—by starting with quality work.

Work has the potential to offer individuals more than an income, benefits, and a way to spend one's day. Ideally, work provides opportunities to use imagination and intelligence, allows workers to achieve goals and develop new skills, and helps workers connect with others and feel capable and accomplished. Work can be an outlet for creativity and passion, and it can provide a way to find meaning in existence. Work has the potential to contribute to worker well-being in numerous ways. NIOSH has defined *worker well-being* as an integrative concept that characterizes quality of life with respect to an individual's health and work-related environmental, organizational, and psychosocial factors. It is the experience of positive perceptions and the presence of constructive conditions at work and beyond that enable workers to thrive and achieve their full potential (Chari et al., 2018). Like the TWH approach, this framework considers the subjective and objective experiences of workers, and reflects the idea that achievement of worker well-being cannot occur through employer-based workplace interventions alone but may require broad-based programs that address different areas of an individual's life and organizational partnerships that cross work and nonwork settings.

Regardless of their age, gender, race, ethnicity, religion, or familial status, workers' labor participation and needs vary across their lifespan, and may change frequently as they pursue personal goals, raise and care for their families, and engage in supplemental learning. Shifting demographics require employers to engage in forward thinking, strategic work design, and workforce planning to assure that current and future workers feel valued, safe, healthy, satisfied, and able to work productively across their lifespan. Based on our review, the following are principles for the design of healthy work that use a TWH approach.

Foremost, work should be safe. Furthermore, work design should be leveraged to promote and sustain worker well-being. Technological advances are increasing the volume of work, but we caution against fitting the worker to the job (e.g., finding employees who can do more at a faster pace). Instead, assure that all work is designed with consideration for the varying makeup and needs of the workforce. There is a continued need to incorporate science and practice across disciplines to advance our understanding of how positive aspects of work, such as opportunity for skill use, economic support, physical security, leadership, and social connections, affect overall well-being (Chari et al., 2018; Tetrick & Peiro, 2017). By embracing integration in practice, jobs can be constructed to protect workers from harm while also providing opportunities for agency, autonomy, personal and professional development, stimulation, the development of positive relationships at work, the flexibility to meet the demands of life and work, and wages that cover the basic costs required for living a safe and healthy life (Chalofsky, 2010; Day, Kelloway, & Hurrell, 2014; United Nations, 2015). Access to health-related programs and resources on the job and in the community can help employees manage chronic diseases (Sorensen et al., 2011). New approaches to return-to-work practices (e.g., comprehensive drug addiction treatment programs), an emphasis on prevention, a reduction in the risk for occupational stress, and attention to the potential for work to address and contribute to mental health (Sauter, Murphy, & Hurrell, 1990; see Chapter 12, this volume) also are recommended. Furthermore, as the nature of the employer and employee relationship changes, employers would benefit by finding new ways to influence and reach workers with OSH information, such as through labor unions, worker centers, and shared office spaces (see Chapter 11, this volume).

Promoting worker well-being through work also offers opportunities for organizations and businesses. At the organization level, well-designed work provides a sustainable way to optimize employee performance, which is essential for all businesses to succeed. Business leaders are becoming more aware that the benefit of integrating safety and health, focusing on positive aspects of health, and improving well-being through work goes far beyond just cost control. There is increasing recognition of worker well-being as a key element that contributes to the organization's success (Malan, Radjy, Pronk, & Yach, 2016). The concept of a culture of health (i.e., workplace leaders *consistently* place value on employee safety, health, and well-being) is emerging as a shared value that holds promise for improving health and job satisfaction, reducing health care costs, and increasing organizational economic performance (Kent, Goetzel, Roemer, Prasad, & Freundlich, 2016; Kwon & Marzec, 2016; see Chapter 16, this volume). Leaders who invest in a culture that supports meaningful work will harvest many benefits seen in recruiting, retaining, and growing workers, thus ensuring their optimum engagement, happiness, and productivity (Berg, Dutton, & Wrzesniewski, 2013). Such a culture lowers risks of turnover, injury, early disability, liability, and long-term health deficits and associated health care costs. And, at the population level, well-crafted work leads to a more productive society that spends less on worker injury, illness, and early disability.

CONCLUSION

As change permeates the American workplace, employers, employees, and their families must continuously adapt to evolving conditions. Employers will look for new ways to organize work to meet production and profit goals while maintaining a safe workplace and sustaining a productive workforce. At the same time, workers may struggle to manage their health, meet their caregiving obligations, and incorporate their personal lives and aspirations into a demanding work schedule that can include long hours and even multiple jobs. NIOSH's TWH strategy for workplace safety, health, and well-being offers a modern and holistic paradigm for achieving improvements in workforce safety, health, and well-being. It does so specifically through an integrated approach that prioritizes safety while simultaneously engaging in other workplace efforts (e.g., healthy work design, employee training and development, injury and illness prevention efforts) to advance the overall well-being of workers. This emerging body of science and practice holds promise to guide the advancement of the safety, health, and well-being of our nation's workers.

REFERENCES

American Psychological Association. (2017). *Stress in America™: The state of our nation.* Washington, DC: Author. Retrieved from https://www.apa.org/news/press/releases/stress/2017/state-nation.pdf

Arora, A., Spatz, E., Herrin, J., Riley, C., Roy, B., Kell, K., . . . Krumholz, H. M. (2016). Population well-being measures help explain geographic disparities in life expectancy at the county level. *Health Affairs, 35,* 2075–2082. http://dx.doi.org/10.1377/hlthaff.2016.0715

Asfaw, A., Pana-Cryan, R., Bushnell, T., & Sauter, S. (2015). Musculoskeletal disorders and associated healthcare costs among family members of injured workers. *American Journal of Industrial Medicine, 58,* 1205–1216. http://dx.doi.org/10.1002/ajim.22500

Benach, J., Vives, A., Amable, M., Vanroelen, C., Tarafa, G., & Muntaner, C. (2014). Precarious employment: Understanding an emerging social determinant of health. *Annual Review of Public Health, 35,* 229–253. http://dx.doi.org/10.1146/annurev-publhealth-032013-182500

Berg, J. M., Dutton, J. E., & Wrzesniewski, A. (2013). Job crafting and meaningful work. In B. J. Dik, Z. S. Byrne, & M. F. Steger (Eds.), *Purpose and meaning in the workplace* (pp. 81–104). Washington, DC: American Psychological Association. http://dx.doi.org/10.1037/14183-005

Black, D. C. (2008). *Working for a healthier tomorrow* [Review]. Retrieved from https://www.rnib.org.uk/sites/default/files/Working_for_a_healthier_tomorrow.pdf

Bradley, C. J., Grossman, D. C., Hubbard, R. A., Ortega, A. N., & Curry, S. J. (2016). Integrated interventions for improving Total Worker Health: A panel report from the National Institutes of Health Pathways to Prevention workshop: Total Worker Health—What's Work Got to Do With It? *Annals of Internal Medicine, 165,* 279–283. http://dx.doi.org/10.7326/M16-0740

Buttorff, C., Ruder, T., & Bauman, M. (2017). *Multiple chronic conditions in the United States.* Santa Monica, CA: RAND Corporation. http://dx.doi.org/10.7249/TL221

Centers for Disease Control and Prevention. (2011, May 20). Ten great public health achievements—United States, 2001–2010. *Morbidity and Mortality Weekly Report, 60,* 619–623. Retrieved from https://www.cdc.gov/mmwr/preview/mmwrhtml/mm6019a5.htm

Centers for Disease Control and Prevention. (2017). *Introduction to public health.* Retrieved from https://www.cdc.gov/publichealth101/public-health.html

Chalofsky, N. E. (2010). *Meaningful workplaces. Reframing how and where we work.* San Francisco, CA: Jossey-Bass.

Chari, R., Chang, C.-C., Sauter, S. L., Petrun Sayers, E. L., Cerully, J. L., Schulte, P., . . . Uscher-Pines, L. (2018). Expanding the paradigm of occupational safety and health: A new framework for worker well-being. *Journal of Occupational and Environmental Medicine, 60,* 589–593. Advance online publication. http://dx.doi.org/10.1097/JOM.0000000000001330

Cocorocchia, C. (2016, January 19). *How the digitization of work affects us all* [World Economic Forum article]. Retrieved from https://www.weforum.org/agenda/2016/01/how-the-digitization-of-work-impacts-us-all

Day, A., Kelloway, E. K., & Hurrell, J. J. (Eds.). (2014). *Workplace well-being: How to build psychologically healthy workplaces.* West Sussex, England: Wiley-Blackwell.

Deutsche Gesetzliche Unfallversicherung. (2016). *New forms of work, new forms of prevention. Work 4.0: Opportunities and challenges* [Position paper]. Retrieved from http://publikationen.dguv.de/dguv/pdf/10002/dguv-nfda_en_accessible.pdf

Dugan, A. G. & Punnett, L. (2017). Dissemination and implementation research for occupational safety and health. *Occupational Health Science, 1,* 29–45. http://dx.doi.org/10.1007/s41542-017-0006-0.

European Agency for Safety and Health at Work. (2016). *Safer and healthier work at any age—Final overall analysis report.* Luxembourg: Publications Office of the European Union. Retrieved from https://osha.europa.eu/en/tools-and-publications/publications/safer-and-healthier-work-any-age-final-overall-analysis-report/view

Feltner, C., Peterson, K., Palmieri Weber, R., Cluff, L. Coker-Schwimmer, E., Viswanathan, M., & Lohr, K. N. (2016). The effectiveness of *Total Worker Health* interventions: A systematic review for a National Institutes of Health Pathways to Prevention workshop. *Annals of Internal Medicine, 165,* 262–269. http://dx.doi.org/10.7326/M16-0626

Fransson, E. I., Keikkilä, K., Nyberg, S. T., Zins, M., Westerlund, H., Westerholm, P., . . . Kivimäki, M. (2012). Job strain as a risk factor for leisure-time physical inactivity: An individual–participant meta-analysis of up to 170,000 men and women: The IPD–Work Consortium. *American Journal of Epidemiology, 176,* 1078–1089. http://dx.doi.org/10.1093/aje/kws336

Ganster, D. C., & Rosen, C. C. (2013). Work stress and employee health: A multidisciplinary review. *Journal of Management, 39,* 1085–1122. http://dx.doi.org/10.1177/0149206313475815

Greiner, B. A. (2012). The public health perspective: Useful for occupational health psychologists and health and safety professionals? In J. Houdmont, S. Leka, & R. R. Sinclair (Eds.), *Contemporary occupational health psychology: Global perspectives on research and practice* (Vol. 2, pp. 184–203). West Sussex, England: Wiley-Blackwell. http://dx.doi.org/10.1002/9781119942849.ch11

Hammer, L. B., & Sauter, S. (2013). Total worker health and work–life stress. *Journal of Occupational and Environmental Medicine, 55,* S25–S29. http://dx.doi.org/10.1097/JOM.0000000000000043

Heikkilä, K., Nyberg, S. T., Fransson, E. I., Alfredsson, L., De Bacquer, D., Bjorner, J. B., . . . Kivimäki, M. (2012). Job strain and tobacco smoking: An individual–participant data meta-analysis of 166,130 adults in 15 European studies. *PLoS ONE, 7,* e35463. http://dx.doi.org/10.1371/journal.pone.0035463

Howard, J. H. (2017a, January 3). Nonstandard work arrangements [Blog post]. Retrieved from https://blogs.cdc.gov/niosh-science-blog/2017/01/03/nonstandard-work-arrangements

Howard, J. (2017b). Nonstandard work arrangements and worker health and safety. *American Journal of Industrial Medicine, 60,* 1–10. http://dx.doi.org/10.1002/ajim.22669

Hymel, P. A., Loeppke, R. R., Baase, C. M., Burton, W. N., Hartenbaum, N. P., Hudson, T. W., . . . Larson, P. W. (2011). Workplace health protection and promotion: A new pathway for a healthier—and safer—workforce. *Journal of Occupational and Environmental Medicine, 53,* 695–702. http://dx.doi.org/10.1097/JOM.0b013e31822005d0

Institute of Medicine. (2014). *Promising and best practices in Total Worker Health™: Workshop summary.* Washington, DC: National Academies Press. Retrieved from https://www.nap.edu/read/18947/chapter/1

Institute of Medicine, Committee on Assuring the Health of the Public in the 21st Century. (2003). *The future of the public's health in the 21st century* [Report]. Washington, DC: National Academies Press. Retrieved from https://www.nap.edu/read/10548/chapter/1

Institute of Medicine, Committee to Assess Training Needs for Occupational Safety and Health Personnel in the United States. (2000). *Safe work in the 21st century: Education and training needs for the next decade's occupational safety and health personnel* [Consensus study report]. Washington, DC: National Academies Press. Retrieved from https://www.ncbi.nlm.nih.gov/books/NBK225528

Jinnett, K., Schwatka, N., Tenney, L., Brockbank, C. V., & Newman, L. S. (2017). Chronic conditions, workplace safety, and job demands contribute to absenteeism and job performance. *Health Affairs, 36,* 237–244. http://dx.doi.org/10.1377/hlthaff.2016.1151

Kent, K., Goetzel, R. Z., Roemer, E. C., Prasad, A., & Freundlich, N. (2016). Promoting healthy workplaces by building cultures of health and applying strategic communications. *Journal of Occupational and Environmental Medicine, 58,* 114–122. http://dx.doi.org/10.1097/JOM.0000000000000629

Kindig, D. A., & Stoddart, G. (2003). What is population health? *American Journal of Public Health, 93,* 380–383. http://dx.doi.org/10.2105/AJPH.93.3.380

Kwon, Y., & Marzec, M. L. (2016). Does worksite culture of health (CoH) matter to employees? Empirical evidence using job-related metrics. *Journal of Occupational and Environmental Medicine, 58,* 448–454. http://dx.doi.org/10.1097/JOM.0000000000000724

Loeppke, R. R., Hohn, T., Baase, C., Bunn, W. B., Burton, W. N., Eisenberg, B. S., . . . Siuba, J. (2015). Integrating health and safety in the workplace: How closely aligning health and safety strategies can yield measurable benefits. *Journal of Occupational and Environmental Medicine, 57,* 585–597. http://dx.doi.org/10.1097/JOM.0000000000000467

Luckhaupt, S. E., Cohen, M. A., Li, J., & Calvert, G. M. (2014). Prevalence of obesity among U.S. workers and associations with occupational factors. *American Journal of Preventive Medicine, 46,* 237–248. http://dx.doi.org/10.1016/j.amepre.2013.11.002

Mack, K. A., Jones, C. M., & Ballesteros, M. F. (2017). Illicit drug use, illicit drug use disorders, and drug overdose deaths in metropolitan and nonmetropolitan areas— United States. *Morbidity and Mortality Weekly Report Surveillance Summaries, 66* (No. SS-19), 1–12. http://dx.doi.org/10.15585/mmwr.ss6619a1

Malan, D., Radjy, S., Pronk, N., & Yach, D. (2016, January). *Reporting on health: A roadmap for investors, companies, and reporting platforms.* Retrieved from http://theinstitute.org/site/wp-content/uploads/2016/01/Vitality-HealthMetricsReportingRoadmap22Jan2016.pdf

Miranda, H., Gore, R., Boyer, J., Nobrega, S., & Punnett, L. (2015). Health behaviors and overweight in nursing home employees: Contribution of workplace stressors and implications for worksite health promotion. *Scientific World Journal, 2015,* 915359. http://dx.doi.org/10.1155/2015/915359

National Institute for Occupational Safety and Health. (2011). From the director's desk— Leading the evolution toward Total Worker Health [NIOSH eNews article]. Retrieved from https://www.cdc.gov/niosh/enews/enewsv9n2.html

National Institute for Occupational Safety and Health. (2015a). *NIOSH* Total Worker Health® *affiliates.* Retrieved from https://www.cdc.gov/niosh/twh/affiliate.html

National Institute for Occupational Safety and Health. (2015b). *Total worker health: What is* Total Worker Health? Retrieved from https://www.cdc.gov/niosh/twh/totalhealth.html

National Institute for Occupational Safety and Health. (2016a, April). *National Occupational Research Agenda (NORA) National Total Worker Health® agenda (2016–2026): A national agenda to advance Total Worker Health® research, practice, policy, and capacity* (DHHS [NIOSH] Publication No. 2016–114). Cincinnati, OH: U.S. Department of Health and Human Services, Centers for Disease Control and Prevention, National Institute for Occupational Safety and Health. Retrieved from https://www.cdc.gov/niosh/docs/2016-114/pdfs/nationaltwhagenda2016-1144-14-16.pdf

National Institute for Occupational Safety and Health. (2016b). Total Worker Health: NIOSH Centers of Excellence for *Total Worker Health*®. Retrieved from https://www.cdc.gov/niosh/twh/centers.html

National Institute for Occupational Safety and Health. (2016c). Total Worker Health: Promising and best practices for *Total Worker Health* [Workshop summary]. Retrieved from https://www.cdc.gov/niosh/twh/practices.html

Occupational Safety and Health Act of 1970, Pub. L. 91 § 596, 84 Stat. 1590 (1970).

Peckham, T. K., Baker, M. G., Camp, J. E., Kaufman, J. D., & Seixas, N. S. (2017). Creating a future for occupational health. *Annals of Work Exposures and Health, 61*, 3–15.

Rehkopf, D. H., Modrek, S., Cantley, L. F., & Cullen, M. R. (2017). Social, psychological, and physical aspects of the work environment could contribute to hypertension prevalence. *Health Affairs, 36*, 258–265. http://dx.doi.org/10.1377/hlthaff.2016.1186

Sauter, S. L., & Hurrell, J. J., Jr. (2017). Occupational health contributions to the development and promise of occupational health psychology. *Journal of Occupational Health Psychology, 22*, 251–258. http://dx.doi.org/10.1037/ocp0000088

Sauter, S. L., Murphy, L. R., & Hurrell, J. J., Jr. (1990). Prevention of work-related psychological disorders: A national strategy proposed by The National Institute for Occupational Safety and Health (NIOSH). *American Psychologist, 45*, 1146–1158. http://dx.doi.org/10.1037/0003-066X.45.10.1146

Schnall, P. L., Dobson, M., & Landsbergis, P. (2016). Globalization, work, and cardiovascular disease. *International Journal of Health Services, 46*, 656–692. http://dx.doi.org/10.1177/0020731416664687

Schulte, P. A., Cunningham, T. R., Nickels, L., Felknor, S., Guerin, R., Blosser, F., . . . Menger-Ogle, L. (2017). Translation research in occupational safety and health: A proposed framework. *American Journal of Industrial Medicine, 60*, 1011–1022. http://dx.doi.org/10.1002/ajim.22780

Schulte, P. A., Pandalai, S., Wulsin, V., & Chun, H. (2012). Interaction of occupational and personal risk factors in workforce health and safety. *American Journal of Public Health, 102*, 434–448. http://dx.doi.org/10.2105/AJPH.2011.300249

Sepulveda, M.-J. (2013). From worker health to citizen health: Moving upstream. *Journal of Occupational and Environmental Medicine, 55*, S52–S57. http://dx.doi.org/10.1097/JOM.0000000000000033

Shi, Y., Sears, L. E., Coberley, C. R., & Pope, J. E. (2013). The association between modifiable well-being risks and productivity: A longitudinal study in pooled employer sample. *Journal of Occupational and Environmental Medicine, 55*, 353–364. http://dx.doi.org/10.1097/JOM.0b013e3182851923

Sorensen, G., Landsbergis, P., Hammer, L., Amick, B. C., III, Linnan, L., Yancey, A., . . . the Workshop Working Group on Worksite Chronic Disease Prevention. (2011). Preventing chronic disease in the workplace: A workshop report and recommendations. *American Journal of Public Health, 101*, S196–S207. http://dx.doi.org/10.2105/AJPH.2010.300075

Tamers, S. L., Goetzel, R., Kelly, K. M., Luckhaupt, S., Nigam, J. A. S., Pronk, N., . . . Sorensen, G. (2018). Research methodologies for *Total Worker Health*®: Proceedings from a workshop. *Journal of Occupational and Environmental Medicine, 60*, 968–978. http://dx.doi.org/10.1097/JOM.0000000000001404

Tetrick, L. E., & Peiro, J. M. (2017). Health and safety: Prevention and promotion. In M. J. Grawitch & D. W. Ballard (Eds.), *The psychologically healthy workplace. Building a win–win environment for organizations and employees* (pp. 199–229). Washington, DC: American Psychological Association.

United Nations. (2015). *Transforming our world: The 2030 agenda for sustainable development* [Resolution adopted by the General Assembly]. Retrieved from https://sustainabledevelopment.un.org/post2015/transformingourworld

U.S. Department of Health and Human Services, Public Health Service, Office of the Surgeon General. (2018, April). *Surgeon General's advisory on naloxone and opioid overdose*. Retrieved from https://www.surgeongeneral.gov/priorities/opioid-overdose-prevention/naloxone-advisory.html

Wang, S., Sanderson, K., Dwyer, T., Venn, A., & Gall, S. (2018). Job stress in young adults is associated with a range of poorer health behaviors in the childhood determinants of adult health (CDAH) study. *Journal of Occupational and Environmental Medicine, 60*, e117–e125. http://dx.doi.org/10.1097/JOM.0000000000001234

World Health Organization. (2010). *Healthy workplaces: A model for action—For employers, workers, policy-makers and practitioners* [Report]. Geneva, Switzerland: Author. Retrieved from http://www.who.int/occupational_health/publications/healthy_workplaces_model_action.pdf

World Health Organization. (2016). *Working for health and growth: Investing in the health workforce* [Report of the High-Level Commission on Health Employment and Economic Growth]. Geneva, Switzerland: Author. Retrieved from http://apps.who.int/iris/bitstream/10665/250047/1/9789241511308-eng.pdf

World Health Organization. (2019). *Social determinants of health: Employment conditions*. Retrieved from https://www.who.int/social_determinants/themes/employment conditions/en/

INDEX

ABOUT THE EDITORS

Heidi Hudson, MPH, is a science communicator and commander in the U.S. Public Health Service. She has led initiatives around the coordination of dissemination and implementation of research, including the creation of practical guidance on integrative approaches to worker well-being. She serves as team leader for the NIOSH Office for Total Worker Health, part of the Centers for Disease Control and Prevention.

Jeannie A. S. Nigam, MS, PhDc, is a research psychologist and advisor to the *Total Worker Health* Program at the National Institute for Occupational Safety and Health. Her research centers on understanding how work organization affects employee health and well-being with emphases in the areas of work–life balance, depression, and benefits of comprehensive organizational programs on worker well-being.

Steven L. Sauter, PhD, is a consultant to the *Total Worker Health* Program at NIOSH. He served previously as coordinator of the NIOSH Research Program on Work Organization and Stress-related Disorders, and he has extensive publications on psychosocial aspects of occupational health.

L. Casey Chosewood, MD, MPH, is the director of the Office for Total Worker Health at NIOSH. He is the author and editor of numerous scientific publications. He lectures extensively on worker safety and health, occupational medicine, health policy, and worker well-being interventions.

Anita L. Schill, PhD, MPH, MA, is a consultant to the NIOSH *Total Worker Health* Program. Prior to retiring after more than 23 years of federal service,

Dr. Schill served as a co-manager of the *Total Worker Health* Program and senior science advisor to the NIOSH director. She received the NIOSH Total Worker Health Founder's Award.

John Howard, MD, MPH, JD, LLM, MBA, is a physician, professor, and public health administrator. Serving in three 6-year terms as NIOSH director, Dr. Howard led NIOSH to expand its research focus to address practical solutions for modern workplace challenges. He also serves as administrator of the World Trade Center Health Program in the Department of Health and Human Services. He speaks and publishes extensively on emerging trends, law, and policy related to occupational safety and health.